The AMERICAN FRONTIER
An Archaeological Study of Settlement Pattern and Process

Studies in
HISTORICAL ARCHAEOLOGY

EDITOR
Stanley South

Institute of Archeology and Anthropology
University of South Carolina
Columbia, South Carolina

ADVISORS

Charles E. Cleland
John L. Idol, Jr.
Mark P. Leone
Kenneth E. Lewis
Cynthia R. Price
Sarah Peabody Turnbaugh
John White

ROY S. DICKENS, JR., (Ed.) *Archaeology of Urban America: The Search for Pattern and Process*

ROBERT PAYNTER *Models of Spatial Inequality: Settlement Patterns in Historical Archeology*

JOAN H. GEISMAR *The Archaeology of Social Disintegration in Skunk Hollow: A Nineteenth-Century Rural Black Community*

KATHLEEN DEAGAN *Spanish St. Augustine: The Archaeology of a Colonial Creole Community*

KENNETH E. LEWIS *The American Frontier: An Archaeological Study of Settlement Pattern and Process*

In Preparation

JOHN SOLOMON OTTO *Cannon's Point Plantation, 1794–1860: Living Conditions and Status Patterns in the Old South*

WILLIAM M. KELSO *Kingsmill Plantations, 1620–1800: An Archaeology of Rural Colonial Virginia*

The AMERICAN FRONTIER

An Archaeological Study of Settlement Pattern and Process

KENNETH E. LEWIS

Institute of Archeology and Anthropology
University of South Carolina
Columbia, South Carolina

1984

ACADEMIC PRESS, INC.
(Harcourt Brace Jovanovich, Publishers)

Orlando   San Diego   San Francisco   New York   London
Toronto   Montreal   Sydney   Tokyo   São Paulo

ACADEMIC PRESS, INC.
Orlando, Florida 32887

United Kingdom Edition published by
ACADEMIC PRESS, INC. (LONDON) LTD.
24/28 Oval Road, London NW1   7DX

Library of Congress Cataloging in Publication Data

Main entry under title:

The American frontier.

    (Studies in historical archaeology)
    Includes index.
    1. Frontier and pioneer life--United States.
2. Frontier and pioneer life--South Carolina--Camden
Region. 3. Land settlement patterns--United States.
4. Land settlement patterns--South Carolina--Camden Re-
gion. 5. United States--Antiquities. 6. Camden Region
(S.C.)--Antiquities. I. Lewis, Kenneth E. II. Series:
Studies in historical archaeology (New York, N.Y.)
E179.5.A48 1984   975.7'02   83-19725
ISBN 0-12-446560-9 (alk. paper)

PRINTED IN THE UNITED STATES OF AMERICA

84 85 86 87   9 8 7 6 5 4 3 2 1

139621

To my parents, who encouraged my interest in the past

Contents

3. The Development of South Carolina as an Insular Frontier

4. Examining the Insular Frontier in South Carolina: Research Directions and Archaeological Hypotheses

5. Examining Hypotheses for the Colony's Establishment

6. Examining Hypotheses for Spatial Patterning

7. Examining Hypotheses for Expansion

List of Figures

List of Tables

List of Abbreviations

BCDRPC	Berkeley–Charleston–Dorchester Regional Planning Council
CMRPC	Central Midlands Regional Planning Council
CPRPC	Central Piedmont Regional Planning Commission
CR	Cemetery Records
CRPC	Catawba Regional Planning Council
DAROCC	Daughters of the American Revolution, Old Cheraws Chapter
LCG	Lowcountry Council of Governments
LCHC	Lancaster County Historical Commission
LSCG	Lower Savannah Council of Governments
NGPPCC	Nathaniel Greene Papers, Papers of the Continental Congress
NRF	National Register File
PDRPDC	Pee Dee Regional Planning and Development Council
SCACG	South Carolina Appalachian Council of Governments
SCRCHAJ	South Carolina, Records of the Commons House of Assembly, Journals
SCDAHSF	South Carolina Department of Archives and History, Survey Files
SCDPRT	South Carolina Department of Parks, Recreation, and Tourism
SCHM	*South Carolina Historical Magazine*
SCRGAABJR	South Carolina, Records of the General Assembly, Acts, Bills, and Joint Resolutions
SCRSSLGCS	South Carolina, Records of the Secretary of State, Land Grants, Colonial Series
SIR	Site Inventory Record
SWPC	Santee–Wateree Planning Council
USDAASCS	United States Department of Agriculture, Agricultural Stabilization and Conservation Service
USDIOAHPI	United States Department of the Interior, Office of Archeology and Historic Preservation, Inventory

USRPDC	Upper Savannah Regional Planning and Development Council	**WRPDC**	Waccamaw Regional Planning and Development Commission

Foreword

The study of frontiers has played an important role in history, geography, and anthropology. Perhaps best known is the *frontier thesis* of American history, proposed in the late nineteenth century by Frederick Jackson Turner to explain certain elements of American culture and personality. Turner's thesis was built on the concept of *adaptation* to a unique frontier environment; *The American Frontier* takes the same concept as a starting point. Unlike Turner, however, Kenneth Lewis searches for general rules or laws for the evolution of all agrarian frontiers. In this way, he follows closely the cultural ecology of Julian Steward. The book draws heavily on economic geography to construct a general model of frontier adaptation. Economic activities are basic to this frontier model because of Lewis's cultural materialist assumptions of the primacy of the social infrastructure in adaptive processes. Most of the book is dedicated to evaluating the model against documentary and archaeological data from colonial South Carolina. The constraints imposed by this data base limit the kinds of change that can profitably be studied; the data are best suited to testing those models based on identification of the function and location of settlements.

Some clarification of the book's scope is necessary. Lewis limits his discussion of agrarian frontiers to those that are expanding. Frontiers are associated with the colonization of new habitats and, for this reason, are unique. Expanding frontiers are mostly shaped by directional processes of change, for example, and the author's use of the *colonization gradient* and other concepts that stress one-way change are therefore appropriate. Green (1979) does much the same thing in his analysis of the expansion of Neolithic peoples into northern Europe. But the reader must understand that not all frontiers are expanding. Indeed, expansion is likely to be only one phase of a larger frontier process taking place over a longer time. Adams's (1965) seminal work on the archaeology of the Diyala Basin in Mesopotamia provides an excellent illustration of how frontier dynamics might be understood on such a "macrotime" scale. Here, frontiers oscillated between expansion on the one hand and contraction or stability on the other hand mostly because of political instability, which on some occasions allowed irrigation farming technology to be used in marginal areas and on other occasions did not. This suggests two things. First, Lewis's book is directed at frontier processes that take place on a limited time scale and not necessarily on all frontiers. Second, we need to think more about nondirectional and stabilizing processes in the evolution of frontiers. Certainly this is not a criticism of the book; it does point out its boundaries.

The reader will find that Lewis discusses a variety of frontiers in addition to the agrarian type and makes an effort to pinpoint similarities and differences. What he proposes is a series of additional models to best explain adaptive change on trading, ranching, exploitative plantation, industrial, military, and transportation frontiers. While in the midst of this section, the reader might contemplate the hierarchical structure of scientific explanation and consider the possibility of building an even more general model of the frontier—one that is capable of handling all these variants. I suspect that greater generality can come from the addition of two explanatory links. The first link would transform the agrarian model within the theoretical framework of evolutionary ecology, making a set of assumptions that human economic behavior is fundamentally no different from that of other species and that all are subject to the principle of natural selection (see Winterhalder and Smith 1981). Current use of least-cost assumptions in some frontier models (e.g., Green 1979) suggests that the transformation would not be difficult. The second link would make a further transformation within the theoretical framework of nonequilibrium thermodynamics. Here, frontiers can be conceptualized as members of a class of general boundary or edge phenomena, which would include all kinds of physical systems that interact with their neighbors. Ilya Prigogine and his colleagues have taken the lead in trying to understand these interactions. Particularly intriguing is the concept of *dissipative structures*, which are temporary systems dependent on a continuous supply of energy from an outside source (e.g., Prigogine *et al.* 1972). For this reason, they are able to change in directions counter to that predicted by the law of entropy; indeed, Prigogine sees all living systems as such structures, and for our purposes frontiers might be thought of in a similar way. That is, frontiers are transitory structures that exist at the edge of or between more stable physical systems and that depend on energy, materials, and information links to those systems.

This book is especially important in three ways. First, it is one of a very few attempts to place frontier studies within a general theoretical framework that is workable for archaeological and for comparative data. Most such studies have not been able to rise above considerations of the frontier's role in the development of historically unique society. Second, the book provides a foundation for a more general theory of frontiers. And third, Lewis gives a wealth of information about archaeological sites in British South Carolina and the means for evaluating their scientific significance, a contribution that is particularly important in this age of cultural resource management. It is my hope that the reader will get as much out of the book as I did.

DONALD L. HARDESTY
University of Nevada, Reno

REFERENCES

Adams, Robert M.
  1965   *Land behind Baghdad: A history of settlement in the Diyala Plain*. Chicago: University of Chicago Press.
Green, Stanton
  1979   The agricultural colonization of temperate forest habitats: An ecological model. In *The Frontier: Volume Two*, edited by William Savage, Jr., and Stephen I. Thompson. Norman: University of Oklahoma Press. Pp. 69–103.
Prigogine, Ilya, Gregoire Nicolis, and Agnes Babloyantz
  1972   Thermodynamics of evolution. *Physics Today*, November, 1972.
Winterhalder, Bruce, and Eric Smith (editors)
  1981   *Hunter–gatherer foraging strategies*. Chicago: University of Chicago Press.

Preface

Archaeology is increasingly called upon to provide evidence of and explanations for past change. This book addresses these tasks by focusing on two topics central to contemporary historical archaeology: the nature and effect of European colonization, and the relation between cultural processes and the material record they leave behind. Frontier processes were integral to the development of colonial societies in the New World and other regions affected by the expansion of Europe. The study of such groups must consider the processes that produced them. Recognizing the material manifestations of frontier colonization processes permits not only the identification of societies undergoing that type of change, but also increases our understanding of their particular historical development. This archaeological study of colonization explores the nature of frontier expansion and demonstrates the increasingly important role of material culture in the investigation of past social change.

The frontier has long been a unifying theme in the study of American history and is still a significant element in the mythology of many former colonial societies. Comparing their histories yields many obvious developmental similarities. This suggests that colonization represents a common response, or several types of responses, to similar situations. The treatment of frontiers presented here is essentially ecological and economic in orientation. It derives from the basic premise that the form, composition, and organization of frontier colonization reflect adaptations to the new cultural environment created by expansion and migration. This discussion is concerned primarily with agricultural frontiers, which constituted a major, and eventually the dominant, form of colonization in North America, the study area for this book.

Processes of colonization possess both temporal and spatial components, which are characterized by rapid growth over relatively large areas. This expansion produces patterning in the material record that is clearly discernible and whose presence permits the recognition of the expansion process. Such patterning is evident in the distribution and composition of settlements, two easily observable elements of the cultural landscape. This study explores the layout and composition of settlements, as well as their change through time, in order to observe the development of an agricultural frontier region on the basis of its material record.

The scale of colonization requires the use of data on regional and larger levels. A phenomenon such as the expansion of Europe involved the growth of a world economy that rapidly absorbed substantial areas within its boundaries. Consequently, the archaeological study of colonization must also employ an equally wide geographic scope. At the same time, the practical limitations of data accessibility require that a study be limited to a region of manageable size. One such area is South Carolina, a region settled by Great Britain largely during the eighteenth century and the focus of study in this book.

The development of the South Carolina frontier may be examined by means of documentary as well as material evidence, yet the key to interpreting either or both is the development of a model that specifies characteristics linked to the colonization process. The frontier model employed here is defined in Chapter 2 and borrows heavily from the work of ethnographers, historians, and geographers. This model describes a process of rapidly expanding agricultural settlement. In Chapter 3, South Carolina's colonial past is examined in terms of the model to determine its degree of conformity with the latter and to set the stage for the archaeological study. Following the development of archaeological hypotheses in Chapter 4, a consideration of the material record is carried out in Chapters 5 through 9. Here, a large amount of data, many from unpublished sources, is brought together to explore such topics as cultural continuity and change; innovation; settlement form, patterning, hierarchy, and organization; economic networks; and adaptive responses to the geographic expansion inherent to the frontier. Agricultural frontiers are the primary focus of this study, yet they are only one form of colonization. Other types of frontiers are characterized by separate developmental processes, and several of these are discussed in Chapter 10 as avenues for future research.

Because of its regional approach and emphasis on the utility of material culture studies, this book should appeal to scholars in several fields, including history, geography, and anthropology. Historical archaeologists should find it especially useful in designing research in former colonial areas and in modeling additional kinds of frontier change. Above all, the characteristics of the model and the material patterning derived from them should encourage comparative research in frontier settings and should result in a fuller understanding of the phenomena associated with this complex cultural experience.

Acknowledgments

During the preparation of this book I have received the assistance of a number of individuals and organizations, without whose help it could not have been completed. The Institute of Archeology and Anthropology of the University of South Carolina provided support for much of my work, including access to its files and collections. Its director, Robert L. Stephenson, maintained a continuing interest in this study and his encouragement and assistance are appreciated.

My work has involved the compilation and analysis of data from a number of sources. I acknowledge the aid of several individuals whose efforts were particularly helpful in assembling this information. They include E. L. Inabinett, Director of the South Caroliniana Library at the University of South Carolina, as well as his assistants, Alice Richardson and Allen Stokes. J. Mitchell Reams, Director of the James A. Rogers Library at Francis Marion College, and Reference Librarian Neal Martin provided access to materials in the library's special collections. I also acknowledge the cooperation of Charles Lee, Director of the South Carolina Department of Archives and History, and his staff for their help in researching information contained in the collections and files under their care. Nancy Brock, John Wells, and Martha Fullington were particularly helpful.

Archaeological data for inclusion in this study were made available by a number of persons. In this regard, I thank Thomas Wheaton of Soil Systems, Inc., Leslie Drucker and Susan Krantz of Carolina Archaeological Services, Trisha Logan of the U.S. Forest Service, and Martha Zierden of the Charleston Museum.

Consultation with scholars in various fields has also played an important role in the development of ideas, concepts, methods, and techniques employed in this study. Several persons have been especially helpful. They are Charles Kovacik of the Department of Geography, Leland Ferguson of the Department of Anthropology, and George Terry of the McKissick Museum, all at the University of South Carolina; H.

Roy Merrens of York University; Donald L. Hardesty of the University of Nevada, Reno; and John Wells of the South Carolina Department of Archives and History. Stanley South of the Institute of Archeology and Anthropology has, as always, been more than helpful in providing comments, criticisms, advice, encouragement, and inspiration throughout the course of this project.

This volume has benefited from the labors of several individuals who reviewed the entire book manuscript. They are Donald L. Hardesty, Carolyn B. Lewis, and Stanley South. To them I owe a debt of gratitude for minimizing the errors and confusion contained in the book's earlier drafts. I also appreciate the efforts of Mark J. Brooks, George Terry, Charles Kovacik, and William Marquardt for reading and commenting on portions of the text.

The computer graphics in Chapters 3 and 7 are based on SYMAPs produced by James D. Scurry from various types of settlement data. His help in constructing these useful maps of settlement expansion is appreciated. Darby Erd drafted many of the line drawings, and the photographs are the work of Gordon Brown. Last, but not least, appreciation is due to Azalee Swindle for typing several drafts of the book manuscript, including the final copy, and to Mary Joyce Burns for typing earlier drafts of several chapters. To all of you, thanks.

The AMERICAN FRONTIER
An Archaeological Study of Settlement Pattern and Process

Introduction

COLONIZATION AS A PROCESS OF CHANGE

Frontier colonization involves the migration of peoples into new lands, bringing these areas and their inhabitants within the social and economic domain of the expanding society. Expansion of this kind has occurred throughout human history and accounts for human occupation of nearly all habitable parts of the earth. The form of colonization has varied greatly, ranging from situations as disparate as the extension of territory by hunter–gatherer groups to the conquest and exploitation of continents by complex, industrial states. Like other aspects of culture, colonization reflects the organizational complexity of the society from which it has originated. The motivations for, as well as the form and scope of, colonization appear to vary with the level of sociocultural integration of the expanding society and the role of that society within the larger economic and political milieu. If we assume that societies, as behavioral systems, adapt in a patterned way to similar situations, then it is likely that regularities in colonization indicate common, or similar, causes and circumstances of migration. Comparative studies of frontiers are capable of revealing such regularities and delineating their causes (Thompson 1973a:3). The results of such research should identify cross-cultural processes of frontier change that will be useful in the investigation of colonization in its many aspects. This study explores processes of frontier change in complex societies, concentrating specifically on the relationship of such processes to the expanding system of which the colonizing society is a part.

Although frontier colonization often involves the interaction of a number of societies in addition to that of the migrants, our focus is primarily on the evolution of intrusive groups. This is not intended to imply that the effects of colonization on aboriginal societies is unworthy of inquiry or that indigenous peoples need not be studied as significant components of an integrated system of interaction. Both of these topics have been successfully explored by anthropologists addressing problems of contact and acculturation (Bohannan and Plog, 1967; Redfield, Linton, and Herskovitts 1936; Spicer 1962; Wells 1973). Their traditional emphasis on the impact of colonization on aboriginal peoples resulted in a neglect, until recently, of the pioneer society as a vital component in processes of frontier change. The investigation of colonization as it affects the intrusive society not only provides information about this important element and its adaptations to the ecological conditions of the frontier, but also offers several methodological advantages that are often unavailable when studying sociocultural change in indigenous societies impacted by colonization (Thompson 1973a:2–3, b:1–3). First, because complex societies capable of large-scale colonization are more likely to have maintained documentary records than the technologically simpler societies they supplant, it is possible to establish a relatively precise "base line" from which to measure subsequent change. Secondly, the often dramatic differences between the environment of the homeland and that of the frontier necessitate a rapid adaptation in which fundamental change may be observed during a short span of time. These methodological advantages should provide basic information about pioneer societies that will allow processes of change to be examined in time and space. The results of such studies may, in turn, shed additional light on larger processes of change affecting frontier regions.

MODELING PROCESSES OF COLONIZATION

This study explores those processes of change associated with overseas expansion of postmedieval European societies, particularly the processes that characterized British colonization in North America during the seventeenth and eighteenth centuries. The colonization of this region was not an isolated event distinct from the larger phenomenon of expansion. Its development, like that of other colonial areas, was linked to the nature and organization of the economic system in which it took place. If we assume that frontier colonization represents behavior adaptive to conditions under which it was carried out, then the early settlement of Britain's North American colonies should exhibit evidence of processes of change found in similar types of colonization. To investigate a particular instance of colonization in terms of such general processes, however, one must construct a comparative model defining their nature and identifying their common characteristics. Such a generalized model may then be employed to analyze data from particular colonial areas, the results of which should identify past processes of change and thereby determine the nature of the colonization that occurred there.

COLONIZATION AND THE ARCHAEOLOGICAL RECORD

The temporal and spatial changes associated with processes of colonization are reflected both in the written records of a literate society and the material remains it has left behind. Each source is a separate reflection of the past reality that generated it; consequently, the type of evidence each contains must be explored by different methodologies. Since our discussion is concerned with the archaeological manifestations of colonization, the models developed seek to describe and explain processes of frontier change that are discernible in the material by-products of such processes. The models focus on aspects of colonization likely to be reflected by the presence of activities whose nature and distribution are recognizable archaeologically. Among the activities most readily identifiable are those related to subsistence, technology, and exchange, aspects of behavior that may be subsumed under the general term *economy* (Clark, 1952, 1957:Chapter VI; Hole and Heizer 1977:264–267). Economic factors are basic to the structure and organization of society and crucial to its understanding from a materialistic viewpoint.[1] Because of the important role played by the economy in the integration of social systems, the remains of its activities are likely to constitute an extensive and highly observable portion of the archaeological record. The models of colonization developed here necessarily will be of an economic nature.

THE FRONTIER AS A REGIONAL PROCESS

A model of colonization must deal with change resulting from the expansion of an intrusive society into a new territory over a period of time. It encompasses a process that involves spatial and temporal variation and must account for both. Only by using the region as a frame of reference can all the components of a frontier system be observed and their processual interrelationships defined. Changes in the size of a frontier region and the organization and composition of its settlement system through time are important in determining the rate and extent of expansion as well as the eventual termination of the frontier process.

Spatial and temporal change in a frontier region should be reflected in patterning revealed by archaeological analysis. Archaeological patterning at both the site and regional level can provide the key to discerning a process of frontier development and provide evidence that may not always be recognizable on the basis of other

---

[1]The primacy of economic factors in the development of cultural systems is based on the premise that the latter undergo selection in favor of their ability to efficiently exploit the natural and cultural environment in which they exist. Because the aspect of culture most closely related to such adaptation involves the activities of subsistence, technology, and exchange, the subsystem basic to the organization of society is economic. The concept of the key role of economic adaptation is both cultural materialistic and cultural ecological in orientation and has been discussed extensively by Steward (1955), Clark (1953), White (1959:54), Childe (1942), Woodall (1972:40–47) and others.

forms of data. As the study of the frontier is important to an understanding of New World history, the use of archaeology is integral to an investigation of frontier settlement. The regional organization of frontier activities requires that their study be carried out on a scale larger than that of the individual site. All critical components of a frontier area must be located and investigated to acquire the data capable of testing assumptions about the relationship between archaeological patterning and sociocultural process. Because of the enormity of such an undertaking, this type of regional approach has usually lain beyond the scope of archaeological research concerned with the historic period in North America. The increasing intensity of such work and its orientation around behavioral problems, however, have begun to make the investigation of such regional questions possible.

RELEVANCE OF FRONTIER STUDIES

Employment of a model of frontier change has relevance to both substantive and methodological questions. Based on comparative studies, the model should reveal behavioral patterning by which frontier processes and their associated geographical components can be identified and analyzed. Awareness of critical variables reflected in patterns of frontier change can expand our knowledge of the composition and function of individual settlements and their larger roles within the entire frontier region. Further, by defining such regions and tracing their evolutionary development, it should be possible to view individual regional histories in the light of larger processes of colonial expansion. The potential value of a frontier model to the study of American history is tied to the significant impact colonization has had on the development of the New World. European settlement of North America was characterized by a continual expansion into new lands, resulting in a virtual repeopling of the continent over a period of several hundred years. This was accompanied by the displacement of its native inhabitants and a drastic alteration of the American landscape. An understanding of widespread expansion is crucial to an interpretation of not only frontier occupations but subsequent historical developments arising out of them.

The methodological value of a frontier model is that it permits the recognition of behavioral information on the basis of material evidence. With the aid of analogies relating to the use and disposal of artifacts by the colonial society, it should be possible to predict and recognize the occurrence of archaeological regularities reflective of sociocultural patterning described in the model. Archaeological patterns revealing settlement form, layout, and function as well as the existence and distribution of activities should emerge from an examination of colonial sites. Intersite comparison of such patterning is likely to show the regular occurrence of larger patterns linked directly to the frontier processes discussed in the model. Such functionally related patterning holds the key to the archaeological analysis of frontiers as regions within which such processes have taken place.

AGRICULTURAL COLONIZATION IN BRITISH NORTH AMERICA

The models employed here are intended to delineate processes of change linked to the postfifteenth century expansion of Europe. Settlement associated with this phenomenon took on many forms, presumably reflecting various types of colonization. Of these, the most widespread form in British North America appears to have been permanent agricultural settlement for the production of export staples (Gipson 1936; Lang 1975:154). This type of colonization not only laid the base for continued settlement of the interior of this continent, but also introduced complex economic, social, and political institutions that permitted the development of a distinct colonial society. A major task of this study is to construct and examine a comparative model of frontier change resulting from overseas expansion of complex societies intent on permanent agricultural colonization.

The model of agricultural frontier colonization is intended to explore the process of change that accompanied British expansion into the Eastern Seaboard of North America. It identifies and describes characteristics of this process that should be discernible through an examination of documentary sources, landscape evidence, archaeological materials, or any combination of them, relating to specific regions where this type of frontier is believed to have existed. Because of the size of the geographical region represented by the Eastern Seaboard and the differential availability of archaeological evidence from the area as a whole, this study is confined to a portion of that region. It focuses on the province of South Carolina, an area that was colonized by Great Britain in the seventeenth and eighteenth centuries. The geographically limited scope of the study, of course, introduces the possibility that conditions unique to this region make the model less applicable to all instances of agricultural frontier settlement. To be inclusive at such a particular level, however, is not the intent of this study. Rather, it is to analyze an individual instance of colonization as an example of a general process to shed light on this larger phenomenon and identify aspects of it that will be useful in refining our models of agricultural frontier development.

THE SOUTH CAROLINA FRONTIER

The data upon which this study focuses are taken from an agricultural frontier region along the Atlantic Seaboard of North America, an area lying largely within the boundaries of South Carolina. The development of this frontier is documented in written sources which spatially and organizationally delimit its growth through time. In addition, the predominantly agricultural nature of the state's economy permitted many features of its early historic landscape to remain intact and undisturbed. This situation provides much useful information relating to the layout and distribution of past settlement. A series of archaeological investigations has been carried out in South Carolina and has explored the sites of many frontier settlements. Although constituting only a small portion of the total settlement of the colonial period, these sites represent components central to the operation of the frontier socioeconomic system and reflect its structure and organization.

The South Carolina frontier may be seen as an individual example of colonization. As such, it illustrates the general processes described in the model of agricultural frontier settlement. On a particular level differences between this frontier and others of similar function are expected. These differences result from diversity in such variables as staple crop requirements, technology, climate, opposition of aboriginal groups, and the degree of social and political integration within the intrusive society. Such differences do not, however, reflect processual variation at the level of the model, but rather adaptations of these processes in response to specific circumstances. The effect of such adaptive variation on the form of the material record must be considered in predicting the form of archaeological patterning in discrete frontier areas. On a broad level, then, an examination of this southern frontier may be treated as a case study designed to investigate processes associated with agricultural frontier settlement in general. The study should also demonstrate the utility of the model in examining specific agricultural frontiers through its ability to incorporate adaptive variations of these processes to local conditions. Finally, it should illustrate the capability of archaeological methodology in discerning frontier processes through an examination of functionally related patterning in the archaeological record.

BEYOND AGRICULTURAL FRONTIERS

The remainder of this study deals with expanding the frontier concept beyond the scope of agricultural colonization discussed in the model. It concentrates on frontiers representing adaptations to economic conditions associated with various types of nonagricultural settlement. These frontiers are likely to have been characterized by different processes of change and have produced distinct behavioral and archaeological patterning. Based on comparative historical, geographical, and archaeological information, it should be possible to construct archaeological models delineating these frontier processes and the patterning associated with them. Archaeological data generated by the systematic investigation of other types of frontiers are only beginning to be assembled. Despite the absence of detailed information, it still may be possible to explore general aspects of patterning in the archaeological record that are likely to vary according to the nature of these diverse types of frontier adaptation. Even without a more refined model, the examination of general functional patterning should demonstrate the existence of meaningful variation in the archaeological record and suggest directions in which such diversification might be investigated.

This book attempts to analyze present data relating to frontier colonization and suggest a design for additional research into this phenomenon. Its intent is to call attention to the existence of processes of frontier change that constitute widespread, if not universal, adaptations to the social and physical environments encountered in colonization and to the fact that such processes can be recognized and monitored archaeologically. At present, we are only beginning to realize the potential material culture studies have for contributing to our knowledge of human behavior. The achievement of this potential depends in large part upon our ability to construct, examine, and refine models that establish links between behavioral processes and the archaeological record (South 1977:24–25). Given the significance of European colonization and its impact upon the intrusive and aboriginal societies involved, an investigation of archaeological models of frontier change appears to be an appropriate beginning step toward this goal.

2

The Development of a Frontier Model

INTRODUCTION

Frontiers associated with European expansion are perhaps the most intensively studied examples of colonization. The grand scale on which European colonization occurred between the fifteenth and the nineteenth centuries marked a departure from earlier expansion and paralleled the economic revolution that propelled the nation states of Europe into positions of world dominance. Processes that accompanied this expansion reflected the role played by colonization in the capitalist economic milieu of this period. Because the intrusive societies were forced to adapt to conditions similar to those encountered by all migrating groups, however, such processes are also likely to disclose behavioral regularities common to colonization in general.

The following discussion examines European overseas expansion to isolate those economic and ecological variables associated with capitalist frontier colonization. On the basis of comparative evidence, it should be possible to recognize general processes of change associated with the settlement of colonial regions and construct models of frontier change capable of describing and explaining the development of such areas. This chapter concludes with the formulation of a model intended to deal with one of the principal types of colonization associated with overseas expansion, agricultural settlement frontiers. Processes outlined in the model are examined subsequently in the light of documentary and archaeological evidence pertaining to a particular frontier. The results of these studies should demonstrate not only the model's ability to predict the nature of frontier change, but also the effectiveness of archaeological methodology in discovering evidence of this behavioral process in the material record.

THE FRONTIER: DEVELOPMENT OF THE CONCEPT

Early Ideas and Historical Studies

The systematic study of the frontier began in the nineteenth century and was encouraged by efforts to understand the nature of European expansion in North America. Early observers of the American frontier noted both a regional and processual component, a distinction that has characterized most subsequent studies of this phenomenon. The notion that American life and character had been shaped by the continual westward movement of population toward new lands was first expressed in the late eighteenth century (Smith 1950:3). By the midnineteenth century this notion had been refined into an argument linking free land to the development of democratic institutions, a process that derived from the frontier's perceived role as a safety valve for discontented elements of society (Tuttle 1967:226). At the same time, the frontier as a region defined by the limits of expansion was being developed as a statistical concept by census scholars so as to aid government researchers in their study of such areas (Mood 1945:24).

Both aspects of the frontier were emphasized by Frederick Jackson Turner's seminal essay, "The Significance of the Frontier in American History," published in 1893. In this influential paper, Turner combined the processual ideas about cultural development with a knowledge of changing geographical landscapes to produce an evolutionary scheme for American frontier settlement. Change was seen as an adaptation to the frontier environment, and its results were the creation of societies fundamentally different from those of the homeland. Turner's (1926) later emphasis on the role of geographic sections in American history grew directly from his contention that each frontier created a new society whose individual development resulted in a sectionally based political and economic selfconsciousness that would continue to characterize each former frontier region. The goal of Turner's inquiry was explanation, yet his arguments failed to provide adequate linkages between the frontier experiences and the behavior attributed to it. This failing, as Miller and Savage (1977:*xxvii–xxix*) have pointed out, is a result largely of the intellectual milieu of the period. The New History of the late nineteenth and early twentieth centuries adopted a presentist–relativist–subjectivist orientation in which the validity of historical interpretation was secondary to its basic purpose, which was, generally, the explanation or justification of present conditions. This particularistic and nationalistic approach placed the emphasis of frontier research on accounting for American uniqueness rather than the explication of general rules of frontier development (Hofstadter 1968:74). Consequently, explanation was lost amid loose generalizations and simplistic notions of social progress (Smith 1950:257). Turner's importance to the study of the frontier lies not in these shortcomings, but rather in his conception of frontier development as an adaptive response to conditions imposed by the physical and social environment of colonization and in his recognition, albeit limited, that certain processes of frontier change might not be unique to North America (Turner 1891:18). It is these aspects of colonization that are most germane to our discussion of the frontier.

The Frontier in Cross-Cultural Perspective

Since Turner, scholars studying frontiers have broadened the earlier parochial view by considering the frontier in cross-cultural perspective. James G. Leyburn proposed a generalist approach to the frontier in his *Frontier Folkways* published in 1935. He stressed both the spatial and processual aspects of frontiers, describing them as those regions on the outer fringe of settlement where pioneer societies are forced to make adaptive changes in order to survive in a basically unmodified environment. By comparing the nature of adaptations associated with various frontiers, Leyburn (1935:2) concluded that it would be possible to recognize "subtypes of social adjustment" based on differences in motives for colonization and the nature of the colony. He defined four subtypes of frontiers based upon a comparative study of a number of pioneer societies around the world. His basic types of frontier societies include small farm, settlement plantation, exploitative plantation, and camp frontiers. The former two are colonies characterized by permanent settlement while the others involve men only and are transitory in nature. Although a simple classification, Leyburn's scheme identified significant differences between frontiers unrecognized in earlier models.

Recent studies of frontiers have concentrated on a more precise definition of the frontier as a region in relation to existing states. Geographers have recognized frontiers as zones, often adjacent to a formal boundary, separating the settled and unsettled portions of a territory under the effective control of a state. Culturally and politically they are zones of transition stretching from the edge of the state core to the limits of its expansion (Kristof 1959:274; Weigert *et al.* 1957:115). The significance of frontier regions as zones of transition has led Prescott (1965:34) to distinguish between them and boundary areas also called frontiers. Frontiers within the bounds of a state's authority, or *settlement* frontiers, constitute regions of colonial expansion, in contrast to *political* frontiers, which refer only to the unclaimed borderlands between two states. Prescott (1965:55) has also recognized two types of settlement frontiers. These are *primary* frontiers, representing settlement regions at the de facto limit of a state's authority and *secondary* frontiers designating those areas originally passed over during initial expansion and settled only later when less suitable land became desirable due to population pressure.

Contemporary Frontier Studies

Interest in defining the processes of frontier change also expanded to include the study of contemporary frontier settlement. The work of Turner and Leyburn had been based on documented historical examples and their models of change were consequently, of a retrospective nature. In an effort to conduct "in process" analysis, other investigators have sought to observe colonization as it was taking place. Among the pioneering works in this field is that of the sociologist C. A. Dawson, whose study of contemporary agricultural settlement in the Peace River country of Alberta (1934) allowed him to observe a four stage sequence of change reflecting population growth, economic intensification, and an increasingly complex system of communications and transportation.

On the basis of their work in Equador and Bolivia, Casagrande *et al.* (1964) and Thompson (1970) postulated a series of regularities that characterize agricultural colonization. This phenomenon of change is characterized by the *colonization gradient,* a term which reflects the process by which the sociocultural system of the homeland is extended, replicated, and reintegrated on the frontier. Colonization is viewed through biological analogy as a process by which an organism establishes itself in a new ecological niche. It is analogous to the spread of a species by radiation to fill the space available within an ecological niche until stopped by a competing species or a boundary situation with which it cannot cope (Casagrande *et al.* 1964:283). The niche into which the colony expands involves the exploitation of various resources within the area of colonization, a region that extends from an entrepôt connecting it with the outside world to the edge of the unfolding frontier.

The colonization process is characterized by a simplification of the social, economic, and political systems of the intrusive society and is reflected in a loss of specialized forms (Harris 1977). This process of "cultural impoverishment" (Thompson 1970:198–199) expresses the revolutionary principle that a generalized, nonspecialized culture is more efficient for dealing with an extensive, relatively open environment (Sahlins and Service 1960:52). Although applicable to the area of colonization as a whole, the degree to which cultural impoverishment affects individual settlements varies according to their proximity to the edge of the frontier and distance from the entrepôt. The extent to which settlements are characterized by a loss of specialized forms is revealed in a gradient of settlement types within the area of colonization. These types exhibit a range of sociocultural complexity that also characterizes an evolutionary process of frontier change through time. The gradient mirrors both the synchronic structure of the colonial region and the diachronic stages through which frontier settlements pass as the area expands and its earliest settled portions achieve a higher postcolonial level of integration (Casagrande *et al.* 1964:314). As a consequence of its spatial and temporal aspects, the concept of the colonization gradient unites the frontier region with the process of colonial settlement. The general conclusions drawn from these studies of contemporary colonization offer a framework within which to analyze past agricultural frontiers more completely.

In an attempt to investigate sociocultural change on the frontier as a general phenomenon associated with all types of colonization, Robin Wells (1973) has proposed viewing the frontier as an interrelated system that extends beyond the intrusive society to include culturally distinct indigenous groups involved in the contact situation. Rather than being focused on adaptation within the colonial society, the effect of frontier expansion is instead measured by observing the extent of change among aboriginal peoples involved in the area's network of communications and differentially incorporated within the expanding system (Wells 1973:9). Because the degree of aboriginal acculturation is generally associated with a society's position in the communication network and distance from the colonial focus, the structure of the frontier system is similar in its spatial arrangement to the zonal patterning observable in the colonization gradient. Like the gradient, Wells's frontier system is constantly expanding so that the adaptation associated with each zone also represents a phase in a succession through which societies in the frontier system must pass (Wells 1973:10).

Colonization in Ecological Perspective

Casagrande *et al.*'s lead in the use of ecological analogy has been followed by others seeking to explain phenomenon of frontier change. Margolis (1977), for example, in studying the behavior of frontier cash crop agriculturalists, likened their short-term adaptive strategies to those employed by "fugitive species" in that they are preadapted to survival in changing environments and thus are able to take immediate advantage of transitory or unstable situations. Certain types of frontier subsistence strategies are, like those employed by fugitive species, unspecialized and highly adaptive to initial occupations. This advantage, however, makes it difficult for them to compete successfully with the more efficient strategies of more specialized groups (or species) who seek to occupy the same niche. This anticipated outcome, together with the general economic uncertainty of frontier life, is believed to encourage the employment of the destructive, quick return strategies characteristic of many frontiers together with the continued expansion of such areas (Margolis 1977:59).

More recently, Donald Hardesty (1980) proposed that models capable of explaining the interactive patterns associated with colonization be built around the use of ecological concepts. He suggested the use of the "ecological community" under transformation as a basic analogy for frontier change. Research problems should be concerned with identifying, documenting, and explaining key processes in this transformation, changes that set these processes in motion, and the impact of the processes on the colonists' social and habitat relations (Hardesty 1980:69).

Frontier development also may be examined in the light of several ecological principles that attempt to explain the adaptive significance of certain aspects of behavior associated with colonization. Two such principles, competitive exclusion and environmental stability, are linked to the diversity of behavior found in different types of frontiers. *Competitive exclusion* refers to the inability of organisms using the same resources to coexist permanently, requiring that they change habitats or environmental lifestyles. This principle varies in importance with the availability of resources to the production units of a frontier population, the organisms within the frontier community. On all frontiers, however, population pressure on resources eventually results in competition requiring one or both of two modifications, the exclusion of competing societies or a change in the patterns of resources used. The latter may lead to ethnic segregation of a resource use as Hardesty (1980:72) has shown, but it also may result in a reorganization of resource procurement and redistribution (Hudson 1969:371). This economic restructuring is one of the basic processes contributing to the increasing level of socioeconomic complexity observed in the colonization gradient.

Environmental stability is linked to the degree of diversity within an ecological community. Success in an unstable environment is less predictable. The employment of a greater range of subsistence-related strategies permits compensation for the increased likelihood that one may fail. The frontier environment is, of course, a result of the social environment of the colonists' own making as much as of the existing physical environment of the area of colonization (Hardesty 1980:74). Diversified economic behavior is adaptive in initial frontier settlement, and it has been argued elsewhere (Lewis 1975a:115) that societies possessing such diversified economics often appear to be preadapted to colonization. Processes introduced to buffer the effects of environmental instability include (1) increasing the complexity and the scale of economic networks in order to increase economic options and (2) technologically modifying the frontier habitat. Both buffering processes are likely to require social and economic adjustments in frontier societies. If the societies also are responding to the effects of competition, these processes may have an immediate ameliorating effect. The specialization and intensification brought about by attempts to increase environmental stability show the trend toward increasing complexity described in the Casagrande *et al.* model.

In addition to the ecological trends toward greater complexity, homogenizing processes are also at work within frontier societies. Hardesty (1980) has recognized that common ideology as well as the dependent role of the colony in the expanding economy of the homeland tend to integrate the frontier. Casagrande *et al.* (1964:283–284) also recognized that participation in a larger socioeconomic system is the principal unifying force in frontier change, because it draws the frontier together through a common tradition and market network.

The simultaneous operation of divisive and unifying processes on the frontier illustrates two principles of growth common to organic systems undergoing change. These are *progressive segregation,* by which the system tends to move toward increasing functional differentiation among its parts, and *systematization,* which is an opposing trend toward wholeness resulting in a closer interrelationship among the system's parts (Hall and Fagan 1956:22). The concurrence of these two processes is not uncommon in societies evolving toward higher levels of sociocultural integration (Hole and Heizer 1977:362). Given the same trend among frontier societies, the operation of these processes does not appear unusual here.

Current understanding of the processes involved in colonization may be seen as a growth out of the refinement of a concept of frontier settlement developed over the past century. From the beginning, the frontier has been recognized as both region and process. Comparative studies overcame early particularistic notions of uniqueness and discovered variability linked with function. Studies of contemporary colonies permitted the definition of processes associated with frontier adaptation and provided models in which to observe such change. Finally, with the employment of ecological concepts, it is possible to examine frontier change in terms of general behavioral processes and begin to explain them.

THE FRONTIER AND EUROPEAN EXPANSION

Frontiers in the World Economy

It is necessary to move beyond the frontier as an isolated entity and examine the larger milieu within which colonization has occurred to produce an expanded model of frontier change built upon earlier studies. Because we are interested in exploring overseas colonization, frontiers must be seen in relation to their role in European expansion during the postmedieval and modern periods. It is useful to examine European expansion in terms of its organization without discussing origins and causes, for it is here that the roots of modern colonization lie.

Perhaps the most comprehensive recent investigation of European expansion is Immanuel Wallerstein's *The Modern World System* (1974). In this study, he argued that the histories of the postmedieval nations of Europe and the territories with which they interacted cannot adequately be explained without recourse to the concept of a *world system,* in which the economics of all the affected areas are enmeshed in a web of mutual interdependence. He chose the term *world economy* to characterize this system because of the particular nature of its organization. Its self-contained economic mode, based on the fact that economic factors operated within an arena larger than that which any political entity could completely control, prevented domination by a single nation. Such a situation gave capitalist entrepreneurs a structurally based freedom of maneuver and allowed continual expansion of the world economy (Wallerstein 1974:348).

A world economy is composed of two basic parts based on the division of labor associated with production. This functional distinction is expressed geographically in the separation of the world economy into the *core states* of Europe at its center and *peripheral areas* at its boundaries (Wallerstein 1980a:21). The latter are distinguished as comprising "that geographical sector of (a world economy) wherein production is primarily of lower-ranking goods (that is goods whose labor is less well rewarded) but which is an integral part of the overall system of the division of labor, because the commodities involved are essential for daily use" (Wallerstein 1974:302). Exchange between peripheral areas and core states is characterized by a "vertical specialization" involving the movement of raw materials from the former to the latter and the movement of manufactures and services in the opposite direction (Gould 1972:235–236). Because the world economy is continually expanding, it is inevitable that its geographical structure will periodically change to accommodate new growth. A process integral to expansion is the formation of *semiperipheral areas* that function as collection points of vital skills and serve to deflect political pressures aimed at the core states from peripheral areas. Because they are still located outside the political arena of the core states, however, semiperipheral areas are prevented from entering into political coalitions in the same manner as the core-area states (Wallerstein 1974:350) and thus remain dependent on them.

Colonization and International Trade

Although European colonization of the New World was conducted with various motives in mind, its chief benefit to the core states was economic. This advantage derived from three sources: gains from international trade, the migration of commercial agents or factors, and commercial policy (Gray 1976:124). International trade in noncompetitive goods permitted the colonizing power to acquire resources unavailable at home and control their production. Wallerstein (1980a:23) characterized the process of controlling such resources as one of incorporation, which involved changes in politico–military and production structures. Factor migration was necessary to control effectively the supply of colonial resources and increase the potential for trade in additional competitive and noncompetitive goods. The movement of factors to peripheral areas permitted the combination of home country capital and local labor required to reorganize indigenous production methods. Their risk could be reduced to an acceptable level only with the establishment of a system of laws recognizing the property right of mother country nationals. The protection of capital and personnel thus encouraged the establishment of a political overlordship (Gray 1976:126–127).

Colonial Settlement and Production

Gray (1976:127–129) argued that, although factor migration is characteristic of colonization, the nature of factor settlement varies in tropical and temperate areas. Colonizing tropical or other nontemperate areas involves the introduction of technology and capital into a nonreproducible climate to produce more efficiently noncompetitive commercial crops or to carry out various extractive activities. Production based on the combination of these elements is a process of industrialization, which is typified by trading, ranching, and industrial activities as well as the exploitative plantation. In such colonies, foreign residence is temporary and characterized by great expenditure on imports to reproduce home life and keep savings in homeland banks. The latter practice resulted in large transfer flows from the colony to the mother country. Foreign factors' control over rent-earning lands and the mother country's influence over the colonial market depresses gains from trade by the indigenous colonial population and creates enclaves instead of spread.

In temperate climates, on the other hand, many important exports are more often competitive with domestic production in the core state. Here production requires migration of labor from the homeland, which is induced by differences in the marginal product of labor in the two areas. The migrants' desire to permanently resettle in temperate colonies creates a different pattern of colonial development. The new pattern is characterized by reduction in the leakages of funds for imports to the mother country and the reinvestment of these funds in real assets in the colony. Both trends encourage economic spread effects (Gray 1976:129–130).

The dichotomy in colonial settlement is also apparent in patterns of commercial policy. Prior to the twentieth century, European expansion was guided largely by mercantilism, a concept which created commercial policies that permitted the mother country to accumulate the largest share of the gains derived from colonial trade. Mercantilistic policies were expressed in trade regulations that distinguished between colonies producing noncompetitive and competitive goods. As a result, there was generally little interference with the former as long as manufacturers from the homeland established a priority on the colonies' imports. The trade of the latter, however, was strictly controlled to protect home industries (Gray 1976:131–132).

Insularity and Colonial Production

When seen in light of the structure of colonial trade, Gray's distinction between tropical and temperate colonization pertains less directly to climate and topography or landforms than to the nature of commodities produced. Different types of production require distinct settlement systems and particular forms of economic interaction with the core state. The two types of colonization were defined by these criteria. The association between settlement forms and economic role in the colonial system of the parent state also was explored by Steffen (1980), who conducted a comparative study of frontier types. These types are defined on the basis of the extent and nature of the interacting links with the homeland, or *insularity*. Insularity, in turn, is shown in the level of change a colonial society has undergone. The fewer or more tenuous the linkages, the greater the insularity and the more likely adaptation will have to be made in the colony's structure and organization.

On the basis of insularity, Steffen (1980:*xii, svii–xviii*) defined two broad categories of frontiers, cosmopolitan and insular. *Cosmopolitan frontiers* are economically specialized and often short term with their success based largely on the colonial policy of the parent state. As a result of direct manipulation in the colony's activities, there is a low degree of insularity and no opportunity for indigenous development. Consequently, no fundamental alteration in economic, political, and social institutions and behavior patterns are likely to arise on cosmopolitan frontiers. Examples of cosmopolitan frontiers in North America are ranching, fur trading, and mining to which might also be added *exploitative plantations* as defined by Leyburn (1935). These frontier colonies generally produce noncompetitive goods of the sort characteristic of Gray's (1976) *tropical colonization*.

Insular frontiers, on the other hand, are economically diverse and long term in nature. Their success requires a more extensive adaptation to local conditions, causing links with the socioeconomic system of the homeland to become fewer and more indirect. The greater degree of insularity associated with a commitment to indigenous development is coincident with the more prevasive change characteristic of such colonies (Steffen 1980:*xviii*). Insular frontiers usually involve specialized and generalized agriculture of the type found Leyburn's (1935) *small farm* and *settlement plantation* frontiers and tend to produce the competitive goods typical of *temperate colonization* (Gray 1976).

The colonization accompanying European expansion was necessary to the development of the emerging capitalist world economy. The colonies' role on the periphery of this socioeconomic system was limited to the production of inexpensive raw commodities for the benefit of the parent state. The states' monopolistic position in colonial trade was reinforced by mercantilist policies restricting colonial production. Differential production requirements affected the types of social and economic linkages between the colony and its parent state. The nature of these linkages, in turn, influenced the structure and organization of the frontier areas. Cosmopolitan frontiers were devoted to the specialized production of noncompetitive goods and are characterized by short-term settlement and limited indigenous development. Insular frontiers, however, involved the production of diverse and often competitive goods and the establishment of long-term settlement. Their looser ties with homeland encouraged the reinvestment of capital and resources in the colony and permitted the development of distinct colonial societies.

The Sequential Development of Colonial Settlement

Although they are distinct forms of colonization, insular and cosmopolitan frontier settlement are not always mutually exclusive developments and may take place in the same area, though usually not simultaneously. Their occurrence generally takes place in sequential order with cosmopolitan frontier settlement representing the initial form of colonization in a region. Colonization varies as the level of interaction between the homeland and the frontier area increases with the length of contact. Activities associated with the level of interaction are determined by the role of the colony in the larger world economy, a role that varies with the duration and complexity of contact.

Meinig (1976) recently proposed a sequence of stages describing the development of European colonization. His initial four stages are exploration, harvesting of immediate coastal resources, barter, and plunder, all of which result only in sporadic and intermittant contact. Because these stages are based on ports in the homeland, interaction is limited and involves no fixed points of contact or settlement within the colonial region. It does, however, permit the accumulation of knowledge about the region and its exploitable resources that affect the direction that subsequent contact will take.

The next two stages involve the establishment of commercial outposts and the imposition of imperial authority. Interaction is increased with the creation and expansion of a fixed focus of colonization in the frontier area and the introduction of a permanent intrusive presence there. The purpose of colonization still is limited largely to the establishment of control to support military, trading, or religious activities. Colonists reside there only temporarily as wealth seekers or agents of state institutions. Interaction of this nature is characteristic of cosmopolitan frontiers. The occurrence of cosmopolitan frontier settlement immediately following the establishment of permanent contact implies an integral role for this type of colonization in the early development of frontier regions as sources of export commodities. Economic and political factors relating to the area's exploitation, however, determine whether this form of interaction will persist or a more permanent, complexly organized social and economic organization will evolve.

Meinig's (1976) final stages of plantation and imperial colonization discuss the organizational adaptations characteristic of insular frontier settlement. Permanent agricultural settlement, factor migration, local reinvestment of capital, and the development of a resident colonial society supported by increased immigration and economic diversification replace the specialized, transient organization out of which the insular frontier evolved. The imperial colony completes the process of colonization by transferring an integrated complex of social, economic, and political interests from the homeland to the area of colonization. This results in the establishment of a self-perpetuating entity physically removed from the parent state.

Although cosmopolitan and insular frontier settlement may occur in sequential order within an area of colonization, each constitutes a seaprate process. The outcome of each is based on the adaptive requirements of the type of colonization. Viewed in the light of the frontier's larger role in the world economy, the processes of change accompanying colonization may be seen as regional developmental processes. These processes are conditioned by the function of the colony in the larger socioeconomic system and the nature of the colony's links with a state at the system's core. Much of the variety observed in the development of individual frontiers may be explained due to their particular economic roles as insular or cosmopolitan frontier regions. Because of the fundamental differences between these two types of colonization, the evolution of each proceeds along different paths. The temporary and restricted nature of the cosmopolitan frontier and the closeness of its ties with the parent state retard change. Long-term effects of such change are consequently more difficult to perceive. Insular frontiers, on the other hand, usually develop into permanent societies at a level of integration comparable to that of their parent states. The evolution of such regions is easier to recognize and, for this reason, most documented processes of colonization have been based on the study of insular frontiers.

Toward a Model of Colonial Settlement

The model of colonization used here is intended to deal with permanent agricultural settlement in British North America, an area that may be defined as a collection of insular frontiers. To examine the historical development of a particular frontier region, the model must be capable of integrating the broad characteristics of insular frontiers with processes of insular frontier change. This may be accomplished by examining insular colonization as a form of agricultural expansion. Viewing frontier development in terms of such a basic process should provide an explanatory framework in which to examine the adaptive significance of individual processes of change and identify those most crucial to the operation of insular frontiers.

THE DEVELOPMENT OF A MODEL OF INSULAR FRONTIER SETTLEMENT

Expansion and Spatial Organization

Insular frontier settlement is essentially a process of agricultural expansion associated with overseas colonization in a world economy. Its existence is a result of the deliberate movement by foreign colonists into a new area to use its resources to produce commercial crops and other commodities. Because of the permanent nature of agricultural settlement, the insular frontier process involves long-term occupation and growth, which require an increasingly complex level of organization. Emphasis on the production of commercial exports and the development of an internal economy are the key elements inherent in insular frontier settlement. These two developments also appear to be common to agricultural expansion in general. This suggests that processes affecting agricultural expansion are also important to the evolution of agricultural frontiers. It is useful to begin our discussion by considering existing models of agricultural expansion.

Economic models of agricultural expansion have attempted to explain this phenomenon in terms of the relationship of distance, costs, and production to the spatial distribution of settlement. Over a century ago, J. H. von Thünen (1966) recognized the significance of these variables in the landscape of his native district of Mecklenburg in Germany. On the basis of data from this area, he postulated that the cost of transport to market increased with distance and that this "economic distance" affected the competition for land and, consequently, the types of activities that could profitably be carried out. Von Thünen's model of an ideal state located on a physically homogeneous plain is characterized by a central market surrounded by concentric zones of production. Competition for the use of desirable zones closest to the market leads to the concentration of the highest rent-yielding farming activities there. Further from the market this competition becomes less intense, permitting lower rent-yielding activities to flourish. The determination of which crop is optimal for each zone is based on comparative land values, crop revenues and production per acre, and crop perishability (von Thünen 1966).

Although von Thünen's model represents a static situation, it describes relationships between variables that resulted in the development of this landscape. This dynamic aspect of the model appears applicable to the study of agricultural expansion. In an attempt to explore the process of expansion, Richard Peet (1970–1971) expanded the von Thünen model.

In Peet's model, spatial expansion of a zonal system is viewed as a process linked to two sets of forces, changes in demand and changes in the technology of supply. Increases in demand permit the distance at which a crop can profitably be grown to be increased. This has a "shunting" effect on other crop zones, producing a larger total agricultural supply area. Advances in transport technology, on the other hand, affect spatial expansion by lowering the rate of revenue-decrease with distance, which permits crop zones to expand and the volume of supply to increase (Peet 1970–1971:188–189).

Changes in demand and the efficiency of supply are not independent processes but are linked in a relationship of mutual reinforcement. Higher prices resulting from greater urban demand provide capital and incentive for technical change in agricultural supply mechanisms. Such change, in turn, increases rural demand for consumer goods and urban services, which enhances urban employment, results in higher wages, and brings about a greater demand for agricultural products. The increase in consumption requires further zonal expansion to enlarge supplies and encourages the repetition of the sequence (Peet 1970–1971:190).

Rises in demand and prices may result from either an increase in exports or an increase in the urban population, both of which are conditions characteristic of colonial areas. The consequent extension of the von Thünen zones provides for expansion in order to incorporate new lands for cultivation. Continued territorial enlargement results in the movement of different kinds of production into new areas which alters the qualitative nature of the demand for transport. The necessity of restructuring the transportation system in the face of increased traffic can provide a favorable situation for the adoption of more efficient methods of movement. The lower cost of operation can help support agricultural expansion during fluctuations in the economy that inevitably follow initial growth. The manner in which the zones advance is closely tied to the speed at which demand increase and production–transportation cost decrease change in relation to each other. When these two components change at a similar rate, prices remain stable and the zones expand in sequence so that all the types of production pass over a given location. When rapid changes occur in the technology of production or transportation, and prices fall, expansion may be undercut, especially in marginal areas, resulting in stagnation or even depopulation (Peet 1970–1971:191, 200).

Expansion, Production, and Transport

Peet's discussion of agricultural expansion reveals the significance of this economic process to insular frontier development. This process is linked to an initial increase in demand for frontier products in previously settled areas, a condition that permits the extension of commercial production beyond its previous extent. Increases in demand, however, can be satisfied in two ways, through geographical expansion or the intensification of present modes of production (Katzman 1975:273). If we assume that the choice of frontier expansion is a decision of economic cost, then it should be possible to view this process in terms of a *least-cost* model. Green (1980) proposed a model in which the two key variables in agricultural production, land and labor, are compared in order to arrive at a range within which a certain level of production is possible. Given that the least expensive of these two variables would be maximized, a high least-cost proportion of land to labor results. The cost of movement to and from fields places an upper limit on the amount of land that can be exploited from existing settlements. If an increase in production becomes necessary, either fission or intensification must occur. Because the higher value of labor would increase the cost of production if used more intensively, fission, or expansion, is the less expensive of the two strategies. If production demands regularly exceed agricultural output, sustained colonization will be the outcome (Green 1980:217–228).

The key to linking economic processes to the nature and distribution of frontier settlement is the relationship between production and transport. The technology of transportation is a significant economic variable in sustaining spatial expansion. The network of trade and communications linkages it develops is primarily responsible for binding the area of colonization together and maintaining its ties with the homeland. Transportation systems shape frontier expansion by encouraging settlement along the routes by which commercial staples may be shipped at least expense to market (Katzman 1975:269). Because the paramount requirement of a frontier transportation system is the funneling of colonial products to markets in the parent state and the redistribution of supplies into the colony, transportation routes generally follow a dendritic pattern focused on the entrepôt connecting the colony with the homeland (Casagrande *et al.,* 1964:312). So important is the organization of this trade that routes facilitating the most direct feasible movement are quickly established even if less efficient precolonial road systems already exist (Rees 1975:334).

The transport pattern on the frontier evolves in response to changing spatial organization of activities that accompanies expansion. Comparative studies of contemporary colonies have revealed that changes in transport structure follow a regular pattern of sequential stages. A model of transport change based on data from colonial states in Africa was proposed by Taaffe *et al.* (1963) and was examined further by Weaver (1977) in the context of the American Southeast. The model describes four stages of transport expansion following initial settlement. Weaver (1977:46) suggested, however, that the continuous and uneven nature of change makes the onset and termination of each stage difficult to distinguish and argued that the development of transport structure may be more accurately portrayed as an unbroken process rather than a series of distinct phases.

The process by which the transport network in a colonial region evolves may be expected to occur in the following manner. Early colonization is characterized by the establishment of a series of ports with few lateral connections between them. Although each has initially only a limited hinterland, major lines of penetration soon appear as the frontier expands into the interior. With their emergence, hinterland transportation costs are reduced for some ports. Markets expand both at the successful ports and their interior centers. Feeder routes also begin to expand from the ports, allowing them to enlarge their hinterlands at the expense of adjacent ports. Nodes begin to form on the major routes of penetration and become focal points for feeder networks of their own. The feeder networks of individual ports and their subsidiary settlements soon begin to mesh. Eventually, they link nearly all of the ports, interior centers, and principal nodes in a region with one another. This complex network of trade and communications contrasts with the simple network of the frontier period and marks the reorganization of the transport structure in response to the greater economic and political integration of postcolonial settlement.

Settlement Pattern and the Organization of Activities

Settlement pattern on the frontier is a direct result of a desire to situate in locations accessible to trade and communication routes and is a consequence of population growth and economic change over time. The process of settlement pattern change occurring in a frontier area was explored by Hudson (1969). He constructed a model defining three developmental stages covering the period from earliest settlement to the incorporation of the frontier area as a part of the parent state. The model is based mainly on analogies drawn from ecological spatial distribution theory and postulates that similar processes affect the morphology of rural settlement during times of rapid expansion. The consecutive occurrence of settlement forms that characterize the model's stages was observed empirically by Swedland (1975) in a study of population growth and settlement expansion in the Connecticut Valley of Massachusetts over a period of two centuries.

Hudson's first stage is one of *colonization,* in which the new area is first occupied by the intrusive population. Settlement density at this time is low and the settlement pattern random but not isolated from the colonial trade and communications network. The second stage is one of *spread,* in which settlement increases as a result of population growth. Because settlement tends to spread out from earlier population centers, its distribution becomes clustered. With increased population expansion, the vacant land is occupied. Finally, readjustment to the pattern of growth also is necessary to achieve a state of equilibrium as settlements approach an optimum size. This process marks a stage of *competition* between settlements over the finite resources of an area of colonization. Competitive exclusion of groups and activities often occurs at this stage, and settlements with a disadvantageous economic position may decline or become abandoned. One result of competition is an even spacing of settlements. The reorganization of a frontier area resulting from competition may be seen, in part, as an attempt to stablize the economic environment to permit maximum settlement density. An increase in the complexity of scale of economic networks and technological modifications of habitat mark the introduction of "buffering" processes necessary to achieve such stability.

Settlement composition reflects the economic organization of insular frontiers, the complexity of which varies with the colony's stage of development. It has been observed that population density is related directly to the social and economic function of communities in the areas they serve. Normally, in a stable settled area, a *hierarchy of community types* is present, each of which performs certain functions. As the area's population density decreases, an upward shift in functions occurs so that services performed by a community at a lower level in the hierarchy must be performed by one at a higher level. When population density increases, the opposite effect occurs (Berry 1967:33–34). In a frontier area, the population density is initially too low to support an elaborate functional settlement hierarchy. Most economic, social, political, and religious activities are concentrated in key settlements called *frontier towns*. These settlements serve as centers of trade and communications within the colony, and by means of their direct connection with the colony's entrepôt, link the frontier directly with the parent state (Casagrande *et al.* 1964: 312–313).

As one moves geographically further from the colony's entrepôt, settlement functions become increasingly less complex. Casagrande *et al.* (1964:313–314) identified three additional types. *Nucleated settlements* are smaller than frontier towns, yet they remain politically organized and serve as subsidiary centers of trade. Economically, they are linked to the entrepôt via the frontier town.

Seminucleated settlements are usually small and more dispersed. Community facilities are absent or occur irregularly because of their lower level of integration.

Finally, *dispersed settlement*, consisting of scattered households, represent the lowest level of the frontier settlement hierarchy. Although isolated, most remain integrated within the larger socioeconomic system of the colony as producers of cash crops. Because the limits of an area of colonization are poorly defined and constantly shifting, a dispersed settlement will lie outside this system on the pioneer fringe.

The expansion of an area of colonization results in continual movement toward new lands on the periphery of settlement. The uneven rate of expansion results in a movement of dispersed settlement beyond the point where transport costs make commercial agriculture unprofitable. Settlement in the pioneer fringe is characterized by subsistence farming carried out by households connected only loosely with the colony. Because the competition for land found in commercial frontier areas is absent here and population density is low, land extensive and destructive types of subsistence strategies often prevail at the pioneer fringe. With the extension of the commercial frontier transportation network into these areas, however, the competition for land resources usually results in the abandonment of such strategies in favor of those yielding a higher revenue (Katzman 1975:269–270). The pioneer fringe may be viewed as a zone of transition in which incipient commercial activities are carried out in anticipation of participating fully in cash crop production (Norton and Conkling 1974:55).

The composition of colonial settlement exhibits gradual loss of specialized forms which is characteristic of the process of "cultural impoverishment" underlying the colonization gradient. Geographically, the gradient progresses from the entrepôt at the frontier's closer edge to the pioneer fringe at the furthest reaches of its transportation network. The frontier is a zone of agricultural expansion, the internal structure of which is continually changing to accommodate the dynamic colonial economy. The roles of individual frontier settlements also change as a consequence of frontier expansion and reorganization. This is not to say that each settlement will pass through each of the settlement types described above, but generally, complex frontier settlements begin as simpler ones. Similarly, structural changes in the transportation network of an expanding frontier may bypass earlier frontier towns, which results in their decline and even abandonment. Ghost towns are not uncommon features in former frontier regions. With the closing of the frontier period of growth, characterized by Hudson's (1969) stage of competition, the colonial region is reintegrated on a level near that of the parent state. This process is accompanied by a restructing of the settlement pattern and the development of a more complex settlement hierarchy. The colonization gradient has moved on. It is an adaptation to the demographic and economic conditions formed at the advancing edge of settlement and is associated only with those areas. Although frontier settlements linger into the postfrontier period, their roles are changed to attest their new positions in a permanently settled region.

Agricultural Production and Markets

The organizational characteristics of insular frontier development describe the process of expansion as a general phenomenon associated with long-term agricultural colonization. The structure of individual frontier systems, however, must remain flexible enough to allow them to accommodate the requirements of regional staple crop resources. These requirements affect both settlement pattern and the social relations of agricultural production. Earle and Hoffman (1976:11, 67) proposed that the size and spatial patterning of colonial settlements are related to the type of staple crops produced. Each staple, because of the particular nature of its bulk, weight, and perishability, necessitates distinct commodity flows and processing demands that differentially encourage the development of various urban functions within the area of colonization. These functions include staple packaging, associated industrial procedures, transportation services, and the provisioning and repair activities related to freight shipment. When expansionary markets result in increased staple flows and where the commodity is bulky, weighty, and perishable, elaborate settlement systems emerge as a result of the commodity's impact on regional transport, manufacturing, and service activities. In contrast, the production of compact and nonperishable commodities require simpler support systems and, consequently, less complex patterns of settlement.

The requirements of regional staple crop production also affect the social relations of production, that is, the manner in which frontier agriculture is organized. Katzman (1975:273) argued that the two basic modes of frontier production, the small farm and the plantation, demonstrate the extent to which the staple crop produced is land intensive rather than capital or labor intensive in nature. Economics of scale also favor the large-scale production of certain crops. The significant factor in determining mode of production, however, may be the crop's annual labor requirements. Earle (1978:54–55) observed that the slave mode of production characteristic of plantations is efficient only if employed on a continuous basis throughout the year, but hired labor associated with small farm production may be more efficiently employed on a short-term basis. Consequently, labor-intensive crops such as tobacco, cotton, and wet rice, which require constant maintenance, are found on plantations, whereas small grains that require only periodic applications of labor are grown on small farms.

The decision to engage in either small farm or plantation production is influenced heavily by the man–land ratio of the frontier (Katzman 1975:274–275). Low density settlement in colonial areas results in a scarcity of labor which causes wages to rise. Even if land ownership is monopolized by a few, labor's high wages tend to lower rents and discourage the large-scale labor-intensive production typical of plantations. If, however, the mobility of labor can be controlled through the imposition of serfdom or slavery, the man–land endowment can be increased, making plantation production feasible. The social relations of frontier staple production may be seen to hinge not only upon the requirements of the staple crop but also on whether or not the landlords can offset labor's market power with their own political power to control its mobility.

A Model of Frontier Change

Based on information contained in the previous discussion, a model of insular frontier change may be constructed. In the model, phenomena associated with the process of agricultural colonization are organized according to six characteristics. These deal with the patterned organization of the frontier region in time and space and the activities likely to have been connected with its various components. The model is designed for the study of insular frontiers in general and has not been constructed solely for the examination of a particular region. Because the model's characteristics reflect processual change rather than a chain of historical events, they describe organizational aspects of culture that should be discernible in either written sources or the archaeological record. The characteristics of insular frontier change are as follows.

1. *Establishment.* The colony must be established as a permanent settlement sustained by the production of competitive export staples destined primarily for markets in the parent state. An insular frontier area remains tied culturally with the homeland; however, the nature of their economic relationship encourages the reinvestment of capital and resources in the colony and the consequent development of a distinct colonial society.

2. *Transport and Spatial Patterning.* The form of a colonial area is determined by the spatial pattern of its transportation network linking the agricultural settlements to the entrepôt and the parent state. The transportation network normally forms a dendritic network which will supercede all those existing previous to colo-

nization. Because accessibility is crucial to successful commercial agricultural production, settlement will follow the transportation system. The geographical size and shape of a particular frontier will depend on the physical and cultural landscape of the frontier and the technology available to the intrusive society.

3. *Expansion.* The frontier is characterized by a regular process of expansion which is an adaptive response to increasing demand for staple export production. Expansion is sustained by improvements in the methods and organization of the transportation system that maintain trade and communications on the frontier. Its increased efficiency supports expanded production during periods of lower demand and serves as a base for the future enlargement of the zone of commercial production.

4. *Settlement Pattern.* The settlement pattern of colonial areas changes through time in response to increasing population density and economic complexity. Three stages of colonization, spread, and competition mark the evolution of a newly occupied territory into a stable area of settlement at a level of integration comparable to that of the parent state. These stages are characterized by a trend toward an evenly spaced settlement pattern. This trend discloses processes of expansion within and readjustment to the limits of the colonial niche.

5. *Organization of Activities.* The initially low population density of a frontier region results in a more dispersed settlement pattern than that in the homeland. This settlement pattern is revealed in the organization of activities in the colony. The smaller number of settlements results in an abbreviated settlement hierarchy which tends to concentrate social, economic, political, and religious activities within the colony at focal points, called *frontier towns.* These serve as termini of the transportation network in the colony and link the scattered settlements of the frontier to the entrepôt. In addition to the frontier town, *nucleated, seminucleated,* and *dispersed* settlements occur, the last of which may extend into the *pioneer fringe,* a zone of transition not yet fully participating in commercial frontier agriculture.

The settlement pattern and social relations of production may vary with the staple crop grown. The cultivation, processing, and transportation requirements of the crops are reflected in the distribution of settlements devoted to their production. Differential labor requirements emerge in the employment of a permanent or seasonal work force and the respective appearance of the plantation or the farm as the primary mode of agricultural production.

6. *The Colonization Gradient.* The hierarchy of settlements within an area of colonization shows a pattern of increasing socioeconomic complexity called the *colonization gradient.* This gradient is visible spatially at any given time, but it also may be observed temporally as the roles of settlements change in response to the region's development into a settled area. As the frontier region expands, the spatial patterning of the colonization gradient is likely to be repeated in newly settled areas. The transport structure within the area of colonization is also apt to mirror organizational changes characteristic of the colonization gradient. The expansion of the frontier is accompanied by an increasingly complex network of trade and communications. Stretching inland from the initial points of contact, linear routes of pen-

etration open the frontier region to settlement. This network begins to branch out to provide more direct access between economic centers and their hinterlands and develop interconnections with adjacent colonial regions.

THE SOUTH CAROLINA FRONTIER: SOURCES OF EVIDENCE

Evidence of the insular frontier colonization process in British colonial South Carolina should be discernible in the documentary record produced by the colonial society and in the patterning of archaeological remains scattered across the frontier landscape. Each type of evidence represents data derived through a separate source of transmission and the way that such data disclose past events varies with the manner in which the events are likely to have been recorded or retained by that source. Neither source forms a complete record of the past but consists of the results of various different transmission processes.

The Documentary Record

Behavior recorded in documents has been consciously preserved by those who compiled accounts of it. The contents of these sources will reveal the significance of the particular events to the individual chroniclers and their motives for preserving them. Obviously, the written record is biased as a result of the social, political, economic, ethinic, religious, racial, and other prejudices of those who compiled it. In societies where literacy is restricted, and even in those where it is not, documentary accounts record only the views of certain individuals belonging to particular segments of the total population (Glassie 1975:8). To interpret the documentary record, the investigator must consider its contents in light of the author's potential bias as well as the accuracy of his information by noting its consistency with comparative accounts (Barzun and Graff 1962:134–135; Bloch 1953:110–116). And historical documents, like any other artifact of the past, are also subject to destruction at the hands of the man and nature. With these qualifications in mind, it should be clear that the historical documentary record has many gaps and contains much misinformation. What are its limitations with regard to the study of culture process?

Processes of change, such as those involved in colonization, are generalizations abstracted from the comparative analysis of situations in which relevant economic, ecological, and other variables are held constant. The characteristics of such processes are manifested in historical events observed and recorded by contemporary individuals and compiled by others who came later. Their accounts, including both public and private documents, can provide information, both direct and comparative, useful in describing and arranging events in sequences relevant to larger processes. These accounts, of course, contain the bias of their authors, but are also subject to limitations based on the interests of the groups for which they were written.

The second point directly affects the completeness of the historical record. This selectivity can severely limit the types of questions that may be posed of particular sets of documentary data. In recent years, attempts have been made to extract additional information from historical sources through the use of quantitative analyses (see, for example, Fogel and Engerman 1974). Such studies have employed these methods primarily to elicit data useful in understanding the economic factors that underlie historical developments. Quantitative, or cliometric, studies have produced a great deal of useful information relating to American economic history. In particular, the economics of slave agriculture in the American South have received a great deal of attention, and the use of quantitative methods has forced the reinterpretation of a number of traditional beliefs regarding this subject (Fogel and Engerman 1974). Cliometric studies, however, require large amounts of quantitifiable source material. As Winius (1980:80–81) has pointed out, such data are available, for the most part, only for the last two centuries. Studies of periods prior to this time, which postdates much of the expansion of Europe, will rarely have adequate quantifiable data available and are limited by the completeness of their source material. Although the expansion of Europe ironically gave rise to the core-state bureaucracies and other organizations that would eventually produce such records, much of the colonization process would be poorly recorded by those who carried it out. This bias in the recording of historical events affects the degree to which documentary information may be used to identify and describe specific historical colonization processes and thereby limits the use of such data in the study of these phenomena.

The Archaeological Record

Archaeologically derived data relating to processes of change are a very different source of historical evidence. Rather than being the result of a conscious effort to record events of the past, archaeological materials are the by-product of activities associated with such events. The archaeological record was formed for the most part unconsciously and unintentionally as a result of everyday activities carried out by all members of a given society. This material record, if undisturbed, is likely to provide a more complete cultural expression than documentary sources because it lacks the bias inherent in the latter.

Although more extensive and less subject to falsification, archaeological evidence presents problems of interpretation more complex than those inherent in historical criticism. Briefly, the analysis of archaeological materials involves an understanding of the relationship between their form and the patterning and behavior that produced them. This relationship is dependent upon activities associated with that behavior and the transformations by which the by-products of past activities enter the archaeological record and are affected by cultural and natural forces after they pass into disuse (Schiffer 1972, 1976). The content and distribution of material on archaeological sites can be used as a basis for inferring the types of behavior that occurred there and identifying the function of the settlements where it took place

(South 1979a). Archaeological inference is not unlimited. It is necessary to develop an understanding of the dynamics of the cultural adaptations involved in the sociocultural system before the relationship between archaeological patterning and past behavior can be established (Binford 1980:4–5).

The identification of settlement function and distribution based on archaeological evidence should also provide information relating to the existence and nature of sociocultural processes. Because they often reflect aspects of past societies that are omitted from documentary sources, archaeological data provide a body of information that can substantially supplement the historical record. Their unbiased nature can also serve to substantiate or repudiate uncertain conclusions based on written sources (for example, see Watkins and Noël Hume 1967). Because our knowledge of the relationships between behavior and its material by-products is still rudimentary and the adaptive significance of many aspects of behavior poorly understood, it is not yet possible to address many of the historical questions that can be answered by looking to documentary sources. Both types of evidence are useful and desirable elements to be employed in the investigation of historical problems, including those dealing explicitly with processes of change. Documentary and archaeological evidence should be viewed as complementary rather than conflicting means for studying such processes. Each is capable of employing its particular strengths to clarify and supplement information provided by the other.

Directions for Research

This study examines the development of the insular frontier in British colonial South Carolina by referring to documentary and archaeological evidence. The use of a documented example of colonization will aid in testing the frontier model, because data from several sources of evidence are available to determine its accuracy as a general explanatory construct. The degree to which the archaeological study supports the historical analysis illustrates the degree to which each methodology can ascertain the occurrence of the insular frontier process and demonstrate the frontier model's usefulness. The study will also emphasize the potential ability of archaeological data to supply information about the settlement of colonial areas for which documentary information is unavailable. The successful employment of archaeological evidence in the investigation of insular frontier development in colonial South Carolina should demonstrate the extent to which general processes of change are reflected both in documentary and material data. It also confirms the necessity of using both methods together to discern the existence of such processes.

Colonial South Carolina, an area settled for the most part during the eighteenth century, was an area of initial permanent European settlement on the Eastern Seaboard of North America and is easily discernible as a physical entity. Adequate documentary sources exist to determine the form and extent of its expansion through time and identify processes of change occurring there during the frontier period. Archaeologically, the region has been extensively explored, and this information with remnant landscape data should also reveal the nature of past processes of change. In the following chapter, the South Carolina frontier will be reviewed through documentary and cartographic evidence and compared to the characteristics of insular frontier change outlined in the model. The results of this analysis may then be used as a basis for examining this frontier region in archaeological perspective.

3

The Development of South Carolina as an
Insular Frontier

INTRODUCTION

The European settlement of South Carolina took place in a period of just over a hundred years. Between 1670 and the close of the eighteenth century, the region was transformed from an area populated by numerous aboriginal societies of varying levels of complexity to one inhabited largely by Europeans and Africans and integrated within the expanding colonial economy of western Europe. The settlement of South Carolina began later than that of many English colonies along the Eastern Seaboard of North America, yet by 1800 it had undergone a process of development similar to that experienced by those established much earlier. Although each colony required an adaptation to local conditions and experienced a distinct regional history, colonization in the 13 British American colonies shared a number of features that suggest a common response to the frontier (Merrens 1964:15–16).

By 1750, all the colonies were characterized by rising Old World populations, which replaced the indigenous inhabitants of the Atlantic Seaboard. These immigrant populations were largely rural and engaged in the extensive production of agricultural and other nonindustrial commodities for an export market. Although the towns and cities were few and the urban population a minority, the role of these settlements was significant because they functioned as collection and distribution points, which supported the agricultural hinterland and encouraged commercial

31

product specialization. These developments are indicative of insular frontier expansion and characterize the insular frontier process throughout most of eighteenth century British North America (cf. Steffen 1980:*xvii–xviii*).

The existence of this process may be observed on the Eastern Seaboard by studying South Carolina as a more-or-less typical example of British colonization. An examination of South Carolina's historical development in light of the model outlined in the previous chapter should permit a recognition of the characteristics of change associated with the insular frontier process. The model is divided into six parts, and our discussion follows a similar format. Although thematic in structure, this format provides a general historical introduction emphasizing aspects relevant to insular frontier development to provide a historical basis for identifying that process. The organization of this discussion proceeds topically from the general to the specific to allow the logical presentation of both historical and processual information.

SOUTH CAROLINA AS A REGION

Before beginning our discussion of South Carolina's development as a colony, it is useful to present a brief description of the region to establish its boundaries and introduce elements of its physiography that will be discussed later in the text. For the purposes of this study, the boundaries of the South Carolina colony are the same as those of the present state. Although the region did not develop in isolation from adjacent colonies, its political boundaries were fixed quite early and serve as a convenient means of delimiting the growth of settlement within this particular colony.

The colonization of South Carolina involved the occupation of a territory stretching from the Atlantic Ocean to the Appalachian Mountains. This region is composed of three physiographic provinces, each of which parallels the Atlantic coast and is oriented on an axis running roughly northeast to southwest (Fig. 3.1). In general, the topography of the land slopes in a southeasterly direction. The region's three principal river systems, the Pee Dee, the Santee, and the Savannah, crosscut these provinces on their way to the sea.

The Blue Ridge Province is the smallest and includes the highest elevations. This mountainous area is confined to the northwest corner of South Carolina and is characterized topographically by great variation in relief. The Blue Ridge Province is underlain by crystalline rock consisting primarily of granites, gneisses, and schists.

Seaward of the Blue Ridge lies the Piedmont Province. Although the two are geologically similar, the latter is topographically distinct. The Piedmont is a gently sloping, dissected upland. Variations in relief are largely a result of stream erosion, with interstream areas forming broad flat-topped or gently rolling ridges. The rocks of the Piedmont are deeply weathered, producing a thick soil mantle characterized by sandy loam soils. Although amenable to agriculture, the sloping topography of this region and its high rate of rainfall present a constant threat of erosion.

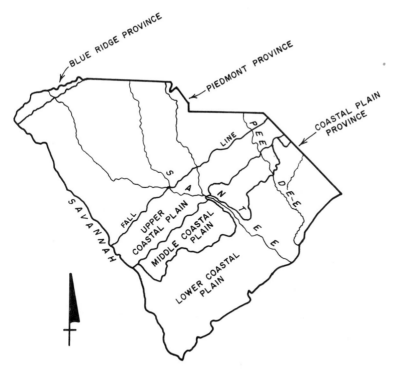

FIGURE 3.1 Physiography of South Carolina.

The Coastal Plain Province is the largest of the three provinces and occupies the southeastern two thirds of South Carolina. Unlike the Blue Ridge and Piedmont provinces, it is underlain by unconsolidated, soft, sedimentary deposits consisting of sands, clays, and marls. The Coastal Plain may be divided into three regional belts that differ topographically. The Upper Coastal Plain lies adjacent to the Piedmont and is characterized by strong relief formed by the deep cutting action of streams. Stream erosion of the less resistant sediments has often formed falls at the boundary of the Coastal Plain and Piedmont provinces and this juncture is referred to as the *Fall Line*. The Middle Coastal Plain lies to the southeast and occupies a lower elevation. Its topography is less a product of erosion than that of the hillier regions inland and there is less variation in its surface. The topography of the Lower Coastal Plain is markedly flatter and is characterized by landforms resulting from both continental accretion or deposition into former marine environments. It is a young area geomorphically, a fact that is reflected in its absence of mature river valleys and the absence of secondary barrier islands and marshes. The present shore is largely primary in type and erosional in nature. Rivers emptying into the Atlantic Ocean form wide valleys and are subject to tidal action. These navigable rivers provide access by water to a large part of the Lower Coastal Plain, although the presence of marsh and swampland might restrict the area actually available for settlement. Soils developed on the unconsolidated Coastal Plain deposits make this region amenable to agriculture and the region as a whole would seem to present no significant barriers to insular frontier settlement (Colquhoun 1969; Cooke 1936; Petty 1943).

SOUTH CAROLINA'S ESTABLISHMENT AS A COLONY

Great Britain's Rise in the World Economy

South Carolina's role as an area of insular frontier development may be examined by observing the manner in which its history reflects the colonization process outlined in the model. Perhaps the most basic characteristic of the insular frontier process is its occurrence in regions lying on the periphery of a world economic system. As such, South Carolina should have been established as a permanent supplier of staple commodities for British markets. Although it must have remained tied culturally to the mother country, its economy is likely to have been marked by a local reinvestment of capital and its society by a perceived social and political distinctness from that of the parent state.

Colonization of this type cannot be attempted outside the context of an expanding world economy such as that centered in Europe after the fifteenth century. England's settlement of the Eastern Seaboard of North America was clearly associated with this expansion. The history of its colonies should reveal England's participation in the European world economy and the role her colonies played as a consequence of it. To comprehend South Carolina's role as an English colony, it is necessary to understand the home country's rise as a colonial power. England's growth came largely after 1600, a time that marked a significant alteration in the European world economy. For the previous 150 years, rapid economic expansion and social change had taken place; however, with the coming of the seventeenth century a period of consolidation set in. The new century saw an economic, social, and political realignment that changed the nature of colonization and the role of the state in it (Lang 1975:221).

By this time, the core of the world economy had shifted from Spain to the states of northern Europe: England, France, and the United Provinces. Although differing in political organization, all had developed strong economies. The economic slow-down of the seventeenth century accelerated their competition for hegemony in the world economy and fostered an intensification of productive efficiency. Hegemony in a world economy is achieved when the products of a core state are produced so efficiently that they become competitive even in other core states. This makes the hegemonic state the primary beneficiary of a free world market (Wallerstein 1980b:37–38).

The rivalry for hegemony in the seventeenth century world economy set the course for England's developing colonial system. England's colonization of the Eastern Seaboard of North America took place prior to and during her rise as a hegemonic power. These colonies reflected both the home country's internal organization and its competitive relationship with other European states. The reorganization of the British economy at a higher level of integration was accompanied by political conflict culminating in the English Revolution. The resolution of this conflict was a compromise that permitted the restoration of the monarchy but transferred much of its power to the landed aristocracy which controlled the parliament as well. This triumph of the aristocracy was also a victory for the capitalistic interests they had come to represent. The leading position of the aristocratic families in the emerging bourgeoisie ensured the power of the class whose interests lay in exploiting the wealth of the world economy (Wallerstein 1980b:121–123).

As a consequence of the political instability that prevailed prior to the Restoration of 1660, the English government played only a minor role in colonization (Lang 1975:146). This activity was instead undertaken by joint stock companies. These organizations, originally developed for overseas trade, pooled the resources of merchants and stockholders and received a monopoly on trade from the crown to help defray the risks of long-distance ventures (Flinn 1965:62). England had successfully used such companies to support colonization in Scotland and Ireland during the sixteenth century (MacLeod 1928:157; Rowse 1957), and similar companies were to provide the framework for the earliest permanent North American colonization in Virginia and Massachusetts (Pomfret 1970:26, 110).

Following the Restoration, England began to actively pursue hegemony in the European world economy and employed its North American colonies in this effort. The year 1660 brought the first of the Navigation Acts, which institutionalized the mercantilist doctrine that subordinated the interests of the colonies to those of the mother country and established a national monopoly over colonial trade (Greene 1970:*xiv*). These acts effectively gave preference to the production of certain staple crops, most of which were noncompetitive. They also indirectly encouraged the establishment of colonial industries in those areas that did not produce any of the enumerated commodities. The latter activities appeared chiefly in New England and the Middle Atlantic colonies where many entrepreneurs turned to the carrying trade as shipbuilders and commercial middlemen. The role of these colonies allowed them to assume a semiperipheral status within the European world economy by the close of the seventeenth century, in contrast to the agrarian staple colonies which remained on the system's periphery (Wallerstein 1980b:237).

The Settlement of the South Carolina Colony

New settlement along the Atlantic Seaboard was carried out with the colonies' economic role as staple crop producers as a paramount consideration. To help achieve this end, and to assume a direct voice in their control, colonial grants were awarded to groups of proprietors who administered their colony for the benefit of the state and for private profit. South Carolina was a proprietary colony, and was settled a decade after the Restoration for both mercantilistic and strategic purposes (Fig. 3.2). The primary intent of the proprietors was to establish a colony for the production of a variety of noncompetitive staples, including ginger, sugar, wine,

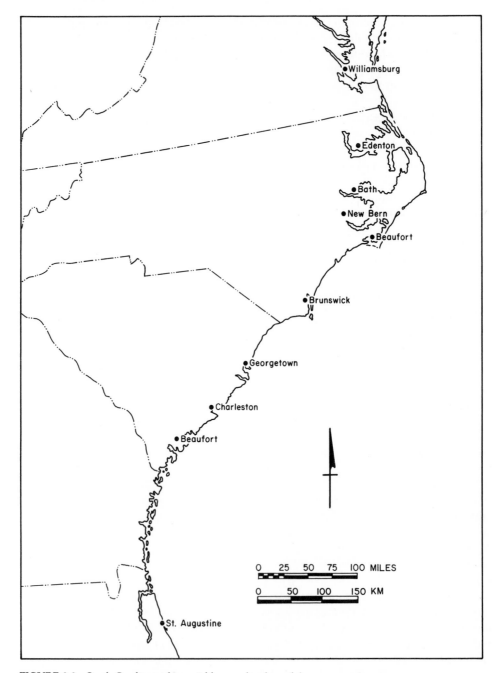

FIGURE 3.2   South Carolina and its neighbors at the close of the seventeenth century.

indigo, cotton, silk, and olives (Clowse 1971:8; Gray 1933:50). The colony's position south of Virginia, also served to establish an English presence in the territory north of the Spanish settlements in Florida (Crane 1929:9–10). As a proprietary colony, South Carolina's political and social culture was laid out along feudal lines. Ownership of land and access to its resources was allotted according to status (Clowse 1971:20).

Initially, the South Carolina colony was established as a permanent settlement to be sustained by the production of export staples. Its cultural and political ties to the homeland were also clearly defined. In these respects, the colonization of South Carolina was already typical of insular frontier settlement. The remaining attributes of this type of colonization: the production of staples, local reinvestment of capital, and the development of a distinct colonial society, would appear later as the colony evolved over the next century.

The Development of Export Staples

South Carolina's economy was linked to the production of marketable staples; however, their selection was not complete until well into the eighteenth century. The early years of the colony involved a great deal of experimentation in subsistence as well as commercial crops, and attempts were made to exploit a variety of resources for export commodities. As a consequence, South Carolina' economy was extremely diversified during the early years. Generally, the amount of its export commodities was small and fell into four categories: (1) livestock and livestock products, (2) food crops, (3) naval stores and lumber, and (4) deerskins and Indian slaves obtained through trade with aboriginal peoples. Its principal market in the early years was the British West Indies. Deerskins were the only commodity exported directly to England (Clowse 1971:60–64, 86–87; Crane 1929:108–114; Gray 1933:57–58).

This pattern of production and exchange did not change until the early years of the eighteenth century when rice emerged as the first major staple crop (Salley 1936:51). Rice cultivation was introduced on a commercial scale by English planters employing the knowledge and labor of Africans skilled in the production of this crop (Littlefield 1981:113–114). Rice exportation rose rapidly, particularly after 1719. The relatively loose control of this commodity granted by the Navigation Acts permitted the extensive exportation of rice to England and northern Europe as well as the West Indies (Gray 1933:286). Rice production on a commercial scale fostered the development of an increasingly complex agricultural technology. Because of the crop's unique irrigation requirements, rice agriculture rapidly evolved toward a more efficient use of hydraulic resources (Fig. 3.3). It quickly shifted from the use of small inland fields fed by freshwater streams to cleared inland swamps where water was impounded. By the latter part of the eighteenth century, rice cultivation had shifted to the tidal portions of the major coastal rivers where it employed an elaborate irrigation system utilizing the tidal flow of fresh water (Hilliard 1975:58).

Rice cultivation was an extremely labor intensive activity requiring continual

FIGURE 3.3 Rice cultivation in the South Carolina lowcountry. The tidal rice fields illustrated in the painting represents the final stage in the development of rice production during the colonial period. The large fields lay adjacent to major coastal rivers subject to tidal influence. Fluctuating water levels permitted the alternate flooding and draining of the fields during the growing season through the use of an elaborate system of dikes, floodgates, and canals. From a painting entitled "Ready for Harvest" by Alice Ravenel Huger Smith. (Courtesy Collection of the Gibbes Art Gallery, Carolina Art Association, Charleston, South Carolina.)

inputs of labor throughout the year (Doar 1936:8). As such, it facilitated the importation of a slave labor force. Slave plantation agriculture had proven immensely successful in the British West Indies, particularly in Barbados, after the introduction of sugar as a staple in the 1630s (Handler and Lange 1978:16–17). Barbadians formed a large part of the European immigrant population of South Carolina during the seventeenth century (Clowse 1971:53). The beginning of slavery there is likely to have been hastened by the presence of settlers who recognized the adaptive advantages of employing unfree labor experienced in the cultivation of rice.

The second colonial staple produced in South Carolina was indigo (Fig. 3.4). Although grown experimentally during the colony's early years, indigo raising did not become profitable until a market for it was created by the decline of its production in the British West Indies. Indigo was reintroduced in the 1740s and soon became a lucrative staple, aided by the War of Austrian Succession (1740–1748), which cut off English supplies from French West Indian sources and prompted a

FIGURE 3.4 Processing indigo in colonial South Carolina. This detailed drawing from DeBraham's map of 1757 illustrates the manufacture of dye substance from the leaves of the indigo plant.

government bounty to encourage production of the crop (Gray 1933:291–292; Pinckney 1977:145–146). Production of indigo increased and it remained a profitable commodity until the American Revolution resulted in the removal of its protected market and artificial price support. At the end of the colonial period, indigo ceased to be a significant staple in South Carolina's economy (Snowden 1920:472).

Indigo also was a labor-intensive crop that could be worked with slave labor in conjunction with rice (Hunneycutt 1949:9–10). It could be grown on high ground not suitable for rice cultivation and be tended, harvested, and processed by the same slaves engaged in other plantation labor (Gray 1933:294). The complementary

FIGURE 3.5   Water-powered grain mill in the South Carolina backcountry. Although of nineteenth-century vintage, this overshot mill is typical of those constructed during the colonial period to process wheat and corn for domestic consumption or export through the entrepôt. (Courtesy South Caroliniana Library.)

nature of its land and labor requirements permitted indigo production to be integrated into the existing coastal plantation rice economy and made its cultivation possible in newly opened areas. This ensured the crop a dominant role in the South Carolina economy as long as an export market for it existed.

The third staple in colonial South Carolina was wheat. Unlike the others, wheat was not tied to the coastal plantation region. It developed as a cash crop in the interior as the area of colonization expanded inland in the fourth decade of the eighteenth century. Wheat never became as important a staple as rice or indigo, yet it represents the major export commodity produced in the backcountry during the colonial period. Colonists in the interior initially grew wheat with other grains for subsistence; however, by the 1750s, wheat had begun to emerge as a cash crop (Meriwether 1940:166). Mills were established at strategic locations in the backcountry to process wheat and other grains. The flour (Figure 3.5) was shipped overland to Charleston for redistribution within the colony and export (Sellers 1934:31). By the 1760s, South Carolina flour had replaced earlier imports from the northern British colonies (Schulz 1972:23) and was exported in quantity to the British West Indies. Although flour production was halted by the Revolutionary

War, it recovered afterward only to be supplanted by cotton in the postcolonial economy of the interior (Ramsay 1809:216–217).[1]

Wheat agriculture was largely in the hands of small farmers (Meriwether 1940:166) in contrast to rice and indigo production in the coastal regions, which was largely carried out on plantations. The different labor requirements of wheat and the plantation staples resulted in a lesser dependence on slavery as an institution of production in the back-country. The differential occurrence of the two forms of production is apparent in the relative proportions of white and black persons in these two regions. In 1790, Negroes constituted over 73% of the population in the three coastal districts of South Carolina, while they averaged only 21% in the four districts of the interior (Petty 1943:69).

Local Reinvestment of Capital

Colonial South Carolina, like other frontier regions, was characterized by the local reinvestment of capital and resources by a population intent on permanent settlement. This is perhaps most obvious in the economic sector of colonial society. Here the pattern of local and regional reinvestment contrasted with that which had evolved in the contemporary cosmopolitan frontier in the British West Indies. The Caribbean economy was geared to the production of virtually a single market crop. Large-scale cultivation of sugar drove out smaller planters. The remaining owners became predominantly absentee entrepreneurs and placed the marketing of their crops in the hands of British factor merchants. The landowners gave little concern to reinvestment in production but worked to reap as much profit as possible during the inevitable decline in production following the exhaustion of plantation lands (Wallerstein 1980b:169–171).

Eighteenth century South Carolina participated in a complex economic system linking the colony internally with England, Europe, West Africa, the West Indies, and the other British colonies of the North American Seaboard. Its trade involved the major export commodities and a variety of other products for export and home consumption (Shepherd and Walton 1972:132). Production during the colonial period was not confined to large estates, and control of both export and internal trade was largely in the hands of resident merchants (Egnal and Ernst 1972:11). Their activities were centered in the entrepôt of Charleston (Fig. 3.6) and in subsidiary centers on the coast and in the backcountry (Sellers 1934:6; Rogers 1969:12). Regional control of commodities favored a greater reinvestment in their production, exchange, collection, storage, and distribution. This situation is reflected in the

[1]Cotton did not emerge as an important staple in the interior until the early nineteenth century following the introduction of the Whitney gin in 1794 (Green 1972:110). Unlike wheat, cotton was amenable to labor intensive plantation agriculture. The economic advantages of large-scale production combined with a growing industrial market to make cotton a more attractive investment and hastened the replacement of small grain farming with cotton plantation agriculture.

FIGURE 3.6   The government customshouse in Charleston. This structure, erected in 1767, was a symbol of royal authority in the economic system of colonial South Carolina. Together with the naval officer who kept the register of shipping and the vice-admiralty court that punished violations of shipping laws, the collector of customs was one of the three elements responsible for carrying out the Navigation Acts regulating trade between South Carolina and the outside world (Rogers 1969:16–17). (Courtesy South Caroliniana Library).

assumption of urban functions by various colonial settlements on the South Carolina frontier. In addition to serving as centers of economic activity, such settlements played a significant role in integrating the colony as a social and political entity (Ernst and Merrens 1973b:554).

This is not to say that no effort was made by home country mercantile interests to dominate the colonial American economy. The expansion of British commerce following the peace of 1748 was accompanied by an attempt by English merchants to gain direct control of American trade by dealing directly with producers. Nowhere was this more obvious than Virginia, where after 1760, the tobacco trade was dominated by Scottish firms (Soltow 1959:85). Their affiliation with semiperipheral regions in the world economy allowed them to undercut English merchants and serve as a direct link between the colonial producers and their European market (Wallerstein 1980b:170). Efforts to infiltrate the colonial American economy were supported by restrictive legislation in the 1760s and 1770s. Uncontrolled importation depressed American markets and encouraged increasingly more radical local responses aimed at regaining control of the colonial economy. Such responses were to contribute substantially to the chain of events that led to the American Revolution (Egnal and Ernst 1972:23–24).

The Rise of a Distinct Colonial Society

The development of a separate colonial society is implicit in the previous discussion. By the mideighteenth century the economy of South Carolina was separate from, though closely intertwined with, that of Great Britain. Other aspects of this colonial society had also developed a distinctness from their counterparts in the mother country. Three areas where such change can readily be observed are in the ethnic composition of the population, the role of the state church, and the colony's political organization.

Although the initial settlers of the colony were English in origin, including some who had resided in the West Indies (Clowse 1971:24), the ethnic composition of South Carolina soon became very complex. Many different groups were incorporated into the colonial society. Indians, including resident groups whose territories were occupied by the expanding colony and enslaved captives brought from the interior (Crane 1929:17–18), formed a substantial segment of the colony's population during the early period of settlement. More significant in their long-term impact were West African Negroes, who were introduced as slaves in the seventeenth century and imported in increasingly larger numbers as labor for the expanding plantation economy (Wood 1974:36). The European population of South Carolina was also heterogeneous. It included Irish and French Protestants as well as emigrants from other English American colonies (Petty 1943:20). Efforts to settle the province's interior during the eighteenth century saw the addition of other groups, including Swiss, Welsh, Germans, Scots-Irish, and Scots, to the colonial society (Gregg 1867; Meriwether 1940; Petty 1943).

The variety of ethnic groups was mirrored by the multiplicity of religions brought with them. The Anglican Church, as the state church of England, was established in South Carolina throughout the colonial period. Its influence, however, was confined mostly to the coastal region, because the backcountry was settled largely by Protestant Dissenters (Wallace 1951:208). The Act of Establishment did not disenfranchise dissenters nor prohibit the practice of their religions (Clowse 1971:155–156). As a consequence, various Protestant groups, including Baptists, Congregationalists, Methodists, Presbyterians, German Lutherans, and French Huguenots, were organized in the colony. Numbers of Roman Catholics, Jews, and Quakers also settled in South Carolina during the colonial period (Ramsay 1809:24–40).

The number and diversity of the ethnic and religious groups in early South Carolina contrasted sharply with the composition of the population of the homeland. This implies the existence of a colonial population distinct in its composition. The makeup of population together with the nature of the colony's economy influenced the political development of South Carolina. This resulted in the formalization of governmental structures that emphasized its internal unity and its separateness from the mother country.

During the colonial period, two opposing forces vied for the administration of the province. The Proprietors and later the Crown through its Board of Trade strove to retain outside control, but a variety of private interests worked to place administrative control in the hands of resident colonial capitalists. These factions were represented by the two major components of the colonial government, the appointed Governor with his Council and the elected Assembly. Because of the colony's early development under negligent and often incompetent proprietary rule, colonial interests were able to establish an active role in the governing process (Wallace 1951:105). Their power manifested itself in the second decade of the eighteenth century when they forced the removal of the proprietary governor as a result of his failure to resolve an economic crisis brought on by the Yamassee War and pirate depredations in the colony. In place of proprietary authority, the colonial assembly invited the Crown to assume direct responsibility for South Carolina (Clowse 1971:194; Sirmans 1966:127).

The assembly retained its power in the governing process under the Royal administrations after 1719 and actually increased it at the expense of the executive (Wallace 1951:231). Despite the generally better management under Crown rule, the conflict between the executive branch and the assembly continued during this period. Following the close of the Seven Years War in 1763, the situation was intensified by the Crown's attempt to exercise a greater degree of imperial power over colonial affairs. The Royal Governor's attempt in 1762 to control election to the Assembly challenged one of the basic rights of that body (Sirmans 1966:252–256). Although unsuccessful, this controversy was soon followed by the imposition of a series of Parliamentary tax laws, beginning with the Stamp Tax of 1765. These generated disputes over the approval of money bills, another prerogative of the Assembly, and accelerated the alienation of the two branches of the colonial government. These arguments helped create the political climate for revolution (Wallace 1899:47–49).

Internal unity within the colony required a political system capable of integrating newly incorporated territories into the jurisdiction of the province. The settlement of the South Carolina backcountry advanced rapidly following the establishment of a series of interior townships in 1731 (Petty 1943:45). This rapid expansion of settlement outstripped the administrative abilities of the Charleston government that had previously ruled a colony confined to the immediate coastal region. Although the newly occupied areas were integrated economically with the rest of the colony, their political administration was neglected (Sirmans 1966:251–252). The absence of civil authority gave rise to the Regulator Movement, an indigenous attempt to provide order in the backcountry (Brown 1963:14–15; Klein 1981:678). A consequence of this movement was the passage of the Circuit Court Act of 1769.

This organized the entire province into judicial districts and located the central government's presence at the seat of each district (SCRGAABJR/1769). By linking the newly settled regions with those of the coast, the Circuit Court Act supported the economic relationship among the colony's settled portions and provided another integrative mechanism that helped create a distinct colonial society in South Carolina (Wallace 1951:218–219).

Historical evidence reveals that South Carolina's colonial development exhibits the initial characteristic of insular frontier settlement. It was founded as an English colony during that nation's rise to hegemony within the European world economy. From its beginning, it was intended as a permanent settlement and was founded for the purpose of providing raw commodities for the benefit of home trade and industry. By the early eighteenth century, rice and indigo had become the staple export commodities of the coastal region, and wheat, the staple of the interior. The variety of agricultural commodities and regional control over the production of commodities encouraged long-term investment in the colonial economy. Such a trend is typical of permanent insular frontier settlement. The economic autonomy of colonial South Carolina was paralleled by the emergence of a society distinct from that of the homeland. Ethnically different as a result of the amalgamation of a large African element, various European groups, and the remnants of the region's native population, colonial society also possessed a diverse religious makeup. Despite the presence of an established church, a larger dissenter population limited its role in the civil life of the colony. The distinctness of colonial South Carolina is also apparent in the colony's political development, which showed trends toward an increasing internal cohesiveness as well as decreasingly effective external control.

Summary

Colonial South Carolina underwent the type of fundamental change associated with insular frontier settlement. Such change is linked to the economic milieu in which the colony was established and reflects an adaptation to conditions encountered in long-term overseas expansion. The characteristics of change discussed above are crucial to the recognition of insular frontier settlement because they describe conditions that must occur for a frontier to appear, and the effect this process has on certain key aspects of the colonial society. Indeed, insular frontier change may be identified on the basis of these characteristics alone. Their presence does not, however, indicate the form of the insular frontier process. The geography of colonization is extremely important, since it allows the process to be viewed in a spatial context. It not only ties past activities to specific locations, but permits the construction of a series of historical landscapes. Because the insular frontier process is one of expansion, the landscape of colonization is perhaps its most visible material manifestation. A knowledge of its continually changing form is necessary to recognize the frontier as well as to comprehend the physical extent of its spread. The relationship between the form of a landscape and the spatial patterning of its material record makes the study of frontier geography especially applicable to archaeology. Because of the rapidly changing nature of frontier settlement, archaeological evidence may often provide the most detailed picture of the colonial landscape. The remaining characteristics of insular frontier change defined in the model are geographical in nature and relate to the content and distribution of settlement through time. In the following sections they will be explored with regard to South Carolina's historical development during the frontier period.

TRANSPORT AND SPATIAL PATTERNING ON THE SOUTH CAROLINA FRONTIER

Insular frontier regions are likely to display patterns of settlement revealing the operation of their central integrating institution, the colonial economy. Economic activities tied to staple commodity production require an efficient network of trade and communications connecting all parts of the frontier with an entrepôt that links the area of colonization with the outside world. Because the frontier expands outward from the entrepôt, its form tends toward a dendritic pattern resembling branches spreading outward from a single trunk. Such a network usually follows the most direct routes of transit, given the available technology, and incorporates or supersedes existing transportation routes in the colonial area. Once established, this network forms the basis for settlement growth throughout the frontier period.

The Entrepôt of Charleston

Colonial expansion by the English in South Carolina centered on the entrepôt of Charleston (Fig. 3.7). Situated at the confluence of the Ashley and Cooper rivers (Fig. 3.8), Charleston's location on a neck of land in a wide natural harbor made it an ideal port. Since it was easily defensible from land or sea attack. This favorable position permitted Charleston to serve as a collection point for colonial export commodities, a distribution center for imported commercial goods, and a receiving point for immigrant settlers and slaves (Sellers 1934:4–5). Not only did Charleston develop as the focus of an expanding plantation economy, it also became the terminus of the British Indian trade in the Southeast (Crane 1929:108). In the beginning, agricultural settlement in South Carolina was confined to the coastal region between the Santee and Edisto rivers. Early land allotments were made along the rivers and tidal inlets, for these watercourses offered the easiest means of trade and communication with the entrepôt as well as protection against potential Indian attack (Petty 1943:20).

The initial thrust of inland movement in South Carolina followed the deerskin and Indian slave trade. Begun in the seventeenth century, the Indian trade became an important segment of the early colonial economy. Its strategic significance was greater than its economic role, however, because it permitted the English to exercise

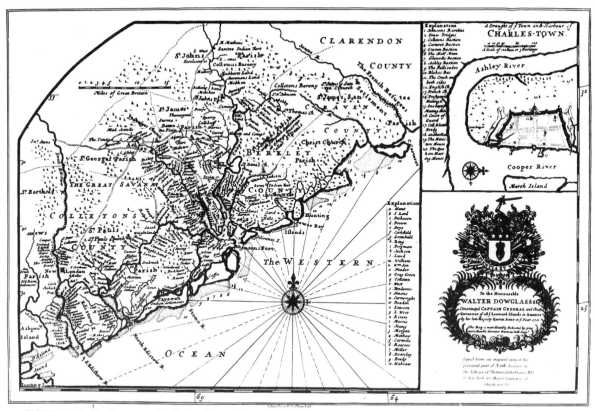

FIGURE 3.7 Settlement in South Carolina in the early years of the eighteenth century. Centered on the entrepôt of Charleston, the early European occupation of the province was limited to the coast between the Santee and Edisto rivers. (Source: Moll 1715.)

FIGURE 3.8 The entrepôt of Charleston in 1762 as seen from the Cooper River. Major public structures are identified as follows: A, Granville bastion; B, Courthouse; C, Council chamber; D, Meeting house; E, St. Philip's Church; F, Customshouse; G, Secretary's office; H, Craven's bastion. The presence of centralizing economic, social, and political activities here, together with its size reflects Charleston's focal role in the development of this colony. (Courtesy South Caroliniana Library.)

control over aboriginal groups in the Southeast and keep them from falling under the influence of England's European rivals, France and Spain (Crane 1929:115). The routes of the Charleston traders penetrated the interior of South Carolina and extended northwest to the Tennessee River and as far west as the Mississippi by the early years of the eighteenth century (Crane 1929:131–136; Phillips 1961/I:429).

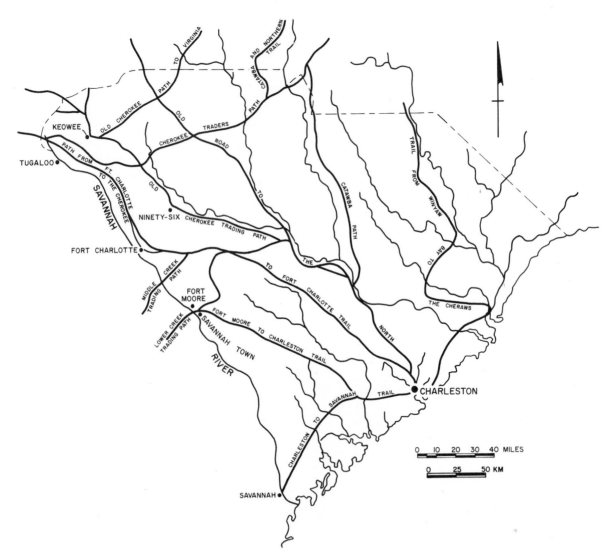

FIGURE 3.9 Indian trade routes in South Carolina in the early eighteenth century. The overland road network linked to the Indian trade was well established prior to the expansion of European settlement inland. This dendritic network, which centered on the entrepôt of Charleston, greatly influenced the pattern of subsequent agricultural settlement. (Source: Myer 1928: Plate 15.)

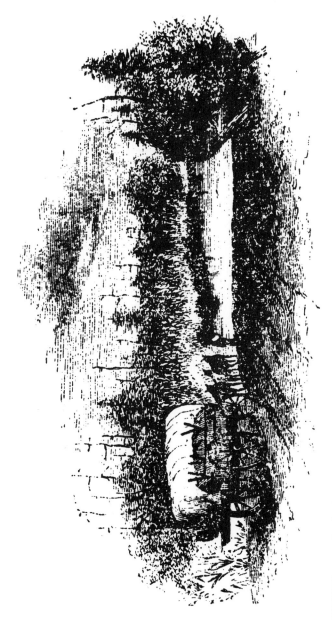

FIGURE 3.10 Overland transportation in the South Carolina backcountry. The drawing depicts a scene on the Catawba path where it crossed Sanders Creek just north of Camden. This road was one of the main overland arteries connecting this frontier town and its hinterland with the entrepôt. (Source: Lossing 1860:461.)

The Overland Road Network

One result of this long distance commerce was the creation of a network of trade routes stretching into the interior from the port of Charleston. These routes (Fig. 3.9) reveal clearly a dendritic pattern characteristic of an economic network organized around a single center. They represented the arteries of most efficient movement to and from the entrepôt. Because of their existence prior to the expansion of settlement inland from the coast, the roads formed a convenient network along which population movement could take place. The routes laid out to facilitate the early Indian trade served equally well as a road system along which manufactured goods and colonial commodities flowed between the entrepôt of Charleston and the backcountry frontier (Fig. 3.10).

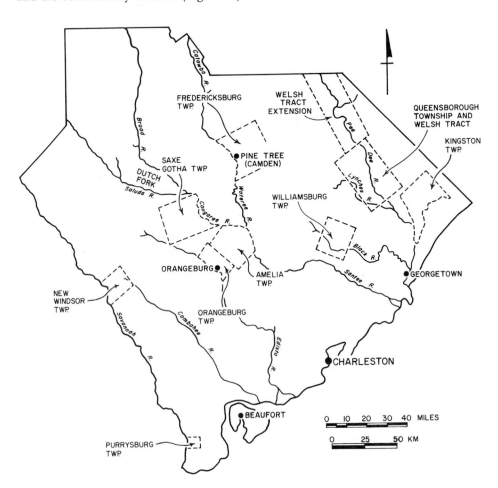

FIGURE 3.11 Layout of the inland townships established in 1731. The dates are those in which the surveys took place. (Source: Petty 1943:38.)

The influence of this early road system on subsequent settlement is illustrated by the location of the earliest areas of permanent agricultural settlement in the interior of South Carolina. In 1731 the colonial governor received instructions to establish a series of inland settlements. These were intended to strengthen the frontier against potential Spanish and Indian threat, increase the production of export staples, and help counterbalance the rising slave population of the coastal plantations. Nine townships, to be settled by small farmers, were to be laid out along the major rivers between the North Carolina border and the Savannah River (Brown 1963:2; Meriwether 1940:19–20; Petty 1943:35). The locations of these townships provided for a fairly even distribution of population across the frontier (Fig. 3.11). Actual settlement in the backcountry did not follow the anticipated pattern (Petty 1943:42). Instead, it occurred only in those townships whose locations were intersected by the road system. This differential development shows the importance of access to the trade and communications network in the determination of settlement pattern in a frontier region. The positions of the occupied townships indicate the basic form of the South Carolina frontier. Its initial settlement followed the dendritic pattern of the overland trade routes, the layout of which would determine the form of the area of colonization until the close of the frontier period.

THE EXPANSION OF THE SOUTH CAROLINA FRONTIER

Agricultural expansion is an integral element in the insular frontier process. The regular enlargement of the zone of staple production, essentially a response to increased demand from homeland markets, is accompanied by a periodic reshuffling of the areas devoted to the production of particular commodities and the improvement of the transportation system to increase efficiency of expanded production. Settlement growth in South Carolina was accompanied by both these trends.

The Townships of 1731

The expansion of colonial settlement received its first boost by the creation of the inland townships in 1731 (Fig. 3.11). The granting of lands in these areas by the provincial government was a conscious effort to encourage inland settlement and influence its form. Differential settlement of these townships according to the pattern of the existing frontier transportation network modified the intended evenly spaced settlement to increase accessibility to the entrepôt. The settlement of the townships and the territories beyond did not occur at once. It took place largely as a gradual expansion inland from the coast prior to 1750 and was subsequently supplemented by overland migration from the northern colonies (Rogers 1969:7). The sequence of this settlement reveals the directional expansion of an agricultural system focused on a central market. The crops produced disclose a zonal allocation of commodity production based on distance and accessibility to that market.

The first township settled was Purrysburg on the Savannah River. It was first occupied by Swiss and German immigrants in 1733, and by the 1740s its white population had stabilized at about 800. Purrysburg's proximity to the coast distinguished it geographically from the inland townships, and it became a moderately successful rice growing region. The growth of plantation agriculture in this region discouraged the formation of nucleated settlements here and hastened the area's incorporation into the economy of the coast (Meriwether 1940:38–41).

Williamsburg Township on the Black River was settled in 1734 by Irish Protestants and Scots. Following an initial period of hardship and slow growth, the region developed a prosperous economy based on grain. After 1745 the introduction of indigo as a staple brought a marked change in the economy from small farm to plantation production. The labor requirements of indigo, however, resulted in a smaller relative slave population than that found in the coastal plantation region (Meriwether 1940:82–83; Petty 1943:39).

In 1735 three townships were occupied: Orangeburg and Amelia between the North Edisto and Congaree rivers and Saxe Gotha on the Saluda River. The first two were settled by Swiss and German immigrants. Amelia and Orangeburg Townships were occupied mostly by small farmers engaged primarily in growing wheat as a staple. Indigo and rice growing were attempted, but neither appears to have been adopted as a major crop. The small settlement of Orangeburg had grown up on the North Edisto by the 1750s, by which time the population of the two townships stood around 1,600 including about 100 slaves (Meriwether 1940:46, 50).

Saxe Gotha was settled initially by German immigrants who were later joined by settlers of English origin. Settlement spread quickly northward onto the Saluda and Broad rivers. Germans settled the "Dutch Fork" at the confluence of these two rivers. Germans, Irish, and immigrants from North Carolina, Virginia, and Pennsylvania moved into the area to the north. Wheat was the major export staple of this ethnically diverse region, which had an estimated population of 800–900 by 1759 (Meriwether 1940:62; Petty 1943:41).

The last of the successful early townships was Fredericksburg on the Wateree River. Fredericksburg Township was the furthest inland from Charleston and settlement here did not begin until 1737. The population grew slowly in the 1740s. Most grants were made to English settlers along the river or its major tributary creeks. In the 1750s a number of Irish Quakers occupied the area near the confluence of Pine Tree Creek and the Wateree River and established a meeting house there. The population increased with the addition of immigrants from the northern colonies and a large number of Scots migrating from Williamsburg Township. By 1757 Fredericksburg had a population of around 900. Wheat and other grains were the major crops grown. By the 1750s a settlement called Pine Tree Hill (later Camden) had grown up near the site of the Quaker grants as a regional milling center and collection point for backcountry wheat (Ernst and Merrens 1973b:561–562; Kirkland and Kennedy 1905:9–10; Meriwether 1940:103–109; Petty 1943:41).

Three of the early townships failed. New Windsor on the Savannah River remained sparsely inhabited as a result of its proximity to the Cherokee. Kingston on the Waccamaw found few immigrants because much of its territory consisted of poorly drained soils and swampy terrain unattractive to the European agricultural colonist. Queensborough Township, at the confluence of the Great Pee Dee and Little Pee Dee rivers, possessed a physical environment similar to that of Kingston. The lands in this township remained largely unclaimed (Petty 1943:39–40).

Despite the failure of the townships in the northeastern part of the province, this region did not remain uninhabited. A group of Pennsylvania Welsh settlers, who had been granted land in Queensborough, successfully petitioned the colonial government to have the area of available land extended further inland to include territory more suitable for agriculture. The resulting Welsh Tract, laid out in 1737, paralleled the Great Pee Dee River as far as the North Carolina border (Gregg 1867:49). Most of the land in the Welsh Tract was taken up by 1746, and Welsh, Irish, and German immigrants from the northern colonies had increased the population of the Pee Dee region to around 4,800 by 1757 (Meriwether 1940:94; Petty 1943:40). Wheat was the major staple crop here as elsewhere on the frontier, although tobacco and indigo were also produced. The small settlement of Cheraw arose as a regional collection point for these commodities (Gregg 1867:112; Merrens 1977:247).

Expansion in Western South Carolina

Although Europeans expanded rapidly into the interior of South Carolina after the 1730s, settlement in the western portion of the province was delayed for several decades. The proximity of this region to territories occupied by the two powerful aboriginal societies remaining in the Southeast permitted the economy of the upper Savannah to remain dependent on the Indian trade later than other parts of the province. Two major trading routes from Charleston passed through this area (Fig. 3.12). The first led to a point on the Savannah River opposite present day Augusta, which served as the terminus of the southern and western trade routes that led to the Creek towns in the Altamaha, Chattahoochee, and Alabama valleys and further west to the Chickasaw and Choctaw settlements (Crane 1929:132–133). A second route passed along the Congaree to the Cherokee towns of Keowee and Tugaloo. By the 1730s, most of the latter trade was centered around the post at Ninety-Six (Meriwether 1940:123–124). Early European settlement was confined to forts and trading posts along these trade routes. Only after the Cherokee War of 1760–1761 had removed the Indian presence and prompted a reorganization of the Indian trade in this area could permanent agricultural settlement of western South Carolina begin to take place (Wallace 1951:180–182).

The successful conclusion of the Cherokee War in 1761 not only created conditions conducive to agricultural expansion on the Savannah River frontier but prompted the provincial government, out of fear of future Indian troubles, to take a more active role in stabilizing this region by encouraging such settlement. It did so by establishing three new townships and offering free passage to European Protestants who would take up lands there (Fig. 3.13).

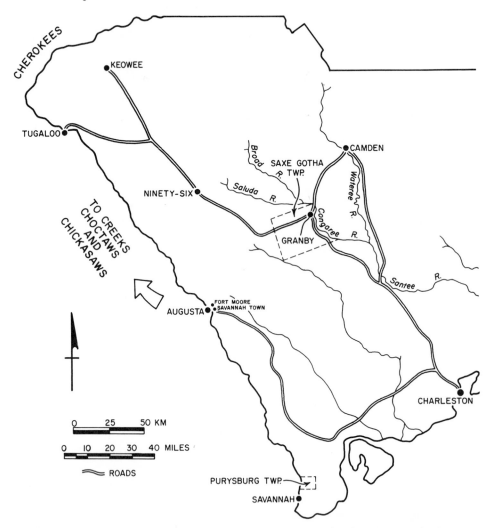

FIGURE 3.12 Major Indian trade routes in the Savannah River region and settlement in central and western South Carolina on the eve of the Cherokee War. (Sources:Hunter 1730; Mouzon 1775.)

In 1726 Boonesborough Township on Long Cane Creek was colonized by Scots-Irish immigrants, many of whom came from Virginia and North Carolina (Cook 1923:6). German settlers occupied Londonborough Township to the southeast on Hard Labor Creek (Bernheim 1872:165). Hillsborough Township, located on Little River, was settled two years later by French Huguenot refugees (Moragne 1857). Despite their ethnic diversity, the dispersed settlement and consequent intermingling of these groups soon led to the loss of their separate identities (Hirsch 1928:102).

Attempts were made to introduce a number of exotic cash crops, including silk

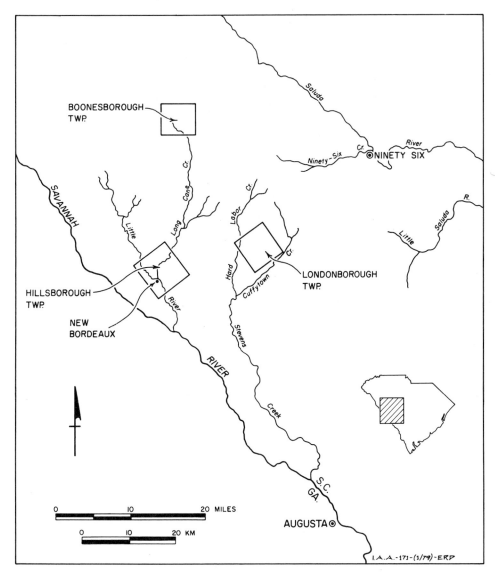

FIGURE 3.13 Post–Cherokee War expansion in western South Carolina. The three townships, together with the settlements of Ninety-Six and Augusta, formed the basis for expansion into this region. (Sources: Meriwether 1940:116; Mouzon 1775; Petty 1943:38.)

and grapes. The intensive labor requirements and destructive effects of plant disease, however, made their cultivation less profitable than grain or indigo (Gray 1933:188; Hirsch 1928:205). As elsewhere in the backcountry, wheat and corn were the major staple crops in western South Carolina (Cook 1923:24).

The close of the Cherokee War brought an end to the immediate threat of

Indian warfare in the South Carolina backcountry. The peace that followed consolidated colonial claims to territory and saw an attempt made to establish a framework for negotiating differences between the province and its aboriginal neighbors (Wallace 1951:182). Coupled with the removal of the French threat to the west following the end of the Seven Years War in 1763, this defeat of a major Southeastern Indian group laid the groundwork for subsequent English expansion.

Post–Cherokee War Expansion

In addition to opening the Savannah River region to agricultural settlement, the Cherokee War allowed an immediate expansion of settlement throughout the colony. The legislation that provided passage and grants of land to encourage settlement in the western part of the province increased immigration to other frontier regions in

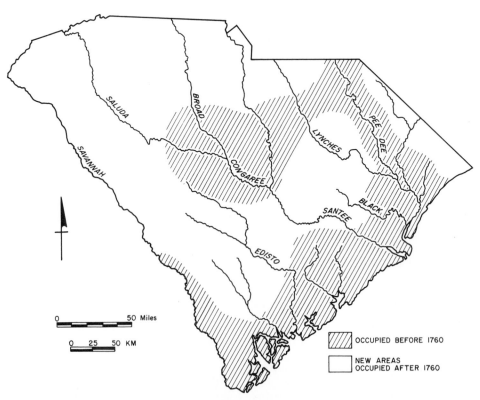

FIGURE 3.14   Expansion of settlement in South Carolina after 1761. The map shows the general spread of population beyond the inland townships and into the upper Savannah River region following the Cherokee War (Sources: Meriwether 1940; Petty 1943.)

South Carolina as well (Meriwether 1940:242–243). Prior to the war, settlement had covered a coastal strip 40–50 miles (64–80 km) wide. The Pee Dee Valley was occupied to the North Carolina line, and the territory from the Pee Dee southwestward through Orangeburg, Amelia, and Saxe Gotha Townships was fairly densely populated. Thinner settlement extended up the Savannah, Saluda, Broad, and Wateree river valleys (Petty 1943:45). After 1761 settlement spread up the Lynches, the Black, the Edisto, and the Congaree to fill in areas passed over in earlier expansion. In the backcountry it moved up the Broad, Saluda, and Wateree–Catawba Rivers and into the Waxhaws region on the upper Lynches (Fig. 3.14). These settlers took up the land between the townships and extended to the western and northern boundaries of the province (Meriwether 1940:256–258). The extent of European immigration into South Carolina after the Cherokee War is reflected in estimates of the colony's white population during this period. From a base of about 33,000 in 1760, it jumped to 45,000 in 1769 and 4 years later had mushroomed to 65,000 (Petty 1943:47).

Expansion and Staple Crop Production

Before the close of the eighteenth century, this figure had more than doubled, and the frontier of settlement had passed beyond South Carolina's borders. European agricultural expansion into the province had taken about a century and proceeded in stages inland from the initial coastal settlements. The occupation of the interior did not greatly extend the range of the colony's principal coastal staples, rice and indigo, because the ecological limits and labor requirements restricted their large-scale cultivation to the densely populated coastal region where the plantation flourished. Instead, the small farming economy of the frontier produced wheat as a third staple. The choice of wheat was linked not only to the presence of a market but to this commodity's capability of being transported to the entrepôt via the existing road system. This system was fully adequate to maintain trade and communications for a small farm frontier economy that supported a small, largely scattered population growing a crop easily transported after initial processing.

The relationship of staple crop to transport efficiency on the South Carolina frontier may be illustrated by the dramatic change that occurred in the trade and communications network following the adoption of cotton as a staple at the beginning of the nineteenth century. The suitability of the backcountry for the growing of cotton and the intensive labor requirements of this crop encouraged the spread of large-scale plantation agriculture, which displaced the small farms characteristic of the colonial period (Edwards 1940:201). The change in the mode of production, accompanied by the adoption of a bulky commodity that could be shipped directly to market without prior processing, required a transport system capable of moving large quantities of this heavy staple. In 1792 the State of South Carolina began a massive canalization project (Fig. 3.15), designed to bring most parts of the interior within a relatively short distance of navigable water (Blanding 1820; Gray

FIGURE 3.15   Stone lock on the Landsford canal on the Catawba–Wateree River as it appeared in 1898. (Courtesy South Caroliniana Library.)

1933:685). When completed in 1828, the system of canals (Fig. 3.16) restructured the transportation network to follow the major river systems. By doing so, it provided adequate support for the growing cotton economy until superceded by more efficient rail transportation in the 1840s (Kohn 1938; Petty 1943:73–74).

Summary

The occupation of the interior of South Carolina may be seen to have occurred as a result of expansion from Charleston along the coast, inland to the townships, and finally into the Savannah River region and the upper portions of the province. A comparison of settlement dispersal with the layout of the overland transportation system of the colonial period clearly shows the relationship of settlement growth to access to market. The postcolonial canal system was intended to maintain the accessibility of inland regions. The canal system successfully sustained the growth of the frontier period by providing the means to market the staple commodities of the plantation system that succeeded it. Canal development, thus, may be seen to mark the termination of the frontier in South Carolina by marking the reorganization of the region's economy at a more complex level of integration.

FIGURE 3.16 The canal system in South Carolina constructed between 1792 and 1828. Concentrated primarily in the Santee River drainage, this network of canals was intended to support the development of plantation agriculture in the central portion of the state. (Sources: Kohn 1938; Schulz 1972:65.)

PATTERNS OF SETTLEMENT ON THE SOUTH CAROLINA FRONTIER

Settlement Pattern and Economic Growth

The form and structure of frontier settlement in colonial South Carolina reveal the movement of an agricultural system inland from its coastal entrepôt. Its expansion was restricted only by the limitations of the transportation network that supported it and, in the west, by the opposition of aboriginal peoples. By the close of the eighteenth century, the system reached its limits. The economic organization of South Carolina was beginning to change from primary dependence on a British export commodity market to a reliance on a variety of foreign and domestic markets and an expansion of internal commerce (Mills 1826:161–162; Ramsay 1809:238–239). The replacement of wheat and indigo by cotton as a staple and the improvement of river navigation accompanied this change. So did a reorientation of the transportation network to reflect the region's postfrontier organization.

The evolution of social and economic organization of the South Carolina frontier is closely linked to the roles played by settlements and the nature of their distribution. The change in the transportation network and the reorganization of trade are associated with a readjustment to the finite resources of this frontier area and indicate a stabilization of the economic environment created by expansion. Such a readjustment is characteristic of the last stage of Hudson's model of frontier development and is likely to be revealed by an evenly spaced pattern of settlement. Because this phase represents the culmination of a general process of settlement pattern evolution, it should be preceded by patterns typical of earlier stages of insular frontier development. The presence of a trend toward an evenly spaced distribution throughout the colonial period is anticipated. Its occurrence may be determined by observing the layout of settlement at different times during the period of frontier expansion.

The Changing Distribution of Settlement in the Eighteenth Century

Reconstructing colonial settlement patterns in South Carolina is hindered by a near absence of cartographic sources showing the actual layout of settlement from the beginning of the frontier period. The earliest comprehensive maps of the province were not published until the occupation of its interior was nearly complete. By this time the pattern of settlement is likely to have taken on a form typical of the later stage of development. Earlier settlement patterns must, therefore, be reconstructed from other documentary data that will permit its observation over time. These reconstructions may be portrayed as a series of maps on which the changing distribution of settlement may be seen. On those maps employing accurate point distributions, nearest neighbor values can be computed in order to observe these changes statistically. A comparison of nearest neighbor values over time should show the trend toward even spacing expected for regions undergoing insular frontier settlement.

POPULATION MAPS

The evolution of settlement pattern during the colonial period may be measured by noting the changing distributions of two types of evidence over time. The first of these is population. Although the locations of individual settlements are unknown, it is possible to ascertain a general distribution of settlement by observing the variation in population density throughout the province. Friis (1940) constructed a series of population maps for the Eastern Seaboard of North America during the eighteenth

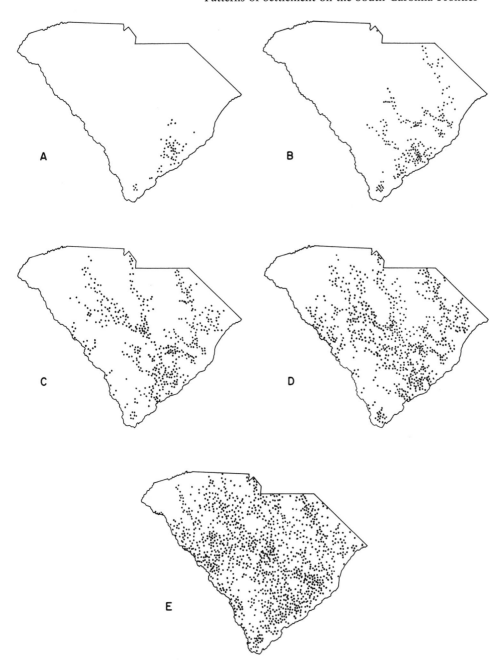

FIGURE 3.17 General distribution of population in colonial South Carolina: A, 1720; B, 1740; C, 1760; D, 1770; E, 1780. (Source: Friis 1940.)

century. Population density was derived from a variety of sources[2] and is portrayed by dots, each representing approximately 250 people. Although of small scale, Friis' maps of South Carolina show a pattern of emerging settlement. In 1700, the population of the province was clustered because it was confined to the coastal region around Charleston and Beaufort, a pattern that was only slightly extended by 1720 (Fig. 3.17A–B). The opening of the interior townships in the 1730s is disclosed by the extension of settlement along three corridors toward the Orangeburg–Amelia–Saxe–Gotha and Fredericksburg regions and the Welsh Tract, with settlement apparently following the roads leading to those areas (Fig. 3.17C). By 1760 this pattern had moved inland as far as the North Carolina line and had begun to spread westward up the Savannah River (Fig. 3.17D). Population growth in new territories opened by the Cherokee War can be seen in 1770 by which time the settlement of the Savannah River frontier was well under way. Overall, a dispersion from areas occupied earlier was beginning to fill in the areas between the townships, creating a more evenly spaced distribution of population (Fig. 3.17E). By 1780, population had expanded to occupy nearly all parts of South Carolina except the northwestern corner which remained Cherokee land until 1777 (Fig. 3.17F).

Although the patterns shown on the Friis maps appear to illustrate a trend toward even spacing as predicted in the Hudson model, there are several problems in applying quantitative methods to his data. First, the scale of the maps makes the measurement of distances between points difficult, if not impossible. Perhaps of greater importance is the uncertainty of the locations of the points relative to the distribution of the 250 persons each represents. Because the data from which these maps were constructed are unavailable, these questions cannot be resolved, and the maps may be used only to gain a very broad view of settlement distribution on the South Carolina frontier.

CHURCH LOCATIONS

The second type of settlement evidence observable through time in South Carolina is locations of churches. If we assume that churches were situated so as to be roughly equally accessible to all members of their congregations, then a church's position is likely to represent a central place within a larger area of dispersed population. By mapping the distribution of churches, it should be possible to observe the layout of settlement during the colonial period and determine its changing patterns.

Maps of church locations through time may be constructed by plotting the placement of individual churches as they were established by decade. The organiza-

[2]Friis (1940:2–3) broke his sources down into the following categories: manuscripts and transcripts; edited and documented archival material; records of town, county, state, and colonial meetings and census tax lists; reputable general, state, county, town, and local histories; generally accepted travel accounts; geneologies; proceedings, transactions, and annual reports of historical and other societies; and bibliographies and guides to the social, economic, and political history of the colonial period. These are listed in detail on pp. 26–31 of his study. In addition, Greene and Harrington's (1932) and Sutherland's (1936) works on colonial population were also employed.

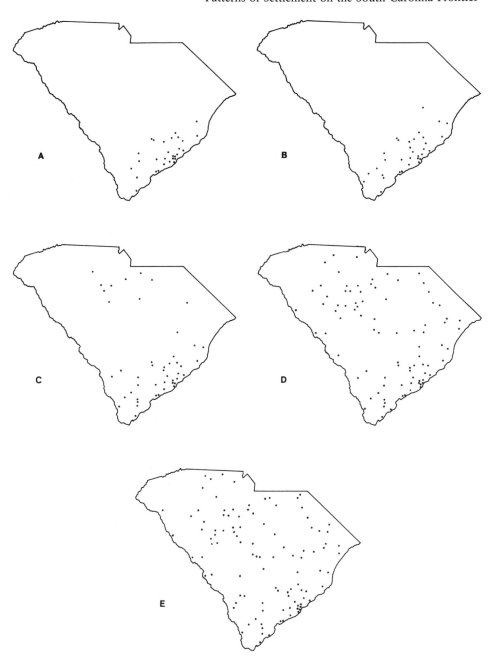

FIGURE 3.18 Distribution of church locations in colonial South Carolina: A, 1740; B, 1750; C, 1760; D, 1770; E, 1780. (Sources: Bernheim 1872; Dalcho 1820; Howe 1870; Townsend 1935.)

tion of churches appears to have lagged slightly behind actual settlement, because in 1740 most are still clustered in the coastal region (Fig. 3.18A). Ten years later, expansion appears to be just beginning with churches established in Williamsburg Township and on the lower Savannah (Fig. 3.18B). Despite the movement of agricultural settlement into several of the interior townships and the Welsh Tract, churches had not yet been established there. This temporal lag between initial settlement and the organization of formal integrating institutions may indicate that a certain population threshold must be reached before their development can take place. The process of organizing churches in areas already settled is manifested in historical accounts of the established Anglican Church and other major denominations (Bernheim 1872; Dalcho 1820; Howe 1870; Townsend 1935). Subsequent maps of church locations by 10-year intervals reveal that by 1760 congregations had been established in the central and eastern portions of the backcountry (Fig. 3.18C). The Savannah River region, still conspicuously vacant in 1760, was occupied during the decade following the Cherokee War, and a number of churches appear on the 1770 map (Fig. 3.18D). After 1760, the density of churches increased markedly throughout the entire province. By 1780, many areas previously vacant had been filled in as settlement expanded into all parts of the frontier (Fig. 3.18E).

NEAREST-NEIGHBOR ANALYSIS

The distribution of church sites through times may be compared statistically by calculating a nearest-neighbor value for each 10-year period. This technique involves calculating the mean observed distance to its nearest neighbor for each point in the study area, in this case defined by the provincial boundaries of South Carolina, and computing the expected mean nearest neighbor distance if the points were randomly dispersed. The ratio of the observed mean distance serves as a measure of the departure from randomness (1.0) toward clustering (0) or even spacing (2.149) (Clark and Evans 1954:451). The results of the nearest-neighbor analysis for church sites by decade are summarized in Table 3.1.

An examination of Table 3.1 shows that in the years prior to the opening of the backcountry to settlement the concentration of church sites in the coastal region produced a distribution with a strong tendency toward clustering. As the occupation

TABLE 3.1 Nearest-neighbor values for South Carolina church sites by decade, 1740–1780

Date range	Nearest neighbor statistic (R)
1740	.5805
1741–1750	.6599
1751–1760	1.0196
1761–1770	1.3964
1771–1780	1.5107

of the interior commenced before midcentury, the pattern of church distribution became more random, reflecting the placement of these structures in scattered locations along the overland trade network of the frontier. The random pattern began to exhibit a trend toward even spacing after 1750 when churches were built in areas previously unsettled. This course suggests a similar development in the overall distribution of settlement in which the random pattern produced by the initial expansion into the interior evolved gradually into a regular more evenly spaced pattern. This statistically defined settlement trend, identified through an analysis of church locations, appears to parallel that described in Hudson's model of colonization and indicates that this region exhibits a pattern of settlement associated with insular frontiers in general.

The trend from randomness to even spacing observed above is supported by synchronic map data representing various types of settlement at different times during the frontier period. One such map displays the locations of regiments of militia as recorded in 1757, two decades after the first townships had been laid out (Petty 1943:45–46). If we assume that the points on this map lie central to the areas in which the militia members resided, then the distribution of these points should

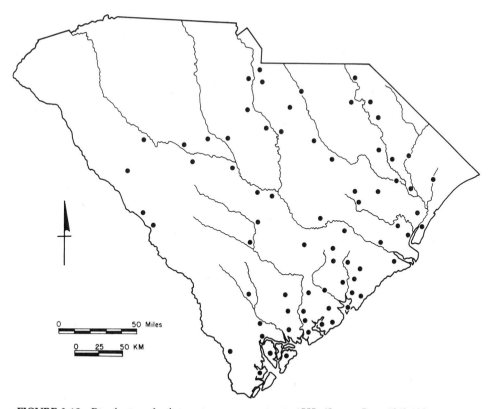

FIGURE 3.19 Distribution of militia regiment muster sites in 1757. (Source: Petty 1943:46.)

display the general pattern of settlement. The Petty map (Fig. 3.19) reveals a distribution reminiscent of that shown on the 1760 Friis map (Fig. 3.17D) and the church map of about the same period (Fig. 3.18C). Settlement appears to have covered a wide coastal strip and extended up the Pee Dee valley. It also occupied the central part of the province and had begun to approach the Savannah River. A nearest-neighbor analysis of this distribution reveals a statistic of 1.1970 which compares well with that derived from the church distribution of 1760 and fits the trend indicated by the church site maps. This correlation suggests a similar time lag between initial settlement and the organization of militia regiments and churches as formal integrative institutions, a factor that must be considered when working with settlement data of this type.

TREND SURFACE ANALYSIS

Settlement information contained in Figure 3.17 may be combined in a single map designed to portray these data as a series of contours representing the extent of English expansion in South Carolina at various intervals during the eighteenth century. Such a map may be produced using the Synagraphic Computer Mapping Program (SYMAP) which has the ability to graphically depict spatially dispersed quantitative variables. It accomplishes this in one of two ways. The first procedure takes the assigned values for the coordinate locations of data values (in this case church founding dates) and interpolates a continuous surface in the regions where there are no data points. These interpolated values are based on the distances to and values of the neighboring data points. This method results in the creation of a *contour surface* (Dougenik and Sheehan 1976/I:1).

SYMAP can also produce a map using *polynomial fitting*. This involves the creation of a *trend surface*, a statistically derived equation explaining variations in given data values distributed either regularly or irregularly in space. Trend surface analysis fits a surface to the values at given data points using polynomial approximation so as to minimize the squares of the deviations between the trend surface and the given data values.

Because trend surface analysis does not fit a surface so that it passes through each data point value, some *residual values* representing deviations not predicted by the trend are likely to occur. Residual maps may be produced by subtracting the trend surface values from the interpolated values of the contour surface. A residual value of 0 is present where the trend and the contour surfaces coincide. Negative residual values occur where the trend surface lies below and underpredicts; the contour surface and positive values are present where the trend surface overpredicts the interpolated values (Dougenik and Sheehan 1976/III:37–38). Consequently, residual maps may be used in conjunction with trend surface maps to reveal anomalies not predicted by the general trend.

A low-order trend surface analysis is most useful in predicting the overall movement of settlement across a region, such as South Carolina, because of its tendency to fit the surfaces to relatively simple geometric forms.[3] This tends to filter out the effects of local variability as well as contour distortions caused by the uneven distribution of data points within the region (Paynter 1982:185–186), permitting the general form of movement to be more easily observed and compared to similar maps of the area constructed from different data sets. Figure 3.19A shows a third order trend surface, which employs a cubic equation that produces a surface with two bends and an approximation of the saddle between four peaks (see Chorley and Haggett 1968:200–201).

A trend surface map of settlement in colonial South Carolina is intended to portray frontier expansion as witnessed by the presence of limited settlement data. The map should be characterized by the appearance of contours reflecting the statistically predicted extent of settlement at various intervals between 1740 and 1780. Because the contours represent a predicted surface, some settlement points, representing residual values, may not fall within the contour for their particular date. The overall trend, however, is likely to mirror the settlement pattern evidenced by the evolving distribution of eighteenth-century churches.

A trend surface map has been generated to estimate the extent of settlement expansion between 1740 and 1780. The contours shown in Figure 3.20A represent the overall pattern of movement. They reveal an initial occupation on a strip of coastline centered on Charleston, followed by an expansion along the coast in both directions and a movement inland as well. After 1764 the rate of interior expansion appears to have increased markedly, reaching the northern boundary of South Carolina by 1772. Two areas still remained conspicuously empty at this time. These are the northeastern fringe along the North Carolina border and the western third of the province lying adjacent to the Savannah River. By 1780 these areas too were occupied, leaving only the northwestern tip of South Carolina vacant of European settlement.

An examination of the residual map (Fig. 3.20B) reveals that a substantial portion of the data values are predicted by the trend surface. This map indicates also where the trend surface has under and over predicted data values. Underpredicted areas would have been settled earlier than shown in Figure 3.19A, while overpredicted areas are likely to have been occupied later than indicated by the trend surface. By observing the distribution of underpredicted data values, it is possible to discern more closely the form of settlement growth in colonial South Carolina. These show clearly that a large portion of the Coastal Plain was occupied earlier than anticipated by the trend surface. This area would include the sites of Georgetown, Orangeburg, Kingstree, and other early settlements in this region. Subsequent ex-

---

[3]There are six orders of trend surface analysis which employ equations of increasing complexity to explain variations in data values. These equations permit surfaces at each order to assume progressively more complex geometrical shapes, each level of which more closely approximates the empirical surface. These shapes and the equations that produce them are described by Chorley and Haggett (1968:200–201) and Haggett, *et al.* (1977:381–382).

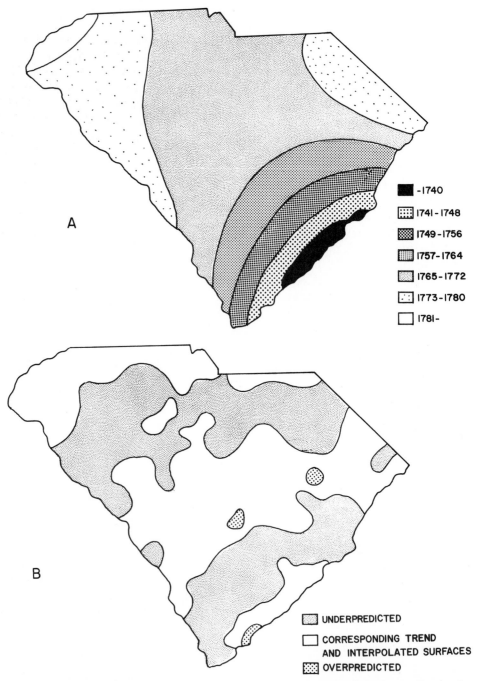

Legend for map A:

- ■ -1740
- ▦ 1741-1748
- ▨ 1749-1756
- ▥ 1757-1764
- ▨ 1765-1772
- ⫶ 1773-1780
- ☐ 1781-

Legend for map B:

- UNDERPREDICTED
- ☐ CORRESPONDING TREND AND INTERPOLATED SURFACES
- ▨ OVERPREDICTED

FIGURE 3.20 Trend surface and residual maps of settlement growth in South Carolina. (A) Trend surface map generated by SYMAP based on church founding dates. The map shows the form of expansion between 1740 and 1780. (B) Generalized map of residual values created by SYMAP showing those areas where the trend surface has underpredicted and overpredicted the occupation times interpolated from the data point values.

pansion into the drainages of the Pee Dee, Wateree, and Broad rivers of the eastern and central Piedmont is reflected by a band of early settlement extending across this region. Camden, Cheraw, and Granby lie here as do the Welsh Tract settlements. The opening of the upper Savannah area and the rise of Augusta as a regional center following the Cherokee War are reflected by the presence of early settlement in the western Piedmont. Areas of overpredicted settlement, on the other hand, are relatively small in size and widely separated. They would appear to represent areas settled after the initial occupation of the Coastal Plain had taken place. Two lie in areas between the major routes of the overland transport network (Fig. 3.10) and may have been avoided because settlement followed these routes as it advanced across the Upper Coastal Plain. A third overpredicted area indicates a later occupation of the coastal area south of Beaufort, another area presumably overlooked during the initial settlement of the region.

A comparison of the trend surface and residial maps allows us to observe the form of settlement expansion in South Carolina during the eighteenth century. This process is similar to that inferred from other documentary sources. Briefly, the map evidence reveals that by 1740 much of the lower Coastal Plain had been occupied by settlement. During the following decade much of the Upper Coastal Plain also appears to have been colonized. Around midcentury the settlement of the interior had begun, and by the 1760s the major river drainages of the central and eastern Piedmont had been occupied. The upper Savannah River region was colonized in the 1770s, and by 1780 only the northwestern tip of South Carolina remained unsettled-by Europeans. The form of frontier expansion revealed by the trend surface and residual maps conforms to that suggested by the church maps and supports statements derived from other documentary sources regarding the sequential occupation of the South Carolina colony.

OTHER MAPS

Another source of settlement data is a series of maps prepared in the 1770s. These maps (Cook 1773; Faden 1780; Mouzon 1775) were attempts to present a comprehensive picture of overall settlement in South Carolina in the late colonial period and show the locations of nucleated settlements and the distribution of some dispersed settlement in addition to roads, rivers, and other physiographic features. The maps also reveal the placement of the courthouse settlements designated by the Circuit Court Act of 1769. This legislation divided the province into seven judicial districts for purposes of administration and established courthouses and jails in each (SCCHAJ/Nov. 28, 1769–Sept. 8, 1770:294). Because of the courts' role as politically integrating institutions, the sites of these settlements are likely to have been chosen so as to be central to the inhabited parts of each district and thus accessible to the greatest number of people.[4] Their locations, then, may be seen as centers of

[4]All but one of the courthouses were established at existing nucleated settlements. Only one, at Long Bluff in the Cheraws District, was deliberately situated at a new location. This was done so that it could be placed more centrally within the administrative region that it was to serve (Gregg 1867:186–187; K. Lewis 1978:23).

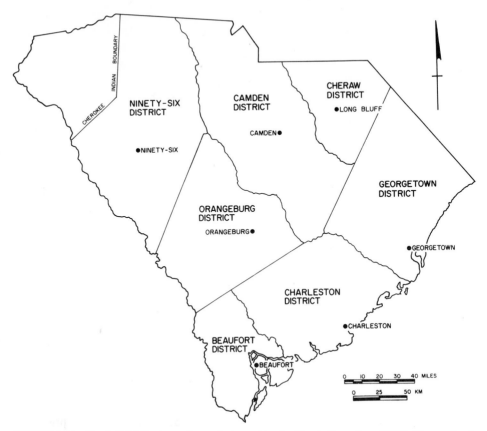

FIGURE 3.21   The judicial districts and seats designated by the Circuit Court Act of 1769. (Source: South Carolina Archives n.d.)

activity from which the general distribution may be measured. The distribution of the seven courthouse settlements (Figure 3.21) depicts an evenly spaced pattern characteristic of settlement in the latter stage of colonization. The nearest neighbor value of 1.6912 reflects the trend already seen in the layout of church sites and further supports the conclusions drawn from other cartographic sources.

Summary

The data derived from documentary sources have revealed that the settlement of South Carolina was characterized by an initial coastal occupation that expanded to the limits of the Upper Coastal Plain by the 1740s. Settlement of the interior progressed rapidly after midcentury, spreading into the eastern and central Piedmont by the 1760s. Following the Cherokee War, migration into the Savannah River region began, and by the time of the American Revolution, Europeans had occupied nearly all parts of South Carolina. The expansion of settlement was accompanied by a change in its distribution. As the population density of the interior increased, filling in the vacant areas, the settlement pattern evolved from one tending toward randomness toward an evenly spaced distribution. This change, discernible both visually and statistically from cartographic data, corresponds to that predicted in Hudson's model of colonization and reveals the occurrence of a similar process of development on the South Carolina frontier.

SETTLEMENT PATTERN AND FUNCTION: THE ORGANIZATION OF ACTIVITIES ON THE SOUTH CAROLINA FRONTIER

Development of the Lowcountry Frontier

The coastal plantation region of South Carolina was colonized in the late seventeenth and early eighteenth centuries. Those portions of it that were amenable to staple crop production were settled prior to expansion into the interior. The coastal region did not develop in exactly the same manner as this later frontier for several reasons. First, rice, its major staple crop, was a relatively compact commodity requiring a simple support system of transport. Secondly, the ecological requirements of rice growing limited its production to the major rivers (Hilliard 1978:Fig. 5). These rivers and their immediate access to the sea permitted rice to be shipped directly from the plantations to a port for shipment (Ravenel 1936:17–18). As for other commodities produced for export, Charleston was the entrepôt for South Carolina's rice crop (Rogers 1969:9).

Frontier Towns in the Coastal Region

Although the marketing of rice did not require as elaborate a settlement system as did grain in the interior, subsidiary settlements did arise as collection points for each of the regions of coastal rice production. Georgetown, on Winyah Bay, was situated in the northernmost rice producing area (Fig. 3.21). Its shallow harbor prevented it from developing as a deep water port to rival Charleston, and its restricted access to the interior via overland transportation routes limited its hinterland (Rogers 1969:8). Its extensive coastal trade, particularly with the entrepôt, permitted it to attain substantial size during the colonial period. Already a frontier town serving as the social and economic focus of this region, it became the seat of Georgetown District in 1769. Although damaged severely during the Revolution, Georgetown grew rapidly after the war and remained a major secondary port well after the colonial period (Drayton 1802:207; Mills 1826:562; Sellers 1934:5–6).

Beaufort, like Georgetown, arose as a subsidiary port to Charleston. Its position in the southernmost rice growing region permitted it to develop as a collection point for this area (Fig. 3.21). Despite its large, deep harbor, Beaufort did not become an entrepôt and like Georgetown remained a relatively small settlement with a limited hinterland (Grayson 1960:14). This was largely because its island location hampered its access to the overland trade network that linked the interior of the colony to the coast. Its situation was adequate for its role as a collection point for local trade by water, and it developed as a fronteir town for the immediate region. Beaufort became the center of social and economic activity for this area, a position it was to maintain throughout the colonial period. It was the logical choice in 1769 as the seat of Beaufort District. Like Georgetown, Beaufort continued to serve as a major subsidiary port long after the colonial period (Mills 1826:368–369; Sellers 1934:4–5).

The Plantation Economy of the Lowcountry

By the mideighteenth century, expansion of plantation settlement in the low-country had occupied most of the coastal region (Petty 1943:45). No longer on the periphery of settlement, the area ceased to undergo intensive colonization. Constant innovation in the methods and extent of rice production, however, permitted the continual expansion of rice agriculture (Hilliard 1975). A stabilized region might be expected to undergo reorganization as a result of increased competition for re-sources by an increasing population. The profitability of rice agriculture and its adaptiveness to the lowland coastal environment, however, allowed this crop to maintain a competitive advantage over other forms of agricultural production (Hill-iard 1978:114; Petty 1943:56). Because of the dominance of this specialized form of large-scale plantation agriculture, the competition for resources and the reorganiza-tion of their procurement and redistribution so often associated with postfrontier development were avoided. Retaining an economic structure that originated in the frontier period also retarded the development of complex institutions that would normally arise in the latter phase of the colonization process. Instead, the mainte-nance of direct economic linkages characteristic of frontier export production was favored.

As a consequence, patterns of settlement and socioeconomic organization be-came relatively fixed as long as the economy of the region remained based on rice. The retention of these patterns into the postfrontier period is indicated by several factors. These include the growth of rice exports (see Gray 1933:1021–1023), the increase in the lowcountry slave population relative to overall population growth (Petty 1943:218; Gray 1933:1025), and the failure of the coastal region to produce more than a few centers of retail trade during the second half of the eighteenth century (Drayton 1802:213–214; Mills 1826:506–507; Sellers 1934:88).

The early stabilization of coastal economy is apparent in the political geography of the region. In contrast to the interior, where a continual subdivision of admin-istrative units parallels the trend toward greater population density and organiza-tional complexity, the lowcountry retained the larger judicial districts of 1769 through the duration of the colonial period.[5] The specialized nature of the lowcountry economy made it a distinct region of insular frontier settlement. The cultural patterns that arose as a result of its separate evolution continued to reinforce this difference long after the close of the frontier in South Carolina.

Development of the Backcountry Frontier

The spread of colonial settlement into the interior of South Carolina reflects the evolution of the region from a largely uninhabited area to one exhibiting a relatively uniform distribution of population. The process of expansion in the backcountry was supported mainly by the growth of commercial agriculture and the development of a transportation network linking the settlements of the frontier to the entrepôt of Charleston. The size and patterning of backcountry settlement were associated with the production requirements of the major agricultural staple. Grain, the primary agricultural staple of the backcountry, was a commodity needing a relatively complex system of transport involving storage facilities, in-transit processing and packaging industries, and shipping services. The necessity of providing such services resulted in settlements capable of carrying them out.

Because of the dendritic structure of the overland transportation network and the adaptability of grain to a wider range of ecological zones, agricultural settlement could expand more or less uniformly across the backcountry yet be linked to the entrepôt in a linear system of exchange. The settlement pattern and social relations of production were also tied to the requirements of this staple crop. As a seasonal crop, grain needed only periodic applications of labor. The extensive nature of its cultivation also made its production on small farms efficient. These two factors only encouraged the dispersal of the agricultural population of the backcountry frontier and deterred the development of a plantation system there. The distribution of the backcountry population is shown by the spatial arrangement of church sites, muster sites, and map data. The small farm nature of this settlement may be inferred from the absence of the large slave population required to have carried out plantation

[5]The establishment of the judicial districts in 1769 represented the first real geographical division of administrative authority in South Carolina. Previously the only units of local government in the province were parishes. These were, however, primarily ecclesiastical units; their only political function was to serve as the basis for electing representatives to the Assembly. Although parishes had proliferated in the lowcountry where the established Anglican Church was dominant and had been extended to the backcountry by the 1760s, all colonial political institutions and the judicial system remained centered in Charleston. The division of the province into judicial districts in 1769 resulted in the dispersal of these institutions to regional centers for the first time (Gregg 1867:182; Mills 1826:192; Sirmans 1966:97–98). The subsequent subdivision of these districts is indicative of a continuing trend toward the localization of authority in the late colonial and postcolonial periods. It mirrored the changing political organization of South Carolina, especially in the backcountry. The absence of a similar trend in the lowcountry during this time suggests a stabilized political organization that was adequate to administer the established plantation economy of this region.

agriculture and, as will be seen, a relative scarcity of nucleated settlements. Even as late as 1790 at the close of the frontier period but just before the introduction of cotton as a staple, the frequency of Negroes in the population of the interior districts of the province was still small and was markedly lower than in the coastal plantation districts (Petty 1943:72–73).[6]

The settlement structure of the interior was determined by the economic demands of staple production and retail distribution. Although Charleston was the entrepôt for nearly all commerce in and out of colonial South Carolina, its retail trade was limited by the technological capabilities of the existing transportation system. In order to extend retail trade into the backcountry frontier and provide for the collection and processing of its staple commodities, subsidiary economic centers developed.

The Frontier Town of Camden

Camden arose from the Pine Tree Hill settlement on the Wateree River as the paramount center of economic activity for the eastern and central portions of the South Carolina frontier (Fig. 3.22). It served as an inland collection point for wheat, corn, indigo, and tobacco grown in the backcountry. By the 1760s Camden had become the principal break-in-bulk point for wheat and was the site of mills and warehouses for processing and storage prior to shipment to Charleston (Fig. 3.23). It surpassed all other nucleated settlements in the interior in this economic role (Mills 1826:589; Schulz 1972:23). In addition to its role as a flour milling center, Camden was the site of other activities that reflected its central position in the economy of the backcountry. These were the establishment of tobacco warehouses and an inspection station (Schulz 1972:25–26), a pottery kiln producing fine British cream-colored earthenwares (Lewis 1976:169; South 1974:180), a brewery (Kirkland and Kennedy

[6]The relative importance of slavery in agricultural production may be inferred from the comparative size of the frequency of Negroes to the total population. The following table shows the frequency of Negroes by district in South Carolina from 1790 to 1830, the period during which the rise of cotton agriculture took place. Charleston, Georgetown, and Beaufort districts had black majorities well before 1790 because of the presence of rice plantation agriculture here. Negroes were still a minority in the interior, but their frequencies increased rapidly with the spread of plantation farming.

District	1790	1800	1810	1820	1830
Beaufort	76.7	79.4	81.5	85.5	84.7
Camden	23.6	30.9	44.4	48.6	54.4
Charleston	77.0	77.2	77.3	77.7	77.0
Cheraw	30.7	28.2	32.1	41.4	47.2
Georgetown	59.9	63.5	63.8	64.3	65.6
Ninety-Six	15.3	17.5	25.5	31.6	42.3
Orangeburg	33.0	31.3	39.9	47.5	50.3

Source: Petty (1943:73).

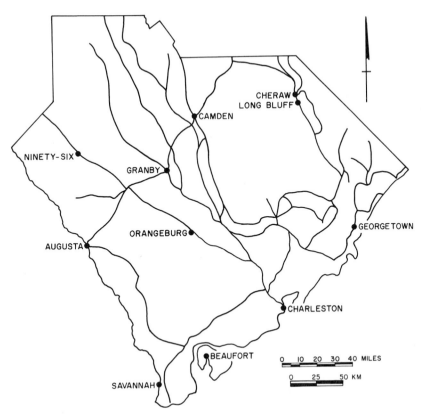

FIGURE 3.22 Principal settlements of the South Carolina frontier and major overland routes of trade and communications. (Source: Schulz 1972:14.)

1905:379; Woodmason 1953:137), a distillery, the stores of at least four merchants, three taverns, a brickyard, a tannery (Kirkland and Kennedy 1905:15), grist and saw mills (Sellers 1934:90), a bakery, the businesses of a tailor and a shoemaker, and a lawyer's office (Schulz 1972:105–106). Camden also was designated as the site of a biannual fair in 1774, and a permanent town market was in existence (Kirkland and Kennedy 1905:12–13, 19; SCRGAABJR/1798/Act 1702). With the establishment of the circuit court system in 1769, Camden became a political and administrative center as the seat of Camden District, an area of considerable size (Fig. 3.21). The presence of a Quaker meeting house and a Presbyterian church assured the settlement a central religious role as well. Land also had been set aside for an Anglican church, but prejudice against the established church prevented its construction (Kennedy 1935:6–7; Kirkland and Kennedy 1905:95; Mills 1826:589; Schulz 1976:93; Woodmason 1953:6).

Camden's early economic role revolved around the activities of its major commercial firm, Joseph Kershaw and Company. The spatial distribution of its mercantile activities reveals the limits of the trade and communications network centered on

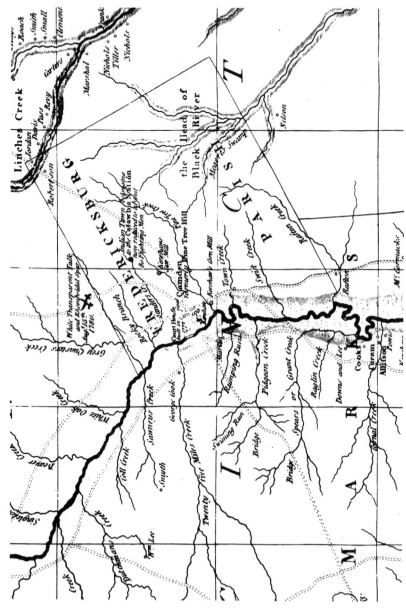

FIGURE 3.23 Camden and vicinity in the 1770s. This detail from Faden's 1780 map illustrates Camden's central location in the overland transportation network leading northeastward to Cheraw, southwestward to Granby, north to settlements further up the Wateree, and south toward Charleston. One of Joseph Kershaw's mills is also shown.

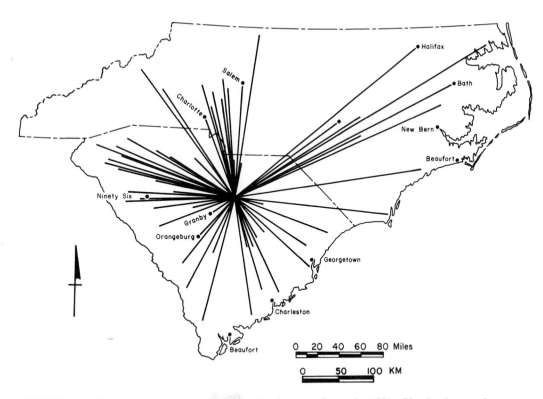

FIGURE 3.24 Sources of customers at Kershaw's Camden store during the 1770s. The distribution of customers illustrates not only the geographic extent of Kershaw's retail trade but its limits as well. The presence of rival frontier towns at Cross Creek and Augusta appear to have eliminated Camden's trade in the Savannah River region and severely restricted it in North Carolina. (Source: Schulz 1976:95.)

this settlement. Kershaw began his business as an agent for the Charleston firm of Ancrum, Lance, and Loocock in 1758. His affiliation with prominant merchants in Charleston and Philadelphia insured an adequate supply of capital to maintain and enlarge his operations at Camden (Ernst and Merrens 1973b:24–25). By 1763 he had established subsidiary stores at Cheraw and Granby, the respective heads of navigation on the Pee Dee and Congaree Rivers (Fig. 3.22) (Sellers 1934:89). Some idea of Camden's economic hinterland in the 1770s may be gained by viewing the distribution of Kershaw's customers. A map of their origins compiled by Schulz (1976:94–95) indicates a trade territory extending more than 120 miles from Camden, with a primary area of interaction confined to a radius of 60 miles (Fig. 3.24).

Camden's Economic Hinterland

The boundaries of Camden's economic region encompassed nearly all of the occupied portion of the South Carolina backcountry and a part of neighboring

North Carolina. These boundaries, however, were not firm, and trade along its outer reaches overlapped with that which focused on other frontier towns. One such settlement was Cross Creek in North Carolina. It had developed by 1770 as a frontier town linking the backcountry settlements of North Carolina with the en-trepôt of Wilmington. Its emergence is significant because it drained away trade that formerly went to Charleston via Camden and thus curtailed further expansion by the South Carolina merchants (Merrens 1964:165–166). As an economic network focused on Cross Creek developed, competition for the trade of the backcountry intensified in those areas along its boundary with Camden's trading network. Its effect was most pronounced in those settlements whose trading networks were likely to be threatened by the encroachment of the other system. Cheraw was such a settlement. Competition from North Carolina traders undoubtedly influenced the legislative decision to locate the district court elsewhere in 1770 and caused Kershaw and Company to close their store there 4 years later (Gregg 1867:119, 186–187). Cheraw remained a small regional trading center that managed to draw at least a part of its trade from North Carolina throughout the colonial period (Drayton 1802:212–213).

Camden as a Military Settlement

Camden's central position in the trade and communications network of colonial South Carolina made it an important strategic military location during the American Revolution. The early years of the Revolution left most of the southern colonies untouched. In South Carolina, the British made an abortive attack on Charleston in 1776, and sporadic partisan warfare occurred early in the backcountry (Nelson 1961:113–114; Weigley 1970:11–12). Not until after the fall of Charleston in 1780, however, was the colony actively involved in the war. The British established a chain of interior posts in South Carolina to secure the province, pacify its inhabitants, and support an invasion of the remaining southern colonies (Fig. 3.25). These served to link the field armies with the principal supply base in Charleston and formed the central elements of a regional defense-in-depth strategy. Camden, to-gether with Ninety-Six and Augusta, formed the major inland strongpoints through which all supplies and communications passed (Lee 1869:163).

Because of its significance, Camden was chosen as the base from which to launch the invasion of North Carolina (Schenck 1889:48). A magazine was estab-lished there in 1780 for the redistribution of supplies, and the town was heavily fortified (Fig. 3.26) (Tarleton 1787:86–88, 103). In the year Camden was occupied, two major engagements were fought nearby, the Battle of Camden on August 16, 1780 and the Battle of Hobkirk Hill on April 25, 1781. Following the second battle, the British Army abandoned Camden and burned much of the settlement (Greene to Continental Congress/NGPPCC/155/II:59). The chain of inland garrisons began to collapse with the loss of Camden. By the fall of 1781 the war in South Carolina was over (Mitchell 1962:201–204). Camden's position remained central to the trade of the backcountry despite the destruction of the settlement and the social and eco-

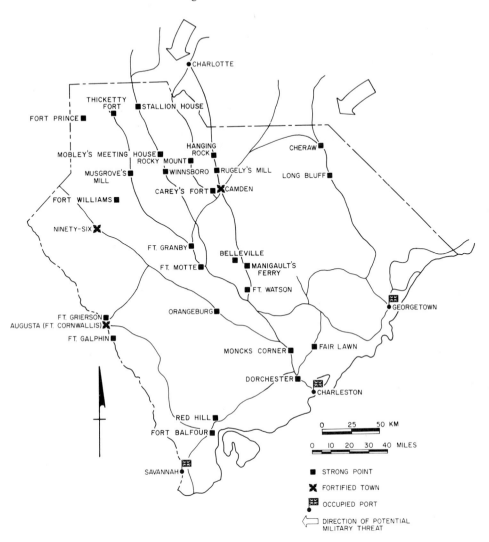

FIGURE 3.25 Distribution of British and Loyalist garrisons in South Carolina, 1780–1781. The layout of these military settlements was intended to provide a support network for field armies, a flexible defense against invasion, and a base from which to pacify the region. (Sources: Hilborn and Hilborn 1970; Lipscomb 1973, 1975, 1977, 1978, 1980.)

nomic dislocations caused by the war. Within 5 years after the war's end it had grown larger than the 1780 settlement and regained its position as a major processing and redistribution center (Schulz 1972:36–38).

Ninety-Six, Augusta, and the Savannah River Frontier

A large part of South Carolina lying outside of Camden's economic hinterland was opened to insular frontier settlement with the opening of the Savannah River

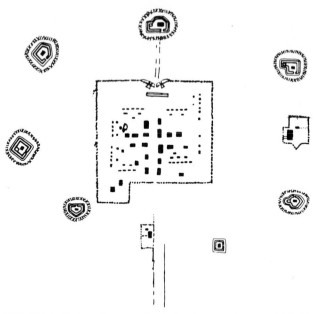

FIGURE 3.26 Camden as a fortified military settlement, 1781. This military plan is also the earliest representation of the town's settlement pattern. The main part of Camden lies within the palisade. The district jail, Joseph Kershaw's house, and the powder magazine lie in separate fortifications respectively to the north, east and southeast of the settlement, forming part of the chain of redoubts defending the town. (Source: NGPPCC/155/II:59.)

region following the Cherokee War. In 1761 Ninety-Six was the largest European settlement in the western backcountry of South Carolina (Fig. 3.22), yet it did not become the frontier town for this region. Its failure to develop as a focus of economic activity is very likely to have been the result of its geographical location which placed it in a disadvantageous position within the colonial trade and communications system. Access to the entrepôt is a key variable in the location of a frontier town, especially one that serves as a collection point for a commodity requiring in-transit processing. Ninety-Six, situated originally so as to provide a link to the Cherokee country, was distant from Charleston and not centrally located within an expanding settlement frontier. The distance and the courses followed by the transportation routes joining it with the entrepôt reduced the potential of Ninety-Six as a frontier town and allowed this role to be assumed by another settlement. Like most other settlements in the backcountry, Ninety-Six was connected to Charleston by routes created for the Indian trade (Fig. 3.12). The first, called the Cherokee Path (Faden 1780; Hunter 1730), passed from Charleston through Granby in the heart of Camden's economic hinterland. The fact that this road passed through one of Camden's subsidiary settlements is likely to have prevented it from becoming a significant avenue for the competitive movement of goods directly to Ninety-Six from the entrepôt.

The second road connected Charleston with Ninety-Six via a point on the Savannah River opposite Augusta, an established center of trade with the Creek Indians in Georgia (Phillips 1908:33; White 1849:513). Augusta maintained direct connections by water and land with the coastal port of Savannah, Georgia. The latter had become an entrepôt in competition with Charleston (Coleman 1976:215), and, when the frontier on the upper Savannah expanded in the 1760s, Augusta's access to the new entrepôt permitted the frontier settlement to expand as the region's frontier town. Augusta's proximity to the second overland trade route to Ninety-Six further isolated the settlement from direct access to Charleston. Its growth precluded Ninety-Six from assuming this role for the newly occupied area. By 1773, the

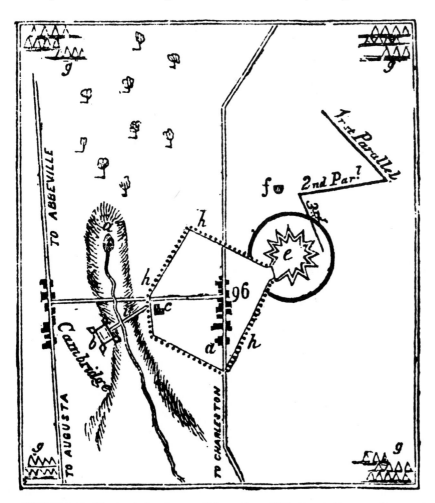

FIGURE 3.27   The fortified settlement of Ninety-Six in 1781. Occupied because of its strategic significance, the settlement was heavily defended by a series of fortifications, including a massive star redoubt. (Source: Lossing 1860:485.)

naturalist William Bartram (1958:201) remarked that "without a competitor, [Augusta] commands the trade and commerce of vast and fruitful regions above it, and from every side to a great distance." Thus, Augusta, while not within the political boundaries of South Carolina, would become the frontier town serving the settlements of this province on the upper Savannah frontier (Drayton 1802:213).

Augusta's role as a key settlement in the South Carolina backcountry was recognized by the British Army which established a garrison there in 1780 to help secure the western portion of the colony. It was beseiged and fell to the Americans in 1781 (Lee 1869:372). Following the war, Augusta, like Camden, quickly arose from its devastation and soon had regained its position as a regional economic center.

Although Ninety-Six failed to develop as a frontier town, it occupied a strategic position in the portion of the new frontier area that lay within the boundaries of South Carolina. The settlement's location within the area's trade and communications system made it a focal point for political and military activity. In 1769, the court for Ninety-Six District was established there. Ninety-Six was the site of partisan encounters early in the American Revolution (Nelson 1961:113–114). It was fortified (Fig. 3.27) and garrisoned by a British force during the military occupation of South Carolina in 1780–1781 (Lee 1869:163–164). Following the loss of Camden and Augusta and an unsuccessful seige by an American army, Ninety-Six was destroyed by its defenders and abandoned. Because of its relative unimportance as an economic center and the subsequent reorganization of the administrative districts, Ninety-Six was not rebuilt, although the small postwar town of Cambridge existed for a time near the site of the earlier settlement (Drayton 1802:209–210; Watson 1970).

Nucleated Settlements on the South Carolina Frontier

In addition to Ninety-Six, several other nucleated settlements appeared in the South Carolina backcountry during the colonial period. The largest of these were Cheraw, Granby, and Orangeburg (Fig. 3.22). The first two served as subsidiary economic centers to the frontier town of Camden. Cheraw on the Pee Dee originally served a wide area but began to decline as an economic center in the 1770s in response to competition from North Carolina. Its diminished role and proximity to the North Carolina border seem to have necessitated a reorientation of activity in this part of the South Carolina frontier. When the region was organized as the Cheraws District in 1769, the administrative center was not placed at Cheraw but at the tiny crossroads settlement of Long Bluff, the location of which seems to indicate a conscious effort to create a political focus in the center of the district rather than on its periphery (Gregg 1867:186–191).

Granby, on the Saluda River, was settled within Saxe Gotha Township around the middle of the eighteenth century. As a subsidiary settlement of Camden, it served as a focus of trade in the central part of the South Carolina frontier. Granby remained an economic center throughout the colonial period and served as a transshipment point for a substantial area until the close of the eighteenth century. Thereafter, it was eclipsed by the new state capital of Columbia situated nearby. During the Revolutionary War, its strategic position led to the establishment of a British garrison at Granby (Drayton 1802:210; Mills 1826:614).

Orangeburg was one of the earliest interior settlements. Established in the 1740s, Orangeburg lay on the Edisto River. Although situated within Camden's trading territory, its early date of settlement, as well as its proximity and direct access to Charleston, permitted it to develop as a subsidiary settlement of the entrepôt. Charleston appears to have been its primary retail market. Because of its geographical position and accessibility via the overland transportation network, Orangeburg was made the seat of Orangeburg District in 1769 (Fig. 3.28). It remained, however, a small settlement of relatively minor importance throughout the colonial period (Drayton 1802:210; Mills 1826:662; Meriwether 1940:47).

Dispersed Settlement

By far the bulk of settlement on South Carolina's colonial frontier was dispersed (Petty 1943:47). Because of inadequate cartographic information for the province, the distribution of this settlement cannot be shown. Its dispersal can be estimated by

FIGURE 3.28　The district courthouse at Orangeburg. This sketch is the only known view of any of the early public buildings erected at the judicial seats established in 1769. (Source: Lossing 1860:490.)

FIGURE 3.29   Detail of the Cook map of 1773, showing settlement in a portion of the Welsh Tract in the vicinity of the Long Bluff courthouse.

plotting the locations of churches, militia units, and other sites of socially integrating activities, as we have done. The distribution of settlement may be observed only in those areas extensively recorded by contemporary mapmakers. In areas where both physiographic and cultural features were recorded in detail, the likelihood of obtaining complete settlement information would seem to be greatest. The vicinity of the Long Bluff courthouse, recorded by James Cook in 1773 is one such area (Fig. 3.29). Clearly shown are the newly built courthouse at a road junction near the river and the dispersed settlements, identified by family names and extending along all the roads as well as some of the waterways. The map and others of the same period (Faden 1780; Mouzon 1775) reveal the predominance of dispersed settlement on the South Carolina frontier as well as its location on the roads making up the overland transportation network of the region.

Reorganization in the Postcolonial Period

The evenly spaced settlement pattern evidenced by the distribution of the district court seats (Fig. 3.30) marked the last phase of frontier development in South Carolina. The next several decades would witness a continued increase in the population density, particularly in the interior (Petty 1943:70), and a reorganization of

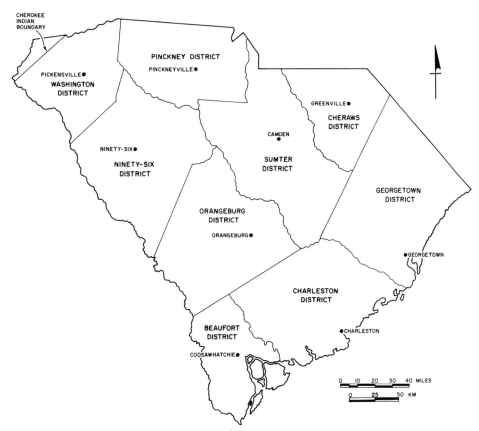

FIGURE 3.30 Judicial districts and seats established in 1791. (Source: South Carolina Archives n.d.)

resource procurement and redistribution systems. Advances in transport technology in the early nineteenth century, such as river canalization and later railroad construction, encouraged the expanded production of cotton by increasing the efficiency and lowering the cost of its shipment.

The reorganization of the network of trade and communications was characterized by a breakdown of the dendritic network by which frontier settlements were tied to the entrepôt through a series of backcountry centers. The linear organization associated with the frontier was replaced by a series of direct linkages between settlements on a much wider scale and over a wider area. A central focus of postcolonial economic activity developed in the interior at Columbia (Fig. 3.31). Rather than being an outlet to the outside world as had the entrepôt of Charleston, it arose as a focal point for economic activity within South Carolina, where trade could now be carried out on a more complex scale. Columbia's location in the geographical center of the state allowed it to assume a central role as capital of the new state (Fig. 3.31) as well as an economic role as the focus of internal trade in South Carolina (Mills 1826:699).

FIGURE 3.31 Columbia in 1794. This drawing, made just a few years after the new capital's establishment, shows the statehouse and adjacent structures. (Courtesy South Caroliniana Library.)

In addition to the loss of internal trade to Columbia, much of the export trade from adjacent former frontier regions in North Carolina and Georgia that had formerly passed through Charleston was now directed through ports in these states such as Wilmington and Savannah (Merrens 1964:165; Phillips 1908:123). By 1820, Charleston's economy was in a slump because of the decline in trade (Derrick 1930:3). Although Charleston would remain as a leading port in South Carolina and the Southeast in the postcolonial period, its role as entrepôt to the interior was eclipsed by Columbia, Augusta, and other inland settlements strategically situated so as to serve new frontier areas further from the coast.

The increasing complexity of the socioeconomic system in this period is revealed by the changing political geography of the region in the last three decades of the eighteenth century. If the administrative districts are seen as units of comparable socioeconomic complexity, then the rate of subdivision of these units should be indicative of the extent to which the overall organizational complexity of the region was increasing. With the exception of the coastal region, whose economy became highly specialized and its settlement pattern fixed relatively early in the colonial period, South Carolina underwent a continual subdivision into progressively smaller administrative units. This process may be observed by comparing maps of the judicial districts of 1769 (Fig. 3.21), 1791 (Fig. 3.30), and 1800 (Fig. 3.32). In a period

FIGURE 3.32 Judicial districts and seats established in 1800. (Source: Coram and Akin 1802; Mills 1825; South Carolina Archives n.d.)

of about 30 years, the number of districts increased from seven to 25, each of which had its own seat that served as a focal point for social, economic, and political activities within its boundaries (Drayton 1802:213–214; Mills 1826).

The fragmentation of the frontier districts coupled with the reorganization of internal trade in the closing years of the eighteenth century radically altered the roles played by individual settlements. As the colonial period ended, so did the need for the types of settlements that characterized its early years.

Summary

Settlement in colonial South Carolina may be seen to have evolved in a manner characteristic of insular frontier regions in general. South Carolina was settled in two phases, an initial occupation of the coastal zone followed by an expansion into the interior of the province. Both regions had agricultural economies, however, the different requirements of their particular staple crops resulted in somewhat distinct forms of insular frontier settlement. The rice economy of the coast was based on a compact, relatively nonperishable commodity that utilized a simple support system and a less complex pattern of settlement. As a result, only two substantial nucleated settlements arose on the coast as regional collection points for rice being shipped to the entrepôt of Charleston. The interior, however, developed a more complex settlement system, which was necessitated by the processing, storage, and shipping demands of grain. Two frontier towns and a number of smaller nucleated settlements arose along the overland transportation network that linked the backcountry to the entrepôt.

The economies of the two regions differed in another way. The coastal lowcountry developed a plantation economy early in the eighteenth century. The environmental limits of rice growing confined its production to a limited area, while its profitability allowed it to maintain a competitive advantage over other cash crops. Its success as a staple permitted the continuation of a large-scale, specialized plantation based economy. It also allowed an unevenly distributed population with a relatively low rate of growth throughout, and after, the frontier period. Competition for agricultural resources characterized the development of the economy in the interior. Grain farming permitted movement into a variety of environments. The expansion of agriculture resulted in an evenly distributed, rapidly growing population. This, in turn, necessitated a reorganization of the economic system at a higher level of complexity.[7] This process is reflected in the progressive fragmentation of administrative units through time, a trend not parallelled in the lowcountry.

Both regions of colonial South Carolina grew as insular frontiers that shared basic similarities in form and organization. As the areas progressed economic differences in production necessitated adaptations that resulted in two distinct economic regions, the contrasting nature of which would endure long into the state's postcolonial history.

SETTLEMENT HIERARCHY: THE COLONIZATION GRADIENT IN SOUTH CAROLINA

As settlement expands within an area of colonization, it is characterized by a spatial distribution that is linked to the organization of its trade and communications system. Because frontier commodity movement on the frontier is centered on a single entrepôt, this organization usually assumes an expanding dendritic pattern that incorporates new areas of settlement. The function of individual settlements

[7]The relative rates of growth for these two regions is evident in the percentage increases in population by district. Using the seven districts of 1790 as a base, the lowest percentage increases in population between 1790 and 1830 are seen in the coastal districts of Beaufort, Georgetown, and Charleston (Petty 1943:70).

within the trade and communications network is related to the economic roles they play in the collection, processing, storage, and redistribution of goods and commodities flowing into and out of the area of colonization. The social and political roles of settlements in the integration of newly occupied territory within the larger system is also influenced by their position within the trade and communications network. The frontier is a transient phenomenon because the forces of expansion that create it also result in its continual movement, bypassing older areas as new lands are occupied. The frontier's spread is often accompanied by an alteration in the transportation network that supports it and necessitates a reorganization that requires individual settlements to take on new roles or even be abandoned.

The relative socioeconomic complexity of frontier settlements is determined by their proximity to the entrepôt. Proximity, in this case, is not merely a measure of direct distance but of distance and accessibility within the existing transportation network and the order in which the settlement is established. The most easily reached and earliest established settlements centrally located within an area undergoing settlement are those most likely to become frontier towns. An important factor affecting the location of frontier towns is the entrepôt's range of direct retail distribution. Within it, the development of competing economic centers is restricted. Frontier towns are associated with their own economic hinterlands. Within their hinterlands, subsidiary centers maintain trade with the dispersed settlements of these regions. The pattern of settlement centered on the frontier towns and their entrepôt represents the colonization gradient, a spatial and organizational continuum of greater to lesser complexity. As the frontier spreads and organizational changes occur, new frontier towns are created and new economic territories are established, while older settlements take on new roles in a more densely populated area organized at a higher level of integration. Individual settlements situated advantageously within the regions pass through developmental stages. These reflect the continuum toward greater complexity seen spatially in the colonization gradient as one moves closer to the entrepôt. The gradient may be observed as a synchronic spatial phenomenon and as an evolutionary process of change in the evolution of the South Carolina frontier.

The Colonization Gradient in the Interior

As we have seen, the colonization of the South Carolina interior was well under way by the middle of the eighteenth century. Following the township surveys of the 1730s, emigrants moved rapidly into accessible portions of the backcountry to take up agricultural lands. The potentially hostile Cherokee presence in the west and the unsuitability of lands on the lower Pee Dee region restricted settlement to those townships on the Wateree, Congaree, and upper Pee Dee systems. These townships[8]

---

[8]The townships were Fredericksburg, Saxe Gotha, Orangeburg, Amelia, Williamsburg, and the Welsh Tract (Fig. 3.11).

also had the advantage of being situated on existing overland transportation routes which linked them to the entrepôt of Charleston. Of these areas, only one produced a frontier town. The reasons for Camden's rise as a social and economic center on the South Carolina frontier are related to its position on the frontier, its accessibility to the transportation network, and the early date of its appearance. When viewed in light of the mideighteenth century area of colonization, Camden was centrally located to serve the Congaree settlements and those in the Welsh Tract. In addition, Camden was strategically situated in the overland transportation network to extend its economic hinterland into the interior of neighboring North Carolina (Merrens 1964:54–55). The road system linking Camden directly with Charleston branched northward and northeastward into the Pee Dee region and the Moravian settlements of North Carolina and westward to the Congarees. Only Orangeburg appears to have been isolated from this network; however, its proximity to Charleston placed this settlement within the territory of the entrepôt's own retail zone (Fig. 3.22).

Camden's origin during the initial period of settlement allowed it to become a regional center with an extensive hinterland well before the Cherokee War opened up the region to the west along the Savannah River. The economic sphere of Camden encompassed potential frontier towns in eastern and central South Carolina. The rapid growth of Augusta as an economic center in the west prevented the development of such settlements in the new frontier region. Cross Creek in North Carolina also arose as a frontier town in the 1760s, establishing a third frontier region in the Carolina backcountry. By the time of the Revolution two decades later, settlement density and agricultural activity in these areas began to reach levels requiring a more complex level of organization than that provided by the existing frontier towns and their network of subsidiary settlements.

In the postwar period, the situation of the South Carolina interior changed dramatically. The removal of British authority, which had confined European settlement east of the Appalachians (DeVorsey 1966), permitted the frontier of the Eastern Seaboard to expand rapidly into the present states of Kentucky, Tennessee, Georgia, Alabama, and Mississippi (Petty 1943:73; Smith 1793:21–22). No longer a frontier region itself, the interior of South Carolina was affected markedly by the introduction of cotton as the principal staple crop. The great demand for this crop in export and in internal markets provided the impetus to increase its cultivation to the exclusion of other commercial crops (Gray 1933:681; Ramsay 1809:215). Cotton production also changed the character of settlement on the old frontier. Given the technology of the eighteenth century, cotton could be grown more profitably on a larger scale than grain. Consequently, the small farm settlement of the interior began to be replaced by plantations, a change which not only altered the form of landholding but the composition of the population as well (Petty 1943:72–73). Realignments of the transportation network were intended to support the expansion of cotton agriculture but would also play a major role in tapping the trade of newly opened frontier regions to the west (Blanding 1820; Logan 1859/I:326; Phillips 1908:123). At the close of the frontier period, the South Carolina backcountry underwent an economic shift, and its population distribution became more evenly spaced with a greater overall density (Petty 1943:69).

The Evolution of Settlement Hierarchy

These demographic and economic changes often altered drastically the roles of individual settlements. Changes in the administrative structure of the state are reflected in the creation of increasingly smaller subdivisions, each with its own seat, and the relocation of the state capital from Charleston to Columbia in the geographical economic center of the state (Lockwood 1832:65; Ramsay 1809:435; Simms 1843:126). In addition to its role as a regional economic center, Columbia became the retail center for the surrounding area. It subsumed the trade of Granby, several miles distant, precipitating the near abandonment of that settlement (Mills 1826:614, 619). Granby, like Cheraw on the Pee Dee, had evolved from an area of dispersed settlement after 1750 to become a nucleated settlement serving as an economic subsidiary to the frontier town of Camden.

The close of the frontier brought a realignment of the colonial transport network and centered the trade of the backcountry on the new capital. This change markedly altered the accessibility of frontier settlements to the entrepôt, restructured retail trade zones, and bypassed some older centers. Some, like Cheraw, declined after reaching a peak in the colonization gradient during the colonial period. Afterward they retained economic influence only over a reduced area (Hammond 1883:702–703; Mills 1826:498). Because of the proximity of Granby and the Saxe Gotha settlements to Columbia, it may be argued that the new entrepôt was in part an outgrowth of them. If so, then they collectively may be seen as having evolved to the pinnacle of the gradient by assuming the role of entrepôt.

Camden, the principal frontier town in South Carolina, also began as an area of dispersed settlement (Kirkland and Kennedy 1905:9–10). Its location on the overland frontier road network and proximity to the Wateree River and several of its tributaries made it attractive as a site for carrying out milling and warehousing activities and for the redistribution of imported retail goods. Camden's position as a frontier town allowed it to assume administrative and social functions for a wide region. The close of the frontier dramatically altered this role. Although it was a major inland commercial center as late as the 1820s, Camden was unable to compete with Columbia as an entrepôt and could not maintain its prominant position in a decentralized economy (Schulz 1972:76). Thereafter, it declined to the status of a regional center, one of several in the state, and its administrative role was limited to that of the seat of Kershaw District (Hammond 1883:702; Haskel and Smith 1846:99; Schulz 1972:85; Simms 1843:89–90).

The nucleated settlements of the frontier period retained varying degrees of economic and political significance in the postcolonial era. Of the circuit court seats of 1769, Orangeburg, Georgetown, Beaufort, Charleston, and Camden remained district seats, although these districts were smaller than their frontier counterparts, and continued to serve as economic centers into the nineteenth century (Hammond 1883; Mills 1826). Cheraw, an economic center since the 1760s, continued to fulfill this role in the upper Pee Dee region, although it never acquired political status as an administrative settlement (Mills 1826:498). Long Bluff and Ninety-Six lost their administrative functions in the closing years of the eighteenth century (Gregg 1867:195; Watson

1970:26). The site of Long Bluff, which was never a commercial center, was abandoned except for periodic use as a landing for the seasonal planters' settlement at nearby Society Hill (McIntosh n.d.:4; Mills 1826:513; Simms 1843:71). Similarly, Ninety-Six could not regain the role it played during the Indian trade. Destroyed during the American Revolution, its site was reoccupied by the small settlement of Cambridge and abandoned permanently about 1850 (Holschlag and Rodeffer 1977:12; Lockwood 1832:84; Mills 1826:351).

The changing economic and social conditions accompanying the close of the frontier in South Carolina affected the old settlements created during the period of initial expansion into the interior and brought about the creation of new ones. These settlements lay in locations strategic to the trade and communications network that was rapidly growing to support the cotton economy. They were situated so as to provide centrally located administrative control for the new districts created in 1800. These districts, made necessary by increased population density and the resulting higher level of social and political interaction, are shown with their seats in Figure 3.32. Most of the seats arose in areas of dispersed or seminucleated settlement and often consisted initially of little more than "a few houses and stores . . . erected . . . in the vicinity of the courthouse" (Drayton 1802:214). Of the more than two dozen nucleated settlements reported by Mills in 1826, all but two of those that arose as district seats at the close of the frontier period had populations of at least 100. Ten had populations of 200 or more; they were Abbeville, Edgefield, Greenville, Lancaster, Laurens, Pendleton, Spartanburg, Union, Winnsborough, and York (Fig. 3.33). Of the new district seats, only Jacksonborough and Winnsborough appear to have been nucleated settlements prior to the beginning of the nineteenth century (Drayton 1802:214).

The rapid evolution of the colonization gradient that created many of the district seats in 1800 also affected other settlements that began to develop but failed and often were abandoned because of their unfortunate positions relative to trade within or administration of the new districts. Among such settlements were Long Bluff and Pinckneyville (Fig. 3.30), both of which were courthouse towns that lay in districts that were subsequently divided (Carrillo 1972). Incipient commercial settlements such as Vienna in Abbeville District, Centerville in Pendleton District, and Granby in Lexington District also arose, often quite rapidly, but were abandoned as a result of changing trade patterns and the successful competition of more favorably situated settlements (Mills 1826:614, 675).

The proliferation of economic and administrative centers at the close of the eighteenth century reflects an evolution of individual settlements toward greater complexity, a process described in the colonization gradient. The gradient is also discernible spatially in the layout of settlement types during the frontier period, a pattern that began to change markedly around 1800. These data correspond roughly to the close of the frontier in South Carolina and the accompanying social, economic, and political reorganization of the old area of colonization. Settlements arising at this time were not the counterparts of these earlier settlements but adaptations to the greater population density and more complex economic organization of a postcolonial region. The emergence of a large number of central place settlements,

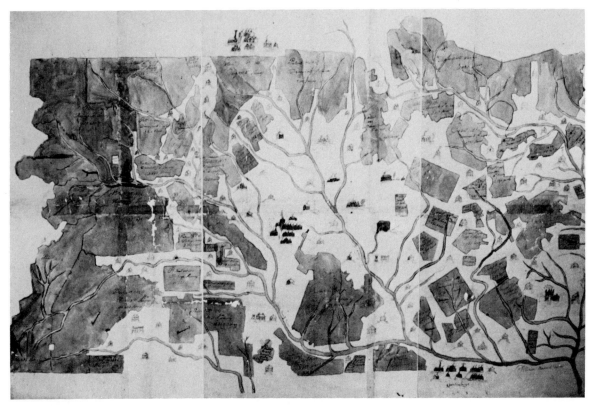

FIGURE 3.33 Spartanburg and vicinity in 1818. The map illustrates the plan of the settlement as well as the layout of landholdings immediately adjacent to it. (Source: Dickey *et al.* 1818.)

many of which served as market centers, in place of the frontier towns indicates the development of a more complex settlement hierarchy with differentiation of market functions at a greater number of levels.

The Evolution of the Transportation Network

The spatial organization of activities in a frontier area is closely tied to the transportation network linking the settlements of the region. Organizational characteristics of the colonization gradient are discernible in the structure of transport. As a frontier region grows, increasing organizational complexity is associated with an intensification of a trade and communications network joining an increasing number of settlements. Changes in transport structure may be observed by constructing a series of schematic diagrams of this network as it appeared at different times during the period of colonization. Because such a study is intended to explore the connections between settlements rather than their distribution, the diagrams may be con-

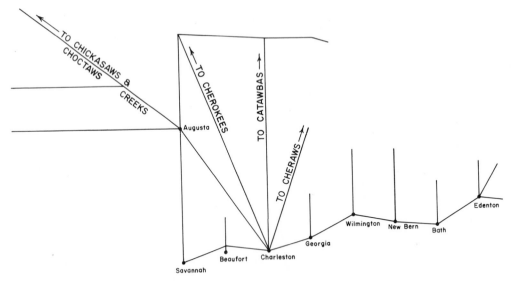

FIGURE 3.34 Schematic diagrams of settlement and transport in the Carolinas and Georgia in 1740. (Source: Weaver 1977:35.)

structed to emphasize directional and geometric aspects of the transport network rather than the absolute geography of the region in which it exists (Weaver 1977:32).[9]

In a study of the evolving transport network on the southern Atlantic Seaboard, Weaver (1977) examined structural changes through the use of a series of schematic diagrams. His diagrams of the region during the colonial period, showing the routes of trade and communication in 1740, 1770, and 1800, reveal a trend from linear links between ports and interior settlements to complex interconnections between an increasing number of economic and political centers.

The first of these diagrams portrays the southern Atlantic Seaboard in 1740. Fig. 3.34 reproduces that portion of the map pertaining to South Carolina and its immediate neighbors. The diagram shows the region prior to inland expansion. At this time, the transportation network consisted of links between the coastal ports and the overland routes of the Southeast Indian trade, the terminus of which was South Carolina's principal port, the entrepôt of Charleston.

By 1770, settlement had proceeded into the interior of South Carolina and its neighboring provinces, supported by immigration from the coast and overland from the northern colonies (Fig. 3.35). A diagram of the transportation network at this time emphasizes these ingress routes as well as the extent of the hinterlands, defined

[9]In the rectangular schematic diagrams, the Fall Line and navigable rivers are portrayed as straight lines with the rivers perpendicular to the Fall Line. Coastal and interior settlements are positioned at distances proportional to their shortest true line distances from the Fall Line. Roads and other transportation routes also appear as straight lines connecting settlements by the shortest distances between them (Weaver 1977:32–33).

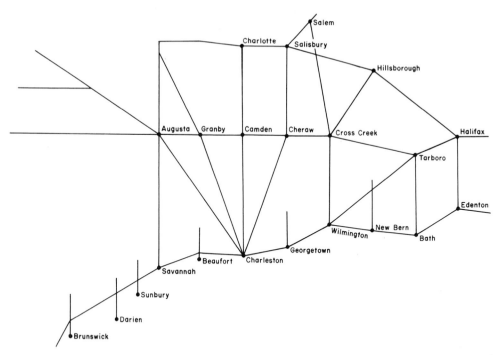

FIGURE 3.35 Schematic diagram of settlement and transport in the Carolinas and Georgia in 1770. (Source: Weaver 177:36.)

by the expansion of feeder routes outward from the inland frontier towns of Camden, Augusta, and Cross Creek. Charleston remained the entrepôt for South Carolina, while Wilmington and Savannah had assumed similar roles in the adjacent provinces of North Carolina and Georgia. The ports of Georgetown and Beaufort still had limited access to the interior as did subsidiary ports in the adjacent colonies. The dendritic structure of the entrepôt-centered frontier transportation networks is clearly illustrated in Fig. 3.35 as is the tendency of their economic hinterlands to intermesh. This increased the number of interconnections between the interior settlements of separate frontier systems.

Fig. 3.36 depicts the transport network 30 years later. By 1800, the pattern of interconnections in the interior had intensified with the creation of new transport links between an increasing number of economically and politically significant settlements. Interior settlements such as Columbia and Augusta and several towns in North Carolina appeared as inland foci of activity. The overall pattern of the transport network was beginning to take on a definitely geometric structure, with most of the major settlements of the region now joined more or less directly with one another. This network formed a grid composed of three northeast–southwest-oriented routes intersected by a series of penetration lines extending from the coastal ports through the Fall Line settlements to the Appalachian Mountains. The begin-

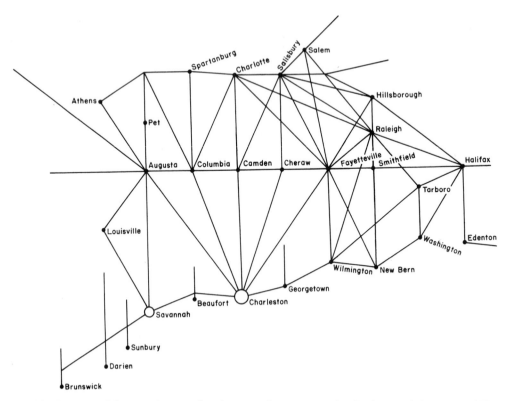

FIGURE 3.36 Schematic diagram of settlement and transport in the Carolinas and Georgia in 1800. (Source: Weaver 1977:37.)

ning of competition for trade territory is discernible in the form of cross-connections in the network. These were created as such settlements as Columbia, Augusta, and Fayetteville sought to expand their spheres of influence (Weaver 1977:37–38).

Changes in the transport structure of colonial South Carolina reflect the economic and political reorganization of the region in response to increasing settlement density. Its evolution from a series of scattered ports through the development of lines of penetration, feeders, and routes of interconnection reveal a trend similar to that outlined in the Taaffe *et al.* model. It also suggests the operation of similar processes of spatial adaptation to conditions encountered in insular frontier colonization.

The relatively rapid evolution of settlement pattern, function, and transport structure in South Carolina at the close of the eighteenth century may be seen as a result of changes related directly to the process of insular frontier colonization. It represents an organizational watershed from which frontier settlements emerged from the colonization gradient at various levels into the more stable structure of the postfrontier period. As a stabilized region organized at a level of integration approaching that of the parent state, South Carolina not only ceased to function as a colony but began to expand its role as a source of emigrants and capital for further frontier expansion (Petty 1943:141–143).

SUMMARY

Colonial South Carolina exhibited formal and organizational characteristics like those described in the model of insular frontier settlement. Although its history represents an adaptation to conditions particular in time and space, the form these adaptations took reflects a strategy employed by other agricultural societies of colonial Europe. Such a strategy is linked to the process of insular frontier change described in the model. In this chapter we have observed aspects of this process revealed in historical sources. These elements are (1) the nature of the colony's economic relationship with its mother country, (2) the development of a staple-commodity resource base supported by local reinvestment of capital, (3) the regular expansion of settlement linked to the pattern of the trade and communications network binding the area of colonization together, (4) the alteration of settlement patterns in response to population density and socioeconomic organizational complexity, (5) the establishment and arrangement of a variety of settlement types reflecting the economic needs of expanding agricultural production, (6) and the evolution of individual settlements in response to their changing roles on the frontier.

The colonization of South Carolina took place during England's rise to hegemony in the expanding European world economy. As a peripheral region within a mercantilistic system, the colony was established primarily for the production of noncompetitive staple commodities. Originally governed by a group of absentee proprietors in the seventeenth century, it evolved into a semiautonomous colony under a royal administration in the early part of the eighteenth. This change was paralleled by the rise of a diversified staple economy characterized by complex internal and external trade linkages and a large degree of local control by resident merchants. Regional control of commodities favored a greater reinvestment in their production, exchange, collection, storage, and distribution. This situation is manifested in the assumption of urban functions by certain colonial settlements on the South Carolina frontier. The trend toward economic autonomy was mirrored politically by the growth of an increasingly powerful representative assembly and a colonial court system that increased local control of the colony's administrative structure.

The evolution of colonial South Carolina as a separate society was encouraged by the diversity of its population, which was composed of a variety of European nationalities, the remnants of the aboriginal population, and Africans imported in increasing numbers to supply labor for agricultural production. This ethnic diversity was complemented by the variety of organized religious bodies introduced, the presence of which mitigated from the beginning the integrative role of the established Anglican Church.

South Carolina's expansion followed the overland trade network developed during the Indian trade that preceded agricultural settlement of the region. The dendritic form of this network, centered on the coastal entrepôt of Charleston, permitted the flow of imported goods and frontier commodities into and out of the area of colonization. Encouraged by the establishment of inland townships in the 1730s, the settlement of the interior spread rapidly up the major river systems of the province. The settlement of the western portion of South Carolina, along the Savannah River, was delayed by the Cherokee presence and did not begin in earnest until the 1760s.

Changing settlement patterns on the South Carolina frontier exhibit a trend from random toward even spacing through time and show a structural response to increasing population density and organizational complexity. Data derived from maps of population aggregates and church sites through time reveal this trend, and are supported by synchronic evidence of settlement distribution, including the locations of administrative centers in the latter part of the frontier period.

The types of settlements that arose in colonial South Carolina are similar to those associated with insular frontier expansion. Because of the physiographic differences between the coastal region and the interior and especially the suitability of the former to commercial wet rice agriculture, these two areas developed separately, although both were served by the same entrepôt. Charleston had two coastal subsidiary centers, Beaufort and Georgetown, which served as collection points for rice as well as foci for the redistribution of goods shipped through the entrepôt. The plantation-dominated economy of the lowcountry, based on the production of an easily transported staple crop, did not require an elaborate settlement hierarchy for support. Consequently, few nucleated settlements developed in this region.

The interior of South Carolina was characterized by a small grain farming economy that needed both frontier towns and a variety of other subsidiary settlements to collect, store, and process this commodity prior to its shipment to the entrepôt. Camden arose as the principal frontier town in central South Carolina around the mideighteenth century, and Augusta, Georgia later fulfilled a similar role for the western part of the colony after the opening of the Savannah River frontier. Each had subsidiary centers through which its retail trade was funneled to and from the dispersed settlements of the frontier.

With time, the population density of the area of colonization increased as did the complexity of its social, economic, and political organization. In response to changes in these variables, the functions of individual settlements were altered to facilitate more efficient trade, communications, and administration. The evolution of particular settlements through time marks the progressive intensification described in the colonization gradient. This is a continuum recording change from lesser to greater complexity that is also manifested spatially at any given time as one moves from the periphery of settlement toward the entrepôt along the primary route of trade.

Colonial South Carolina underwent intensive settlement of the type described in the model of insular frontier colonization. Characteristics of change associated with this colonization process are evident in the historical sources relating to the early development of the region. These sources reveal not only the broad economic, social, and political changes that occurred on a regional basis but also the form these changes took in individual settlements on the frontier. Because of the interrelated nature of these spatial components, it is possible to study a frontier system as a regional phenomenon through an examination of its parts. The ability to do this offers a particular advantage when conducting archaeological research. Its site-specific nature requires a data base built from geographically separate observations assembled within a larger regional framework.

The employment of a regional approach in archaeology permits a past society to be observed more or less in its entirety as a system of integrated parts, the nature of which defines its content, structure, and range (Binford 1964:426). Societies, especially those that are technologically complex and areally extant, are participated in unevenly by their constituent parts. Activities associated with various components, likewise, may occur at different places and at separate times (House 1977:243). Because such activities are likely to be recognizable in the archaeological record, their sequence and distribution should be discernible when viewed at the regional level. There it will reveal larger elements of structure and organization as well as processes of continuity and change. Insular frontier colonization is such a process and should be recognizable in the archaeological record laid down in regions where it has taken place.

In the following chapter, the archaeological record of the settlement frontier in South Carolina will be examined in light of the process of insular frontier change. The existence of this process and the boundaries of the region in which it occurred have been established and the loci of various activities associated with this process delineated on the basis of documentary evidence. These phenomena should also be recognizable archaeologically, here and elsewhere, on the basis of the material record alone. The distribution and sequence of activities reflecting the occurrence of the insular frontier process may be discerned through the discovery and analysis of functionally significant archaeological patterning. Such patterning is a by-product of particular activities and their interrelationships and also of the various transformations by which the material they generate moves into and out of the archaeological record. Through the use of historical, ethnographic, and archaeological analogies at different levels of inference, the nature and layout of archaeological patterning likely to be associated with particular processes within specific cultural contexts may be predicted with some degree of reliability. An understanding of the behavioral significance of such patterning should make it possible to discover and explore processes archaeologically without the benefit of a particular historical record as extensive as that available in the case of South Carolina.

4

Examining the Insular Frontier in South
Carolina:
Research Directions and Archaeological
Hypotheses

INTRODUCTION

Documentary and cartographic evidence has been employed to demonstrate the
occurrence of insular frontier change in colonial South Carolina, a process associated with the presence of certain activities and organizational characteristics set
forth in the frontier model developed in Chapter 2. Historical sources, however,
represent only one record of this past. The material remains generated by colonial
period settlement are also likely to reflect evidence of the insular frontier process.
Formed independently of the written record and not subject to the intentional biases
that so often alter the content of documents, the structure and content of these
remains can reveal functionally significant patterning that may be used to verify and
complement statements derived from other types of historical data. Both of these
capabilities are utilized in the following chapters, which examine the settlement of
South Carolina as an example of insular frontier colonization on the basis of its

archaeological record. Material evidence from sites of colonial period settlement is explored through the use of archaeological hypotheses derived from the characteristics of the insular frontier model. The extent to which the patterning anticipated in these hypotheses is present in the archaeological data should demonstrate the potential of this form of evidence as an information source and its value in exploring problems of culture process.

The procedure followed here involves the testing of a historical model through an examination of archaeological hypotheses. It is not intended to establish this model as the best or only explanation of frontier change. To do so would require a comparison of competing frontier theories that represent propositions at the same level of logical inclusiveness. Testing a theory against data produces probablistic rather than absolute results and thus cannot entirely prove or disprove the former (Price 1982:711–712). This type of testing is, however, a necessary first step in measuring the adequacy of a given theory and is especially useful when alternate theories have not yet been formulated. This is the case with the explanation of frontier change. The analysis of the archaeological data from South Carolina will serve principally to examine the theory of change set forth in the insular frontier model.

BASIC ASSUMPTIONS

The archaeological analysis will seek to identify the characteristics of insular frontier change in colonial South Carolina, a region where written sources have shown this process to have taken place. In order to accomplish this, it will be necessary to seek archaeological evidence indicative of the appearance and distribution of activities associated with the structure and function of settlement as described in the frontier model. Change in the organization of activities over time is an integral part of the frontier process, and it too much be discernible archaeologically.

The archaeologist's ability to obtain behavioral information from material evidence is based on several assumptions regarding this type of data. The first is that societies operate as *systems* composed of interacting components, both cultural and natural, that are continually acting and reacting with one another to produce variation and change. A systemic organization also presupposes the existence of cultural mechanisms that regulate change and maintain behavior within certain limits or boundaries. To deal with a phenomenon as complex as human culture, it is necessary to adopt an approach that stresses the organizational interrelationship of all variables in the system rather than between isolated characteristics of man and his environment (Buckley 1967:41; Geertz 1963:9–10). Approaching the past from a systems perspective emphasizes the organizational aspects of culture as opposed to its static elements. Because a cultural system consists of the organizational framework within which events and behavior happen, rather than a summation of these events, our investigation of the past must assume an organizational perspective (Binford 1981:201).

Just as human behavior may be seen as part of an interrelated system, separate activities not involving all parts of the system or all members of the society may be defined as *subsystems*. The number of subsystems increases with the complexity of the cultural system and, concommitantly, with the degree of specialization within it (Binford 1965:205). Colonial societies created by the expansion of Europe were components of a complex, worldwide economic system the investigation of which may best be carried out through an examination of those subsystems most closely associated with its economic organization.

Because behavior is not random, it is possible to observe patterns in human activities. A recognizable *structure* may be seen in the systemic organization of technology, economics, religion, social organization, and other specialized activities. Changes in these patterns may be traced through time and variation in systemic structure viewed as a historical phenomenon.

Of crucial importance is the final assumption that the archaeological record will exhibit particular *patterns* reflecting organizational aspects of the cultural system that produced it (Longacre 1971:131). The archaeological record should also reveal temporal changes in patterning that indicate variation in the structure of the system over time. In order to examine the relationship between a cultural system and the material record it leaves behind, archaeologists have sought to delineate the relationship between the organization of behavior and the nature of the deposition it produces. In particular, they have focused on the linkages between functionally significant sets of activities and the form of their archaeological by-products.

PROCESSES AND PATTERNS

The search for systemic structure in the archaeological record has followed two lines of inquiry. One has involved the definition of processes by which the archaeological record is formed, and the other has attempted to recognize behaviorally significant patterning in the composition and distribution of archaeological materials. Both can provide data relevant to the organization of past culture systems and their change through time. Such information is crucial to the recognition of processes on the basis of material remains.

Processes affecting the formation of the archaeological record are important to understanding the manner in which that record was produced. *Formation* processes identify specific types of deposition that result in the accumulation of archaeological materials. Because deposition of some kind results from nearly all activities, formation processes are likely to be universal. Single processes may be linked to a variety of activities and in themselves cannot identify particular activities. If the processes likely to be associated with an activity are known, however, it should be possible to predict the composition and distribution of the archaeological remains of that activity. Formation processes can provide a link between our knowledge of the structure of an existing cultural system and the form of its material by-products.

Schiffer (1972, 1976) described several basic processes involved in the formation of the archaeological record. These are discard, loss, and abandonment. *Discard* may be defined as the deposition of waste material. It may accumulate at its location of use as primary refuse or be deposited elsewhere as secondary refuse (Schiffer 1976:30–31). Secondary refuse may reflect the deposition of single as well as multiple activities, and the size and nature of its content may vary with the distance the material is moved to its place of deposition (South 1977:179, 1979a:218–219). *Loss,* the second formation process, involves the inadvertant deposition of items and may vary with the object's size, portability, and function (Schiffer 1976:32–33). Finally, the process of *abandonment* is the accumulation of artifacts that remain in a given area after it is no longer in use. Abandoned material may include the de facto refuse of production or habitation that is left behind because it is inefficient or impossible to remove (Schiffer 1976:33–34). An important type of abandonment refuse is architectural in nature, consisting not only of standing remains but also material that has accumulated as a result of construction, repair, or demolition of structures (Green 1961:53). Abandonment may also modify other cultural formation processes, such as discard, resulting in the development of refuse disposal patterns different from those associated with an activity area still in use (Schiffer 1976:33; South 1977:61).

The formation processes outlined by Schiffer provide a basis for exploring the relationship between past activities and the archaeological record they leave behind. These processes are, however, general and do not specify in detail the form the archaeological record is likely to take as a result of discard, loss, or abandonment. In order to relate particular past activities to their material remains, it is necessary to define the means by which the by-products that activity generates are disposed. This may be accomplished by examining the various types of deposition that are associated with each formation process. An outline of such types has been presented by South (1979a:220), who has called them *disposal modes.* Each mode is linked with the occurrence of particular refuse types, the size and condition of artifacts likely to be present, and the probable spatial patterning of the archaeological evidence. Disposal models provide a key linking site structure to activity occurrence by describing the manner in which the by-products of activities pass into the archaeological record. A knowledge of these processes can help the investigator interpret the nature of the archaeological deposition from a given activity. If the composition and organization of the activity are known, or can be inferred accurately through analogy, and the disposal modes can be specified, it should be possible to anticipate the content and distribution of the archaeological record the activity has generated.

Archaeological patterns delineated through an understanding of formation processes and their associated disposal modes can allow the identification of past activities on the basis of archaeological evidence. These patterns yield information useful in determining the form and function of past settlements. Such patterns, which consist of the regular association of similar archaeological elements, may be found to relate directly to specific subsystems of the past culture. The occurrence and layout of structures of English settlements in the colonial American South, for example, reveal patterns of architecture, differential artifact use, and spatial distribution that relate to the organization of social, economic, technological, and other subsystems operating in this region of the European world economy (Lewis 1980a; South 1979a:223–224). If archaeological site components are viewed as elements of such subsystems, then the combination of subsystemic elements at a site should be indicative of the settlement's role in the past culture system (South 1979a:227–230). Archaeological patterning resulting from the various subsystemic combinations associated with different types of settlements can permit the identification of settlement function on the basis of the material remains generated by past activities. These patterns reflect activities occurring as a result of the structure of the cultural system within which they took place. Changes in the complexity and organization of this system through time should also be readily discernible in such patterns, permitting the extent and nature of the change to be observed archaeologically. Insular frontier change involves radical shifts in the systemic structure of the intrusive society's culture as it adapts to the environment of the frontier. South Carolina, as a region of insular frontier settlement, should exhibit the characteristics of such change in composition, form, and distribution of its archaeological remains.

HISTORICAL ANALOGY AND ARCHAEOLOGICAL INVESTIGATION

Crucial to the effective use of archaeological data for investigating the systemic structure of past cultures is the development of adequate analogies linking the use and deposition of material items to the operation of specific activities. Given a knowledge of formation processes and disposal modes, it should be possible to anticipate the form and content the remains of an activity will take if we are aware of its nature, organization, and technology. Correlations between aspects of a past activity and the archaeological record are indirect observations that must be supported by bridging arguments (Binford 1968:19–20). The relevance of such arguments derives from the strength of the analogs used to construct them and is reflected in the prior probability of the hypothesized relationship between behavior and archaeological data. The prior probability of such a hypothesis is a measure of its likelihood, independent of testing, arrived at through an examination of its implications (Salmon 1976:379). For the archaeologist dealing with the historic past, arguments based on documentary and ethnographic analogies provide an effective means of accomplishing this and, in so doing, play a pivotal role in determining the plausability of archaeological inferences (Orser 1979:5).

The use of documentary and ethnographic sources in archaeological situations offers a great advantage, since it allows precise recognition of certain variables present in particular contexts at specific times in the past (Harrington 1952:337). Analogies based on both types of evidence may be employed to make inferences concerning the interpretation of particular artifacts or other forms of material evidence and about organizational and behavioral aspects of extinct societies (Deetz 1971:123; Longacre 1971:136). Gould (1971:175) has pointed out that ethnographic knowledge can be brought to bear at three levels of archaeological research. In each case, the use of historical documentation may be substituted for ethnographic sources. The first level of *practical interpretation* involves the use of informants (documents) to locate and provide background information about sites. The second level of *specific interpretation* is directed toward solving particular problems within the context of an individual site. An example might be the functional interpretation of a tool type. Finally, *general interpretation* attempts to present broad explanations of culture history and process.

In the previous chapter, documentary sources were employed at the general level to provide evidence for the process of insular frontier change in colonial South Carolina. The analysis of the archaeological data will seek to produce information supporting these conclusions. In order to avoid circular reasoning, however, its use of analogies must be confined to those at the practical and specific levels. Documents may be used to aid in establishing the locations of sites and approaching specific problems within site context. Because of the geographically extensive nature of British colonial society and the widespread occurrence of common cultural practices associated with it (South 1977:124–125), behavioral relationships and their accompanying archaeological patterning are also likely to be similar throughout regions colonized by Great Britain. Specific documentary analogies regarding such behavior need not be confined to interpreting activities occurring at single sites. Behavioral analogies are likely to relate to aspects of colonial culture that were widespread. The use of such analogies can aid in the functional interpretation of material remains found at most sites of British cultural affiliation that were occupied during the same period. Documentary data used to establish links between behavior and material evidence should consist of sources general enough to have a broad degree of application, yet particular enough to allow the interpretation of individual archaeological data sets.

EXAMINING THE ARCHAEOLOGICAL RECORD

The recognition of the characteristics of insular frontier change in the archaeological record of South Carolina depends on an effective employment of historical analogies and an understanding of pertinent archaeological formation processes. These conceptual tools allow bridging arguments to be made linking behavioral patterning reflecting the systemic organization of the past culture and archaeological patterning representing the material record generated by such behavior. Proper bridging arguments should permit the prediction of archaeological data sets disclosing the conditions described in each characteristics of the frontier model. These expectations may be set forth as hypotheses, each of which is accompanied by a series of test implications specifying the form the archaeological record is likely to assume if the hypothesis is valid. The degree to which the archaeological data support the hypotheses should illustrate the ability of archaeological methodology to reveal the occurrence of regional processes without the assistance of a separate form of evidence.

The characteristics of the insular frontier model show organizational change within a sociocultural system. Because the model is largely economic, it stresses those aspects of culture related most closely to the economic subsystem. Both documentary and archaeological evidence are likely to reflect economic activity, however, each does so differently and their results are not identical. Just as the bias of the recorder distorts the content of documents and must be taken into account, there are several factors that affect our ability to discern information about the economic organization of a past society from a study of its material remains. This is not to imply an incompleteness in the archaeological record, but rather to recognize the nature of this source of data and the limitations that currently exist in our ability to utilize it.

Perhaps the most significant factor affecting the type of information preserved derives from the nature of the archaeological record itself. Briefly, material evidence represents the cumulative result of the operation of numerous processes relating to the transfer of objects during and after their use. Because it is formed as a result of such processes, the archaeological record tends to mirror general systemic changes rather than those associated with specific events. Its patterned structure, then, does not indicate an accumulation of events, but the basic organizational constraints or determinants operating on them (Binford 1981:197). Consequently, archaeological hypotheses should be designed to explore the organizational aspects of processes such as frontier change and not to elicit evidence of individual historical events reflecting the change. In our discussion of insular frontier change, archaeological questions will be addressed primarily to the organization of colonial society and its evolving form and distribution on the changing frontier landscape.

A second factor affecting our use of the archaeological record is the inadequate development of studies addressed to problems of relating behaviorally significant activities to patterning in the archaeological record. Activity patterning on historic sites has only begun to be explored (see for e.g. Binford 1978; Dethlefson 1981; Dickens and Bowen 1980; Ferguson 1977; Lewis 1976, 1977b; Otto 1977; Price and Price 1978; Rathje and McCarthy 1977; Schiffer et al., 1981; South 1972a, 1977, 1978, 1979a; Stevenson 1981). These studies and others demonstrate the existence of functionally meaningful patterning in the archaeological record and show the persistence and variation of such patterning in response to cultural variables. The recognition of functional artifact patterns is still in its infancy, however, and many of the patterns already observed need additional refinement that only comparative studies can provide. In the absence of an established body of data relating behavior to archaeological patterning, it will be necessary to employ patterns derived largely from historical analogies and a knowledge of site formation processes.

Finally, the archaeological study of a region as large as South Carolina requires the use of data obtained from a large enough sample of sites to measure the variables of frontier change in the area as a whole. Such a sample should ideally include sites of settlements representing key economic features of the frontier system as well as those capable of revealing change in the system through time. Unfortunately, conditions for obtaining an unlimited sample of such data rarely exist, and one is obliged to settle for a less than optimal sample. Such is the case with South Carolina. Urban development has restricted access to a number of sites of known colonial settlement, and many parts of the state remain unsurveyed for the remains of early European occupation. Available funding has also not permitted extensive investigations at many colonial period sites. The paucity of information is partially a result of the fact that prior to the 1960s only limited archaeological excavations had been carried out in South Carolina, and almost none on sites of the colonial period (Stephenson 1975:8). In the past two decades, however, a great deal of work has been accomplished in locating and investigating historic sites. These investigations have produced much new information about colonial settlement in every part of the state and have included the exploration of several settlements which documents have identified as having played central roles in South Carolina's frontier development. Although the sample provided by these data is incomplete and information about many settlements described in documentary sources is not yet available, the areal extent, morphological variation, and temporal range of the sites represented appears adequate to permit an investigation of the processual questions posed by the insular frontier model.

Based on the use of historical analogy, a number of hypotheses will be proposed in the following section to examine the characteristics of the insular frontier process on the basis of archaeological evidence. Archaeological test implications for each hypothesis may then be deduced, specifying the form such material evidence is likely to assume if the hypothesis is supported. Because of limitations resulting from our less-than-perfect knowledge of functionally related archaeological patterning and an incomplete sample of sites of frontier settlement, this study will not be able to examine every aspect of insular frontier colonization in South Carolina. The hypotheses should address the central problems of each of the frontier model's characteristics because insular frontier change as a regional process may be recognized in data representing its salient features only. An information base that includes all sites occupied during the colonial period is not required to identify the existence of a frontier.

The following chapter will examine each of the hypotheses using archaeological data obtained from the sites of colonial settlement in South Carolina. Its results should verify the occurrence of the characteristics of insular frontier change presented in the model. Our success in recognizing this process on the basis of archaeological evidence should illustrate not only the advantage gained by employing processual models in archaeological studies but also the explanatory capability of archaeological methodology to aid in the investigation of past cultural systems.

THE DEVELOPMENT OF ARCHAEOLOGICAL HYPOTHESES

A Definition of Subsystems

The model of insular frontier settlement exhibits six basic characteristics that have been readily identifiable in an examination of documentary sources pertaining to colonial South Carolina. The characteristics describe the nature, distribution, organization, and evolution of activities associated with this process of frontier change. Such activities are usually described in written sources and make it unnecessary to examine the systemic structure of colonial culture in order to identify insular frontier change. The use of archaeological evidence in the study of colonial societies, however, requires a knowledge of the parent culture's systemic structure to enable the formulation of hypotheses linking material patterning to past activities on the frontier. Because activities are generally subsystemic (in that they involve components of only part of the total system), the archaeological hypotheses should examine those subsystems most likely to exhibit evidence of frontier change. The insular frontier model is focused largely on the development of colonies as permanent bases for the production of commercially marketable commodities. Activities associated with this development may be defined in terms of three broad subsystems: economic, sociopolitical, and trade and communications.

The *economic subsystem* includes those activities which result in the production of material artifacts including agricultural commodities beyond the subsistence level. Its components are people, material resources, and the finished products (Renfrew 1972:22–23). Because the frontier model is economically oriented, this aspect of the colonial culture system will figure prominantly in the archaeological analysis. The model, however, is not confined exclusively to economic activity and will deal also with the following two subsystems.

The *sociopolitical subsystem* consists of behavior patterns in which the defining activities are those that take place between people. Sociopolitical activities may overlap into other aspects of culture, but may be distinguished as a separate subsystem that seeks to define patterns of interpersonal behavior (Renfrew 1972:22–23). The sociopolitical subsystem deals with those activities that regulate the functioning of societies. These are activities related to: maintaining internal order, validating and maintaining patterns of authority, and regulating the competition for power, the welfare of the society as a whole, foreign relations, and defense from external attack (Trigger 1974:95–96).

The *trade and communications* subsystem is identified by those activities that involve transferring information or material goods between or within settlements. This subsystem encompasses all activities that entail travel by any components of the system whether people or artifacts (Renfrew 1972:23). Because of the importance of trade to the existence of frontier settlement, this subsystem assumes a significant role in colonization and is closely bound to the operation of both economic and sociopolitical subsystems.

Each of the characteristics of the frontier model involves at least one of these three subsystems. In order to explore archaeologically the process of change described in the model, hypotheses may be used to examine the manner in which subsystemic organization is apt to be affected by the conditions associated with each of the model's characteristics. Hypotheses should link patterns of change to adaptive cultural responses in each aspect of colonization under consideration and indicate the accompanying subsystemic variation. Test implications for each hypothesis will specify, in turn, the particular type of archaeological evidence that these subsystemic changes are likely to have produced.

The Organization of the Archaeological Analysis

The archaeological analysis will proceed in a manner similar to that found in the historical discussion in Chapter 3. Our discussion will follow the format of the frontier model, the characteristics of which have been arranged so as to permit the process of insular frontier change to be examined in progressively greater detail. It begins by addressing static structural features of the region's content, layout, and organization. These are the phenomena that permit the identification of an area of colonization in time and space. Once these basic characteristics are defined, a framework exists within which it is possible to measure change through time. The opportunity to observe change throughout a colonial region allows one to explore the dynamic aspect of the frontier process which, in turn, reflects the evolution of a complex sociocultural system adapting in a patterned manner to its position at the periphery of a world economy.

Archaeological hypotheses of insular frontier change will broadly address the effect of the conditions described by the model's characteristics on three basic subsystems of English colonial culture. The frontier model involves a process of change wide enough in extent to be measured over the region as a whole, yet so pervasive as to affect the development and composition of individual components of colonial settlement. The subsystems may also be observed at different levels within the area of colonization. On the one hand, they are regional phenomena whose operation takes place throughout the frontier area. Subsystems are also site specific in that their related activities are found in most settlements, permitting the recognition of subsystemic components on a much smaller scale as well. Because this study deals with such a wide range of variation in both the scope of change and in the regional structure within which it occurs, archaeological hypotheses and test implications should be general as well as specific. They should deal with the area of colonization as a whole, yet also be concerned with the form, composition, and role of individual settlements.

The archaeological hypotheses and test implications are intended to link patterning in the existing material record with the organization and operation of a past cultural system. This record involves two types of evidence, (1) archaeological remains and (2) standing structures and other intact cultural landscape features. The study of the former requires the excavation and analysis of buried artifacts, architectural remains, and other features, while the investigation of the latter is concerned with the identification of remnant structural evidence. Because archaeological analysis deals with the remains of the activities carried out at a settlement as well as the structures in which they were housed, it provides a more comprehensive view of the past than the study of architecture alone. Ideally archaeological investigations should accompany architectural studies to provide the greatest amount of information. By itself architecture may provide clues regarding function and date of construction as well as the origin, status, and ethnicity of its inhabitants (Glassie 1968, 1975; Kniffen 1936; Kniffen and Glassie 1966; P. Lewis 1975). Many colonial period structures still exist in South Carolina as remnants of its early historic landscape. Although constituting only a portion of the material record at their sites, they often represent all that is presently available for study. Architectural structures and features form a significant part of the available archaeological record in this former colonial region and can supply important information capable of greatly supplementing data derived from excavated archaeological sites. In the following section, material evidence from both archaeological and architectural sources will be employed to examine the phenomenon of insular frontier change in colonial South Carolina.

Eleven hypotheses have been formulated to present the characteristics of the frontier process in terms of the subsystemic organization of eighteenth century British colonial culture. Each hypothesis specifies the types of activities that are likely to be associated with the various aspects of insular frontier change. The remains of such activities should be discernible in the archaeological record and the hypotheses enumerated here will form the basis of archaeological test implications to be considered in the following section. The hypotheses will be grouped into categories based on the frontier model. This arrangement will form the organizational format for the next five chapters.

Hypotheses for the Colony's Establishment

The first set of hypotheses is concerned with the establishment of the colony as a distinct region of settlement. As defined in the model, establishment is characterized by the maintenance of cultural and economic ties with the homeland concurrently with the development of a distinct society with an economy geared to the production of export staples. These facets of colonization will form the basis of the first four archaeological hypotheses. Because establishment must occur for a frontier region to exist, its characteristics must, likewise, be recognized archaeologically if the study of such a region on the basis of material evidence is to take place. Establishment is a general phenomenon involving the area of colonization as a single entity and the frontier period as a unit of time. Consequently, the hypotheses will focus on evidence capable of portraying space and time in a similar manner.

1. The first hypothesis is that the social and economic ties between the colony and the homeland will be discernible in the archaeological record. Evidence of such ties may take the form of nationally or ethnically distinctive artifacts as well as patterns of artifact use. Culturally significant artifact patterning should reflect not only the operation of an efficient and extensive system of trade and communications but also the continuation of social and economic practices relating to the use of artifacts.

2. The emergence of a distinct colonial society should be evident despite the retention of social and economic ties with the homeland. This distinctness results from an adaptation to conditions encountered at the periphery of the world economy. It is most likely to appear in the aspects of colonial culture related most closely to the region's peripheral role in that system. Distinctness should be characterized by

the adoption of new artifacts and patterns of behavior, often borrowed from other societies with which contact has taken place.

3. Finally, the presence of a permanent colonial society should be recognizable in the long-term occupation of the region it settled. Archaeological evidence should reveal continuous settlement in South Carolina from the late seventeenth century onward.

Hypotheses for Spatial Patterning

The following hypotheses deal with the frontier region as a spatial phenomenon. An area of colonization reflects the spatial patterning of its trade and communications network, which links its settlements together socially, politically, and economically. This network is likely to exhibit a dendritic form centered on the colony's entrepôt. Settlement should show this spatial pattern throughout the period of colonization. Because we are again dealing with a synchronic phenomenon, the two hypotheses will be concerned with the frontier period as a single block of time.

4. An entrepôt must be established at the accessible edge of the area undergoing colonization. In the case of South Carolina and other British colonies on the Atlantic Seaboard, such entrepôts would have been ports. Because of the entrepôt's role as focus of social, political, and economic activity, it is expected that this settlement will be larger than others in the colony and exhibit evidence of centralizing institutions associated with its position.

5. The spatial pattern of a frontier region may be defined by the dendritic form of its trade and communications network. This linear network's form, centered on the coastal entrepôt, is apt to be evident both in remnants of the transportation routes themselves as well as the colonial settlement pattern.

Hypotheses for Expansion

The next two hypotheses relate to the dynamic aspect of frontier settlement. They deal with the expansion of the colonial region through time and the concomitant changes in settlement pattern and the organization of trade and communications. These changes are integral to the process of expansion and a recognition of their presence provides a spatial and temporal framework in which to examine the organization of activities within the frontier.

6. Viewed through time, English settlement in South Carolina should exhibit continuous expansion throughout the colonial period. Earliest settlement should be concentrated around the entrepôt with subsequent expansion occurring progressively further from it along the dendritic pattern defined earlier.

7. If the settlement pattern of the frontier region is observed cumulatively at different intervals, it should exhibit a trend toward even spacing. This trend man-

ifests an increasing density of settlement and a growing competition for land and resources as the area of colonization begins to near its capacity to support an agricultural population.

Hypotheses for Settlement Pattern and the Organization of Activities

The changing structure of trade and communications in a frontier region is related closely to the organization of activities and the roles of the settlements in which such activities are carried out. Settlement structure during the frontier period spatially illustrates the organizational patterning described in the colonization gradient. During the period in which colonization takes place, the dendritic transportation network supports a hierarchy of settlements that permits the efficient exploitation of a sparsely settled region. This hierarchy is revealed in the function of each settlement and its position within this network. The nature of frontier settlement is discussed in the following three hypotheses.

8. The existence of frontier towns is crucial to the maintenance of economic, political, and social organization in a frontier region. These settlements serve as foci of activities and link large portions of the frontier directly with the entrepôt. As a result of their role, frontier towns should be the largest settlements in the area of colonization except for the entrepôt. These settlements should exhibit evidence of their central position in the frontier economy. In addition to being domestic settlements, frontier towns should also be identifiable as centers of politically, socially, and economically integrating activities throughout the period of frontier settlement.

9. Nucleated settlements should also be found in the area of colonization. These settlements, which are smaller than frontier towns, contain few of the frontier towns' integrating institutions. They are mainly domestic settlements, yet they should exhibit evidence of some specialized economic or political activity.

10. Dispersed settlements are occupied by the remainder of the frontier population. These should include individual family or small group settlements possessing a largely domestic function as units of agricultural production. The nature of these settlements may vary considerably with the type of commercial agriculture carried out and should reflect the social relations of production. Although dispersed settlements themselves are smaller than frontier towns and nucleated settlements, they are often associated with the control of large landholdings. In the case of slave plantations, they may also involve a substantial population. Because of their specialized agricultural nature even these should be discernible from other types of settlement.

Hypothesis for the Colonization Gradient

The frontier is not a static phenomenon and rapidly evolves in response to increasing population density and agricultural expansion. Nowhere is this change more evident than in the composition and distribution of settlement in the area of colonization. The colonization gradient, in which settlements are ranked hierarchically according to their roles in the frontier economic system, may also be seen as an evolutionary scheme through which settlements pass as the region becomes integrated at a higher level. Change in the settlements of the frontier should be of the types specified in the final hypothesis of insular frontier colonization.

11. Colonial settlements will vary in response to their roles in the changing economic system of the frontier period. Those which are situated strategically in the evolving trade and communications network will usually assume additional economic and political functions and grow in size as related activities are drawn to them. Alterations in the transportation network cause earlier settlements to be bypassed and create advantages for the growth of new ones. It is anticipated that evidence for the abandonment of older frontier settlements and the creation of others in new locations will characterize the latter part of the frontier period.

SUMMARY

Eleven archaeological hypotheses have been derived from the characteristics of the frontier model. Each hypothesis indicates expected changes in one or more of the three subsystems that play important roles in the organization of colonial societies. These hypotheses describe the insular frontier process as a cross-cultural phenomenon, applicable generally to the study of overseas agricultural colonization. In order to define this process in terms of the particular case of the South Carolina frontier, it is necessary to further deduce a series of test implications for each hypothesis. These will describe the specific types of evidence one would expect to encounter in the material record left behind by a permanent British agricultural colony in eighteenth century South Carolina. This evidence should assume the form of predictable patterning in the archaeological record at the sites of actual settlement. In the following section, the hypotheses developed here will be examined archaeologically in analyses designed to obtain such evidence. The success of the analyses should demonstrate the potential of archaeological methodology as a means of exploring this as well as other widespread processes of sociocultural change.

5

Examining Hypotheses for the Colony's Establishment

INTRODUCTION

Eleven archaeological hypotheses for insular frontier change have been set forth in the previous discussion. Each hypothesis deals with a different aspect of this process as it is likely to affect intrusive colonial societies. This chapter and the five to follow examine material data from an insular frontier region in order to provide evidence in support of those hypotheses. The hypotheses specify conditions that are expected as a result of the operation of the process of insular frontier change on the systemic structure of the intrusive British society that colonized South Carolina in the late seventeenth and eighteenth centuries. This chapter examines hypotheses for the colony's establishment as a permanent area of settlement. Establishment is crucial to the existence of insular frontier colonization and must occur if the other characteristics of this process are to take place.

To examine each of the hypotheses in this and subsequent chapters, it is necessary to develop a series of archaeological test implications based on information derived from ethnographic and historical analogies. Sets of test implications will specify the particular types of observations necessary to support the statements contained in the hypothesis. Each set should contain at least one crucial test implication which, if confirmed by the archaeological data, will definitely substantiate the hypothesis under consideration (Hill 1972:83). The usefulness of material data in the recognition of frontier change may be demonstrated if all of the testable hypotheses are confirmed. The examination of the archaeological implications for each hypothesis constitutes a basic test of archaeological methodology as a tool for the study of culture process. Our successful employment of this methodology should demonstrate its potential usefulness in conjunction with or in the absence of other types of historical information.

HYPOTHESIS 1: CREATION AND MAINTENANCE OF CULTURAL TIES WITH THE HOMELAND

The first hypothesis predicts that archaeological data will provide evidence for the establishment of a British colony in South Carolina and the continued maintenance of economic and social ties between the colonial society and the parent state throughout the period of colonization. Evidence for establishment must reveal both cultural affiliation between the colonial population and that of the homeland and its continuation over a sustained period. Both cultural continuity and temporal association are likely to be manifested in the occurrence of particular classes of artifacts that are sensitive to these two variables. It is anticipated that the patterning exhibited by these classes will permit the identification of the colonists' nationalities and the time in which the colonization took place. South Carolina is known to have been open for settlement as a colony in the second half of the seventeenth century when English occupation of the southern Atlantic Seaboard began. The terminal date of colonization in South Carolina, as in the other British North American colonies, occurred in the last decades of the eighteenth century after it achieved political independence from Great Britain. Archaeological evidence should indicate a continuous English occupation there during this period. Because the Atlantic Seaboard had come under the scrutiny of all the principal colonizing states of Europe prior to this time, contact by any of these societies at some time after the fifteenth century is possible if not likely. An occupation by one of these competing states, however, could not exist coterminously with a British colony. Consequently, if such an occupation is found, it should have a termination date before 1670. Material evidence supporting these statements may be explored through an examination of two archaeological test implications.

Ceramic Use

In order to establish the national affiliation and chronological limits of a colonial occupation, it is necessary to consider types of artifacts which exhibit diagnostic temporal variation and those that differ in frequency of occurrence or in appearance according to the sociocultural ties of the settlers. Perhaps the category of artifacts that best meets both these criteria is ceramics (Miller and Stone 1970:98), an item present in great abundance in European sites of the postmedieval period. Ceramics are especially useful in archaeological studies because these artifacts' composition and method of manufacture lend them to wide variation in form (Shepard 1956:334) and their fragile nature insures a continual deposition in the archaeological record at sites of their use.

By the seventeenth century, the Eastern Seaboard was an area peripheral to the emerging European world economy. Three European states—England, France, and Spain—were rivals for the control of this territory and its resources. Each attempted to establish colonies to secure and exploit its claims. The key to identifying the colony's homeland lies in recognizing the manner in which socioeconomic differences are reflected in each nation's use of ceramics.

ORIGINS OF COLONIAL CERAMICS

As mercantilist states, England, France, and Spain encouraged the export of the products of home industries, while excluding import of competing products from its colonial possessions. Consequently, the sites of colonial settlements occupied by each of the European states should be characterized by a predominance of ceramic artifacts emanating from the homeland, its trading partners, or its other colonial possessions. Archaeological evidence from English, French, and Spanish settlements in the New World (Deagan 1978:33; Griffin 1962:36; Lister and Lister 1974; Lunn 1973; Noël Hume 1970:5) has revealed a pattern of ceramic use in which each country's colonies were limited to the products of their own colonial systems. Because South Carolina was settled permanently as a British colony, archaeological sites produced by this settlement should be characterized by collections of ceramics imported from or through English ports.

The ceramic industries of each of the European colonial states produced a variety of types reflecting regional stylistic differences. Associated ceramic types formed complexes that changed through time as local industries arose and declined. Ceramic technology, however, remained basically similar prior to the eighteenth century, resulting in the production of only a few basic wares. These consisted largely of unglazed, lead-glazed, and tin-glazed earthenwares and stonewares (Lister and Lister 1974; Noël Hume 1970:102, 139). During the eighteenth century, English manufacturing underwent a marked technological change characterized by rapid innovation and increased industrialization (Clow and Clow 1958:328–329). This resulted not only in the proliferation of British goods, including ceramics, but also in an enhancement of these products' ability to compete with those of other European countries on the international market. Industrialization in ceramic manufacturing even led to the decline of some foreign industries, most notably the production of French faience (Haggar 1968:165). As a result, British colonial settlements of the eighteenth century saw the use of a wide variety of new ceramic wares including fine white stonewares, unglazed red and black stonewares, refined earthenwares, and perhaps most notably the ubiquitous creamwares and later pearlwares (see Noël Hume 1970). These ceramics reflect technological as well as stylistic and regional differences. The revolution in English ceramic technology should be observable in the archaeological remains generated by those settlements. Because of the failure of French and Spanish industries to develop similarly at this time, such a diversity should not be repeated in the eighteenth century colonial sites of these nations. South Carolina, as a British colony settled largely during the eighteenth century, should be characterized by the presence of archaeological sites exhibiting the wide variety of English ceramics manufactured and used during this period.

REEXPORTATION OF FOREIGN CERAMICS

Although the European colonizing states usually gave preference to their native ceramic industries, the reexportation of foreign wares was also a feature of colonial trade. This trade usually did not involve the ceramics of competing states but reflected the extensive trading links between the core states and nations not conducting their own colonial expansion. Inter-European trade in Italian tin-glazed wares, for example, made these ceramics a common component of Spanish material culture in the New World (Lister and Lister 1976:29–30). Together with northern European earthenwares, they were regularly imported into English colonies prior to the enactment of the restrictive Navigation Acts in the midseventeenth century (Noël Hume 1970:138). The reexportation of Oriental porcelains was carried out by all of the major colonial states of Europe. Spanish trade with China and the establishment of Dutch commercial ties with Japan in the seventeenth century initiated a growing traffic in porcelains that was dominated by England after 1708 (Palmer 1976:10–11).

The commercial expansion of England in the seventeenth and eighteenth centuries brought an increase in the amount of foreign goods shipped through British ports (Darby 1973:381), yet the restrictive nature of trade regulations greatly reduced the vareity of products reaching its colonial possessions. After the passage of the first Navigation Act in 1651, non-English ceramics exported to British settlements in North America were confined to Oriental porcelains and substantial amounts of German and Flemish stonewares known collectively as Westerwald (Noël Hume 1970:141). The exclusive nature of the ceramic trade should have produced a distinctive pattern of ceramic usage on sites of British colonial settlements occupied during this period. A comparison of the ceramic collections from eighteenth century British colonial sites suggests that the Westerwald stonewares generally comprise less than 6% of the total Old World ceramics, while Oriental porcelains may account for up to 20% of these artifacts.[1] Oriental porcelains are also present in both Spanish and French North American colonial sites (Deagan 1978:41; Fairbanks 1973:170; Miller and Stone 1970:81); however, Westerwald

[1]The figures are based on an analysis of the ceramic collections from several widely scattered eighteenth century settlements in British North America at which extensive archaeological investigations have taken place (Lewis 1976:151). These sites represent a variety of settlement types, including forts, trading posts, and domestic structures. They are Brunswick Town, North Carolina (South 1972a); Spalding's Lower Store, Florida (Lewis 1969); Fort Michilimackinac, Michigan (Stone 1970); and the Trebell cellar in Williamsburg, Virginia (South 1972a).

stoneware occurs in French sites only in small numbers (Lunn 1973:185–187; Miller and Stone 1970:76).

It is anticipated that sites of late seventeenth- and eighteenth-century British settlements in South Carolina will be recognizable archaeologically by the regular occurrence of Oriental porcelains and Westerwald stonewares in frequencies comparable to those of other English colonial sites occupied during this period. Earlier English sites, particularly those existing before the enactment of the Navigation Acts, are likely to exhibit a wider variety of reexported foreign wares that formed a substantial part of the English ceramic inventory in settlements of this period (Caywood 1955; Cotter 1958; Deetz 1973). English ceramics, however, should remain the dominant component recovered from all British sites.

CERAMICS AND COLONIAL CHRONOLOGY

The ceramics recovered from the sites of colonial settlements should reveal the time at which their occupations took place and the duration of their occurrence. These artifacts were exported in great quantities to colonial regions where their broken pieces accumulated rapidly as part of the archaeological record. Because of their relatively short use life, ceramics were continually imported, and newer types replaced older ones as ceramic technology changed over time. The simultaneous appearance of new ceramic types throughout extensive colonial regions was noted by South (1972a:72; 1977:232–233) who viewed the sequential occurrence of types as archaeological horizon markers useful in accurately dating the occupations of individual sites. The presence of such a temporally sensitive class of artifacts permits the calculation of both a reasonably accurate chronological range and a median date for an archaeological occupation.

A technique useful in establishing a site's temporal range based on ceramics involves a collective comparison of the use spans of all types present. This "bracketing" technique (see South 1977:214–216) places the *terminus post quem*, or date after which the earliest objects are likely to find their way into the ground, at the point beyond which the beginning dates of half of the ceramic types extend. A *terminus ante quem*, or date by which the last archaeological materials would have been deposited, is established similarly by determining the date by which the manufacture of half of the types had terminated. In some instances the bracket may be narrowed further if certain ceramic types are conspicuously absent from a site's collection.

The median date for a site's occupation may be obtained using the South (1972a) formula, which derives a mean ceramic date based on the frequencies of occurrence of datable ceramic types recovered from an archaeological context. Because the technique is quantitative, it is influenced by the relative intensity of output into the archaeological record occurring during a site's occupation. Consequently, it is likely to reveal the median date of the period of that occupation having the heaviest output. If we assume that this period normally occurs at the midpoint of an occupation, the mean ceramic date is likely to represent the median historic date of the settlement.

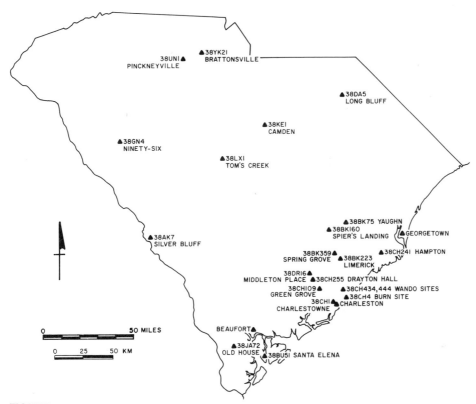

FIGURE 5.1   Locations of South Carolina archaeological sites discussed in this chapter. (Source: SIR.)

EXAMINING THE ARCHAEOLOGICAL RECORD

Based on the discussion above, it is anticipated that archaeological data from sites in South Carolina (Fig. 5.1) will show a British occupation characterized by a wide variety of English ceramic types, a near absence of ceramics manufactured by competing European colonial states, and the presence of specific types of reexported wares. This occupation should be temporally distinct, commencing in the last half of the seventeenth century and lasting until at least 1800.

In order to identify the presence of a continuous British occupation in South Carolina, it is necessary to examine the ceramic contents of a number of extensively excavated European settlement sites with regard to their ethnicity and temporal position. A group of 12 such sites will be used. They are situated throughout the present state and should constitute a geographically representative sample of settlement in this region as a whole (Fig. 5.1). Table 5.1 illustrates aspects of each site's ceramic contents. These aspects should permit the identification of their past occupants' national affiliation. The accompanying Table 5.2 shows the mean occupants' national affiliation. The accompanying Table 5.2 shows the mean ceramic dates and the estimated occupation spans of the same group of sites.

TABLE 5.1 Frequencies of ceramic types by site

Site	Percentage frequency				English ceramic types (N)	Total European ceramic specimens
	English ceramic types (%)	Oriental porcelain (%)	Westerwald stoneware (%)	Other foreign re-exported ceramics (%)		
Charles Towne, 38CH1 (South 1972a)	19	0	1	80	4	151
Santa Elena, 38BU162 (South 1980)	0	0.1	0	0	0	955[a]
Camden, 38KE1 (Lewis 1976)	96	3	1	>0.1[b,c]	32	11,242
Long Bluff, 38DA5 (Lewis 1978)	97	2	1	0	20	1,055
Middleton Place, 38DR16 (Lewis and Hardesty 1979)	87	12	1	0	37	2,729
Hampton, 38CH241 (Lewis 1979a)	90	9	1	0	29	1,816
Ninety-six, 38GN4 (Holschlag and Rodeffer 1977)	97	2	1	0	20	1,082
Silver Bluff, 38AK7 (Scurry et al. 1980)	83	14	3	0	25	2,201
Green Grove, 38CH109 (Carrillo 1980)	89	9	2	0	37	10,803
Spiers Landing, 38BK160 (Drucker and Anthony 1979)	99	1	0	0	22	970
Limerick, 38BK223 (Lees 1980)	98	Unknown	2	0.5[c]	33	6,466
Wando plantations, 38BK434 and 38BK444 (Scurry and Brooks 1980)	91	9	4	0	19	469

[a] This collection includes 13 Spanish or Spanish colonial ceramic types in addition to the Oriental ceramics indicated in the table.

[b] Indicates the occurrence of Iberian olive jar fragments.

[c] Indicates the presence of "debased" Rouen faience fragments.

TABLE 5.2   Dates of early historic sites in South Carolina

Site	Estimated range[a]	Mean ceramic date
Santa Elena, 38BU162	1550–1600	1573
Charles Towne, 38CH1	1640–1700	1667
Wando, 38CH434, 444	1720–1850	1785
Green Groe, 38CH109	1740–1810	1785
Silver Bluff, 38AK7	1740–1820	1785
Middleton Place, 38DR16	1740–1820+	1796
Hampton, 38CH241	1760–1810+	1793
Ninety-six, 38GN1–5	1760–1820	1777
Spier's Landing, 38BK160	1760–1820	1798
Camden, 38KE1	1760–1820+	1791
Limerick, 38BK223	1760–1830+	1795
Long Bluff, 38DA5	1770–1820	1793

[a] The estimated ranges have been computed using the mean ceramic dating formula and the bracketing tool described in the text.

The sites illustrated in Table 5.1 may be separated into groups based on the frequency distributions of the ceramic categories discussed above. Ten of the sites (Numbers 3–12) exhibit ceramic frequencies anticipated in British eighteenth century settlements. The chronological positions of these sites, as illustrated in Table 5.2, indicates that all were occupied after 1700, and a comparison of their temporal ranges reveals that a British occupation of South Carolina persisted throughout the eighteenth century.

In each of the 10 sites, British ceramics represent more than 83% of the total Old World ceramics recovered. Specimens produced by competing European colonial states occur only occasionally and in very small numbers. These artifacts consist of Iberian olive jars, found on most of the sites, and "debased" Rouen faience, present on sites occupied in the late eighteenth century. The regular use of the olive jar as a general transport and utilitarian container in British colonies as well as throughout northern Europe (Watkins 1973:192–193) would seem to account for its appearance here. The latter may be seen as a minor supplement for English ceramics that was made possible by a removal of the embargo on foreign earthenwares in 1775 (Noël Hume 1970:142). In both cases, these ceramic types are special cases. They may be grouped functionally with other reexported foreign wares that reached England's colonies via the international trading network and do not in themselves provide evidence for direct colonial contact by either France or Spain.

Although the number of English ceramic types present at each of the sites varies from 19 to 37, with a mean frequency of 27 types per site, the variety represented in every case reveals the predicted diversity of wares anticipated at sites of permanent British colonial settlement. The occurrence of up to 37 distinct types of British ceramics illustrates the diversity of wares expected in English sites. These include earthenwares, stonewares, and porcelains, the products of three distinct methods of manufacture. Earthenwares run the gamut from heavy-bodied, coarse-paste lead or tin-glazed slipwares to refined creamwares and pearlwares developed in the last half of the eighteenth century. Stonewares range from heavy utility wares to fine white and "scratch-blue" salt-glazed tablewares in use by the 1720s. Unglazed black "basalt" and red stonewares, produced after the 1750s, are present as are the black-glazed "Jackfield" stonewares manufactured from 1745 to 1790. British porcelains consist primarily of "teawares." In short, the variety of ceramics recovered clearly illustrates the proliferation of ceramic technology characteristic of the British potteries in the eighteenth century and mirrors the diversity of ceramic types found on English colonial sites of this period.

The presence of a noticeable quantity of reexported foreign pottery is also apparent in the collections from the South Carolina sites. The two principal categories present are Westerwald stoneware and Oriental porcelain. The former comprises from 0 to 4% of the total ceramic inventory, whereas the latter accounts for 1 to 20% of these artifacts. The occurrence of both types falls within their expected ranges on British colonial sites.

The second group of sites contains only one example, Charles Towne, a seventeenth-century settlement that yielded a collection containing a small number of English ceramic types and a large number of reexported Italian earthenwares and stonewares. Only 19% of the total ceramic specimens were English. Oriental porcelains are absent, although a single specimen of German stoneware was recovered (Table 5.1). The composition of this collection is similar to that found on other seventeenth-century English colonial settlements (see, for example, Caywood 1955; Cotter 1958), however, the low incidence of English ceramics here is unusual. It may be explained by the fact that the Italian ceramic specimens represent fragments of several vessels broken in place, and the remainder of the collection is composed of the scattered fragments of many vessels (South, personal communication, 1981). Because of the relatively small sample size, the presence of many pieces of a few vessels has skewed the relative frequencies of English and foreign ceramics at Charles Towne. If this factor is considered, the reexported wares may be seen to represent a much smaller portion of the ceramic inventory, the majority of which would have consisted of vessels of English origin.

The third group consists of the remaining site, Santa Elena, which exhibits a complete absence of English ceramics. Its ceramic collection is composed of 13 Spanish types and reexported Oriental porcelain, an assemblage characteristic of Spanish colonial settlements elsewhere in the New World (Deagan 1978; Lister and Lister 1974; South 1980:30–31). The presence of a Spanish settlement in an area assumed to have been English appears at first to raise questions about the cultural affiliation of the area's frontier inhabitants. When this site is placed in chronological perspective, the range and mean date of its occupation are seen to occur a half century earlier than the beginning of any English settlement in South Carolina (South 1979b:17). Santa Elena's early date and an absence of any later Spanish sites imply that this site represents an aborted short-term Spanish attempt to settle this region. Documentary evidence suggests that this site was not associated with the subsequent colonization carried out by England.

An examination of ceramic evidence at 12 historic sites in South Carolina has revealed patterns that support the hypothesis for the establishment of a permanent English colony here in the late seventeenth century and its continued existence throughout the eighteenth. The composition of the ceramic assemblages shows anticipated changes accompanying Britain's expanding economy and rise to power within the European world economy. South Carolina's cultural affiliation should also be indicated by other types of evidence, as is discussed below.

Architecture

Another class of artifact likely to reflect the cultural background of its creators consists of the structures erected by members of the intrusive society in the area of colonization. This is not to say that colonial architecture mirrors the range of construction found in the homeland and remains unmodified by the functional demands of the frontier environment or changing stylistic taste. Migration into a new area at the periphery of the European world economy is apt to have fostered a great deal of innovation in building, which engendered the development of a distinct vernacular architecture. The retention of building forms characteristic of the parent state is likely to occur where conditions exist that encourage the use of traditional styles and provide the resources to produce such structures.

Architectural styles and their attendent forms, like other art styles, have a tendency to show great persistence, especially if their function in the cultural system remains relatively unchanged (Herskovits 1948:398; Linton 1936:419). The employment of traditional architectural styles in a colonial region is likely to occur widely where the colonists' cultural homogeneity is maintained and a functional similarity between colonial structures and their homeland counterparts persists. Traditional styles are likely to appear in structures occupied by individuals whose ties with the homeland remain closest and who are able to afford reproducing often complex architectural forms in a region where specialized technological capabilities are often restricted. Of course, only those structures durable or fortunate enough to have survived are available for study. These usually consist of buildings that have remained in use until the present, often in their original function.

The domestic structures of high-status individuals residing in an insular frontier region are likely to fall into this category of structure. Because of the economic and social roles of such persons, their ties with the homeland would have remained close and their relative wealth would have permitted the construction of substantial dwellings, a function these buildings could have continued to fulfill long after the colonial period. Numerous early structures exist in South Carolina and an examination of existing high-status architecture is expected to reveal similarities with that found in contemporary English buildings of the seventeenth and eighteenth centuries. The presence of structures exhibiting such architectural styles would establish the cultural affiliation of their builders and provide useful information regarding the dates of the buildings' construction.

ARCHITECTURE IN ENGLAND: ANTICIPATING COLONIAL STYLES

By the midseventeenth century, academic architecture in England had been transformed from Gothic to a Renaissance style heavily influenced by the use of Palladian design elements adopted from Italy. The seventeenth century English mansion was a rectangular or H-shaped structure with a symmetrical plan. A main entrance was situated in the center, opening into a reception hall through which access to separate rooms was gained. The exteriors of these buildings were also symmetrically arranged and generally unornamented. Windows were placed uniformly in long ranges, and roof cornices were continuous. Turrets or towers were also employed occasionally, and the main entranceway often passed through a centrally located full-height porch or stair tower (Waterman 1945:4).

Italian design elements were popularized in England chiefly through the works of two major architects, Inigo Jones and Christopher Wren. Jones's Palladian style brought the enlargement of windows and their arrangement in equal tiers and the introduction of a hipped roof with dormers, architrave trim, columned loggias, pediments, and tall, rectangular, paneled chimney shafts with cornice caps. English Palladian architecture was modified further by Wren, who introduced baroque decorative elements such as broken and scroll pediments, resticated quoins, and elaborate carving as well as a more private arrangement of the interior plan. The latter was achieved by emphasizing access to rooms through hallways instead of other rooms and by placing kitchens, pantries, and offices in wings flanking the house (Kimball 1922:53–54; Waterman 1945:7–13).

The dissemination of architectural styles after the late seventeenth century was aided by the publication of design books and architectural guides, which described rules of proportion and design of details and provided sample plans and elevations. The distribution of these publications had a tremendous influence on English architecture, particularly in provincial and colonial areas, because they standardized the style employed in high-status domestic architecture throughout the British colonial system (Kimball 1922:59–60; Waterman 1945:16). As a consequence, we may expect to find evidence of the developing Palladian architectural tradition of Jones and Wren in English colonial regions where high-status individuals are likely to have established a permanent residence. An examination of colonial period structures in the British colony of South Carolina should reveal the employment of these styles in the domestic structures of such persons.

SURVIVING ARCHITECTURE IN SOUTH CAROLINA: AN EXAMINATION

To observe the extent of Palladian architectural influence in colonial South Carolina, a sample of high-status domestic structure was examined for evidence of relevant stylistic elements. Because the survival rate of these structures is unknown, it was impossible to predict if any remained from the earliest period of colonization in the third quarter of the seventeenth century. It is probable that growth after initial

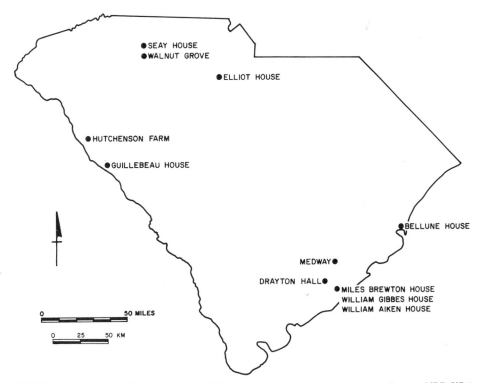

FIGURE 5.2 Locations of South Carolina standing structures discussed in this chapter. (Sources: NRF; SIR.)

settlement would have produced an increasingly larger number of such structures and that most would date from a later part of the colonial period. This discussion does not attempt to be comprehensive in its treatment of colonial architecture as a spatial phenomenon because temporal and distributional aspects of architecture are examined later. It is intended merely to examine enough examples from a wide area to demonstrate the occurrence of English architectural styles in South Carolina as evidence of the cultural affiliation of the frontier region's dominant social group.

An examination of the architectural styles of high-status structures in South Carolina was facilitated by an interest in surviving early buildings arising as a result of their form, age, and, often, association with particular historical events or personalities. As a consequence, a number of surveys of seventeenth- and eighteenth-century buildings have been carried out. The architectural data presented here, and elsewhere in this chapter, are drawn in large part from these studies.[2]

Architectural surveys revealed several seventeenth-century structures, all of

[2]The results of these surveys have been included in such published sources as Lachicotte (1955), Stoney (1938), Kimball (1922), the Architects' Emergency Committee (1933), Smith and Smith (1917), and Simons and Lapham (1927), as well as reports of the various regional planning councils of South Carolina and the entries contained in the National Register of Historic Places maintained by the U.S. Department of the Interior (NRF).

FIGURE 5.3   Medway house on Back River, an example of early English Palladian architecture. The wings on either side of the central stair tower are later additions to the original structure. (NRF photograph.)

which reflect the style of contemporary English architecture (Fig. 5.2). One example of early high-status domestic architecture is Medway (Fig. 5.3) on Back River. It exhibits the symmetrical layout common to examples of English Palladian architecture as well as large windows, placed in even tiers; a columned loggia; tall, rectangular, paneled chimneys with cornice caps; and a hipped roof. The unornamented façade of the house shows an absence of later Palladian decorative elements. A tower enclosing the central entranceway is situated in the center of the front wall. The plan of this structure reveals a symmetrical layout of rooms, all of which are entered directly from the entrance hall or through other rooms (Stoney 1938).

Eighteenth-century mansions in both urban and rural settings in South Carolina demonstrate the continued influence and increasing elaborateness of English Palladian architecture in this colonial region. Several examples from various locations illustrate this statement. Two urban structures in Charleston, the William Gibbes house and the Miles Brewton house, date from the third quarter of the eighteenth century (Figs. 5.4 and 5.5). Both buildings are two-storied and nearly square in plan. Each exhibits a central entranceway opening into a hall running to the rear of the house. From the hall access is gained to a set of two rooms on either side. Both

FIGURE 5.4 The William Gibbes house on South Battery in Charleston, an example of later Palladian architecture in an urban setting. (NRF photograph.)

FIGURE 5.5 The Miles Brewton house on King Street in Charleston, another urban double house in South Carolina. (NRF photograph.)

FIGURE 5.6 Drayton Hall on the Ashley River, a Palladian double house in a rural setting. (NRF photograph.)

structures are set on raised basements with divided staircases leading to the main entranceway. The Miles Brewton house has a mansard roof and a two-storied pedimented portico with a columned Palladian architrave surrounding the doorway. Waterman (1945:350) suggested that such roofs are a variation of the Palladian deck on hip. The entrance way of the William Gibbes house, which opens onto a pavilion, is surrounded by an architrave frame supporting a frieze and pediment. Each of the paired windows is surmounted by a pediment, and the hipped roof contains a pediment centered over the main entrance (Architects' Emergency Committee 1933:34–42). The plan and façade of these two structures are typical of eighteenth-century high-status architecture in Charleston and represent a style known regionally as the "double house" (Smith and Smith 1917:93; Stoney 1937:21). Its formal affiliation with later English Palladian architecture is clear, indicating a maintenance of close cultural ties between the builders of such houses and their contemporaries in England.

The architectural form employed in the Charleston double house is also found in surviving eighteenth-century houses elsewhere in South Carolina. Drayton Hall, on the Ashley River (Fig. 5.6), is a rural example of this form. It is a brick structure with a mansard roof similar to that of the Miles Brewton House. The front façade of Drayton Hall contains a two-storied pedimented portio reached by a double staircase. The rear of the structure exhibits a central roof pediment, window pediments, and a columned architrave with pediment and frieze at the entranceway that opens onto a pavilion. This house also has the symmetrical central hall plan, however, the entrance hall has been widened into a large room with a separate stair hall to the rear (Architects' Emergency Committee 1933:24–29; Stoney 1938:55–56, 120–133). Unlike its urban counterparts, Drayton Hall is surrounded by space adequate for the placement of dependency structures. The house is flanked by two such structures placed to either side and slightly forward of a line formed by its axis, an arrangement that follows the contemporary Palladian pattern (Waterman 1945:17). These structures housed activities associated with the domestic function of the mansion (Stoney 1938:56; L. Lewis 1978).

A survey of colonial-period high-status architecture has revealed a definite English presence in South Carolina. Both urban and rural structures have stylistic elements that developed in the English architectural tradition of the seventeenth and eighteenth centuries. Chronological change reflecting those occurring in English architecture indicate a continuous association of the colonial architectural tradition with that of the homeland. The dominance of this style in high-status architecture and the absence of styles characteristic of the other competing colonial states of Europe support the assumed British cultural affiliation of this region throughout the colonial period by demonstrating the maintenance of an important social link between the governing classes in England and South Carolina.

HYPOTHESIS 2: INNOVATION AND THE FRONTIER ENVIRONMENT

The second hypothesis relating to the establishment of a colony states that despite the maintenance of cultural ties with the homeland, conditions encountered at the periphery of the world economy will result in the modification of behavior. The degree of such change reflects the insularity of the frontier region. Changes consist of functional adaptations to the colony's marginal position in the economic network of the core state or to the need to exist and carry out production in a region whose environment and resources vary from those of the homeland. Change of little or no adaptive value, or stylistic change, is also anticipated as a result of innovation stemming from relative social isolation, the mixing of cultural traditions on the frontier, or random innovation.

The archaeological test implications for such innovation deal with two aspects of adaptation apt to be recognizable in the material record of colonial South Carolina. Both involve basic functional changes to the colonial environment, although stylistic innovation is also evident in both types of evidence to be considered. The first implication involves technological adaptation to the economic isolation of the frontier. The second attempts to observe changes in architecture as a response to the social and natural environment of the frontier region. Both adaptations are likely to have resulted in the appearance of new artifacts and the modification of those in use by the intrusive society. The form and nature of such material change are addressed in the following discussion.

Economic Adaptation: Ceramic Use on the Frontier

The role of an insular frontier region in the world economy is primarily that of a producer of raw commodities, dependent upon the parent state for most of its finished goods. Its physical separation from the homeland, together with the growth of a complex resident society, often creates markets that cannot be satisfied solely through imports. This situation results in the development of colonial industries producing goods to supplement and occasionally to compete with those of th homeland. Archaeological evidence of these industries' by-products should be discernible in sites occupied during the colonial period.

A major finished import into British overseas colonies in the eighteenth century was ceramics. Demands for this product appear to have outstripped the merchants' capacity to supply it, resulting in the local manufacture of ceramics in the New World (see, for example, Barka 1973; Caywood 1955; Watkins and Noël Hume 1967). Because ceramics are an artifact that is widely used, easily broken, and nonrecyclable, evidence of colonial ceramic industries should be readily available in the archaeological record. An examination of colonial period sites in South Carolina yielded several varieties of ceramics useful in demonstrating the existence of regional and local industries during the frontier period.

THE MORAVIAN TRADITION

Colonial ceramics recovered from sites of British settlements in South Carolina may be divided into three traditions, each of which employed different manufacturing techniques and originated from a geographically separate source. One tradition centered in the Moravian settlements of North Carolina and appears to have come into being in the 1750s. Archaeological excavations at kiln sites in Bethabara yielded a collection of vessels and wasters large enough to illustrate the variety of thrown and press-molded forms made during the 20 years the potteries were in operation (South 1967). The Moravian ceramics (Fig. 5.7) include a variety of utilitarian culinary vessels as well as some delicate wares, lighting devices, and smoking pipes (Bivans 1972; South 1965). Both red and white pastes were employed with various combinations of slips and glazes to produce 15 distinct types (South 1967:37–38). These ceramics contrast markedly with those imported from England during the same period and are easily recognized on three colonial period archaeological sites in South Carolina (see Fig. 5.8).

Moravian ceramics have been identified at the sites of only three South Carolina settlements: Camden (Lewis 1976:171), Ninety-Six, and Charleston (South, personal communication, 1981). Two are interior settlements occupied before 1760, whereas the third is an earlier coastal example. Because of their contemporaneity with the Moravian potteries and their distance from the coastal settlements, it is probable that inhabitants of these settlements supplemented imported English wares at least in part with locally manufactured ceramics.

FIGURE 5.7 Examples of Moravian-tradition ceramics from Bethabara, North Carolina: (A) plate, (B) bowl, and (C) candlestick forms. (Photograph courtesy of Stanley South.)

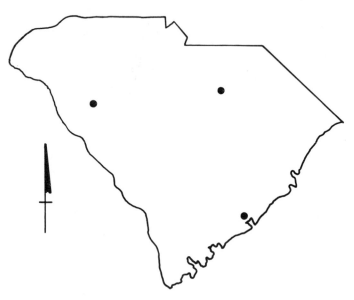

FIGURE 5.8   The distribution of Moravian-tradition ceramics in South Carolina. (Source: SIR.)

THE ENGLISH COLONIAL TRADITION

The second colonial ceramic tradition centered in South Carolina and later spread northward to supplant the earlier Moravian tradition at Bethabara. Its origins and the spatial distribution of its products were identified through the excavation of a number of eighteenth century archaeological sites (Fig. 5.9).

English colonial ceramics in South Carolina consist of molded, white paste, cream-colored earthenwares similar to those manufactured in England by Wedgwood and others after 1760. Specimens represent, for the most part, finely made utilitarian culinary vessels, often incorporating sprig-molded decoration and other delicate appliqué elements. In addition, decorative forms and sprig-molded pipes were also produced in North Carolina. These vessels were finished in clear or various colored glazes, sometimes applied in a mottled, or "tortoiseshell," pattern (Bivans 1972; South 1971a) (Fig. 5.10).

Three kiln sites were identified archaeologically through the presence of kiln remains or wasters (Fig. 5.9). The earliest of these is situated in coastal South Carolina in Berkeley County and appears to date from the 1760s (South, personal communication, 1981). A second source of these ceramics lies in the interior at Camden, a settlement where these wares were produced between about 1770 and 1780 (Lewis 1976:169). Finally, the third site of production is at Salem, North Carolina, where the manufacture of English colonial ceramics displaced the earlier Moravian tradition in the late 1770s (South 1971a:172). In addition to being found at these kiln sites, English colonial ceramics produced there were recovered from a number of sites in South Carolina that were occupied in the second half of the

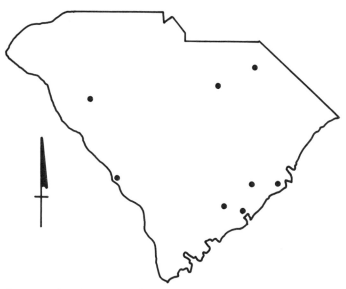

FIGURE 5.9 The distribution of English colonial ceramics in South Carolina archaeological sites. (Source: SIR.)

FIGURE 5.10 Examples of English colonial-tradition ceramics from North Carolina, illustrating culinary and serving forms. (Photograph courtesy of Stanley South.)

eighteenth century (Fig. 5.9). Although English colonial wares never constituted a major portion of the ceramics used in these settlements, their widespread occurrence indicates that this pottery was an integral element of internal trade during the latter part of the colonial period and may have played a significant role as an industrial product in the frontier economy.

THE COLONO TRADITION

A third indigenous ceramic tradition in colonial South Carolina produced a variety of unglazed, low-fired, often burnished, and generally undecorated earthenwares known collectively as Colono wares. These ceramics consist mainly of flat-bottomed pots and bowls and many European culinary forms (Baker 1972; Ferguson 1980), several of which are illustrated in Fig. 5.11. Colono wares are common in assemblages from historic sites in South Carolina and appear to have been used from the late seventeenth through the early nineteenth centuries. Although similar in composition to prehistoric Indian pottery, the form of Colono ceramics, the occasional use of punctate decoration, and extensive surface burnishing have led Ferguson (1980) to suggest that they represent an amalgamation of more than one ceramic tradition.

The form, decoration, and surface treatment of Colono ceramics are similar to those found in West African ceramic traditions. Their presence here suggests that these traditions were transplanted to North America along with the importation of large numbers of African slaves. African slave-manufactured pottery was produced in colonial settlements in the British West Indies as early as 1650 (Handler and Lange 1978:140–141), and it is reasonable to anticipate that it was manufactured elsewhere in colonial areas where substantial African slave populations were present. The association of Colono ceramics with European sites and their absence on

FIGURE 5.11 Examples of Colono ceramic vessels from Bluff plantation on the Black River in South Carolina. (Photograph supplied by the author.)

aboriginal sites of the colonial period further suggest that most of these wares were produced by potters heavily influenced by Old World ceramic traditions (Ferguson 1980:79). The enslavement of Southeastern Indian groups during the early colonial period presents the possibility, if not the likelihood, that aboriginal ceramic technology also contributed to the development of the Colono tradition in South Carolina.

Similarities between some Colono ware and later Catawba Indian trade pottery led Baker (1972) to postulate that at least a portion of these ceramics was produced by remnant Indian groups as an adaptation to their absorption into the colonial economy. Lurie (1959:60) observed this phenomenon among aboriginal groups in eastern Virginia who produced specialized trade goods to supplement increasingly inadequate native procurement systems. An aboriginal trade pottery, collectively termed *Colono–Indian* ware (Noël Hume 1962), occurs as an element in the material culture of Virginia and other British colonies on the southern Atlantic Seaboard (Baker 1972:16). At present, no definitive studies have permitted the distinction of separate types of Colono ceramics so they remain lumped together as a single tradition on the basis of their similar morphology.

Colono ceramics are assumed to have supplemented European pottery in the colonial economy. Because of their distinct forms, absence of glazing, and often crude workmanship, these wares may be assumed to have been less expensive to produce and intended for use largely by members of the lowest socioeconomic groups in the area of colonization (Baker 1972:16; South 1974:188). Consequently, Colono wares may generally be expected to occur in the sites of settlements where such groups were most numerous. The distribution of sites of Colono ceramic occurrence (Fig. 5.12) reveals that its use was heaviest in the coastal region. Its concentration here contrasts with the more widespread distribution of European and

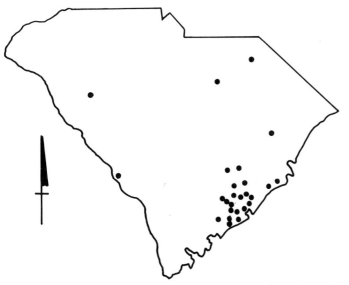

FIGURE 5.12   The distribution of Colono ceramics in South Carolina archaeological sites. (Source: SIR.)

English colonial ceramics. This geographical disparity, together with the similarity of Colono ware to African and aboriginal ceramics, implies the presence of a large slave population in this area; however, its occurrence here and elsewhere does not preclude its having played a wider role in the colonial economy.

The presence of three distinct colonial ceramic traditions in South Carolina indicates the existence of local industries that supplemented the supply of manufactured goods in this frontier area. Each tradition has its roots in a separate geographical area—England, Central Europe, West Africa, and aboriginal North America—and their presence reflects the cultural diversity of the frontier region's inhabitants. Their appearance also reveals a collective response to conditions brought about by the colony's peripheral position in the world economy. The rise and decline of these three ceramic traditions during the colonial period attests to adaptations characteristic of functional change in an insular frontier context.

Architectural Adaptation on the Frontier

Adaptive change on the frontier can involve dramatic stylistic modifications in artifacts to make them more suitable for use in the area of colonization. Change of this type involves a response by the intrusive society to both the natural and cultural environments of the frontier region. These environments include not only the climate and resources of the new land but also the available technology, economic resources, and cultural heterogeneity created by immigration from diverse sources. Adaptive change may be observed through an examination of architectural innovation on the South Carolina frontier, a phenomenon through which the effects of these variables can be measured against the known architectural traditions of seventeenth and eighteenth century England.

URBAN ARCHITECTURE: THE SINGLE HOUSE

As we have seen, the Palladian tradition of English architecture was transported intact to the colony of South Carolina where it manifested itself in the dwellings of high-status individuals. Examples of this architecture were noted in both urban and rural contexts throughout the colonial period. English Palladian architecture was developed in northern Europe and incorporated many features unnecessary in the warmer climate of South Carolina. Architectural style, however, is one of the most conservative elements of culture. It is highly resistant to modification that would alter its overall appearance despite the obvious utility of such changes (P. Lewis 1975:2). Colonial high-status domestic architecture was no exception. It is probable that adaptations to architectural style would have consisted of more minor modifications to make it more amenible to its new environment.

An adaptation of English Palladian architecture may be seen in the Charleston "single house." Like its larger counterpart, the double house, it embodies a symmetrical plan with a central entranceway, paired windows, and various Palladian

FIGURE 5.13 The Governor William Aiken house in Charleston, an urban single house in South Carolina. (NRF photograph.)

decorative elements. The single house differs, however, in several respects that change its appearance but not its basic style. The structures are one room deep instead of two, which permits more efficient ventilation in a humid climate; they are generally set at right angles to the street for greater air circulation between buildings; and they have open galleries on each floor along their south or west walls to catch the prevailing sea breezes (Stoney 1937:20). The Governor William Aiken house, built at the beginning of the nineteenth century in Charleston, illustrates these features (Fig. 5.13). Similar high-status urban dwellings were common in colonial Charleston and Georgetown (Fig. 5.14) and later in some of the inland settlements, for example Camden (Sweet 1978).

Although the urban single house appears to have been confined to the coastal cities, the adaptive advantages of this house type to the South Carolina environment may be reflected in the appearance of its rural counterpart, the I-house (Kniffen 1936:185; P. Lewis 1975:72). Two basic forms of this structure, the "hill planta-tion" with two-storied porches and the "Carolina I-house" with a one-story porch (Newton 1971:10–11), occur in colonial and postcolonial contexts throughout the southeastern United States.

The use of materials in English colonial houses in South Carolina also shows an adaptation to the resources available for construction. Brick and stone were favored building materials in England during the eighteenth century (Waterman 1945), and

FIGURE 5.14   The Bellune house in Georgetown, another example of a single house in an urban setting. (NRF photograph.)

the former was also used to some extent in South Carolina. The availability of lumber in the extensive forests of the region, however, permitted the substitution of wood in the local architecture. This material was adaptable to both single and double house styles, and several of the examples illustrated are of frame construction. In addition to wood, urban architecture of the coast occasionally employed coral limestone blocks and tabby, a lime-and-oyster-shell cement poured in forms (Simons and Lapham 1927:20). Both materials were used previously in the British West Indies and Spanish Florida (Manucy 1962a:66–69), and their appearance in South Carolina undoubtedly derives from at least one of these sources.

RURAL VERNACULAR ARCHITECTURE: THE LOG HOUSE

In addition to the English Palladian architectural tradition and its derivatives employed in high-status structures, we may expect the surviving architecture of the colonial period to exhibit vernacular styles. Such styles represent folk traditions that may be seen as expressions of shared ideas regarding houses by people residing in a region (Kniffen 1936:192). Folk house styles mirror cultural heritage, current fashions, functional needs, and various aspects of the natural environment (Kniffen 1965:549). Because folk housing is a cultural–geographical phenomenon rather than an academic style, its use is more apt to be widespread in an area of colonization. The cultural diversity of a frontier region's inhabitants, however, is likely to result in the introduction of more than one venacular tradition and perhaps the amalgamation of several.

One type of vernacular architecture that characterized rural settlement in colonial South Carolina involved the use of horizontal log construction. The log house, composed of a pen or series of pens, was an architectural type found widely in Europe (P. Lewis 1975:7), although most American examples employed British floor plans (Jordan 1980:179). The log house was apparently introduced in North America by German immigrants who settled in Pennsylvania and was spread southward along the Piedmont by their descendents and Scotch–Irish settlers during the eighteenth century (Kniffen and Glassie 1966:59).

Log architecture in the Piedmont South is characterized by rectangular pen structures with gable ends facing sideways and a roof ridge running parallel to the front. Such structures were usually single story, although some had two, and were raised above the ground on log, brick, or stone piers. Enlargement of log buildings was almost always horizontal and usually involved the addition of another log frame or pen (Zelinsky 1953:175). Common types of log houses are: (1) the single pen, containing a single room with a chimney at one end; (2) the double pen, composed of two single pen structures joined at the gable end with chimneys at opposite ends; (3) the saddlebag, a double pen with a single chimney in the common wall; (4) the dogtrot, a double pen with a raised central hall separating the pens (Newton 1971:6–11). All of these types follow British floor plans except the dogtrot, which appears to have a Swedish–Finnish antecedent (Jordan 1980:165). Various types of corner-timbering were used in the construction of log houses in the southern Piedmont. Saddle-notching, V-notching, and half-dovetail notching were the most common (Kniffen and Glassie 1966:63–64).

Surviving colonial-period log houses are not numerous in South Carolina. Only five examples of such structures remaining in a relatively unmodified state were available for study. These buildings, all constructed before 1800, lie in the interior and their distribution (Fig. 5.2) seems to reflect the diffusion of an indigenous architectural tradition along the southern Piedmont rather than inland from the coastal settlements.

The first of these structures is the Guillebeau house in McCormick County (Fig. 5.2). Its original section, which dates from the 1760s, is a single-pen log building of two stories resting on fieldstone piers (NRF). Sockets in the exterior wall suggest a full-length porch on one side (South 1979c). The roof is supported by rafters laid on purlins, which are anchored in and protrude through the gable walls. The use of purlins contrasts with the normal practice in British log architecture in the American South (Zelinsky 1953:180) and may represent the adoption by recent immigrants of a feature usually associated with rural architecture in Central Europe (Doyon and Hubrecht 1964:52; Jordan 1980:164–165). The large, double-stepped brick chimney located at one end of the structure is another unusual feature in log houses. It is a Medieval element normally found in the brick architecture of the Middle Colonies (Forman 1948:102). Corner-timbering in the Guillebeau house features full dovetail notching. At present, the log structure is surrounded on three sides by later frame additions, and its exposed surface is covered by weatherboarding (Lewis 1979b).

FIGURE 5.15   The Walnut Grove house in Spartanburg County, a rural, two-story, clapboard-covered log house. (NRF photograph.)

The Elliott house in Chester County (Fig. 5.2) was constructed in the late eighteenth century. It is a two-story, single-pen structure set on stone piers with a brick chimney at one end. The logs are joined with full and half-dovetail notching at the corners, and a one-story porch runs along the front side of the house (NRF).

The Walnut Grove house (Fig. 5.15) in Spartanburg County dates before 1770. It is a large, two-story, log house constructed as a single pen divided into two rooms. The structure rests on brick and stone piers and has a brick fireplace at both ends. The walls are joined by full and half-dovetailed corner-notching, and the entire exterior was covered with clapboards at the time of its construction (NRF).

The Seay house (Fig. 5.2), also in Spartanburg County, was built around 1780. It is a single-story, single-pen structure set on stone piers. Corner-timbering consists of half-dovetailed notching. A stone chimney is situated at one end of this structure (NRF).

The Hutchenson farm house (Fig. 5.2) in Abbeville County is a dogtrot structure constructed around 1800. It is a two-story building composed of two log pens set on stone piers. A brick chimney laid on stone foundations is located on the outside wall of one of the pens. Half-dovetail notching again is the technique of corner-timbering used in this structure (USDI/OAHP/I).

These specimens of eighteenth-century log architecture share a number of technological attributes that link them to an indigenous tradition of colonial American architecture originally introduced in the Middle Colonies and diffused, with modifications, along the Southern Piedmont. Although not unique to South Carolina, log architecture here represents the adoption of a building technique well suited to the forested environment of the region. The abundance of timber allowed this architectural tradition to continue throughout the nineteenth century and possibly later (Zelinsky 1953:181).

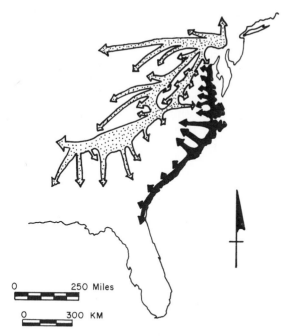

FIGURE 5.16 Diffusion of building traditions on the Eastern Seaboard. The solid color represents the indigenous English architectural tradition that developed on and spread inland from the coast. The stippled pattern shows the movement of vernacular log architecture south along the Piedmont from its Pennsylvania source. (Source: Kniffen and Glassie 1966:60.)

The log tradition contrasts sharply with the indigenous architecture of the coastal region not only in its form but also in its geographical extent. Kniffen and Glassie (1966:60) plotted the distributions of these two architectural traditions on the Eastern Seaboard (Fig. 5.16). The coastal tradition may be seen to have developed and diffused inland along the entire seaboard region. The log tradition spread south and westward along the eastern edge of the Appalachians. Although log construction did not penetrate to the coast, the indigenous coastal tradition, characterized by the I-house, eventually diffused through the interior of South Carolina. In at least one instance, at the Walnut Grove house, this style was adapted to log construction.

The development of two indigenous architectural traditions in colonial South Carolina reflects adaptive change in a basic component of British material culture. Each tradition represents the permanent modification of European architectural styles and techniques to conditions encountered at the periphery of colonial settlement. This type of adaptation provides evidence of the behavioral change anticipated on an insular frontier, change that is revealed in the patterned remains of the surviving material record.

HYPOTHESIS 3: LONG-TERM SETTLEMENT IN THE AREA OF COLONIZATION

The permanent nature of insular frontier colonization implies a continuous occupation. Such a long-term occupation of the area of colonization encourages an intensification of the economic base and the development of complex institutions associated with insular frontier settlement. An increasing population density and an increasingly complex economic structure form the base for further frontier expansion and promote organizational change within previously settled areas. The third hypothesis states that evidence of such long-term settlement should be evident in colonial South Carolina.

Because a frontier grows outward from an initial point of settlement, its oldest and longest occupation should be in South Carolina. This area is also likely to have played a central role in the continued economic development of the colony and should contain the site of its entrepôt. Additional settlements of progressively shorter duration should be found at increasingly greater distances from the entrepôt. The beginning dates of their occupations should mark the time expansion had spread into a particular area. Such settlements usually persisted into the post colonial period. The archaeological test implications deal with two aspects of colonization, the establishment of the entrepôt and the development of its hinterland.

In colonial South Carolina, long-term, continuous settlement should be found at the site of its entrepôt on the Atlantic coast. Here an occupation dating from the last half of the seventeenth century should be discernible. If the original site has remained in use continuously, this occupation will extend into the postcolonial period. In addition to establishing a continuous occupation of the colony's entrepôt, it should be possible to observe long-term settlement in other parts of the colony. Because we are not yet attempting to define the form and boundaries of the frontier region, only a sampling of sites need be examined. It will include sites found throughout the present state whose beginning dates indicate that they were the earliest in their area and whose occupations are long enough to demonstrate continuous settlement through the frontier period.

The archaeological date ranges of site occupations may be estimated in several ways. One of these involves the mean ceramic dating and range bracketing techniques described earlier. Here the ranges of a number of extensively excavated sites were examined to demonstrate an English cultural affiliation. Examining the ceramic date ranges from these sites and others also may provide a basis for establishing a long-term English occupation of South Carolina.

A second clue to the date of an area's occupation lies in the architecture of standing structures. Buildings used to date occupations may be assigned chronological positions on the basis of their architectural style, methods of construction, component artifacts, and association with other structures. In some cases, dates of construction have been inscribed on buildings. Noncomponent artifacts associated with early structures may also be used to establish dates of construction. Although these buildings may not always represent the earliest settlement in a particular area, their presence can aid in establishing a minimal *terminus post quem* for a site in the absence of other material data.

Finally, cemeteries can provide information regarding the range of a site's occupation. If one assumes that cemeteries came into use not long after the initial settlement of an area took place, the interment dates inscribed on the tombstones are likely to mark the period of its earliest occupation. Because evidence of a cemetery's earliest use may not always have survived, dates derived from their markers can reflect a period subsequent to that of pioneer settlement. In the absence of additional data, however, cemeteries can provide a minimal *terminus post quem* date for an area's occupation.

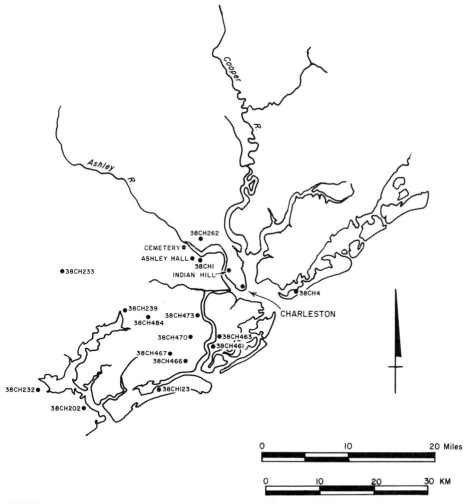

FIGURE 5.17   Sites of seventeenth- and early eighteenth-century settlement in South Carolina. The entrepôt of Charleston lies at the confluence of the Ashley and Cooper rivers, adjacent to a large natural harbor that facilitated overseas trade. (Sources: SIR; CR; NRF.)

Tracing the Entrepôt

The location of South Carolina's entrepôt should be indicated by the site or group of sites having the earliest *termini post quem* and occupations extending through the period of colonial settlement. Because the entrepôt is likely to grow in size with time, it may be represented by a cluster of sites in close proximity to one another that have coterminus or overlapping date ranges. Such a site or sites should be identifiable on the basis of material evidence of its initial date of occupation as well as its temporal range.

An examination of archaeological sites in South Carolina reveals that the site of British settlement with the earliest occupation date is Charles Towne on the Ashley River (Fig. 5.17). Ceramic evidence suggests that it was occupied from the midseventeenth century to around 1700 (Table 5.2). Within 20 miles lie at least 17 other colonial sites occupied before or around 1700 (NRF; SIR; South 1962; South and Hartley 1980). This cluster of sites indicating the area of earliest English settlement in South Carolina includes only one locale likely to represent an entrepôt. This is the present city of Charleston. Charleston contains several surviving structures dating before 1720 and a number of others constructed throughout the eighteenth century (NRF). Cemeteries in Charleston were in use at least as early as 1729 (Webber 1928). Archaeological sites in Charleston have also revealed an occupation from the late seventeenth century onward (SIR; South 1962).

Charleston's location on the coast adjacent to a large natural harbor is an ideal site for an overseas entrepôt. Its size and density, early date of occupation, and continuous settlement throughout the colonial period make it the paramount candidate for this role based on the available material evidence. Because no other site in South Carolina exhibits similar characteristics, it is possible to identify Charleston as the central settlement in this frontier region.

Long-Term Settlement Outside the Entrepôt

Evidence of a continuous occupation in the area of colonization as a whole throughout the colonial period may be obtained by examining chronologically sensitive archaeological materials from sites located in various parts of this region. These sites should represent the remains of successful agricultural settlements that were established as the frontier expanded. Consequently, the beginning dates of these settlements should vary, with those closer to the entrepôt being earlier than those further from it.

Because we are not yet seeking to establish patterns of overall settlement or define the temporal sequence of the frontier's occupation, an extensive examination of the archaeological record is unnecessary. By observing the ceramic date ranges of a small number of sites from which substantial collections have been made, it is possible to estimate roughly the duration of settlement for the general area in which

TABLE 5.3   Dates of selected archaeological sites in South Carolina

Site	Estimated date range[a]	Source (if first citation)
Burn Site (38CH4)	1700–1810+	(SIR)
Good Hope (38JA72)	1720–1810	(SIR)
Wando Sites (38CH434, 444)	1720–1850+	—
Green Grove (38CH109)	1740–1810	—
Silver Bluff (38AK7)	1740–1820	—
Middleton Place (38DR16)	1740–1820+	—
Thom's Creek (38LX2)	1760–1810	(SIR)
Hampton (38CH241)	1760–1810+	—
Ninety-Six (38GN4)	1760–1820	—
Spier's Landing (38BK160)	1760–1820	—
Camden (38KE1)	1760–1820+	—
Limerick (38BK223)	1760–1830+	—
Long Bluff (38DA5)	1770–1820	—
Bratton House (38YK21)	1780–1820+	— (Carrillo *et al.* 1975)

[a] The estimated ranges have been computed using the mean ceramic dating formula and the bracketing tool described in the text.

they existed (Table 5.3). The sites chosen are distributed throughout South Carolina (Fig. 5.1) and provide a sample of the entire area of potential colonization.

The date ranges shown in Table 5.3 reveal that each of the sites was first occupied at some time during the eighteenth century and remained in use at least as late as the first decade of the nineteenth. Their relatively long occupations, lasting until after the close of the colonial period, indicate the presence of permanent English settlement throughout South Carolina from the eighteenth century onward. Variation in the beginning dates of their occupations reveals a progressive expansion over the area of colonization. The earliest settlement occurred along the coast in the vicinity of the entrepôt. An examination of long-term settlement in colonial South Carolina suggests patterns of expansion that are discussed at length below. More important, however, the duration of their occupations demonstrates the establishment of permanent colonial settlement and provides a framework within which to examine further processes of insular frontier development.

6

Examining Hypotheses for Spatial
Patterning

INTRODUCTION

Archaeological analysis has permitted us to recognize an English colonial presence in late-seventeenth- and eighteenth-century South Carolina. In order to investigate this region further, it is necessary to define it as a spatial entity possessing a pattern of settlement reflecting the organization of an insular frontier economy. Two main elements of spatial patterning should be recognizable here. The first is the presence of a centrally placed entrepôt with direct access to the metropolitan area. As the social, political, and economic focus of the area of colonization, the entrepôt should lie at the hub of a dendritic network of trade and communications that affects the distribution of pioneer settlement. The establishment of a dendritic settlement system is the second element of spatial patterning crucial to the recognition of an insular frontier region. In the discussion of the following hypotheses, both of these elements are examined through an analysis of archaeological evidence from South Carolina.

HYPOTHESIS 4: DEFINITION OF THE ENTREPÔT

The entrepôt is the integrating hub of an insular frontier region. It is established as the first settlement of substantial size in an area of colonization and serves as the focal point of economic, social, and political activities there. The entrepôt usually evolves into the region's largest settlement. Archaeological data have indicated that Charleston falls within the area of earliest English settlement in South Carolina. If this settlement fulfilled the role of entrepôt, we may expect that it possessed integrating functions associated with these centers of frontier activity. The fourth hypothesis predicts that material evidence capable of recognizing this aspect of the entrepôt's role will be present here and that an examination of the material record will confirm our assumption that Charleston represents this type of frontier settlement. The material evidence is examined here through two test implications, each of which pertains to a different aspect of the entrepôt's role.

Because Charleston remains an urban area and has not yet been systematically explored archaeologically, its role as an entrepôt must be investigated largely through the use of other types of material data. In South Carolina, surviving colonial architecture is extensive and provides a source of evidence relating both to settlement size and content in early Charleston and in other coastal settlements. Architectural evidence forms the basis for exploring questions of settlement function addressed in the following discussion.

Size

The entrepôt, as the principal port of entry into the area of colonization, the focus of its trade and communications network, and the center of social and religious activities, is expected to be the largest settlement in the region. Because it serves as the paramount transport link to the homeland, the entrepôt must be situated in a position accessible to the transport network of the parent state. In colonial North America such settlements would have been located on the coast at sites offering anchorage to oceangoing vessels and unimpeded access to the interior. As we have seen, Charleston was a densely settled coastal site with an adjacent harbor. Archaeological, architectural, and cemetery evidence have revealed that the earliest occupation by English settlers occurred here, marking it as a likely site for South Carolina's entrepôt. Material evidence shows that several other early coastal settlements also came into existence in the early eighteenth century at locations possessing good harbors as well as having access to the interior via navigable water. These sites lie in the present cities of Georgetown and Beaufort, and their material record consists of standing architecture and cemeteries.

As the colony's oldest port settlement, Charleston should have become the entrepôt. Because of the various functions associated with this role, it is also likely to have been the largest port settlement. The comparative size of these early settlements may be measured by observing the distribution of material evidence in each location. Three maps have been prepared, showing the distribution of architectural and archaeological remains and cemeteries in Charleston, Beaufort, and Georgetown (Figs. 6.1, 6.2, and 6.3). Because the maps are not based upon complete surveys of the cities in which the early ports were situated, colonial settlement patterns cannot be

FIGURE 6.1 Distribution of structures, archaeological sites, and cemeteries in Charleston, dating from the colonial period. These data indicate both the size and form of the early settlement. (Sources: Elzas 1903; Jervey 1906; NRF; SIR; Stoney 1944; Webber 1928; Honerkamp et al. 1982.)

reconstructed precisely. If we assume, however, that the condition of the material data base from each site is similar, then the distributional patterns these data reveal should be comparable, permitting us to ascertain the relative size of the three port settlements.

A comparison of the distributions of available material evidence in Charleston, Beaufort, and Georgetown shows that the settlement were relatively small and lay adjacent to the harbor waterfronts. Of the three sites, the remains of Charleston encompassed the largest area. Its area of approximately 42,000,000 square feet (3,906,000 m²) surpass the 10,900,000 square feet (1,013,700 m²) of Beaufort and the 24,000,000 square feet (2,232,000 m²) of Georgetown. In terms of overall settlement size, these data indicate that Charleston served as the entrepôt for colonial South Carolina.

Centralizing Institutions

As the central settlement in the area of colonization, the entrepôt serves as the hub of the transport network and the focus of the various centralizing institutions that link the colony together economically, socially, and politically. Material evidence for these activities at the three colonial port sites should consist of surviving structures once devoted to activities associated with centralizing institutions. Each site may contain structures of this type, however, the entrepôt should exhibit the most and the greatest variety. If the condition of the material data base in each of the port settlements is comparable, then a comparison of the surviving structures in

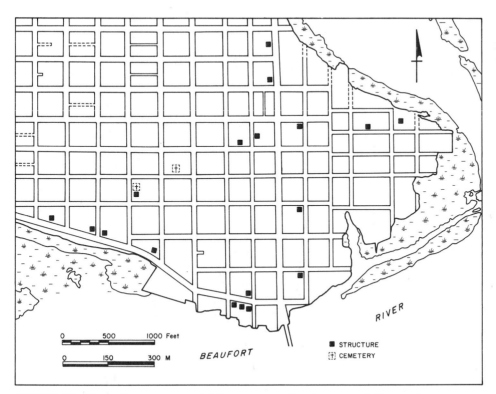

FIGURE 6.2 The settlement pattern of eighteenth-century Beaufort as revealed by standing structures. (Source: LCG 1979; NRF.)

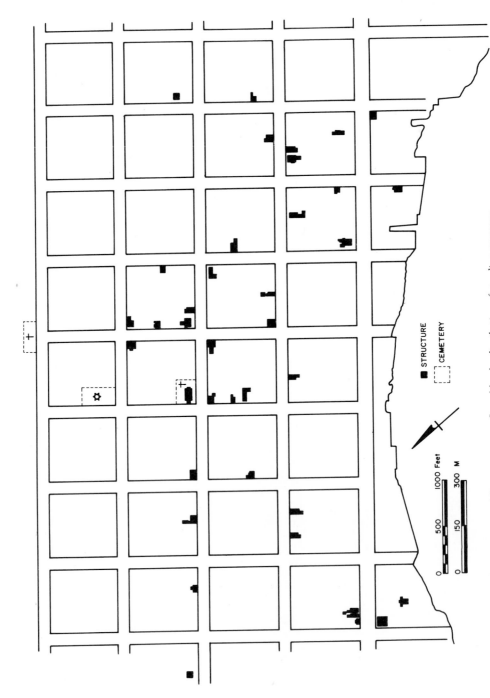

FIGURE 6.3 The settlement pattern of Georgetown as reflected by the distribution of standing structures. (Sources: Lawson 1974; NRF; WRPDC 1971.)

Charleston, Beaufort, and Georgetown should reveal the former as the site of the entrepôt.

Not all centralizing activities were housed in specialized structures, the design or architecture of which makes them recognizable. In the absence of other types of material evidence it is possible to identify only those types of activities likely to have left distinctive architectural remains. These actvities may be divided into several categories: (1) economic activities that would have required the construction of warehouses, mills, or other processing structures, store and market buildings, and offices; (2) centralizing political activities that would be associated with buildings housing administrative activities, including governor's houses, state houses, custom houses, courthouses, and other government structures; (3) religious activities, identified by churches, churchyards, and their related buildings; and (4) the presence of a social hierarchy best represented by high-status domestic architecture. Finally, a protection of a coastal entrepôt from attack by the forces of competing European states or pirates might require the establishment of (5) a permanent military garrison near the settlement or its harbor. This should be evidenced by the presence of magazines, forts, or other defensive works in or near the site of the entrepôt.

The past function of an early structure is recognizable generally on the basis of

FIGURE 6.4 The colonial statehouse building at the intersection of Meeting and Broad streets in Charleston. This administrative structure is presently the Charleston County courthouse. (Author's photograph.)

its architecture. Most substantial public buildings employed designs following the Palladian style popular in seventeenth and eighteenth century England. The function of a structure would have been most closely linked to its layout and size. The identification of colonial South Carolina buildings was accomplished by comparing these structures to contemporary European structures used for a variety of purposes (see Forman 1948; Waterman 1945). Fortifications of the period were identified through a comparison with those discussed in Muller (1746), Hughes (1974), and Duffy (1975).

An examination of the standing structures at the sites of the three colonial ports reveals that Charleston contains structures representing all of the categories outlined

FIGURE 6.5   St. Michael's Episcopal Church on Meeting Street in Charleston. This colonial-period religious structure reflects the presence of the State Church of England in this colonial entrepôt. (Author's photograph.)

FIGURE 6.6 The Charleston powder magazine, an early eighteenth-century military structure on Cumberland Street. (NRF photograph.)

above. These include business structures consisting of offices, stores, and taverns; two political structures, the statehouse (Fig. 6.4) and the exchange custom houses; two churches (Fig. 6.5) and five cemeteries; over 100 high-status dwellings; and one defensive structure, a powder magazine (Fig. 6.6) (Elzas 1903; Jervey 1906; NRF; Simons and Lapham 1927; Stoney 1944; Webber 1928). If one expands the scope of settlement to include the approaches to Charleston Harbor, two eighteenth-century forts, Fort Moultrie and Fort Johnson, may be seen to flank either side of the harbor's entrance (South 1974; 1975). Their remains were identified on the basis of archaeological evidence uncovered in extensive investigations carried out at these sites.

Georgetown, in contrast, contains no eighteenth-century political or military related structures. Its surviving buildings include those devoted only to economic, social, and religious functions. These consist of a substantial number of high-status domestic structures, a warehouse, and a church. Three eighteenth-century cemeteries are also present (Lawson 1974; NRF; WRPDC 1971). Similarly, Beaufort lacks structures associated with political activities that would be expected in the entrepôt.

Its architectural remains include structures devoted to economic, social, religious, and military activities (LCG 1979). These consist of a tavern, a church and two cemeteries, numerous substantial domestic structures, and a fort located 1½ miles (2.4 km) south of the settlement along the approach to its harbor (Lepionka 1979).

Material data reflecting the extent and nature of eighteenth century occupations in Charleston, Georgetown, and Beaufort revealed that each of these colonial ports was a site of certain centralizing institutions characteristic of key settlements in an insular frontier system. Charleston contains evidence of a greater variety of such activities than either of the others and is the only one of the three to have possessed a political function. The presence of political activities there identifies this settlement as the seat of administrative power in the colony. This is one of the most important roles of an entrepôt. Its association with the port of Charleston identifies this settlement as the entrepôt for colonial South Carolina, a conclusion supported by the settlement's size, location, and early emergence in this frontier region.

HYPOTHESIS 5: THE DENDRITIC FORM OF SETTLEMENT

The area of colonization is tied together by a network of trade and communications routes centered on the entrepôt. Because the settlement lies on the periphery of the colonial region, this transport network tends to be dendritic in form, spreading outward from a single point as it leads inland. The basic layout of settlement established by the transport network usually persists throughout the colonial period. Increasing population density and intensified agricultural development, however, bring about shifts in settlement pattern and economic organization. These, in turn, affect trade by reorienting transportation routes around new economic centers with additional ties to the outside world. The fifth hypothesis states that such a dendritic settlement pattern should be observable in colonial South Carolina.

In South Carolina an entrepôt was established at the port of Charleston. As the focus of the trade and communications network, Charleston should constitute the central point of a settlement system radiating into the interior. The following two test implications are intended to investigate types of material evidence capable of indicating this pattern of settlement in colonial South Carolina.

Patterns of Settlement on the Frontier

The distribution of settlement in an area of colonization should reflect the dendritic layout of the trade and communications network emanating from the entrepôt. Material evidence of settlement should be easily discernible in the archaeological record, which should permit the identification of sites of structures and activities distributed in a linear arrangement focusing on the port of Charleston. The compilation of a complete site record would require a survey of the entire state of

South Carolina, a task that is presently far from complete. Surveys of other types of material evidence, however, have been carried out in many areas and may be used to supplement the archaeological record. These surveys of standing structures and cemeteries, like those of archaeological sites, do not cover the whole state and are subject to the bias of the researchers who conducted them. Because each type of survey was concerned with a different kind of evidence, the results of each may help offset the others' biases. Together the distributions of these three types of data should provide a reasonably accurate picture of settlement during the colonial period. If we observe the geographic patterning of these data in the latter part of the colonial era, their distribution should reveal the dendritic form described in the

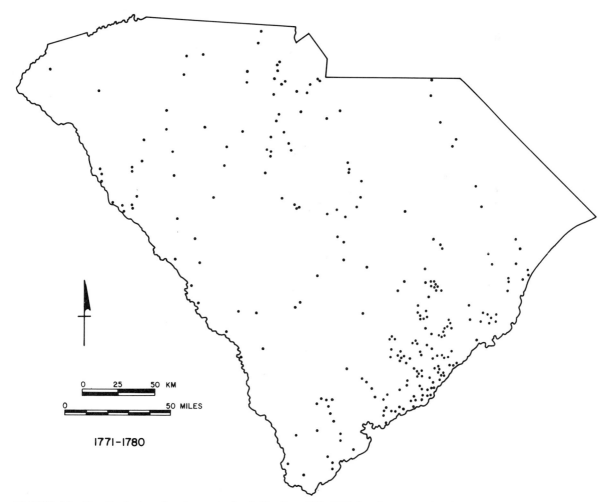

FIGURE 6.7 The distribution of settlement in South Carolina, 1771–1780, based on material evidence. (Sources: see Note 1.)

model of insular frontier settlement. A map of settlement in 1780, as indicated by material evidence, is shown in Figure 6.7.[1]

The distribution of settlement sites in 1780 clearly shows a clustering in the coastal area centered on Charleston. Spreading outward from the entrepôt are at least four branches of settlement. The westernmost runs along the coast toward Beaufort and turns inland along the Salkehatchie drainage toward the Savannah River. A second branch follows the Edisto River but appears to stay close to the coast. A third branch moves inland directly from Charleston, following the Ashley and Cooper rivers, and the Santee as far as the confluence of the Congaree and Wateree rivers. Here it divides, turning northward up the Wateree drainage, northwestward into the territory between the Wateree and Broad rivers, and westward toward the upper Savannah. The fourth branch parallels the coast to Georgetown, then turns inland along the Pee Dee River reaching as far as the North Carolina border.

These branches form a dendritic pattern of settlement centered on the entrepôt of Charleston. At least two, and possibly three, major routes of interior migration are indicated. Although they are associated generally with the larger river drainages, only the easternmost branch along the Pee Dee River appears to have taken the path of a single watercourse. The central branch, in contrast, crosses several drainages as it spreads inland across north and central South Carolina. Similarly, the westernmost branch crosses over to the Savannah River from the upper Salkehatchie drainage. This distribution of migration routes suggests that rivers did not play a paramount role in the settlement of the interior. In order to connect the settlements revealed in Figure 6.7, an overland road system would have been necessary. With the exception perhaps of the Pee Dee region, such a road network is likely to have carried the bulk of traffic of the South Carolina frontier to its coastal entrepôt.

Settlement in the coastal region, unlike that of the interior, seems to have clustered along the drainages of major rivers of the Lower Coastal Plain. In addition to the Cooper and the Ashley rivers, which empty into Charleston Harbor, the

[1]The locations of archaeological sites, standing structures and other cultural features, and cemeteries have been assembled for Figure 6.7 and Figures 7.1–7.10 from the following sources: Anthony and Drucker 1980; Asreen 1975; BCDRPC 1979; Brockington 1980; CMRPC 1974; CPRPC 1971; CR; Crockett 1965; Crowder 1970; CRPC 1975, 1976a,b,c; DAROCC 1977; Daugherty 1961; Drake and Rainwater 1970; Drucker 1980; Drucker and Anthony 1980; Drucker and Fulmer 1981; Ebenezer Memorial Association 1975; Elzas 1903; Garrow *et al.* 1979, 1981; Glover 1939, 1940, 1972; Goodyear 1975; Harley *et al.* 1978, 1979, 1980; Herold 1981; Herold and Knick 1979; Herold and Thomas 1981; Heyward 1929; Hough 1963; House and Ballenger 1976; Jervey 1906; Johnson and Rosa 1971; Lachicotte 1955; LCG 1979; LCHC 1974; Lees and Michie 1978; Logan 1980; LSCG 1972; McClendon 1977; Middleton 1941; Muse 1980; Neely 1959; NRF; PDRPDC 1972; Readling 1970; Reid 1977; Runnette 1936, 1937, 1950; Russell *et al.* 1981; Salley 1925; SCACG 1972; SCDAHSF; *SCHM* 1913, 1917a,b, 1925, 1926, 1937; SIR; D. Smith 1981; H. Smith 1909; South and Hartley 1980; Stoddard 1963, 1965a,b, 1966a,b; Stoney 1938; SWPC 1972; Taylor and Smith 1978; Todd 1931; Trinkley and Tippett 1980; USRPDC 1972; Walker 1939, 1941; Waring 1926; Watson and Watson 1972; Webber 1928; Whaley 1976; Widmer 1976; Wood 1977; WRPDC 1971; Zierden 1981, 1982.

Dates for the historic occupations of the sites used to construct this and the other settlement maps to follow have been derived using the techniques described earlier in the discussion of long-term settlement.

drainages of the Edisto, Wando, Stono, Santee, and Black rivers exhibit evidence of such settlement, suggesting that water transport routes played a larger role in the occupation of this region. Rivers of the Lower Coastal Plain are wide and deep, and terminate at the heads of bays formed by their drowned lower valleys (Petty 1943:4). Such navigable waterways would have formed ideal transport routes, unhindered by the shallower waters found further inland.

A comparison of settlement in colonial South Carolina suggests the development of two patterns of transport, a waterborne system on the Lower Coastal Plain dissected by deep, navigable rivers and an overland system in the interior. This geographic distinction does not preclude the use of either type of transport elsewhere in the area of colonization but rather indicates a predominance of each type in a separate region. Such a broad division should be reflected by evidence for the actual transport routes which will be examined below.

Colonial Transport Routes

Material evidence of overland transport routes consist primarily of actual remnants of the roadways themselves. Although clearly visible elements of the cultural landscape, roads are difficult to place in time because they are generally zones of low-density activity that produces little archaeological deposition even when in use over long periods. The age of roads can be estimated, however, if they associate with settlements of known age or transport activity areas such as river crossings.

No systematic survey of early roads in South Carolina has been carried out, but the presence of abandoned and unimproved roadways have been noted in the vicinity of many colonial settlements under investigation (Fig. 6.8). Although most evidence consists of road fragments that have not been fully traced, it suggests their general direction and provides clues to their possible destinations. By linking these segments, it is possible to reconstruct a conjectural map of the basic road network based on material data. A map showing the locations of identifiable early road traces appears as Figure 6.9. Routes in this figure have been drawn along the shortest direct distances between points, following high ground between river drainages and avoiding swamps and other impassible areas. A minimum number of river crossings have been included.

The map shows a dendritic road network extending inland from the entrepôt of Charleston along three main branches. One thrusts northwestward towards the Savannah River, then parallels it into the western portion of the present state. The second branch is more complex. It runs in a northerly direction toward the Santee River, where it turns westward, dividing into two branches. One heads northward again, west of the Wateree River, and the other continues westward, splitting several times as it expands into the northern part of South Carolina. Its westernmost segment appears to intersect the Savannah branch of the road's network, forming an inland link between these two major elements of the overland transport system. The third branch splits off the central branch near the coast and turns eastward where it is likely to have intersected a road running from the port of Georgetown up the western side of the Pee Dee River. In addition to the three major branches described, a fourth branch extending westward from Charleston along the coast is indicated. The length of this branch is uncertain, but it is likely to have led to the port of Beaufort, joining this coastal settlement by land with the entrepôt.

It is immediately apparent that the overland transport network of colonial South Carolina was designed mainly to provide coastal access to the interior. Routes

FIGURE 6.8   Trace of the Charleston road at the Ninety-Six site in Greenwood County. This and many other colonial road segments remain as visible features on the present landscape. (Author's photograph.)

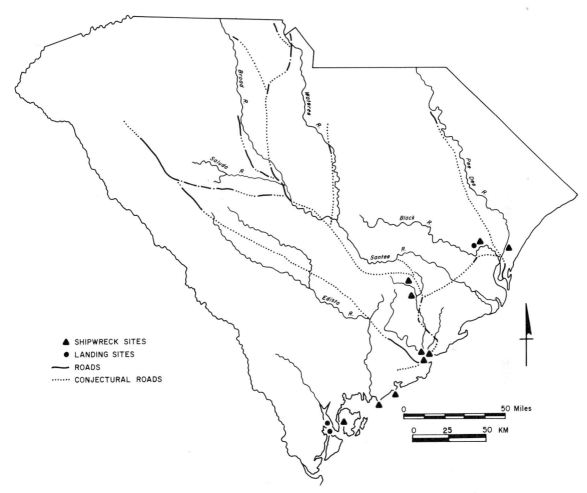

FIGURE 6.9 Conjectured overland transport network of colonial South Carolina, based on road traces. The extent of the coastal riverine network is reflected by the locations of shipwrecks and landing sites. (Sources: BCDRPC; CMRPC; Consulting Associates 1976; CPRPC; CRPC; NRF; PDRPDC; SIR; USRPDC.)

from the entrepôt to other port settlements are circuitous in nature as a result of their having to avoid areas of low terrain, open water, and swampland on the Lower Coastal Plain. Because of the region's access to the sea and navigable coastal waterways, there was extensive use of water transport. Shipping, especially in the relatively shallow draft vessels of the eighteenth century, would have required no modification of these watercourses except at landing sites. Consequently, the material record of such traffic is likely to consist of deposition generated by the movement of goods along these routes. Unlike roads, water routes are capable of accumulating and preserving undisturbed a great deal of cultural material because of the difficulty of retrieving material that has fallen into deep water. Shipwrecks are perhaps the most obvious example of such accumulations. They not only provide datable information through their cargoes and form but are, in themselves, evidence of water transport. Underwater surveys of major South Carolina coastal rivers (Stephenson 1975:52) have resulted in the discovery of a number of such wrecks, some of which have been investigated and assigned specific date ranges.

The locations of these wrecks appear in Figure 6.9. This map reveals shipwreck sites near each of the eighteenth-century ports on South Carolina's coast: Beaufort, Charleston, and Georgetown. In addition, wrecks have been found in the Waccamaw, Black, Cooper, and Beaufort rivers. Several river landing sites have also been identified on the Stono, Black, and Broad rivers. Based on the data available from archaeological surveys, a pattern of river transport emerges. Its layout indicates a coastal trade among the entrepôt and other ports as well as movement into the Lower Coastal Plain via a number of navigable rivers.

A comparison of the inland and water transport networks inferred from material evidence reveals a clear pattern. The transportation network of colonial South Carolina consisted of a dendritic inland system of roads emanating from the entrepôt to the far extremities of the area of colonization. Settlement along the coast followed the watercourses of the Lower Coastal Plain, implying the great importance of waterborne trade and communications in this region. The presence of shipwrecks and landings along major coastal rivers and an absence of evidence for an elaborate coastal road system seems to support this assumption. Overall, the form of the colonial transport network appears to conform to the entrepôt-centered pattern predicted in the model of insular frontier settlement. The layout of this network defines the form of settlement within the area of colonization and provides a framework in which to explore diachronic aspects of settlement expansion.

7

Examining Hypotheses for Expansion

An examination of the spatial patterning of settlement in colonial South Carolina has revealed that the region was characterized by a dendritic settlement distribution centered on the coastal entrepôt of Charleston. One implication of this patterning is that settlement occurred first on the coast in the vicinity of the entrepôt and then spread inland along a series of overland routes. Expansion is the dynamic aspect of insular frontier colonization, and through it we may observe the evolution of settlement systems. The hypotheses to be addressed in this section deal with colonial expansion and the changes it is likely to have brought about in settlement patterns and the organization of transport. The anticipated changes are integral to the insular frontier process, and material evidence of their occurrence should be discernible. The recognition of change will document South Carolina's development as a spatial entity and provide a framework in which the organization of frontier activities may subsequently be examined.

HYPOTHESIS 6: EXPANSION AS A CONTINUOUS PROCESS

The process of insular frontier colonization is essentially one of agricultural expansion in which new lands are occupied for the commercial exploitation of their resources. Although the rate of expansion varies with market demand and transport efficiency, the growth of an area of colonization is generally continuous and resuls in the relatively rapid spread of settlement through the available territory. The sixth hypothesis predicts that such a continuous movement should be observable in the material record of colonial South Carolina. The following test implications examine two aspects of settlement expansion in this region.

Material Patterns of Agricultural Expansion

Because of the entrepôt's central position in the transport network of the frontier, it serves as the major point from which expansion originates. The entrepôt is the initial area of settlement and its position determines the direction in which further colonization must move. In South Carolina we have seen that Charleston, on the Atlantic coast, was established as the entrepôt in the late seventeenth century. It lay at the hub of a dendritic transport network that stretched overland to the boundaries of the present state and spread by water along the entire Lower Coastal Plain. Settlement in the latter part of the frontier period corresponds to the layout of this

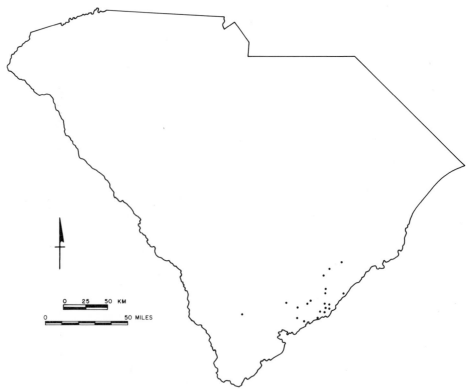

FIGURE 7.1   The distribution of settlement in South Carolina, 1670–1700, based on material evidence. (Sources: see text.)

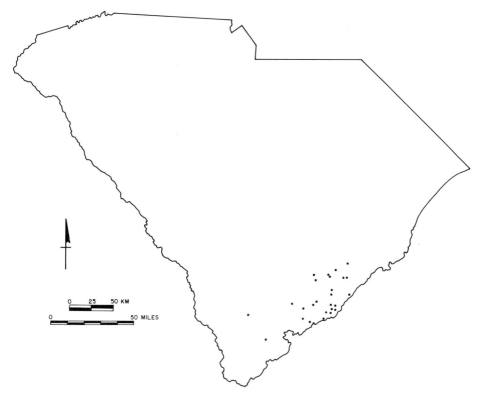

FIGURE 7.2 The distribution of settlement in South Carolina, 1701–1710, based on material evidence. (Sources: see text.)

network. This suggests that direct expansion outward in all landward directions from the entrepôt took place during the eighteenth century. The actual process of expansion, however, must be observed at shorter intervals which allow the movement of settlement to be traced from the time of initial colonization to the close of the frontier period.

SETTLEMENT EVIDENCE FOR EXPANSION

It is necessary to plot the sites of material evidence of British settlement at relatively short time intervals in order to observe the hypothesized progressive expansion inland from its coastal entrepôt. The evidence of earliest settlement dates from the last half of the seventeenth century and may include sites occupied as early as 1670, the date by which the colonization of South Carolina is known to have begun. The period 1670–1700 will serve as the base line for our study of settlement growth. Sites of settlements occupied before 1700 are shown in Figure 7.1. They are represented by archaeological remains, standing structures, and cemeteries in use at this time. Nine additional maps (Figs. 7.2–7.10) portray the distribution of settlement remains at 10-year intervals during the next century. These maps are derived from the same sources used in Figure 6.7 (see Note 1, Chapter 6). When viewed as a series, the maps allow the distribution of settlement in South Carolina to be traced throughout the colonial period on the basis of material evidence. A definite pattern of expansion may be seen to emerge from these data.

In the years before 1700, European settlement in South Carolina was confined to a small area around the entrepôt of Charleston (Fig. 7.1). All settlements appear to have been scattered along rivers of the Lower Coastal Plain: the Cooper, the Ashley, the Stono, the Edisto, the Coosawhatchie, and Goose Creek. An initial expansion outward from the entrepôt appears to have occurred along the navigable watercourses that may have constituted its major transport links.

Ten years later, the occupied area of South Carolina had not increased greatly over that of 1700 (Fig. 7.2). Settlement had proceeded up several of the coastal rivers, and the site of Beaufort was now occupied. The northern end of the Lower Coastal Plain was still vacant at this time with no settlement yet along the major drainages of the Santee and Pee Dee rivers.

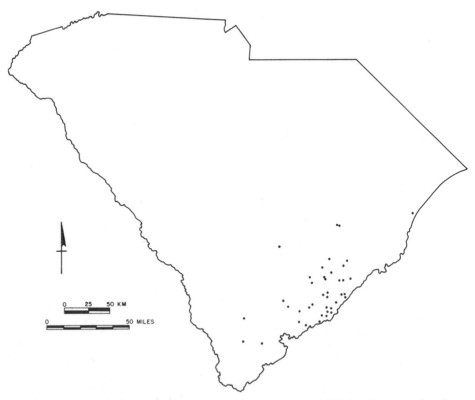

FIGURE 7.3 The distribution of settlement in South Carolina, 1711–1720, based on material evidence. (Sources: see text.)

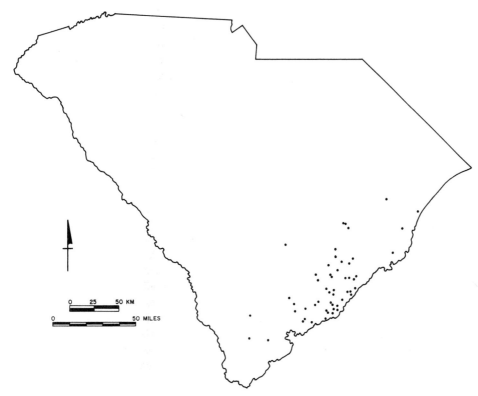

FIGURE 7.4 The distribution of settlement in South Carolina, 1721–1730, based on material evidence. (Sources: see text.)

By 1720, a relatively dramatic expansion had taken place. Although still largely confined to the Lower Coastal Plain, settlement had spread northeastward to the mouth of the Pee Dee and northward to the Santee (Fig. 7.3). Inland migration along the rivers occupied earlier had increased as had the overall density of settlement in the vicinity of Charleston. Most settlement appears still to have been accessible by water along the coastal rivers.

After its initial northward thrust, expansion in South Carolina appears to have entered a period of consolidation (Fig. 7.4). Settlement along the Santee grew, and the site of Georgetown on Winyah Bay at the mouth of the Pee Dee was occupied. Inland colonization had not yet taken place, however, and the frontier remained largely a coastal region. The greatest concentration of settlement lay in those areas closest to Charleston, which implied an intensification of land use there as a consequence of its proximity to the entrepôt's markets.

The decade ending in 1740 witnessed the first movement into the interior of South Carolina (Fig. 7.5). Settlement had extended up the Pee Dee River past its confluence with the Lynches. The vast Santee drainage was beginning to be oc-

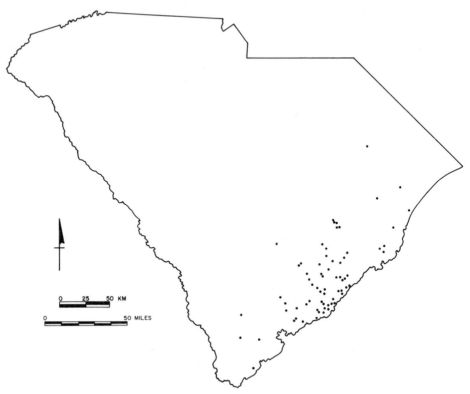

FIGURE 7.5 The distribution of settlement in South Carolina, 1731–1740, based on material evidence. (Sources: see text.)

cupied, and settlement had progressed as far as the Congaree River. The site of Orangeburg was also settled by this time. Inland expansion reflected by these settlements also reveals the beginnings of a dendritic pattern of colonization. Although most coastal settlements still lay close to major rivers, the overall distribution suggests the development of overland links between the river systems. Such land routes would be necessary to extend the transport system beyond the Fall Line, which marks the head of river navigation.

The 10 years prior to the middle of the eighteenth century saw an extension of settlement further up the Pee Dee and into the Wateree River region (Fig. 7.6). Settlement in the west appears to have stablized, and the northern portion of the colony remained unoccupied. Along the coast, settlement density increased, and the site of Kingstree was occupied. Newly colonized sites in the coastal region were mainly along major rivers or on the coastal islands. They continued the riverine pattern of settlement established early in South Carolina's history. Many of the inland settlements appear to have been located away from navigable water. Those situated on rivers did not follow the river's course as on the coast but were situated at isolated points, perhaps representing places of intersection by overland routes.

Between 1751 and 1760, inland settlement experienced another spurt of growth, which pushed colonization into the north-central portion of the province and the upper Savannah region (Fig. 7.7). All the major rivers—the Savannah, the Congaree, the Wateree, and the Pee Dee—were inhabited at least as far inland as the Fall Line. The first archaeologically demonstrable settlement at Camden dates from this decade. Settlement in the interior was not noticably removed from the rivers as well, implying the development of a complex interior road system stretching inland to the boundaries of the colony. Settlement density also continued to increase along the coast and produced a cluster pattern centered around the ports of Charleston, Beaufort, and Georgetown.

In the 1760s, growth occurred along the frontier in the northern portion of South Carolina (Fig. 7.8). All the major river drainages were occupied beyond the Fall Line, and settlement had expanded throughout the Piedmont region, except the northwest corner of the colony. The density of occupation appears to have varied within the interior, but nowhere did it approach that of the coastal region.

The following decade saw settlement in the interior of South Carolina begin to intensify (Fig. 6.7), particularly in the north-central region and along the Savannah

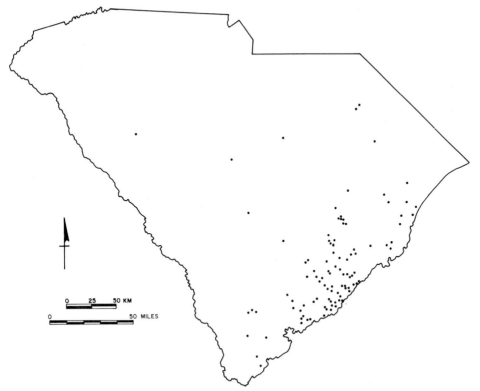

FIGURE 7.6 The distribution of settlement in South Carolina, 1741–1750, based on material evidence. (Sources: see text.)

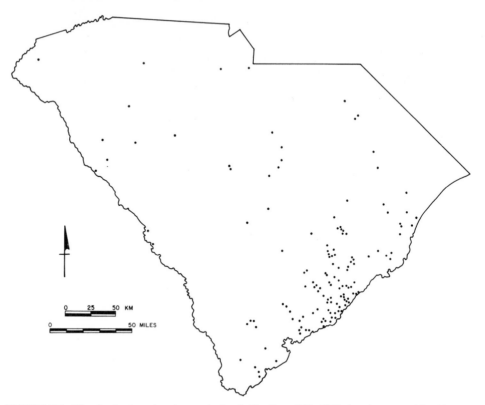

FIGURE 7.7   The distribution of settlement in South Carolina, 1751–1760, based on material evidence. (Sources: see text.)

River. The sites of several modern cities had been occupied by this time including Abbeville, Allendale, Barnwell, Cheraw, Chester, Spartanburg, and Winnsboro. The distribution of settlements in the interior had begun to assume a linear form independent of the river system. This pattern suggests the development of an elaborate overland transport network as discussed earlier. Only one portion of the province, its northwest corner, remained uninhabited by European agricultural settlement by 1780.

The closing decades of the eighteenth century mark the end of the colonial period in South Carolina. The distribution of occupied sites during this time (Figs. 7.9 and 7.10) shows a dramatic increase in the density of settlement throughout most of the interior, particularly above the Fall Line. For the first time, the northwest corner of the present state was occupied as were the sites of several more modern cities and towns, including Chesterfield, Columbia, Conway, Lancaster, Lexington, and York. The linear pattern of settlement seems to have become even more complex. This implies a further intensification of the overland network of trade and communications in the closing years of the frontier period. Settlement along the coast had intensified around the three major ports and occupied the principal river courses of the Lower Coastal Plain. By 1800, settlement was still far from evenly distributed across the entire area of colonization. In general, the distribution of material evidence reveals a pattern of settlement characterized by an intensive, clustered occupation of the Lower Coastal Plain. Settlement tapered off to a much less dense occurrence on the Upper Coastal Plain and a moderately dense and somewhat more evenly distributed occupation in the Piedmont.

TREND SURFACE ANALYSIS

The form of settlement expansion indicated by the maps presents a complex picture of movement that generally agrees with that predicted by the insular frontier model. In order to visualize this movement more clearly, it may be portrayed graphically through the use of SYMAPs such as those employed in Chapter 3. Because of the extremely uneven spacing of the data points on the base maps, a trend surface map would again appear to offer the best means for presenting this information. A third-order trend surface map and a map of residual values appears as Figure 7.11.

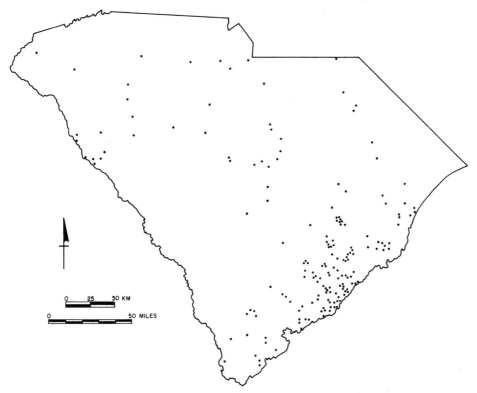

FIGURE 7.8 The distribution of settlement in South Carolina, 1761–1770, based on material evidence. (Sources: see text.)

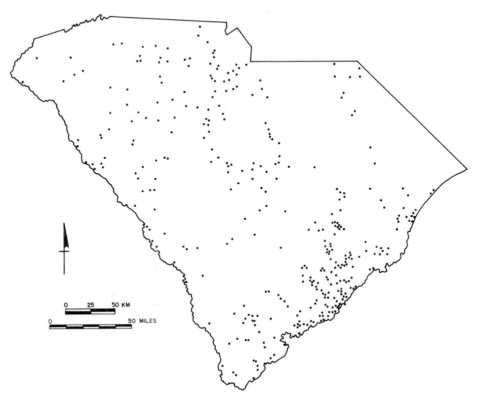

FIGURE 7.9   The distribution of settlement in South Carolina, 1781–1790, based on material evidence. (Sources: see text.)

Figure 7.11A, the trend surface map, illustrates settlement movement by 20-year intervals beginning in 1700. The map shows an initial occupation of the coast in the vicinity of Charleston, followed by expansion outward from that point along the coast prior to 1740. By 1760, settlement had turned inland. The trend continued during the following two decades. The northeastern portion of South Carolina was occupied at this time, as was an area stretching westward to the Savannah River. A large portion of the northwestern and north-central part of the state, however, does not appear to have been settled until the closing decades of the eighteenth century. This trend surface reflects the general movement of settlement across the area of colonization as predicted in the model and the form revealed in the church trend surface map (Fig. 3.20). It also reflects the general movement observed in the settlement maps (Figs. 6.7, 7.1–7.10), although a few anomalies are present.

A perusal of the residual map (Fig. 7.11B) shows that a substantial portion of the data values are predicted by the trend surface. The residuals indicate also where the trend surface has under and overpredicted values, thereby identifying those areas settled respectively earlier and later than shown in Figure 7.11A. Several areas of earlier settlement appear. These include portions of the Lower Coastal Plain north-east and southwest of Charleston, the Upper Coastal Plain northwest of Charleston, the Pee Dee drainage, a portion of the Piedmont and Upper Coastal Plain stretching westward from the Pee Dee to about the center of the state, a pocket of settlement along the northern border, and two similar pockets along the Savannah River. Areas of settlement occupied later than predicted by the trend surface appear in several places on the Coastal Plain and in two pockets in the northeastern part of the state.

A consideration of the residual values allows us to observe several aspects of settlement in greater detail. In particular, the early horizontal movement along the Lower Coastal Plain is more clearly evident, as are the initial thrusts of inland expansion in the vicinity of Orangeburg and along the lower Pee Dee drainage. Early settlement along the Savannah River, presumably linked to the rise of Augusta, is also discernible. A prominant area of early settlement lies in the central interior, reflecting the initial occupation of the region crossed by the drainages of the Broad, Wateree, and Pee Dee rivers. Areas of overpredicted values, on the other hand, are likely to show regions avoided by the initial movement of settlement. Their presence

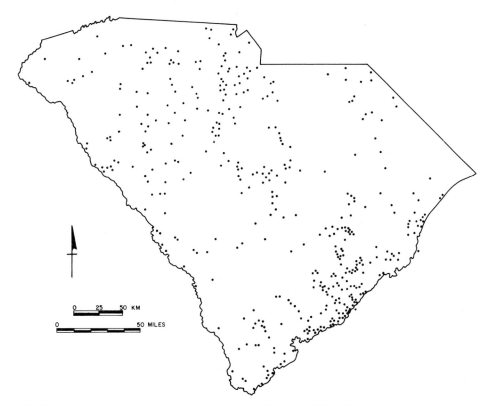

FIGURE 7.10   The distribution of settlement in South Carolina, 1791–1800, based on material evidence. (Sources: see text.)

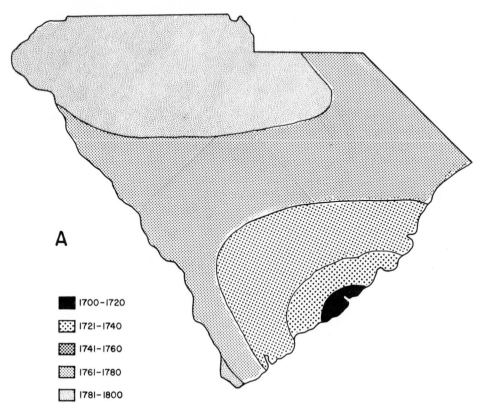

A

- ■ 1700-1720
- ▦ 1721-1740
- ▨ 1741-1760
- ▨ 1761-1780
- □ 1781-1800

FIGURE 7.11   Trend surface and residual maps of settlement growth in South Carolina. (A) Trend surface map generated by SYMAP, based on archaeological sites, standing structures, and cemeteries. This map shows

may also indicate the linear course of settlement produced by the dendritic trade and communications network characteristic of insular frontier areas.

A comparison of the trend surface and residual maps has revealed the overall form of colonial expansion in South Carolina during the eighteenth century. Several characteristics of the development are evident. First, the initial occupation spread from the entrepôt of Charleston into its immediate surrounding area along the coastal rivers. Second, following the naviagable rivers of the Lower Coastal Plain, settlement spread outward from the entrepôt along the Atlantic coast. Two other port sites, Georgetown and Beaufort, became centers of secondary settlement clusters. Third, although the density of settlement in the coastal region continued to increase throughout the colonial period, the most intensive occupation appears to have remained associated with the principal rivers. Fourth, settlement of the interior began after much of the coastal region was colonized. The first occupation of the Upper Coastal Plain took place in the 1740s, over a half century after the settlement of the coastal region began. Fifth, interior expansion proceeded along the drainages of the major river systems, but it did not produce a riverine pattern of settlement

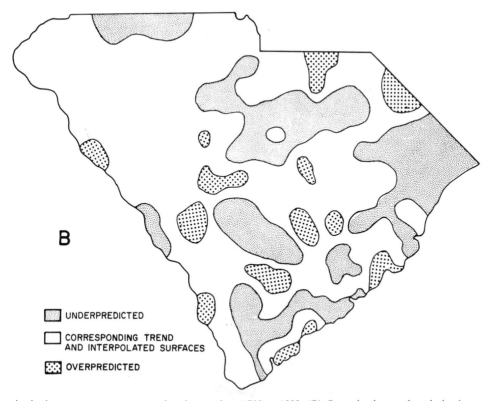

clearly the continuous expansion of settlement from 1700 to 1800. (B) Generalized map of residual values created by SYMAP showing where the trend surface has underpredicted and overpredicted the period of occupation interpolated from settlement sites.

similar to that of the coast. Instead, settlement seems to have followed a dendritic system of overland routes from which it branched out to cover intermediate areas. Such a pattern facilitated the colonization of a region that increased in size as the distance from its focal point, the entrepôt, increased. Finally, the occupation of the interior was a rather rapid process and encompassed the entire Piedmont in less than 40 years. The northwest corner of South Carolina, however, remained a curious exception to this phenomenon, remaining unsettled until after 1780. This anomaly to what appears to have been an otherwise continuous process of inland expansion and the initial delay in the interior's settlement are questions that bear additional comment and are addressed further below.

Barriers to Expansion

The expansion of South Carolina from its coastal entrepôt to the borders of the present state was characterized by the continuous movement of settlement anticipated in the frontier model. The colony's rate of expansion, however, was not constant. As we have seen, South Carolina appears to have been settled in three phases: first the occupation of the Lower Coastal Plain, followed by an expansion into the interior, and finally the colonization of the northwestern corner. This uneven rate of expansion suggests the presence of barriers to settlement that took time to overcome before movement along the frontier could continue. Once each barrier was passed, expansion proceeded unimpeded until another was encountered.

Barriers to colonization by complex, semiindustrial states such as those of seventeenth and eighteenth century Europe may be divided into three general categories: environmental, cultural–political, and economic.

ENVIRONMENTAL BARRIERS

Environmental barriers to settlement, such as extreme climate, infertile soils, and various topographical obstacles to migration, do not seem to have existed in early South Carolina. The region's level Coastal Plain extends up to 150 miles (240 km) inland from the coast and rises to a series of uplands which mark the beginning of the Piedmont. This gently sloping, dissected province encompasses nearly all of the remainder of the state. Its topography rises to form the low mountains of the Blue Ridge Province only in South Carolina's extreme northwestern corner. The two major provinces are cut by extensive river systems. Soils of both regions were developed under the cover of a mixed conifer and deciduous forest, high rainfall, and warm temperatures, and are generally suitable for the production of most European crops (Eleazer 1955; Frothingham and Nelson 1944; Petty 1943). Rather than a barrier to migration, the physical environment of South Carolina is likely to have been conducive to agricultural expansion.

CULTURAL–POLITICAL BARRIERS

A second potential barrier may be termed *cultural-political* and consists of impediments to settlement arising from the resistence of peoples already occupying the area of colonization. Archaeologically, the presence of such groups may be witnessed by the existence of sites of protohistoric aboriginal settlements that were contemporary with those of the English colonists. Additionally, the proximity of these groups might be indicated by the remains of trading posts and forts constructed to maintain contact with, control over, and defense against the former. The location of such sites should delineate the boundary of the territory occupied by both native and intrusive groups. The presence of aboriginal groups would antedate the European presence in the colonial area, and the terminal dates of sites occupied by such native peoples may delineate the boundaries of expansion at a given time. If such sites are associated with evidence of the institutions of external political control mentioned above, then their spatial distribution is likely to reveal the presence of temporary barriers to frontier growth.

In South Carolina, several types of noninsular frontier settlements have been identified on the basis of archaeological evidence. These include protohistoric ab-

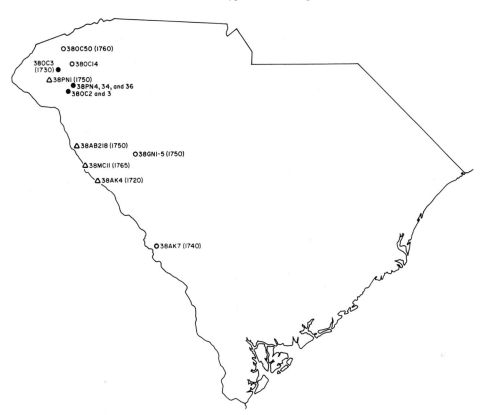

FIGURE 7.12   Distribution of (○) English trading posts, (△) forts, and (●) protohistoric aboriginal settlements in South Carolina. (Sources: see text.)

original settlements characterized by the occurrence of an assemblage of trade goods similar to that found on sites of similar function throughout British North America. Trading posts and forts, distinguished by distinctive architecture and artifact assemblages, are also present (Caldwell 1974; Combes 1969; Neill 1961; SIR).[1] The date ranges of these sites have been computed using the mean ceramic formula and the bracketing technique described earlier. All predate the earliest evidence of per-

[1]British Indian trade artifacts recovered from South Carolina sites represent an assemblage similar to that present at a number of eighteenth century protohistoric aboriginal and trading settlements and described in contemporary documents pertaining to the British Indian trade (cf. DeJarnette and Hanson 1960; Georgia 1805; Grimm 1970; Lewis 1969; Quimby 1966; Smith 1956). Although the American Revolution resulted in the creation of a number of forts in South Carolina, it is possible to distinguish frontier fortifications associated with Indian trade and defense by the dates of their occupations. The Revolutionary War, fought from 1775 to 1782, postdates expansion in all parts of South Carolina, a process that was essentially complete by 1770. Consequently, all frontier forts would have been occupied before this time.

manent English settlement in the areas where they occur. The locations of these sites and the dates of their occupations appear in Figure 7.12.

The distribution of sites reveals that protohistoric aboriginal settlements and English trading posts and forts were situated in the western and northwestern portions of South Carolina. Dates derived from material evidence recovered from these sites show that all were occupied in the eighteenth century, but they preceded the movement of agricultural settlement into their locales. All the aboriginal settlements that were situated in the northwestern corner were abandoned before the European occupation of that region after 1770. The presence of native groups and the potential threat of their hostility, witnessed by the presence of the English forts, probably prevented earlier colonization of this region. Consequently, a cultural–political barrier may be assigned as the likely cause of the delay preceding the last phase of settlement expansion.

ECONOMIC BARRIERS

The absence of environmental and cultural-political barriers to the interior's initial settlement implies that the delay in inland migration resulted from economic causes. Transportation networks play a key role in the development of a frontier region. Their growth is linked to increases in market demand for frontier commodities which make feasible the costs of expanding such networks. Because separate categories of agricultural commodities require different types of transportation systems, the cost of expanding transport networks would increase dramatically with the incorporation of new crops. The extension of areas of older crop production into regions where new methods of transport are necessary would also increase costs. Given these limitations, it is likely that agricultural expansion would occur first in regions where the previously developed system of transport could be maintained. It is reasonable to expect that the boundaries of such regions would influence agricultural growth and that the expansion of settlement beyond their limits might be delayed by the necessity of organizing new transport systems.

Material evidence from South Carolina has revealed the development of different systems of trade and communications in the coast and the interior. The former is characterized by deep river channels that permitted extensive water transportation in this region. Interior transport, on the other hand, was dependent on overland routes linking inland settlements to the entrepôt. If we compare the zones of riverine and overland transport with the regions of expansion shown in Figure 7.11, the former may be seen to coincide with the region of initial expansion prior to 1760. This suggests that expansion was linked to the sequential development of transport systems and that the lesser comparative cost of developing a region with one system before moving on to another favored limiting early expansion to the coast region of South Carolina. Subsequent movement into the interior would have been postponed until the creation of a system of overland transport became economically feasible. The pattern of transport system growth in colonial South Carolina strongly implies that a substantial economic change accompanied the expansion of coastal settlement into the interior. This shift is likely to have produced a temporary delay in the rate of overall expansion such as that which occurred prior to the rapid growth of interior settlement in the second quarter of the eighteenth century.

The rate of expansion in colonial South Carolina appears to have varied in response to both economic and cultural–political variables. Material evidence suggests that these were responsible for delays in the initial settlement of the interior and the occupation of the northwest corner of the colony. The changes associated with interior expansion are basic to the growth of insular frontier regions, because they influence the development of the economic structure on which the colony's survival is dependent. Although economic change may serve as a temporary barrier to expansion, its overall effect is beneficial because the diversification it brings increases the region's environmental stability and ultimately enhances the rate of colonial settlement.

An examination of settlement in colonial South Carolina has shown a gradual expansion outward from the entrepôt, first along the coast and then inland. The distribution of settlement sites in the area of colonization indicates that expansion apparently progressed along linear routes that, in turn, define the form of the transport network. Maps of the cumulative occupation of South Carolina from 1670 to 1800 show a pattern of initial expansion that resulted in scattered settlement in the newly occupied area, followed by a secondary spreading out of settlement to fill in areas between the points of initial occupation. With time, the density of settlement increased until its distribution became more uniform across much of the area.

HYPOTHESIS 7: PATTERNS OF SETTLEMENT DISTRIBUTION

The sequential patterning of settlement revealed in the 11 maps shows an increasing density of settlement through time. This pattern suggests a trend away from an initial clustered distribution toward one that is more evenly spaced. The seventh hypothesis predicts that such a trend toward even spacing will be discernible statistically. This reflects a readjustment of settlement spacing in response to the growing competition for land and resources as the area of colonization moves nearer its capacity to support a maximum agricultural population.

The degree of even spacing at any given time during the frontier period may be determined statistically by calculating a nearest-neighbor value for the sites then occupied. Distributional tendencies may be observed over time by comparing the nearest-neighbor values of site distributions at regular intervals throughout the frontier period. Nearest-neighbor values for colonial South Carolina have been calculated for each of the settlement distribution maps presented in Figures 6.7 and 7.1–7.10, which represent 10-year intervals from 1700 to 1800. These values appear in Table 7.1.

The nearest-neighbor values reveal the predicted trend from a clustered toward a more evenly spaced pattern of settlement, a trend similar to that evidenced by

TABLE 7.1 Nearest-neighbor values for settlement sites in South Carolina

Date of settlement distribution	Nearest-neighbor value
1700	0.3124
1710	0.3563
1720	0.5324
1730	0.5363
1740	0.6038
1750	0.7473
1760	0.9123
1770	0.9379
1780	1.0149
1790	1.0666
1800	1.1258

documentary data relating to the settlement of this region. This statistical trend is shown graphically in Figure 7.13. The slope of the curve suggests that the rate of change during the frontier period, though continuous, was uneven. The greatest change appears to have occurred between 1710 and 1720 and again between 1740 and 1760. The dates correspond to the two periods of greatest expansion in South

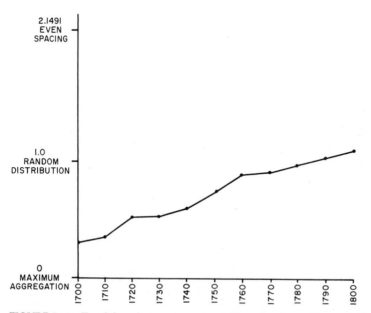

FIGURE 7.13 Trend through time of nearest-neighbor values for settlement distributions in colonial South Carolina.

Carolina. A rapid increase in the slope of the curve at these points reflects the markedly greater settlement spread that took place at these times, increasing both the distance of dispersal and its rate. The remainder of the eighteenth century is marked by a steady trend toward even spacing, implying a continuous growth throughout this period.

Statistical data derived from settlement maps of South Carolina have revealed a pattern of settlement change that conforms to the trend predicted in the model of insular frontier colonization. These results corroborate the conclusions drawn earlier regarding the form and nature of expansion and have helped refine our knowledge of changing patterns of settlement within the colony as a whole. Information derived from these material data provides both a spatial and temporal framework within which to view frontier change in this region. Thus, with the area of colonization defined in time and space, it is now possible to consider the organization of the frontier system and the evolution of its structure.

8

Examining Hypotheses for Settlement
Pattern and the Distribution of Activities

INTRODUCTION

The sequential occupation of sites in South Carolina has permitted us to observe
the development of English settlement in this colonial region. These data imply a
general expansion outward from the entrepôt of Charleston along the coast and then
inland along the major river drainages. The distribution of structures, archaeological
sites, and cemeteries show a settlement system tied together by a dendritic network
of transport routes focused on the principal port. The overall pattern of settlement
alone, however, reveals little about the system's organization. To investigate this
aspect of insular frontier colonization, it is necessary to examine the remains of
individual settlements themselves according to their position within the trade and
communications network and their form and content.

The function of a frontier settlement is linked largely to the economic activities
associated with it. Such activities reflect its role in the production of staple commodities which is related, in turn, to the settlement's position in the network of trade
and communications. Settlements may be ranked according to their relative economic function into three basic categories: frontier towns, nucleated settlements,
and dispersed settlements. Each type is associated with specific activities of production and occupies a position in the transport network that facilitates carrying out
these tasks. The results generated by the testing of the following three hypotheses
should permit us to identify each type of frontier settlement in South Carolina on the

basis of available material data. The investigations focus on three aspects of settlement that are tied to a site's role in the frontier system. These are its size, layout, and composition. Test implications for each are addressed in the discussion of each hypothesis. Then they are compared with data from extensively investigated sites in order to demonstrate the existence of the three settlement types and their positions within the trade and communications network. The investigation of settlement types is conducted in descending order of their economic significance, beginning with the frontier town.

HYPOTHESIS 8: FRONTIER TOWNS, SECONDARY CENTERS OF ACTIVITY

The frontier town serves as the focus of economic, social, and political activity for a substantial portion of the area of colonization. As such, it occupies a status similar to that of certain contemporary settlements in the metropolitan area, in this case eighteenth century Great Britain. Because the frontier town exists at the edge of the world economy in a region of low population density, the role it plays varies from that of its European counterpart. Its role in a colonial region requires the frontier town to maintain certain functions while at the same time adapting to frontier conditions by restructing its integrating institutions and, consequently, altering its form.

The role of the frontier town as a focus of activity in colonial South Carolina may be compared to that of settlements in a contemporary European settlement hierarchy. Blouet (1972) defined six levels of settlement based on degree of economic development. Only at the third level, called the *town,* do we find functions comparable to those of the frontier town, for only here is exchange conducted on an *inter-* rather than an *intra*regional basis. The town is characterized by a greater specialization of production, an increase in the variety of employment, and the marketing of a greater range of goods than is found in settlements lower on the urban scale (Blouet 1972:5–7). In addition to its interregional economic functions, political and social functions may be added to the role of the frontier town. Towns may also be assigned separate relative statuses within an urban hierarchy based upon the spatial extent of their influence (Grove 1972:560–561). In a settled region, extent of influence and size appear to be directly correlated (Jones 1966:87–88). Thus, settlements dominating as wide an area as a frontier town are likely to rank highly and be of a substantial size.

In terms of size, the frontier town should differ markedly from its European counterpart. The smaller size of the frontier town is related to the nature of colonial expansion, specifically the rapid spread and consequent widely dispersed settlement pattern and low population density. In the traditional process of European settlement evolution, a settlement's relative status as a center for socioeconomic activity is tied to its population density and economic complexity, so that settlement growth may be seen as a reflection of urban function (Fox 1973:76). The frontier town, however, comes into existence very rapidly. It does not arise solely to integrate settlements economically within a specified area on an intraregional basis, but also serves to tie such settlements into the network of a complex and far-reaching inter-regional economic system. The frontier town is established as an economic center without having first passed through a series of intermediate growth stages and without taking on the roles and the forms of less complex settlement types. Consequently, the frontier town need not be as large as an English market town. It is not necessarily a population center that assumed urban functions but a market center set up primarily to coordinate social, economic, and political activities.

It may be best to view a frontier town as part of a larger, dispersed social entity. It serves as the nexus of the socially integrating institutions of the area of colonization. The notion of *community* in an anthropological sense, defined as the basic unit of organization and transmission within a society and its culture (Arensberg 1961: 248), is useful in dealing with a settlement of this type. Arensberg's definition stresses function rather than form and sees the community in an organizational rather than a spatial sense as, for example, does Murdock (1949:79). Thus, a community may include more than a single settlement and its form may even vary periodically according to the adaptive mode of the particular society (Trigger 1968:60–61). A frontier town seems to represent the focal point of a dispersed community, the limits of which are somewhat difficult to define. Yet, within it, primary subsistence production and, to a large extent residence, lies outside the area of nucleated settlement.

If we view the frontier town as a part of a community that is a regional economic, social, and political center, then its form and content are likely to vary from those associated with communities of similar function in Europe. Material manifestations of these differences are set forth below in the form of archaeological test implications for size, layout, and content. Together the implications embody characteristics that should permit the identification of the frontier town as an entity by distinguishing diagnostic elements of its internal patterning.

Size

The size of a settlement is related to the activities carried out there and to the distribution of persons normally involved with them. The larger, localized supporting population associated with market towns in Europe should not be present in the frontier town. An abundance of land on the frontier and an absence of a need for defense of cooperative subsistence activities in the frontier town fail to provide the adaptive pressures that commonly resulted in the concentrated settlement pattern of European towns (Page 1927:450). Consequently, the frontier town should be smaller than its European counterparts with fewer structures and activities in its area of concentrated settlement.

Settlement size may be determined archaeologically by observing the number of structures and activity areas. The number of structures in a frontier town in eighteenth-century British North America is presumed to be less than the low end of the range of structures found in functionally comparable settlements in England. Comparative information on the size of eighteenth century English market towns indicates that these settlements varied greatly in size. While provincial centers such as Liverpool and Bristol engaged in extensive overseas trade and respectively supported populations of 60,000 and 50,000 persons by midcentury, medium-size towns like Leicester, Northampton, and Exeter contained less than 12,000. Smaller centers supporting only periodic markets often had populations ranging from 800 to several thousand (Patten 1973:129–130). A rough conversion of these figures to the number of structures in a given settlement may be made by dividing the mean family size of 4.75 (Laslett 1972:126) into the total population of the settlement, assuming that most structures housed at least a single family. The results of this computation with regard to the settlements mentioned above indicate that the number of structures ranged from 168 to 12,630. These figures agree with those derived by F. M. Eden (1973:32–33, Table 8), who in 1800 published an estimate of the number of houses in contemporary English towns. His figures show a range from 116 to 12,000.

Within the frontier towns of colonial South Carolina, however, the population and consequently the number of structures are likely to have been less than those in the smallest English market towns. An examination of maps of contemporary frontier towns in North Carolina provides comparative information about the size range of similar eighteenth century frontier settlements. Three inland settlements, Cross Creek, Halifax, and Salisbury contained respectively 46, 50, and 28 structures (Merrens 1964:157; Sautier 1769a, 1770a,b), whereas the coastal settlement of Brunswick consisted of about 40 buildings (Sautier 1769b). The size of these settlements falls well below the range of English market towns and provides an estimated range to aid in the identification of similar settlements in South Carolina.

The size of sites of colonial-period settlements is evidenced by the number of standing structures and ruins as well as their subsurface material remains. Counting structures on the basis of aboveground evidence is straightforward; however, identifying subsurface remains has required the use of various archaeological techniques capable of defining building locations. Archaeological investigations have been carried out at the sites of a number of colonial period settlements and have employed several aerially extensive techniques capable of delineating site boundaries and structural evidence. These include the stripping of large areas to uncover foundations and other features not discernible in other types of excavations in order to reveal spatial relationships over large areas (South 1971b:48). Employing stratified, systematic, unaligned testing and other techniques to sample archaeological sites has yielded functionally significant patterns of artifact occurrence, the form of which has been linked to the distribution of structures and activities in past settlements (Lewis 1980a). Finally, the survey of sites using proton magnetometry and soil resistivity techniques has helped define site boundaries and isolate structural remains for intensive examination (Peters 1982; Ralph and Borstling 1965; South 1982). The results of these investigations have produced data useful in defining frontier towns and other types of colonial settlements in early South Carolina.

Three settlements have been found to fall within the assumed size range of frontier towns. They are the coastal settlements of Georgetown and Beaufort and the inland town of Camden (Fig. 8.1). The first two settlements lie within the present cities of the same names and, in the absence of archaeological work there, must be identified solely by the presence of eighteenth century structures and cemeteries. Figures 6.2 and 6.3 show that 41 colonial-period structures are present in George-town and 20 remain in Beaufort. These structures are likely to represent only a portion of those originally found in the eighteenth-century settlements. Without an extensive archaeological examination of both townsites, the actual sizes of these early settlements cannot be determined. If the remaining structures represent even

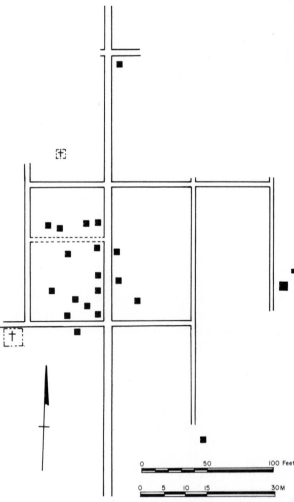

FIGURE 8.1 Camden, showing the locations of structures and cemeteries discernible through material evidence. (Source: see text.)

two-thirds of those in existence at any one time during the colonial period, both settlements would fall within the range of contemporary frontier towns.

The settlement of Camden has been analyzed on the basis of archaeological data alone. In order to ascertain the number of structures and activity areas in Camden, all accessible parts of the site (about 75% of the town's area) were examined utilizing an exploration technique designed to gather a representative sample of the archaeological materials distributed over this area. A stratified systematic unaligned sampling technique was chosen in order to achieve a maximum dispersal of the sample units within this area (Haggett 1966:196–198). Redman and Watson (1970:281–282) suggest that this technique is the best for revealing overall artifact patterning because it prevents the clustering of sample units and assures that no parts of the survey area are left unsampled. It is capable of discovering patterning in the archaeological record occurring both at regular and irregular intervals. It accomplishes this by dividing the area to be sampled into a series of square units (strata) based upon the coordinates of the site grid and then sampling a smaller unit within each stratum. The positions of the smaller units are determined by the intersection of coordinates selected along both axes of the grid from a random numbers table. The relative sizes of the units involved determine the percentage of the site area sampled. Naturally the greater the size of the sample the more reliable will be the results; however, the difficulty of enlarging the sample increases in direct proportion to the size of the site.

At Camden, a sample of 1% of the site contents were recovered. In order to observe the occurrence of activity patterning within the settlement as a whole, it is necessary to interpolate the frequencies of archaeological variables across the entire site. This may be done using SYMAP to generate contour maps depicting the relative counts or weights of particular artifact classes.

Structure locations at Camden were observed by mapping the distribution of architecturally related materials across the site. This class of artifacts would include bricks, nails, window glass, and other items associated with the construction of buildings. Even where extensive demolition of a structure has occurred, the distribution of these artifacts has been found to provide adequate evidence of its existence (Carrillo et al. 1975:57; Lewis 1975b:67–70).

Archaeological investigations at Camden uncovered evidence of 17 structures in the accessible portion of the settlement. It is estimated that as many as eight more may be covered by modern construction (Lewis 1976:102). In addition to the structures identified in the sampling excavations, several more were discovered nearby through the use of magnetometer and geohm surveys (Ralph and Borstling 1965) followed by intensive archaeological investigations (Calmes 1968; Lewis 1976, 1977a, 1981; Strickland 1971). Three structures were uncovered in these excavations, bringing the total estimated number of buildings in colonial Camden to about 28. Two colonial-period cemeteries lie adjacent to the settlement as well (Fig. 8.1). With at least 30 structures and activity areas, Camden's size also falls within the range of frontier towns in the region. Its size suggests that Camden, like Georgetown and Beaufort, served as frontier towns in South Carolina.

Layout

The function of a settlement is reflected in part by the patterned layout of its structures and activities. Market towns of eighteenth-century England grew from earlier smaller settlements and accumulated large supporting populations. Growth had brought pressure on land in these settlements, resulting in a contiguous arrangement of their structures. The layout of these medieval towns developed around a haphazard arrangement of streets organized around such central elements as the marketplace, church, or castle (Jones 1966:45). Open spaces were usually associated with these foci of activity and would themselves become a central element in the planned towns of the Renaissance (Zucker 1959:79).

The development of conscious city planning in Europe after the midfifteenth century introduced the regular polygon as a basic unit for organizing the layout of new settlements. One of the most common forms employed in the design of planned towns was the gridiron. This pattern focused on a square in the center of the town into which roads entered at a right angle. Government buildings, church lands, and markets were usually situated just off the central square. Perhaps because of its simplicity, the gridiron plan was employed in towns established in newly occupied areas of Europe. English colonial settlements in Ireland were also laid out along gridiron plans with a central square, and this plan subsequently appeared in larger seventeenth-century settlements in British North America (Price 1968:39; Reps 1965:177, 1972:22).

Because of its popularity and simplicity, it is likely that the gridiron plan would have been employed in the design of settlements in colonial South Carolina. Its use, however, would have varied with the settlement's function on the frontier. As we have seen, the complexity of frontier settlements is related to their size. The necessity for organizing settlement in a gridiron layout, or other regular pattern, varies with its size and density of population. A regular layout permits greater access by a maximum number of people to a town's major thoroughfares. A settlement having a sizable population is likely to have been arranged in this manner. Colonial settlements, however, usually lacked the large supporting populations of their European counterparts, and only the largest would have required a regular arrangement of its structures to accommodate its inhabitants and activities.

The entrepôt and its subsidiary frontier towns constitute the largest settlements in a frontier region and are the most likely to support an occupation dense enough to require the planned allocation of space. An examination of colonial plats in neighboring North Carolina supports this assumption. It reveals that a gridiron pattern formed the basis for the layout for the entrepôt of Wilmington (Sautier 1969c); the frontier towns of Halifax, Cross Creek, and Salisbury; and the port of Brunswick. These settlements correspond in size roughly to their counterparts in South Carolina and it is anticipated that the latter will share a similar layout.

The entrepôt of Charleston and the ports of Beaufort and Georgetown have been examined largely through their architectural remains. The distribution of standing colonial period structures and other material evidence at these three sites clearly reveals that each of these settlements was laid out on a gridiron pattern (Figs.

6.1–6.3). At Camden, the layout of settlement is reflected by the distribution of structural remains in the archaeological record alone. Here also a grid pattern is indicated by the orientation of structural artifact clusters along three roads lying at right angles to one another and by the alignment of nearby structural remains along the axes of this grid (Fig. 8.1).

All three of the settlements identified as frontier towns on the basis of size exhibit a layout assumed to be associated with major centers in a colonial region. This layout is apt to reveal not only the denser populations found in these settlements, but also the greater number of activities concentrated there. The extent of such activities has been touched upon briefly in the discussion of the entrepôt and is elaborated below in an analysis of the content of frontier towns.

Content

Frontier towns serve as centers of specialized economic, political, and social activity within the area of colonization and should exhibit evidence of such in their material record. Because specialized activities are also found in the entrepôt and some nucleated settlements, evidence of their occurrence alone may not permit the three types of frontier settlements to be distinguished from one another. Their absence, however, would preclude a settlement's having been a frontier town or an entrepôt.

The extent to which specialized activities dominated life in a frontier town is likely to be manifested in the archaeological record, but the nature of the evidence is likely to be varied. Many of the processing and small-scale manufacturing activities associated with frontier agricultural production would normally have been situated away from settlements to be near sources of raw materials or water power (Thirsk 1973:103). Frontier towns are more likely to have contained structures for the storage and transfer of both raw agricultural commodities and finished imported goods as well as repair and maintenance facilities linked to such commercial activities. Central political and religious activities should also have taken place within the frontier town where the confluence of trade and communications routes would have occurred. Although the frontier town would have had a much smaller supporting population than its European counterparts, the resident occupation of the former is still likely to have been substantial, and these settlements would have included much space devoted to domestic activities.

ARCHITECTURAL EVIDENCE

If we assume that most activities were associated with structures, then it should be possible to identify the presence of such activities by analyzing the architecture of standing structures or ruins and by examining the contents of activity areas lying adjacent to them. Of the three settlements tentatively identified as frontier towns, Georgetown and Beaufort are represented only by standing structures, while Camden is known only through its archaeological remains. Architectural evidence in the first two settlements revealed several specialized activity structures in each. These reflect the occurrence of centralizing economic and religious activities here. Colonial-period political structures are absent in Georgetown; however, the presence of a fort near Beaufort suggests a government administrative presence here. In both settlements, specialized activity structures represent a minority of the total surviving buildings, 20% or less. The remainder of the structures were built to serve a domestic function. Because these results are based solely on counts of standing structures, the circumstances of whose survival are uncertain, it is difficult to determine if the relative proportion of domestic to specialized activities accurately reflects that prevalent in the colonial-period settlements. The presence of a substantial component of specialized activity loci within each settlement does conform to the expectation for the content of frontier towns.

ARCHAEOLOGICAL EVIDENCE

Unlike Beaufort and Georgetown, the locations of all colonial-period structures in Camden and its immediate vicinity have been ascertained. Because of the extensive nature of the archaeological excavations there, only small portions of the site have been excavated in detail. Architectural data helpful in defining function are unavailable for much of Camden, and the identification of activities is based on an analysis of the contents of individual activity areas. These areas have been defined on the basis of the occurrence of subsurface features, formed as a result of both domestic and specialized activities, in relation to structural features. These activities would have been characterized by two basic disposal modes, dumping and maintenance–storage. Each is associated with a different type of archaeological feature.

Studies of medieval and postmedieval living sites in England have shown that such sites were used generally for the disposal of refuse which was buried in pits or scattered on the surface (Hurst 1971:116). A similar pattern of disposal has been noted in English colonial sites in North America (South 1977:47–48). In addition to their use for disposal, activity areas were heavily utilized in connection with the function of their associated structures. These areas usually contained outbuildings in which activities were concentrated and tools and materials were stored. Such outbuildings might include privies, wells, wagon sheds, workshops, storage sheds, barns, warehouses, and general purpose sheds (Hurst 1971:115; Noël Hume 1969; Sloane 1967). Archaeological evidence of such outbuildings may consist of regular pits, if the building extended below the surface in the manner of a privy, and postholes dug to secure the supporting members of structures. Concentration of structural materials or foundations may be present if an outbuilding was of substantial construction, and it is possible that some of the structures defined on the basis of architectural materials represent such structures.

A comparison of the distribution of pit and posthole features with the pattern of structural remains at Camden was produced by combining SYMAPS of these three variables (Fig. 8.2). It reveals 10 clusters of these features, which implies the existence of as many activity areas. They permit the site of Camden to be divided into smaller units for the purpose of activity analysis (Lewis 1976:107).

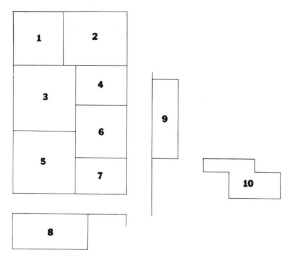

FIGURE 8.2   Plan of structure-based activity areas at Camden. (Source: Lewis 1976:107.)

Intrasite Activity Variation   To isolate domestic and specialized activity areas at Camden, it has been necessary to predict patterns assumed to be associated with the domestic–nondomestic functions of the site. These patterns are based on relationships between classes of artifacts and activities linked to these functions.

A domestic occupation in an eighteenth-century urban British colonial site should be associated with a specific group of domestic related activities involved with the production, preparation, consumption, and distribution of subsistence products. These activities comprise a subsistence activity set centered upon a structure. The archaeological record of a domestic occupation may be expected to represent the by-products of this activity set. A commercial, industrial, or other nondomestic activity area would involve a technological activity set that results from the manufacture, repair, modification, storage, and shipment of goods and commodities. It may be expected to contain evidence of activities related to the movement of goods and commodities rather than to these products themselves. Industrial structures likewise should not be characterized by the finished goods they produced but by the presence of by-products of manufacturing processes and perhaps distinctive architectural form. It must be remembered that nondomestic structures, especially those situated within a nucleated settlement, are likely to have served as living quarters for those who worked there. Therefore, such a structure is apt to include some elements of both subsistence and technological activity sets, and its by-products will reflect this dual nature.

The archaeological record does not yield a total inventory of past activities but only the residue of such activities resulting from the operation of cultural formation processes. At Camden these processes would most likely include discard and loss. One may assume that loss is related to artifact size and portability and discard is a function of the fragility of the artifact given normal use and the degree of lateral cycling and recycling that it may undergo during its normal use life (Shiffer 1972:158–159). If true, it should be possible to predict the general types of artifacts that form the by-products of various past activities.

As the surviving by-product of domestic and specialized activity sets, the archaeological record should permit observation of the occurrence of these sets among Camden's activity areas. If each area contains the refuse produced by one or more of the sets, then we may assume that the relationship between the artifacts associated with each set will reflect statistically the functional difference between the areas' occupations (see Schiffer 1976:64). It is expected that the proportional relationship between functionally significant groups of artifacts varies according to the nature of the activity that produced them. In order to distinguish between domestic and specialized activity sets, three activity categories have been constructed. They include *Subsistence* activities, which are likely to occur in the context of a domestic activity areas; *Subsistence–Technological* activities, which may occur in areas that supported both a domestic and nondomestic occupation; and *Technological* activities, which would have taken place only in a nondomestic, specialized activity context. The artifact classes associated with these categories and the relationship of both to the domestic and specialized activity sets are summarized in Table 8.1.

It is assumed that artifact deposited together are the by-products of a single activity or group of related activities. Their rate, and hence relative amount, of deposition is expected to vary with the nature of the activity that produced it. For example, domestic household activities and some types of manufacturing such as potting, brickmaking, or smithing, would be characterized by a substantial discard of waste material (South 1963, 1967, 1977:47–48). Light industries producing a perishable by-product or activities concerned with the transfer, repackaging, storage, or exchange of goods or commodities, on the other hand, are not likely to leave behind a substantial residue of either discarded or lost material. In the case of most

TABLE 8.1 Activity sets, subsistence activity categories, and associated artifact classes

Activity sets	Activity category	Activity class
Domestic	Subsistence	Food storage containers Food processing tools Cooking and eating utensils Floral and faunal remains Fishing and hunting equipment
Specialized	Subsistence–Technological	Architectural artifacts Personal artifacts
	Technological	Tools Processing equipment Storage containers

specialized activities, it is probable that all usable tools and equipment were valued too highly to deliberately discard into the archaeological record. It is probable that the distinguishing characteristics of a specialized technological activity might not consist of a high-frequency occurrence of specialized artifacts. Rather, the presence or absence of these items themselves might be more meaningful. In a small sample, such as that examined at Camden, technological artifacts are likely to represent only a small portion of the total artifacts recovered unless high discard output activities were present. The probability of sampling error is high when the expected occurrence of a particular class of items is low. Therefore, it seems best not to rely entirely upon this class of data to identify the presence of a nondomestic occupation.

The low rate of deposition of specialized activity artifacts makes the statistical measurement of Technological activity occurrence difficult. Further, it gives the Subsistence category may be used to measure the intensity of the domestic component. It is assumed that the Subsistence–Technological component of an area will remain constant regardless of the activity performed there. Thus, the larger the existence of a particular Technological activity; however, its size relative to the subsistence category may be used to measure the intensity of the domestic component. It is assumed that the Subsistence–Technological component of an area will remain constant regardless of the activity performed there. Thus, the larger the relative size of the Subsistence activity category, the greater the likelihood that the domestic activity set constituted the major activity in that particular area. An area characterized by this activity set very likely contained a domestic occupation. Conversely, the smaller the relative size of the Subsistence activity category, the less likely the domestic activity set is to represent the principal activity there. Because we are concerned with discovering the presence of a nondomestic, specialized occupation that is characterized chiefly by the absence of an archaeological by-product of its own, it is logical to expect that evidence of a Technological activity set indicative of such an occupation will constitute a minor part of the archaeological record. The presence of a specialized activity occupation, then, is likely to be evidenced by the reduced size of the area's Subsistence activity component.

Activity Variation at Camden We may now examine the relative occurrence of artifacts by activity category at Camden. The numerical counts and percentages of these artifacts by area are shown in Table 8.2. An examination of the percentage frequencies of the three categories reveals wide variation in the frequencies of the two larger categories (Subsistence and Subsistence–Technological), together with very low percentages in the Technological artifact category. When compared graphically (Fig. 8.3) the percentages of the two major categories cluster into three groups.

The first group of areas exhibits a high frequency of Subsistence artifacts (79–81%) and a lower frequency of Subsistence–Technological artifacts (18–20%). Technological artifacts total no more than 1% of the artifacts in any area. On the basis of this relationship, it is possible to assign a domestic occupation to Areas 2, 3, and 6.

The second group includes Areas 1, 4, 7, 9, and 10. Here the percentage of

TABLE 8.2   Companion of Activity Categories by Area at Camden[a]

Activity category	Area										Total
	1	2	3	4	5	6	7	8	9	10	
					COUNTS						
Subsistence	813	4191	3782	1311	1693	2130	1665	1316	1119	651	18671
Subsistence–Technological	317	1088	874	461	825	478	612	841	392	224	6112
Technological	20	48	25	20	1	18	42	29	38	3	244
	1150	5327	4681	1792	2519	2626	2319	2186	1549	878	25027
					PERCENTAGES						
Subsistence	71	79	81	73	67	81	72	60	72	74	75
Subsistence–Technological	28	20	19	26	33	18	26	38	25	26	24
Technological	2	1	1	1	0	1	2	1	2	0	1
	101	100	101	100	100	100	100	99	99	100	100

[a] Source: Lewis (1976:124).

Subsistence artifacts is somewhat lower (71–74%), whereas that of Subsistence–Technological artifacts is higher than in the previous group (25–28%). Technological artifacts range from less than 1% to 2% of the totals. Although the relative relationship of the two larger artifact categories is similar to that in the first group, the areas in the second group form a distinct cluster apart from those in the first. No intermediate areas are present (Fig. 8.3). For this reason, it is possible to identify tentatively these areas as sites of less intense domestic occupations, which perhaps represents combination residence–businesses.

The third group is composed of two areas (5 and 8) that contain a sizably lower percentage of Subsistence artifacts (60 and 67%) and a much higher percentage of Subsistence–Technological artifacts (33 and 38%). Technological artifacts constitute no more than 1% of the totals. The marked difference between these areas and the other two groups is clearly discernible in Figure 8.3. The relative frequencies of the artifact categories in these areas suggests the presence of a greatly reduced domestic occupation as might be anticipated in an industrial area. The absence of manufacturing debris seems to preclude the presence of an industry characterized by a nonperishable by-product. It is probable that the two areas represent the remains of a specialized, nondomestic occupation of an unknown type (Lewis 1976:122–126).

A comparison of the percentage frequencies of functionally significant artifact categories has resulted in the division of the 10 areas defined by the sample excavations at Camden into three groups. Although we cannot identify precisely the activities revealed by the archaeological remains in each area, it has been possible to distinguish those areas that contain a high Subsistence artifact component. They would appear to be the by-product of domestic occupation areas. The second group of areas contains a relatively smaller percentage frequency of Subsistence artifacts. Although this material also was probably generated by a domestic occupation, the latter is likely to have shared the area with another nondomestic activity. In the two areas falling into the third group, the domestic occupation seems to have comprised an even smaller portion of the total activities there. This last group of areas is likely to represent specialized activities, the presence of which is crucial to the identification of Camden as a frontier town.

In addition to the main area of the settlement examined through the use of sampling, several adjacent areas were intensively explored. Architectural remains found in these areas are shown in Figure 8.4. All are identifiable as to function. The southernmost area contained the foundations of a brick structure the form of which identifies it as a magazine used for the storage of munitions. Two earthen redoubts lay northeast and southwest of the settlement, which was surrounded by a palisade wall (Calmes 1968; Strickland 1971). Two structures situated just east of the settlement were also surrounded by a single palisade wall. The presence of these military features indicates that Camden was heavily fortified against attack, a situation that was not shared by other colonial-period settlements in this part of the South Carolina interior. The military structures have produced ceramic collections that indi-

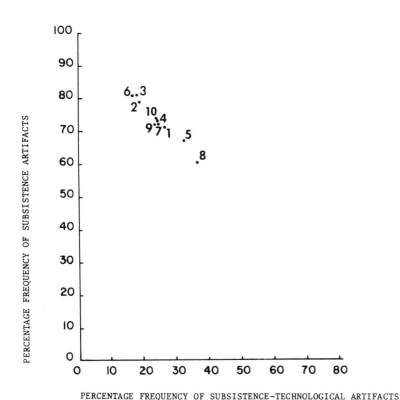

FIGURE 8.3 Activity areas at Camden by occurrence of Subsistence and Subsistence–Technological artifacts. (Source: Lewis 1976:125.)

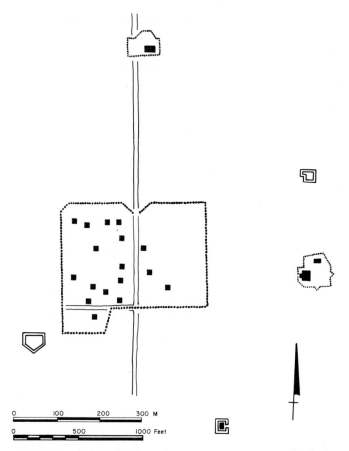

FIGURE 8.4 Military features and contemporary structures at Camden as revealed by archaeological evidence. (Sources: see text.)

cate all were occupied for only a short period in the 1780s (Lewis 1977b; Strickland 1971), a time corresponding to the period of the American Revolutionary War. Because these specialized activity structures represent only a short segment of the settlement's history, they would not have played an integral part of its long-term role as a frontier town. Their presence does suggest that Camden's position was central enough to have permitted it to serve as a fortified military base for a wide region. A frontier town lying within an area of military operations is likely to have been used for such a purpose.

The area surrounded by the palisade wall just east of the settlement contains two large structures and an adjacent activity area encompassing several outbuildings and other features. The foundations are those of domestic structures, a saddlebag house and a double house (Lewis 1977b:77).

The remaining structure was situated north of Camden. Only a portion of this building has been investigated; however, the configuration of its exposed foundation is similar to that found in public buildings in England and other parts of British North America (Holschlag *et al.* 1978; Lewis 1981). On the basis of this limited architectural information it is possible to identify the site of this structure as a specialized activity area.

If we ignore for the moment the temporary military structures, we find that the archaeological investigations have produced evidence of two domestic and one specialized activity areas. This increases the total probable domestic areas to 10 and the specialized activity areas to three. If one included the two eighteenth-century cemeteries situated adjacent to the early settlement (CR) within the latter group, specialized activity areas may be seen to have constituted about one third of the areas. The relative importance of such activities in this settlement conforms to the expectation for a frontier town and implies that Camden functioned in this role during the eighteenth century.

In our discussion of settlement content, it was predicted that because a frontier town is a socioeconomic center in an area of colonization, a substantial component of specialized, nondomestic activity areas would be present in the sites of these settlements. Surveys of architecture in Georgetown and Beaufort and extensive archaeological investigations at Camden revealed that each of the settlements possessed such a component. The proportion of each site's activities thus supports the identification of the three settlements as frontier towns.

Status

The central role of the frontier town in trade and communications activities and the administration of the colonial region is likely to have made such settlements home to individuals involved in the buying, selling, and processing of goods and commodities as well as those persons holding local political office on the frontier. If such individuals resided in the frontier towns of South Carolina, it is expected that the structures or living areas they occupied would yield archaeological evidence reflecting their high socioeconomic status. In a stratified society, status is usually associated with the unequal distribution of scarce goods and services. Evidence of this differential allocation should be readily discernible in the material record.

ARCHITECTURE

One of the best indicators of status is architecture. Structures inhabited by wealthy individuals in an eighteenth-century British colony are likely to have emulated contemporary styles of architecture fashionable in the homeland. These styles have been discussed in detail earlier and include both the Palladian double house and the colonial single house. They are relatively large structures with distinctive floor plans that should make their presence easily distinguishable as standing structures or archaeological features. In Georgetown and Beaufort an analysis must focus on the architecture of standing structures alone, but at Camden a study of architectural remains must be supplemented by other types of material data.

A survey of architectural evidence in the three settlements produced ample support for the presence of high-status individuals in Georgetown, Beaufort, and Camden. In the first two settlements, both single and double houses exist among the surviving buildings shown in Figures 6.2 and 6.3 (NRF). At Camden, the Kershaw house site, situated just east of the colonial settlement (Fig. 8.2), yielded the remains of a double house of substantial size (Lewis 1977b:37). Architectural similarities with a contemporary structure in Charleston and graphic evidence of the building prior to its destruction in the nineteenth century permitted the reconstruction of the Kershaw house as an example of an early high-status dwelling on the frontier (Fig. 8.5).

PORTABLE ARTIFACTS

Archaeological investigations in Camden are likely to have produced evidence of additional high-status occupations in the frontier settlement. One form of evidence consists of portable artifacts associated with this social class. If we assume that such items are likely to be found in areas frequented by high-status persons, then the distribution of such artifacts should provide a key to identifying those areas. Unlike architecture and other permanent landscape features, portable high-status artifacts are transferred into the archaeological record in a somewhat more complicated manner. This is because these items are usually highly valued objects that are subject to a high rate of retention. For this reason, the occurrence of such items in the

FIGURE 8.5 Replica of the Kershaw house reconstructed on the site of the original structure in 1976. This building is an unusual example of the Palladian double house in a rural setting in the South Carolina interior. (Author's photograph.)

archaeological record is not usually the result of discard or abandonment as is often the case with less valuable artifacts. Rather, their appearance there is nearly always a consequence of loss. With regard to the process of loss, Schiffer (1976:32) suggests that certain regularities are likely to affect the probability of an object's entering the archaeological record. First, the probability of loss should vary inversely with the object's mass. Small objects are more likely lost than larger ones. Second, loss probability varies directly with the artifact's portability. An item more frequently moved or moved longer distances is more likely lost than one that is stationary. It may be added that the probability of loss is also directly related to its usable condition as the result of age or wear. Thus, a worn-out valuable is more likely to be exposed to conditions leading to loss than a new one.

One class of artifact that would fall into the category of small, portable items subject to wear is that of personal objects, especially those associated with dress. In the last half of the eighteenth century, a great disparity existed in the nature of Englishmen's dress. This was closely tied to the individual's status. In general, persons of higher status wore elaborate costumes adorned with fasteners of precious metals in contrast to the relatively simple dress of lower-status commoners (Steel and Trout 1904/I:327–328). Because of the perishable nature of clothing, only certain parts such as buttons, buckles, and other fasterners are likely to be retained in the archaeological record. Due to their generally small size, these items most probably represent loss or, if worn, discard. These artifacts should be particularly indicative of status because the materials of which they were manufactured seem to have varied according to the wealth of the wearer. Buttons, for example, were made of a variety of materials including lead, bone, pewter, brass, glass, and wood (see Olsen 1963; South 1964), but those worn by higher-status individuals would more likely have been of silver, silver plate, or pearl (Steel and Trout 1904/I:319, 328). Similarly, clothing buckles were made of materials ranging from iron for the cheapest buckles to pewter, brass, and silver, the latter being associated with persons of wealth and higher status (Abbitt 1973:26; Noël Hume 1970:86). It is predicted that the occurrence of high-status clothing and personal items will identify high-status living areas on the site.

An examination of the archaeological data from Camden provides the following results. The patterned distribution of high-status artifacts in the archaeological record is clearly discernible due to the small number of items falling into this category. Four artifacts of assumed high intrinsic value were recovered in the archaeological excavations. Area 2 contained a silver-plated brass button with an engraved floral design on its face (see South 1964:117, Type 7). A worn silver cane tip with the initials *RH* engraved on its head was also recovered from this location. The second area containing high-status artifacts is Area 6, where a brass button (Type 7) engraved with the initials *GB* and a silver-plated brass button (Type 7) were recovered. On the basis of the occurrence of these objects, Areas 2 and 6 may be identified as high-status locations (Lewis 1976:128–129). Excavations at the Kershaw house site yielded 24 high-status items, including stemware fragments, wig curlers, and silver objects (Lewis 1977b:89).

CERAMIC VARIETY

High economic status within a stratified society is usually correlated directly with the variety of property possessed by persons in that society (Tumin 1967:40). The variety of property may be expressed in terms of the addition of wealth goods to the normal assemblage of artifacts associated with a domestic occupation. Such items are discussed elsewhere. Perhaps of greater significance is the relative diversity of items within use classes of artifacts. Such classes are common to all socioeconomic levels, but the greater diversity of artifacts within them is likely to be correlated directly with higher status.

A class of artifacts having a potential for great diversity is ceramics. The range of variation here reflects differences in form and function, both of which vary with the socioeconomic status of the owner. The association of high-status and large, diverse ceramic holdings is noted in colonial inventories (Brown 1973:60). It is predicted that an increase in the variation in type and quantity of ceramic specimens is directly related to the status of the persons who occupied the area in which the specimens are found (Deetz 1973:20).

The relative variety of ceramic types may be examined by comparing the total number of ceramic types recovered from each area. Table 8.3 shows that of the 31 ceramic types present at Camden, the number appearing in individual areas varies from 19 to 29. This range forms two clusters, the first containing areas possessing from 19 to 22 types and the second containing areas with 25 to 29 types. Four areas (1, 4, 8, and 10) fall into the first group and seven areas (2, 3, 5, 6, 7, 9, and the Kershaw house site) may be included in the second. This nearly equal division of the areas suggests that the ceramic variety criterion may be somewhat less sensitive to high economic status and instead tends to separate wealth at a lower level. The inclusion of Areas 2 and 6 in the upper status locations based on ceramic variety is significant in that it supports the results obtained from the distribution of high-status artifacts.

EVIDENCE OF LOW STATUS

Just as it is possible to observe a correlation between high status and artifacts of greater value, it is equally reasonable to postulate an inverse correlation between the occurrence of artifacts of low value and a high-status occupation. Rather than being artifacts of specialized function, as are many of the items associated with high-status individuals, artifacts related to low-status persons are likely to be common items in widespread use. They may be differentiated mainly by the presence of certain distinguishable forms which for social, political, or religious purposes are restricted to use by low-status persons.

An example of a class of artifacts to which a status distinction might apply is locally made ceramics. Despite the apparent availability of imported English ceramic products, locally made American ceramics were manufactured, often in the face of official government policy, and managed to compete favorably with the British products they imitated. The lower cost of local pottery would have made it a less-

TABLE 8.3 Comparison of ceramic type occurrence by area at Camden[a]

Ceramic type	\ Toft area										Kershaw house
	1	2	3	4	5	6	7	8	9	10	
Lead-glazed slipware		x	x	x	x	x	x	x	x	x	x
Ironstone-whiteware	x	x	x	x	x	x	x	x	x	x	x
Mocha		x						x			x
Jackfield ware			x		x	x	x	x	x	x	x
Bisque earthenware		x	x			x			x		x
Coarse red earthenware	x	x	x	x	x	x	x		x		x
Delft	x	x	x	x	x	x	x	x	x	x	x
Creamware	x	x	x	x	x	x	x	x	x	x	x
Finger-painted creamware					x						x
Annular creamware	x	x	x	x	x	x	x	x	x	x	x
Overglazed enameled creamware	x	x	x	x	x	x	x	x	x		x
Transfer-printed creamware		x	x		x		x				x
Pearlware	x	x	x	x	x	x	x	x	x	x	x
Underglaze polychrome pearlware	x	x	x	x	x	x	x	x	x	x	x
Finger-painted pearlware		x	x		x	x	x		x	x	x
Transfer-printed pearlware	x	x	x	x	x	x	x	x	x	x	x
Annular pearlware	x	x	x	x	x	x	x	x		x	x
Hand-painted pearlware	x		x	x	x	x	x	x	x	x	x
Edged pearlware	x	x	x	x	x	x	x	x	x	x	x
Carolina creamware	x	x	x	x	x	x	x	x	x	x	x
Nottingham stoneware		x	x	x	x	x	x	x	x	x	
British brown stoneware	x	x	x	x	x	x	x	x	x	x	x
Westerwald stoneware	x	x	x	x	x	x	x	x	x	x	x
White salt-glazed stoneware	x	x	x		x	x	x	x	x	x	x
Scratch-blue stoneware		x	x	x	x	x	x	x	x		
Black balsaltes stoneware		x	x	x	x	x	x		x	x	x
Engine-turned stoneware	x	x			x	x	x			x	x
Brown stone bottles									x	x	
Porcelain	x	x	x	x	x	x	x	x	x	x	x
Colono ware	x	x	x	x	x	x	x	x	x	x	x
Total types present	19	26	26	22	29	26	26	22	25	22	27

[a] Source: Lewis (1976:130).

expensive alternative to imported ceramics (Noël Hume 1970:99), especially to those persons of lower economic status. The manufacture of good quality local cream-colored earthenware in South Carolina prior to the American Revolution found a ready market with the residents of this colonial region. The availability of local pottery here would have favored the widespread use of its products. Due to their lower cost, local ceramics probably composed a greater proportion of the ceramic inventories of persons of lower economic and social status. The lower relative occurrence of this artifact in the archaeological record should be directly associated with the presence of higher status occupations.

An examination of the frequency distribution of the percentages of Carolina

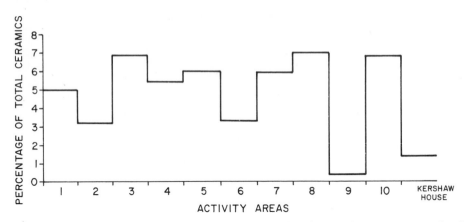

FIGURE 8.6 Relative frequencies of Carolina cream-colored earthenware by activity area at Camden. (Source: Lewis 1976:131.)

cream-colored earthenware to all ceramics by area (Fig. 8.6) clearly reveals a marked disparity in the occurrence of this artifact across the site. Four areas (Areas 2, 6, 9, and the Kershaw house site) exhibit a low frequency of locally made ceramics relative to the other areas in Camden. On this basis, it is possible to identify these areas as locations of high-status occupations in this colonial settlement (Lewis 1975c:36–42, 1976:169).

A comparison of archaeological remains from the site of Camden indicates that three areas are likely to have contained high-status occupations. Areas 2, 6, and the Kershaw house site yielded high-status artifacts as well as a wide variety of ceramic types and a low frequency of locally produced ceramics. The presence of the last two characteristics in Area 9 suggests that persons of high status also occupied this area in the past. Since all of these areas have been identified as sites of domestic activity, it seems likely that they represent high-status residences (Lewis 1976:132).

The archaeological data from Camden and the architectural data from Georgetown and Beaufort reveal the presence of a substantial high-status occupation in each of these colonial settlements. This confirms our expectation for frontier towns and provides further evidence that these settlements once served in that role.

Frontier towns on the South Carolina frontier are likely to have been characterized by a distinctive size, layout, and content and by the presence of high-status individuals. Although these characteristics may be found individually in other frontier settlement types, the combination of all four are unique to the frontier town and the entrepôt. In addition to the entrepôt of Charleston, the occurrence of these characteristics has been confined to three colonial settlements in South Carolina. They have permitted us to identify these frontier towns on the basis of their material record. The presence of frontier towns, in turn, identifies an important element in the settlement pattern associated with the insular frontier process.

HYPOTHESIS 9: NUCLEATED SETTLEMENTS ON THE FRONTIER

Nucleated settlements represent secondary centers of activity in the area of colonization. They generally rank below frontier towns in the settlement hierarchy of a colonial region because they are functionally less complex and their range of influence is more restricted. Although nucleated settlements are usually the focus of one or more specialized activities, the variety or extent of such activities in a frontier town is not present here. As a consequence of their more limited socioeconomic role, nucleated settlements should be noticably smaller in size and population. Like the frontier town, the nucleated settlement should have its functional counterpart in the metropolitan area from which useful comparisons regarding form and composition may be made. The nucleated settlement is expected to reflect its cultural heritage as well as any adaptive changes derived from its role.

The limited economic role of the nucleated settlement places it at a level of complexity below the frontier town. In a European urban hierarchy, it corresponds roughly with the village (Blouet 1972:4–5). Villages are defined as centrally placed settlements where intraregional exchange takes place on a regular basis. As a result of the need to manage such exchange, economic specialists and trading institutions develop and additional specialized activities may be supported by surpluses derived from this exchange. In addition to the agricultural village, which was the most common type in eighteenth century Europe, nonagricultural settlements were also present. Most were of two types. The first includes settlements that arose in areas of special resources and centered around activities such as mining, quarrying, or fishing. Such activities are unlikely to be of great significance in the economy of an insular frontier region like South Carolina. In areas of dispersed agricultural settlement, specialized, nonagricultural agglomerations often developed around isolated, usually noneconomic, centralizing institutions, such as a church, that were situated at crossroads or other points central to the areas they served (Flatres 1971:176–179).

The second type of nonagricultural rural settlement seems to share much in common with the nucleated settlements of an insular frontier region. While neither type possesses the substantial resident population of an agricultural village, each serves as a focal point for certain centralizing activities normally associated with it. The nucleated settlement, like the European rural agglomeration, has a relatively limited specialized function because it serves as an intraregional center in a region dominated by a larger settlement. The similarity between the nucleated settlement and this rural agglomeration seems to show a common adaptive response to a need for establishing integrating institutions in areas of dispersed agricultural population. Analogies drawn from the latter should be useful in studying its counterpart in insular frontier regions.

The function of the nucleated settlement should be manifested in the material record. Archaeological test implications regarding size, layout, and content are developed below. These focus on pertinent kinds of material patterning that should permit the identification of nucleated settlements on the South Carolina frontier. The sites of three colonial-period settlements which may have played this role have been identified on the basis of their archaeological remains. An analysis of their archaeological remains follows.

Size

Nucleated settlements on the frontier are smaller than frontier towns, reflecting their more limited socioeconomic role in the area of colonization. The size range of these settlements is uncertain but is apt to approximate that of functionally similar settlements in Europe and to be smaller than that of frontier towns. Specialized rural agglomerations in Europe were usually organized around a centralizing institution and consisted of structures housing activities related directly or indirectly to it. Often these settlements were not situated to assume an active role in the economic regions they served and were quite small. Such settlements acquired only a few additional structures, and these were related to the settlement's function as a site for public activities. Examples of ancillary structures would typically be an inn, a smithy, or a school (Flatres 1971:177). A settlement used as an economic center in an area of dispersed settlement is likely to be somewhat larger in order to accommodate the people and activities involved in trade. An examination of the archaeological record of colonial sites in South Carolina has revealed several sites whose size suggests that they were nucleated settlements.

Perhaps the most extensively investigated nucleated settlement is Ninety-Six (38GN1-5), situated in western South Carolina (Fig. 5.1). Archaeological investigations were conducted there between 1970 and 1976 (Holschlag et al. 1978; Holschlag and Rodeffer 1976a,b, 1977; South 1970a, 1971b, 1972b). This work was intended to uncover evidence of the eighteenth-century settlement as well as associated military features. It involved the use of extensive trenching to locate subsurface features followed by the subsequent removal of the overlying plow zone to expose them (Holschlag and Rodeffer 1977:44–47; South 1971b:39–40). Intensive excavations were confined to structural features defined in this manner. On the basis of such features and their accompanying building debris, nine structures were defined at Ninety-Six (Holschlag and Rodeffer 1976a:75–78; Holschlag et al. 1978:90–100; South 1971b). All are grouped in loose clusters around a crossroads formed by the intersection of two roadbeds (Fig. 8.7). Two military fortifications lie adjacent to Ninety-Six, and the defensive work connecting them appears to have encompassed the settlement (Holschlag et al. 1978:81–85). Most of the enclosed area has been explored archaeologically. Given the density of the settlement as a whole, the portion that has not been examined is likely to contain no more than three or four additional structures. In all, about a dozen buildings appear to have existed at Ninety-Six, substantially fewer than those found in the frontier towns and well within the size anticipated for nucleated settlements.

Another likely site of a nucleated settlement is Long Bluff (38DA5) on the Pee

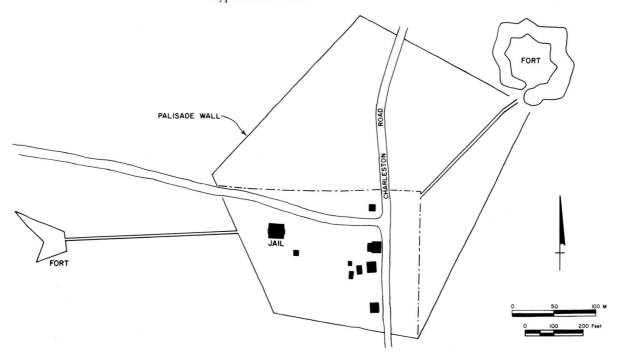

FIGURE 8.7 Ninety-Six, showing the locations of structures and other cultural features revealed by archaeological investigations. (Sources: see text.)

Dee River (Fig. 5.1). Extensive archaeological investigations were carried out there in 1974 and 1977 in an attempt to define the size and form of the colonial-period occupation. A portion of the site was explored by removing the topsoil in search of features. The remainder was examined through the use of various sampling techniques that included stratified, systematic, unaligned and systematic samples of the subsurface remains and a systematic sample of surface materials. Because of the exploratory nature of these excavations, which aimed at delineating overall patterns of distribution within the settlement, it was not possible to examine individual features, and intensive investigations were not carried out (Lewis 1975d; 1978:43–45).

An examination of the distribution of structural artifacts across the site revealed nine concentrations situated on both sides of a road leading to a river landing and one intersecting a road at the top of the bluff (Lewis 1978:66). The occupied area at Long Bluff, as defined by the distribution of nonstructural artifacts, does not appear to have extended far beyond the crossroads, and like Ninety-Six, the settlement appears to have been fairly restricted in size (Fig. 8.8). The number of structures also compares favorably with that at Ninety-Six and falls below that found in the frontier towns. On the basis of size, Long Bluff corresponds to our expectations for the nucleated settlement.

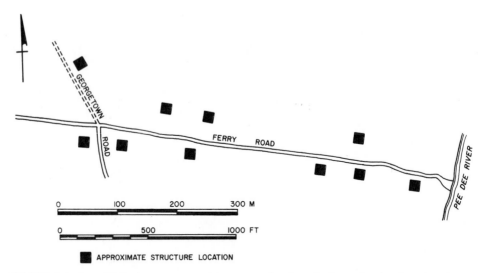

FIGURE 8.8 Long Bluff, showing structural locations inferred on the basis of archaeological evidence. (Source: Lewis 1978:67.)

The site of a third nucleated settlement is that of Pinckneyville (38UN1) in Union County (Fig. 5.1). It was examined extensively in 1971 through the excavation of a series of exploratory trenches in the vicinity of a standing structure and a number of visible ruins. The purpose of these excavations was to investigate as wide an area as possible so that the form and layout of the settlement might be determined (Carrillo 1972:25). Several areas were examined in the course of this work, but as in the case of Long Bluff, large-scale, intensive excavations were not carried out. It is estimated that approximately half of the settlement's occupied area was explored (Carrillo 1972:35).

The archaeological excavations at Pinckneyville uncovered the remains of six structures in addition to the one still standing (Fig. 8.9). All were clustered relatively close together as were structures in the other nucleated settlements. If the remaining unexcavated portion of the settlement contained an equal number of structures, Pinckneyville would have been a small settlement comparable in size to Ninety-Six and Long Bluff. Its estimated size of 12 buildings falls well below the limits of the frontier towns and within the expected range for nucleated settlements.

Layout

Just as the frontier town's layout reveals the influence of European traditions, the patterning of smaller frontier settlements is likely to have followed the form of their Old World counterparts. Specialized nonagricultural settlements performed a limited integrating function similar to that of nucleated settlements on the frontier. The former, imposed in isolated locations in Europe, were placed centrally within the areas they served, often at crossroads offering access in several directions (Flatres 1971:179). Perhaps the most common patterns of small settlements in such locations is the placement of structures along both sides of the roads (Page 1927:448). Beresford and St. Joseph (1958:126–127) observed that such "row settlements" offer the most compact form and provide equal access to the road for all inhabitants. It was an arrangement especially convenient in forested areas, such as much of eighteenth-century South Carolina, since it involved a minimum of clearing. Row settlements, in general, were confined to areas secure from hostilities, because their elongated form did not facilitate an easy defense. This form of settlement would have been well suited to the dispersed economy and relatively secure conditions present in much of the South Carolina frontier during the eighteenth century.

The function of a nucleated settlement appears related to its size, which is linked, in turn, to its layout. A comparison of the structure distributions at the sites of Ninety-Six, Long Bluff, and Pinckneyville (Figs. 8.7–8.9) reveals that each settle-

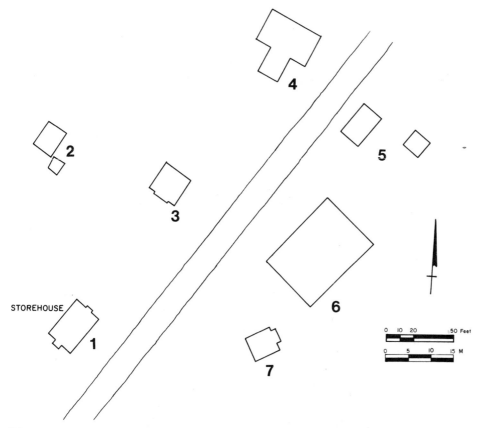

FIGURE 8.9 Pinckneyville, showing structures revealed by archaeological investigations. (Source: Carrillo 1972.)

ment consisted of a series of buildings placed along one or both sides of a road. Each site lies adjacent to a crossroads. The placement of structures along at least two of the intersecting roads suggests that the crossroads may have constituted the focus of activity for these settlements. In addition, Long Bluff, and Pinckneyville were situated near navigable water, the Pee Dee and Broad rivers respectively, which provided an additional route of access to these settlements.

Ninety-Six is unique among the three in that it represents a row settlement that was fortified. The awkward form of the defensive works, designed to enclose a linear settlement, show that the latter was not originally intended for this type of protection and strongly implies that the fortifications were a later addition to an established nucleated settlement.

Content

All three of the sites examined exhibit the anticipated size and layout for nucleated frontier settlements. Their content, which should include the presence of some specialized nonagricultural activity, is also likely to be discernible in the archaeological record. Content must be approached in terms of different criteria at each site because of the various ways in which it was excavated. Ninety-Six, where features were exposed and excavated, provided a wealth of architectural data as well as some information about artifact patterning. Long Bluff is represented by sample data alone. Pinckneyville, on the other hand, yielded both architectural and archaeological information.

At Ninety-Six, the architectural remains permitted the identification of a number of specialized activity structures. Three are of a military nature and appear to have been superimposed on an existing settlement (Fig. 8.7). They include a star redoubt (38GN3) situated northeast of the town. It is a large earthwork surrounded by a defensive ditch and contains an internal traverse embankment. Associated with this fortification are a series of siegeworks, which include both parallels and approaches to the redoubt's north side (Holschlag and Rodeffer 1976b) and a mine excavated to permit the destruction of its north salient. The traverse inside the redoubt would have been thrown up to counter such an event (South 1970a:18–19). The siegeworks followed standard eighteenth-century practices (see Smith 1779; Vauban 1740), though on a reduced scale, owing to the smaller size of the fortification, and clearly identify a siege conducted against the settlement in the European tradition (Holschlag and Rodeffer 1976b:77–78).

Additional fortifications at Ninety-Six include an irregular redoubt at the western end of the settlement (Holschlag and Rodeffer 1976a; South 1971b:47–48); two separate walls enclosing the settlement itself, each consisting of a ditch and stockade (Holschlag et al. 1978:81–83; South 1971b:41–43); and a caponier, or communications trench, at each end of this fortified area linking it with the two redoubts (Holschlag and Rodeffer 1976a:78–79, b:84–85). Within the town fortification lies another military structure, a log blockhouse, which appears initially to have been a

TABLE 8.4 Comparison of activity categories in
the jail and settlement of Ninety-Six (%)[a]

Activity category	Area	
	Jail	Settlement
Subsistence	65.2	84.5
Subsistence–Technological	34.4	14.6
Technological	0.4	0.9
	100.0	100.0

[a] Source: Holschlag and Rodeffer (1977); Holschlag et al. (1978).

separate fortification surrounded by its own ditch and stockade (South 1971b:43–44).

The remainder of the structures at Ninety-Six relate to its nonmilitary occupation. Of the architectural remains uncovered, only one foundation has been identified as a specialized activity area. This is the jail, a brick structure whose form corresponds to functionally similar contemporary buildings (Holschlag et al. 1978:68). This conclusion is supported by artifact evidence as well. A comparison of the materials recovered from the fill of this structure and those found in the fill overlying the remainder of the settlement[1] (Holschlag et al. 1978) may be used to determine the relative importance of domestic activity in these two areas in a manner similar to that employed at Camden. The results of this comparison are shown in Table 8.4. They indicate clearly that a higher percentage frequency of subsistence artifacts is present in the settlement. The frequencies of Subsistence and Subsistence–Technological artifacts from the jail and the settlement at Ninety-Six fall respectively within the ranges of the low and high domestic content activity areas at Camden. The similarity of these frequencies and the association of lower domestic activity content with a nondomestic structure supports the conclusions regarding function and artifact content. It also suggests that the distinction observed reflects a broad functional pattern of artifact usage and discard.

Another area at Ninety-Six is characterized by the occurrence of a large quantity of blacksmithing debris. It lies just southeast of the jail (Holschlag et al. 1978:99; South 1970a:23). Although this material was not quantified, its presence suggests another specialized activity at Ninety-Six and, together with the jail, demonstrates the diverse content anticipated in a nucleated settlement.

At the site of Long Bluff, no architectural features were exposed because of the exploratory nature of the excavations. Likewise, the extremely small size of the sample, designed principally to define the limits of that settlement, is inadequate to

[1]Artifact totals from the exploratory excavations in the settlement have not been broken down beyond this point in the excavation reports.

distinguish the broad activity categories observed at Ninety-Six and Camden. As a consequence, the data presently available from this site can provide little information regarding settlement content. Long Bluff's location between a river landing and a crossroads, however, suggests the presence of transport activities and the centralizing institutions that are likely to have accompanied them.

The content of Pinckneyville is indicated both in architectural remains and the patterned archaeological record observed at this site. Pinckneyville contains a single standing structure of eighteenth-century construction (Fig. 8.10) whose function can be discerned on the basis of architectural data alone. It is a 1½ story brick building, the form of which suggests that it served as a specialized activity structure, presumably a storehouse (Carrillo 1972:42). Although evidence of several other structures was encountered in the exploratory excavations, only two of the ruins were sufficiently intact to determine function based on architectural form. These structures (Numbers 4 and 5) appear to have been domestic in nature (Carrillo 1972:34, 45).

The occurrence and distribution of specialized activities at Pinckneyville is likely to be reflected in the relative frequencies of Subsistence artifacts recovered from each of the areas examined at the site. A comparison of the artifacts by area is presented in Table 8.5 (cf. Figure 8.9). This table includes data from all areas except Area 4, from which no artifacts were collected. An examination of the percentage frequen-

FIGURE 8.10 The brick storehouse at Pinckneyville, the only remaining structure of the early settlement. (SIR photograph.)

TABLE 8.5 Comparison of activity categories by area at Pinckneyville (%)[a]

Activity category	Area					
	Storehouse 1	2	3	5	6	7
Subsistence	49.5	86.9	74.3	80.8	80.9	63.9
Subsistence–Technological	50.5	12.5	22.9	19.2	18.9	36.1
Technological	0	0.6	2.8	0	0.2	0
	100.0	100.0	100.0	100.0	100.0	100.0

[a] Source: Carrillo (1972).

cies reveals that in Areas 2, 3, 5, and 6 Subsistence artifacts predominated, while in the other two areas they occurred at lower levels. In the first groups of areas, the percentage frequencies of both Subsistence and Subsistence–Technological artifacts fall within the ranges of the high domestic content activity areas at Camden and Ninety-Six, which suggests that these areas encompass the remains of domestic structures. One of the remaining areas (Area 7) exhibits frequencies within the ranges of low domestic activity areas at the other sites and is likely to be a specialized activity structure. The last area (Area 1) shows an even lower percentage frequency of domestic activity artifacts and should also denote a nondomestic occupation. Area 1 lies adjacent to the storehouse structure, and its artifact content appears to confirm the architectural conclusions regarding its function.

An examination of the material remains at the sites of Ninety-Six, Long Bluff, and Pinckneyville has revealed that at least two of these contained the specialized activity areas characteristic of nucleated frontier settlements. Investigations at Long Bluff were not extensive enough to provide adequate data for architectural or quantitative artifact analysis. Both structural and artifactual data from the remaining two sites, however, have provided corroborative evidence of the content of the settlements and have affirmed the patterns of domestic and specialized activity occurrence observed in the archaeological record at Camden.

Archaeological evidence obtained from investigations at the sites of three colonial period settlements in South Carolina has permitted their identification as nucleated settlements, a type integral to the settlement structure of insular frontier regions. All were small settlements, consisting of little more than a dozen structures. Each was situated centrally at a crossroads, with its buildings distributed along the converging roads. Long Bluff and Pinckneyville also lay adjacent to or near a navigable watercourse that could have provided an additional trade and communications route linking these settlements with areas around them. In the two sites where archaeological work sufficient to define architecture and activity loci had taken place, specialized, nondomestic areas were discernible. This provided evidence of the integrating institutions found in nucleated settlements. Ninety-Six's central position in the trade and communications network is emphasized not only by its proximity to transport routes but also in its having been chosen as a site for extensive military fortifications on a scale comparable to those at Camden, a frontier town. Although the settlements discussed here represent only a portion of the nucleated settlements likely to have existed in colonial South Carolina, their presence is sufficient to demonstrate the occurrence of this settlement type in the region and provide further evidence of its development as an insular frontier.

HYPOTHESIS 10: DISPERSED FRONTIER SETTLEMENTS

The majority of insular frontier settlements are dispersed throughout the area of colonization. They consist of individual farms and plantations where settlers live and where the production of agricultural commodities is carried out. Consequently, while the sites of dispersed settlements should be the most numerous in a frontier region, they are also likely to be the smallest and often the most briefly occupied. Dispersed agricultural settlements may include both small farms as well as larger, more specialized agricultural complexes. The farm and plantation represent two basic modes of commercial agricultural production, and their occurrence varies with the requirements of the staple crop produced. By the time of South Carolina's founding in 1670, both types of agriculture had been introduced into British North America (Gray 1933:301–303). It is probable that farms as well as plantations would have developed in this colony.

In order to recognize the presence of these two types of dispersed settlement in the archaeological record, it is necessary to consider the form and content of the activities associated with each and the nature of the material record they are likely to have produced. The size, form, and content of plantations and farms are linked to the organization of activities in these two settlement types. Although both produce agricultural commodities for a largely export market, they are distinguished by their scale and the manner in which production is carried out. These organizational differences resulted in the development of separate "occupance forms"[2] that allow the production activities of each to be carried out most efficiently. Farm and plantation occupance forms reflect their organizational differences, and these forms define the size, layout, and content of the activities each settlement type contains.

The Farm

The farm is the smaller and less complex of the dispersed settlement types found in an insular frontier region. It is basically an agricultural production unit centered on the residence of the owner. Although the farm's function is reflected in the nature and arrangement of the activities associated with it, specific patterns of activity

---

[2]The term *occupance form* refers to settlement types as defined by their spatial patterning and function. It implies a dependent relationship of form to function in which the former may be seen as a result of the role played by the settlement in the larger colonial system.

distribution may also vary with the cultural background of the colonists. Because South Carolina was settled by pioneers whose roots lie mainly in northern Europe and the British Isles, it is reasonable to assume that the farms they built in the new country would attempt to replicate patterns of that part of the Old World. The eighteenth century saw the close of the postmedieval period of British farming and the beginning of the Agricultural Revolution. Farms prior to 1750 tended to be generalized in production and form and consisted of a complex of separate structures to accommodate persons, animals, goods, and the processing of crops (Nigel 1970:55–58). Unprecedented population growth and the concentration of persons in urban centers as a consequence of the Industrial Revolution began to place an increasingly greater demand upon agriculture. The larger output required of agriculture was made possible through organizational rather than technological improvement. It involved the use of (1) convertible agriculture, the alternation of arable lands and grass, and (2) alternative agriculture, farming for fodder crops that enriched the soil both by the chemical action of the fodder plants as well as manure of the grazing animals (Chambers and Mingay 1966:4). At the same time, the enclosure movement hastened the consolidation of holdings and movement of farms from the village to the field (Hoskins 1970:22). The farm occupies a relatively small, limited area that must be continuously reused in the production of crops. The process of change in small-farm agriculture brought about by the Agricultural Revolution may be seen as an attempt to increase the yields of farmlands through an intensification of soil rejuvenation. The introduction of the new methods of farming entailed a reorganization of the farm as a productive unit and resulted in the development of a distinctive occupance form.

The critical component in the improvement of soils in the eighteenth century was manure. In order to obtain, collect, and store this commodity, it became necessary to reorganize the farmyard into a "manure reservoir." This was accomplished by assembling the following parts of the farmyard into a compact arrangement: a barn where corn was threshed and straw distributed, a collection of livestock buildings where the straw and hay were transformed into manure, and a yard bordered by these structures where stock was exercised and manure accumulated (Nigel 1970: 76–77). The farmyard generally formed a square to the rear of the house and kitchen (Downing 1850:223). It served as the center of agricultural activities on the farm and was usually subdivided by fences into separate activity areas (Favrelli and Favrelli 1978:13). Ideally, the farmyard faced south to catch the sun and was protected on the north side by its most substantial structure, the barn. Storage sheds were often located in the same range as the barn, while the remaining two ranges contained buildings used for livestock and storage. Working animals were placed to face the early morning sun, and pigs and poultry were located near the house to provide easy access to household waste products. If present, farm processing machinery was installed in existing structures to involve little change in previous working routines. Not until much later did the massive use of inorganic energy force the rearrangement of farm buildings around the farm equipment (Nigel 1970:79, 93). Construction materials used in farm buildings varied throughout Britain with the availability of local materials. While timber and wattle-and-daub construction were still common, they were beginning to be replaced by locally manufactured brick (Nigel 1970:98).

A composite plan of a typical eighteenth-century British farmyard is illustrated in Figure 8.11. This arrangement represents an ideal layout for mixed farming and might be expected to vary with the precise nature and scale of the farming carried out (Favrelli and Favrelli 1978:14; Hoskins 1970:22). Although this general square arrangement was retained in British colonial America, new crops introduced different structures into the yard, climatic differences made the cardinal orientation less mandatory, and the variety in size of frontier farms undoubtedly affected the composition of the farmyard. The defining criteria of the farmyard are its rectangular shape, its position adjacent to the farmhouse and kitchen, and the functions of its structures. Material evidence of these should be recognizable in an examination of the archaeological record.

The Plantation

Like the farm, the plantation's role is centered around the commercial production of agricultural commodities. It differs, however, in scale and organization of production. Plantations exist to efficiently and cheaply produce staples on a large scale for a substantial nondomestic market (Wagley and Harris 1955:435). The competition of agricultural staples for suitable land, labor supplies, and markets favors the location of plantations to minimize cost while maximizing access to markets. These conditions are found on the periphery of a world economic system where native resources can be cheaply exploited for raw commodities that may be then shipped directly from a colonial entrepôt to markets in the parent state (Smith 1973:2; Thompson 1959:29–30).

A plantation is "a capitalistic type of agricultural organization in which a number of unfree laborers are employed under unified direction and control in the production of a staple crop" (Mintz 1959:43). The organization of a plantation is marked by (1) a relatively large population and territorial size, (2) an emphasis on the production of specialized cash crops, (3) a use of labor beyond the owner-family, and (4) a dependence on the authority principle as the basis for collective action (Pan American Union 1959:190). To these may be added (5) a centralized control of cultivating power, (6) a relatively large input of cultivating power per unit of area, and (7) a necessity of producing subsistence crops to at least in part support the plantation population (Prunty 1955:460). These characteristics reflect the manner in which agricultural activities are organized to facilitate production. The plantation not only provides a setting for these activities but also an arrangement to facilitate carrying them out. This arrangement is manifested in the form of the plantation settlement.

The necessity of managing a large labor force engaged in specialized agricultural work directly influenced the occupance form of the plantation. Prunty (1955:490) pointed out that on the antebellum plantation management controlled all cultivating

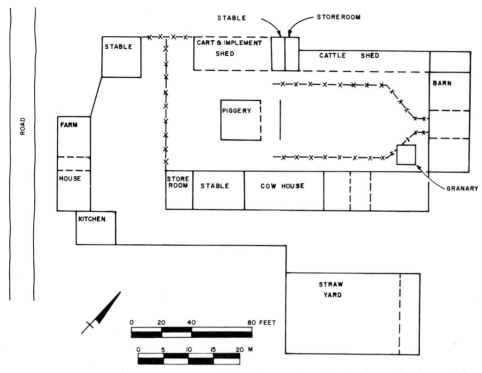

FIGURE 8.11   Typical eighteenth-century English farm, showing the enclosed yard situated to the rear of the house and kitchen. (Sources: Favrelli and Favrelli 1978:13; Nigel 1970:80.)

power and solely decided the manner of its employment. This is denoted spatially in the general layout of a plantation.

> The owner's or manager's house customarily was situated near a cluster of service buildings and slave quarters. Such houses were grouped compactly in rows along short roads, forming a square or, more frequently, a rectangle of buildings. . . . Together these buildings formed a nucleated plantation village, a settlement type noteworthy because of the large area within which it was distributed. (Prunty 1955:465–466)

Although the plantation itself might be areally extensive, its occupied area was compact. The actual layout of buildings within this area varied but seems generally to have followed the same pattern. Waterman and Barrows (1969:*xiv*) note that eighteenth century plantations in the American Southeast centered around a main house and its dependencies. Throughout the eighteenth century these structures exhibited a basic Palladian symmetry in their arrangement (Waterman 1945:17). The house and its forecourt were flanked by the dependencies, which were sometimes attached by passages to the main house (Kimball 1922:79). In the last quarter of the century, the dependencies shifted from a position on either side of the forecourt to one in line with the orientation of the house. Dependencies apparently did not possess definite functions in every plantation and served variously as offices, kitchens, overseers' quarters, libraries, servants' quarters, as well as housing for other support activities related to the main house (Waterman 1945:61, 259, 341).[3]

Farm and service buildings, consisting of shelters for work stock and plantation tools, were situated in a cluster apart from but adjacent to the main house complex. They were generally placed in a linear or geometric arrangement (Phillips 1929:332; Waterman and Barrows 1969). Their proximity to the main house complex, which also placed them near the pasture, cropland, and labor quarters, ensured that cultivating power was centrally located within the area to which it was applied and among the human elements whose effective employment depended on it (Prunty 1955:466).

The slave quarters were generally situated near the agricultural buildings to one side of the main house. They were commonly arranged in rows facing a cleared square at one end of which the main house and its dependencies stood. Quarters varied in size and method of construction from one room huts to larger buildings of log, frame, or brick (Rawick 1972:70–71, 77). Often its relative proximity to the main house reflected the status of the structure's occupants on the plantation (Anthony 1976:13).

The entire plantation complex was not like the farm, situated directly on a main road linking settlements, but would have been placed along a branch road leading into the plantation lands (Phillips 1929:335). The complex was usually adjacent to the earliest cultivated land. The exhaustive effect of continuous cropping of cotton required a continual clearing of new land for planting (Dodd 1921:25). This resulted in a constant expansion of cultivated lands accompanied by a general movement away from the site of the original plantation settlement (Olmstead, 1957:53).

Mt. Vernon, in Fairfax County, Virginia, a plantation that had assumed its final form by the 1770s (Architects' Emergency Committee 1933:70–73),[4] clearly illustrates the layout of the plantation settlement pattern. The geometric layout of the structures at Mt. Vernon is highly visible (Fig. 8.12) with the main house and dependencies situated at the center of a U-shaped plan. Service buildings lie in a row stretching to either side of the forecourt. Quarters form a block oriented at a right angle to the service buildings. The U-shape of the layout is further emphasized by the positions of entrance roads, paths, walls, and ornamental and vegetable garden plots.

---

[3]The pattern of plantation settlement outlined here is derived from a comparison of the layout of structures on the following plantations in British North America: Tryon's plantation in Brunswick Town, North Carolina; The Hermitage, Savannah, Georgia; Mt. Vernon and Gunston Hall, Fairfax County, Virginia; Bremo, Fluvanna County, Virginia; Lower Brandon, Prince George County, Virginia (Architects' Emergency Committee 1933:23, 70–71, 95, 107); Amphill and Stratford, Westmoreland County, Virginia; Carters Grove, James City County, Virginia; Westover, Charles City County, Virginia; Mount Airy and Menokin, Richmond County, Virginia; (Waterman and Barrows 1969:179–183); and Rosewell, Glouscester County, Virginia (Noël Hume 1962:161–162; Waterman and Barrows 1969: 181); and Uncle Sam, St. James Parish, Louisiana (Newton 1972:81).

[4]Although it may appear irregular to choose as an example a plantation that has achieved such notoriety as has the estate of George Washington, the amount of architectural information generated as the result of this intense interest has made it possible to construct an accurate picture of the plantation's form and structure.

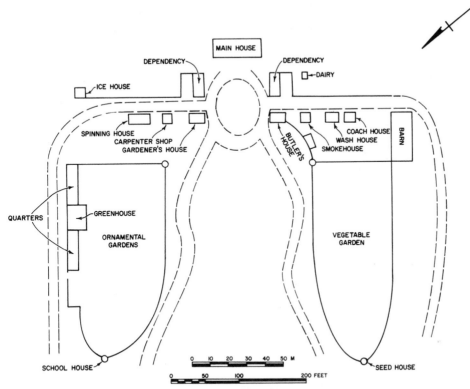

FIGURE 8.12 Mt. Vernon in Fairfax County, Virginia, illustrating the basic layout typical of eighteenth-century plantations. (Source: Architects' Emergency Committee 1933:70–71.)

The plantation may be seen as an institution designed to produce and process raw agricultural commodities on a large scale through the extensive use of unfree labor. An organization of activities necessary to accomplish this purpose is reflected in their spatial distribution on the plantation site. This distribution exhibits a uniform pattern characteristic of an occupance form that should be recognizable in the archaeological record.

Farms on the Frontier

Although farms undoubtedly constituted the most numerous type of settlement in an insular frontier region such as South Carolina, few are identifiable as such on the basis of extant material evidence. Many of the isolated eighteenth-century sites as well as standing structures are likely to represent farming settlements; however, an absence of information about associated outbuildings and overall settlement plans makes their past function difficult to ascertain. In order to identify the presence of early farms, it is necessary to obtain archaeological evidence capable of revealing critical aspects of settlement layout and content. Archaeological investigations at three early sites in South Carolina have provided information useful in identifying farm settlements of the frontier period.

THE KERSHAW HOUSE SITE

Perhaps the most exhaustively examined farm settlement is the Kershaw house site centered on the foundations of a large double house lying just east of Camden (Fig. 5.1). Although situated near the town on a road aligned with the town grid, the site is physically separated from the settlement by a zone of unoccupied land and appears to have developed as a separate farm complex (Lewis 1977b:16). The Kershaw house site was examined archaeologically between 1968 and 1974. After initial exploratory excavations located the site of the double house, the investigations were expanded to encompass much of the surrounding area, and exposed and examined adjacent structural features (Strickland 1971:66; 1976:6). Archaeological and structural features and the material collected from them formed the data base for an analysis of the site's occupation (Lewis 1977b:26).

In order to delineate the role of the Kershaw house site as a farm, the layout and function of these features may be examined with regard to expectations for this type of settlement. The architectural remains have revealed the presence of several structures normally associated with farm settlements of this period. These include a frame kitchen building and a smokehouse, both of which rested on brick foundations, a brick cold cellar, and a log storage building that was constructed directly on the ground. These structures were arranged in two rows facing each other to the rear of the house (Fig. 8.13). The excavations were not extended far enough from the house to determine if another range of structures intersected the ends of the two rows to form a rectangular arrangement. The distribution of the structural remains and their function as shown by their architecture indicate, however, that the Kershaw house represents a farm settlement.

In order to examine further the function of several of the structures, an analysis may be made of the archaeological materials associated with them. Three structures at the Kershaw house site, identified architecturally as a house, a kitchen outbuilding, and a smokehouse, contained collections of contemporary materials from the colonial occupation of the site.[5] These artifacts are sufficiently numerous to permit a comparative analysis of past activities to be carried out. Because subsurface deposits are not likely to include items lost or discarded as primary refuse, it is anticipated that only those activities producing substantial amounts of nonbiodegradable secondary refuse deposited in the ground would appear in the surviving archaeological record. Of the four general activities carried out on a farm—domestic, animal accommodation, repair and processing, and storage of agricultural items and products—only the first is likely to have resulted in such deposits. This is due to the

---

[5]Archaeological excavations at this site did not retain materials recovered from the plow zone. Consequently, artifactual analyses of this settlement are limited to the use of materials contained in subsurface deposits.

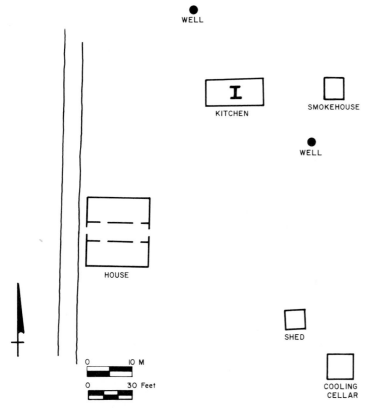

FIGURE 8.13 Structures at the Kershaw house site. (Source: Lewis 1976:26.)

continuous production of large amounts of refuse as a result of day to day domestic activity. Table 8.6, which summarizes the percentage of archaeological materials by activity class, tends to confirm this assumption. In each of the areas, domestic activity artifacts constitute more than 97% of the total archaeological materials recovered. Farming activity artifacts are present in all three areas. The low frequencies of these artifacts reflect their anticipated lower rate of accumulation and the possibility that the activities that produced them were concentrated outside the excavated area of the site (Lewis 1977b:85).

The three areas examined have been identified architecturally as three farm structures associated with domestic–subsistence activities. Because each structure is likely to have had a different domestic role, it would also have participated differentially in these activities. An examination of the quantitative relationships between artifact groups sensitive to these differences should permit the identification of activities associated with the structures.

Architectural evidence indicates that the house, where food was consumed, and the kitchen, where it was prepared, were separate buildings. The spatial distinction

TABLE 8.6 Comparison of percentage frequencies of artifacts in each
activity class by area at the Kershaw house site[a]

Activity class	House	Kitchen	Smokehouse
Domestic	99.7	98.6	97.2
Animal accommodation	0.1	0	0
Repair and processing	0.1	0	0.1
Storage	0.1	1.4	2.7
	100.0	100.0	100.0

[a] Source: Lewis (1977b).

between these two activities is likely to appear in the relative frequencies of food
preparation and consumption artifacts. A larger portion of the former characterized
the kitchen, and a greater frequency of the latter was found in the house. Areas of
other specialized activity are expected to exhibit a lower total frequency of both food
preparation and consumption artifacts.

A comparison of the percentage frequencies of food preparation and consumption artifacts in the three areas is shown in Table 8.7. It indicates the hypothesized
relationship between the two artifact groups in the house and kitchen and suggests
their respective functions. The lower relative frequencies of both groups of artifacts
in the smokehouse suggests that it contained a more specialized activity (Lewis
1977b:87).

The distribution of faunal remains is likely to be directly related to the function
of an area either as a locus of food consumption or of food preparation and processing. South (1977:179) noted that faunal remains are usually deposited at a distance
from living areas because of their odors. Other areas where food items were used,
stored, or processed would also have been associated with faunal remains, yet
because they were not living areas the disposal of such material would probably have
been heavier and in closer proximity to structures. Therefore it is likely that living
areas will exhibit a lower frequency of occurrence than areas of food processing or
storage. Areas not containing activities related to food production should be characterized by an absence of faunal material.

TABLE 8.7 Comparison of percentage frequencies
of food preparation and food consumption artifacts at
the Kershaw house site[a]

Activity group	House	Kitchen	Smokehouse
Food preparation	3	8	1
Food consumption	93	81	76
	96	89	77

[a] Source: Lewis (1977b).

A comparison of the percentage frequencies of faunal remains in the house, kitchen, and smokehouse reveals frequencies of 15.4, 45, and 54%, respectively, for these areas. This implies that the house has the greatest likelihood of being a living area, but areas of food storage or processing are represented by the kitchen and smokehouse (Lewis 1977b:86).

Wine bottles in the eighteenth century were primarily used as vessels for storing, serving, and decanting beverages rather than as containers in which such beverages were shipped from manufacturer to user. Because the heaviest use, and consequently breakage, of bottles would have been associated with living areas, it is expected that the greatest rate of discard would also have occurred there. For this reason it is expected that areas marked by the greatest relative occurrence of wine bottle fragments in the archaeological record would have been used most exclusively as living areas, whereas those areas with a lower proportion or an absence of such artifacts will represent centers of other sorts of activity as well.

An examination of the relative percentage frequencies of wine bottle glass to all other artifacts in the three activity areas at the Kershaw house site indicates that the former comprises 9.1% of the total artifacts in the house. In the kitchen and smokehouse this percentage drops to 6.5 and 5.7%, respectively. The relatively larger frequency of wine bottle glass in the house suggests that this area is more likely to have been used more exclusively as a living area than the others (Lewis 1977b:88).

Structures used as living areas would have constituted the principal depository for the class of artifacts collectively termed furniture hardware. Unlike many types of artifacts, furniture is a durable item that is not likely to have entered the archaeological record at a high and constant rate. Consequently, the percentage frequency of furniture hardware to other artifacts in the archaeological record may be assumed to be quite low on any site. The spatially restricted use of such artifacts would nearly preclude their occurrence in areas that lacked a domestic occupation. Areas of specialized, nondomestic activity should be characterized by an absence of furniture hardware in the archaeological record. An examination of archaeological materials from the Kershaw house site reveals that furniture hardware is present in the house and kitchen and is absent in the smokehouse. On the basis of this observation, it appears that the latter did not constitute a living area.

Of the structures that served as living areas in a settlement, it is likely that the one inhabited by high-status individuals generated a discard composed of a greater proportion of high-status artifacts than would have those living areas occupied by servants, slaves, or other persons of lower socioeconomic status. An inspection of the archaeological remains of the three areas at the Kershaw house site is expected to reveal a higher frequency of high-status artifacts in the living area of the site occupied by upper-status persons and a lower occurrence or absence of such items in living areas of persons of lower status and in specialized activity areas.

A list of upper-status items recovered from the Kershaw house site by area appears in Table 8.8. It clearly shows a preponderance of high-status items to be associated with the house, but few or none were recovered from the other two areas. On the basis of the marked differential occurrence of these artifacts, it seems proba-

TABLE 8.8 Comparison of high-status artifact occurrence at the
Kershaw house site[a]

Artifacts	House	Kitchen	Smokehouse
Stemware fragments	10	—	3
Porcelain buttons	1	—	—
Silver ornament plate	1	—	—
Etched-glass fragments	2	—	—
Silver plate objects	1	—	—
Silver buttons	3	—	—
Wig curlers	1	—	—
Total artifacts	19	0	3

[a] Source: Lewis (1977b).

ble that the house was the high-status living area at the site, whereas occupations by
lower-status persons may have been present in the other two areas (Lewis 1977b:
89).

Closely related to the status of the site's occupants is their differential use of
Colono ceramics, a ware assumed to be generally associated with lower-status persons and perhaps the preparation of certain foods. The appearance of Colono ware
in the archaeological record should indicate the existence of food preparation and
processing activities as well as the presence of persons of lower economic status.
Changes in the relative frequency occurrence of this artifact in different parts of the
site should reveal the extent to which the two characteristics are present. In the case
of an upper-status dwelling with separate kitchen, Colono ceramics should occur in
greatest quantities in the refuse of the kitchen and other structures devoted to food
preparation. Living areas occupied by servants would also be expected to exhibit a
higher frequency of this artifact than would the residence of the owner. The main
structure, lacking both food preparation and lower-status living areas, is expected to
contain the lowest relative frequency of Colono pottery.

An examination of the percentage frequency of Colono ceramics to all other
ceramics in the three areas of the Kershaw house site indicates that the occurrence of
these artifacts varies greatly across the site. They comprise 3.5% of the total ceramics at the house, 9.7% at the kitchen, and 21.2% at the smokehouse. This
suggests that the least amount of food preparation and the highest-status occupation
took place, as expected, at the house, and the other areas served as food preparation
and processing loci presumably associated with persons of lower status (Lewis
1977b: 90).

Finally, the extent to which storage activities were carried out within a settlement complex should be reflected by the relative degree to which artifacts falling in
this class occur throughout the site. It is anticipated that storage-related artifacts will
have their highest frequency of occurrence in structures that did not serve as living
areas and that they would be present in increasingly lesser frequencies in structures
that served to an increasingly larger degree as living areas.

An examination of the three areas at the Kershaw house shows that the percentage frequency of storage related artifacts to all other artifacts is low throughout the site (Table 8.6). Their frequency is lowest at the house, higher at the kitchen, and highest at the smokehouse. This suggests that the house is most likely to have served exclusively as a living area, while the smokehouse was probably the site of storage activities. The kitchen exhibits a percentage frequency between the others and may have contained both activities (Lewis 1977b:90).

A comparison of the relative frequencies of a variety of functionally significant artifact groups in the three activity areas of the Kershaw house site has suggested that the Kershaw house represents the remains of a high-status living area where storage and food preparation and processing activities occurred to a lesser extent than in the other two areas examined. The smokehouse, on the other hand, appears to have been the locus of storage and processing activities as well as the preparation of food. The kitchen seems to have had a mixture of the types of activities found in the other two areas. It presumably served a multipurpose function as a lower status living area as well as one devoted in part to food preparation, processing, and storage. An overlapping of activities is also evidenced by the distribution throughout the site of artifacts from nearly all of the groups discussed. Although the artifacts utilized in the functional analysis of the Kershaw house site represent the archaeological record of only a portion of that site, they provide evidence that indicates the presence of living areas and specialized activity areas corresponding to those indicated by architectural evidence. The nature and distribution of these areas permit the identification of the Kershaw house site as that of an eighteenth-century farm on the South Carolina frontier.

THE PRICE HOUSE SITE

Another farm site may be identified on the basis of the arrangement of its architecture. It is the Price house (38SP1), a standing structure situated on a through road in Spartanburg County (Fig. 5.1). Exploratory excavations, conducted at the Price house in 1970, were confined largely to one side of the area at the rear of the house and were designed to uncover evidence of architectural features. The investigations revealed three additional eighteenth-century structures: a brick kitchen and a cold cellar placed in a linear arrangement, and a well to one side of these buildings (Fig. 8.14).

Several of these structures were excavated and found to contain refuse primarily from the nineteenth century and later, reflecting the structure's long occupation (South 1970b:27, 33, 36). Although these artifacts mostly postdate the colonial period when the house was constructed, they may still be used to identify the earlier structures if the buildings retained the same functions over time. The relative appearance of functional artifact categories may be measured by comparing collections from three areas at the site: the Price house, the kitchen, and the cellar.

The kitchen and cellar, like those structures adjacent to the Kershaw house, are likely to have been associated most closely with the domestic–subsistence function

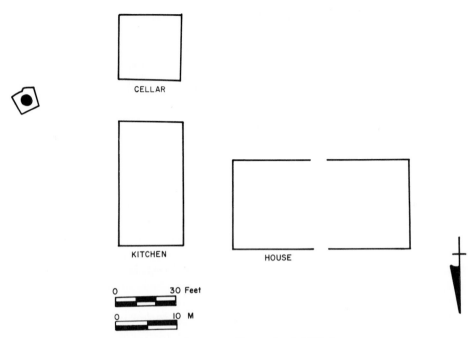

FIGURE 8.14 Structures at the Price house site. (Source: South 1970b.)

of the house. Yet, because of their proximity to other farm structures, they are likely to have accumulated some materials generated by agricultural activities. An examination of the contents of the three areas in terms of the activity classes that are likely to characterize the contents of a farm site appear in Table 8.9. Here we find that domestic activity artifacts constitute more than 94% of the artifacts in each area. At the house, the only other activity represented is storage; however, agricultural items were found in both other areas, and animal accommodation artifacts are associated only with the area furthest from the house (SIR). The presence of these items, representing the last two activity classes, indicates the existence of farming activities

TABLE 8.9 Comparison of percentage frequencies of artifacts in each activity class at the Price house site[a]

Activity category	House	Kitchen	Cellar
Domestic	94.3	95.9	95.7
Animal accommodation	0	0	1.1
Repair and agriculture	0	4.1	2.0
Storage	5.7	0	1.2
	100.0	100.0	100.0

[a] Source: South (1970b).

TABLE 8.10 Comparison of percentage frequencies of food preparation and food consumption artifacts at the Price house site[a]

Activity groups	House	Kitchen	Cellar
Food preparation	17.6	19.3	36.6
Food consumption	82.4	80.1	64.4
	100.0	100.0	100.0

[a] Source: South (1970b).

near, but not at the areas investigated. The discard of their refuse here shows, however, the expected overlapping of farm activity areas observed also at the Kershaw house site.

Variation in the nature of domestic activity between the kitchen, where food was prepared, and the house, where it was consumed, may be observed archaeologically by examining the distribution of material discarded as a result of these activities. Table 8.10 presents the percentage frequencies of food preparation and consumption artifacts found in these two areas. An examination of the relative occurrence of the artifacts in these activity groups indicates an increase in the occurrence of food preparation artifacts and a decrease in that of consumption artifacts as one proceeds from the house to the kitchen and cellar (SIR). This trend corresponds to that observed at the Kershaw house site.

A comparison of artifacts uncovered in the limited excavations at the Price house does not provide as comprehensive a picture of activities as that available from the Kershaw house site data. An analysis of these materials has, however, allowed us to observe the spatial distribution of food preparation and consumption activities on the site and demonstrate its proximity to agricultural activities normally associated with farm settlements. The occurrence of domestic farming activities is reflected in the architectural evidence which has revealed a cluster of buildings whose arrangement and functions correspond to that attributed to farms. The Price house site, although only partially explored, would appear to offer a second example of farm settlement in eighteenth-century South Carolina.

THE HUTCHENSON FARM SITE

Both the Kershaw house site and that of the Price house represent relatively high-status dwellings that remained standing long after the close of the eighteenth century (Lewis 1977b:88–89; South 1970b:14).[6] Most other eighteenth-century standing structures likely to have been farmhouses tend also to be large, substantial buildings, whose architecture would seem to indicate the higher status of their

[6]The Kershaw house was destroyed in 1865 (Kirkland and Kennedy 1905:279) whereas the Price house was occupied well into the twentieth century (South 1970b:42). Both buildings have since been restored as historical exhibits.

builders. Only a few examples of lower-status rural architecture remain. One of these is the Hutchenson farm house, a log structure built in Abbeville County about 1800 or before (Fig. 5.1). A contemporary log smokehouse is situated behind the house, and their arrangement is similar to that found in farm settlements. These two structures lie adjacent to a through road and form the focus of a farmyard composed of late nineteenth- and early twentieth-century buildings (Fig. 8.15). They may well have formed the nucleus of an earlier farm complex (USDIOAHPI). Because this site has not been explored archaeologically, questions regarding its original form and composition cannot be answered at present; however, the layout of its surviving architecture suggests that it was first established as a farm settlement and continued to function as such in the present century.

THE DISTRIBUTION OF FARMS

Three early farming settlements have been identified through an examination of their material remains. Although none of these sites was excavated completely, all contained architectural evidence of structures arranged in a manner normally found in a farm context. At each of these sites, the presence of outbuildings placed to the rear of the principal domestic structure in linear fashion implies the existence of the rectangular complex of structures characteristic of farmyards. Because the archae-

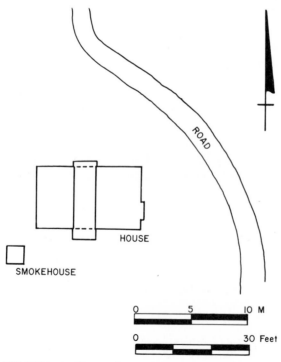

FIGURE 8.15   The Hutchenson farm house site. (Source: USDIOAHPI.)

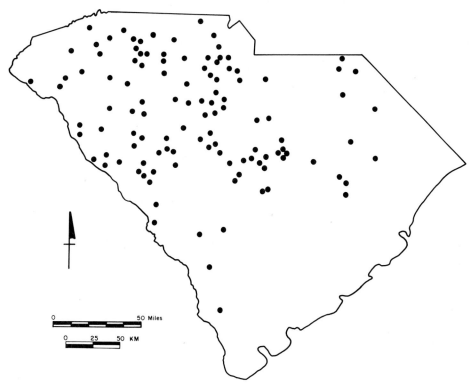

FIGURE 8.16 Distribution of farm settlements in South Carolina in 1800 based on material evidence. (Sources: see text.)

ological work conducted at two of the sites was mostly architecturally oriented, much of the interpretation of settlement form and content has relied upon structure-based archaeological data. Material evidence capable of delineating the nonstructural activity areas critical to the definition of farm settlement has been unavilable. Artifact assemblages collected from structural contexts, however, have permitted the identification of domestic activity variation within the settlements and detected the occurrence of agricultural activities, the refuse of which overlapped into these areas of the sites.

The small number of farm sites investigated reflects a lack of emphasis on this type of settlement rather than an absence of early farms in South Carolina. The state contains a large number of standing rural, domestic structures situated on through roads, which are likely to mark the locations of eighteenth-century frontier farms (Fig. 8.16). They, like the Kershaw and Price houses, usually represent upper-status dwellings, which presumably constituted a minority of the farms of this period. The size of even this portion of the total dispersed settlement is sufficiently large to indicate the relative numerical importance of farms relative to other types of frontier settlements.

The distribution of these structures is limited largely to the Upper Coastal Plain and Piedmont regions of South Carolina. Their absence from the Lower Coastal Plains suggests that this type of frontier agriculture was less efficient there than in the interior. This geographic disparity reveals either an avoidance of the coastal region, which is unlikely because of the presence of other settlement there, or the adoption of plantation agriculture in those areas where farm sites do not appear. In order to explore this question, we now examine the occurrence and distribution of colonial plantation settlements in South Carolina.

Plantation Settlements

Plantations differ from farms as a result of their scale and organization of production, attributes that are reflected in the size and layout of their settlements. The central feature of most plantations is the main house, lying at the terminus of a branch road leading into the settlement. These structures were usually constructed to advertise the wealth of their owners. Because of the size and elaborate architecture often exhibited in such houses, many eighteenth century plantation sites in South Carolina may be identified on the basis of standing architectural remains. Often other structures accompanying the main house have also survived, which permits the recognition of an entire element of the plantation settlement. The main house complex represents only a small component of the plantation. Its remaining parts, the areas where production was carried out and where tools, work stock, and labor were housed, are less likely to have survived. Consequently, their study has required archaeological investigations aimed at defining the various settlement components.

Archaeological investigations have been conducted at several sites each of which is characterized by the presence of structures of high-status rural architecture located at the terminus of a branch road. These investigations have included both extensive exploration of wide areas to locate, identify, and delimit elements of plantation settlements and intensive excavation of particular site components to examine more closely smaller-scale activity patterning. The results of the investigations should permit the definition of critical components of plantation settlements and demonstrate their association with particular site types. Data from eight archaeological sites are examined (Fig. 5.1). Large portions of three sites, Middleton Place (38DR16), Hampton (38CH241), and Limerick (38BK223), were examined through the use of various sampling techniques, but only parts of the others, Drayton Hall (38CH255), the Spier's Landing site (38BK160), Spring Grove (38BK359), and the Yaughn (38BK75) site, were intensively excavated or surveyed. This information is used to examine respectively the formal and functional aspects of plantation settlement in South Carolina.

SETTLEMENT PATTERN

The layout of the plantation follows the organization of these settlements as centers of labor-intensive commercial agricultural production. It should consist of areas devoted to various activities arranged in a regular manner to one or both sides of a central residence complex. Plantation settlements are also characterized by their compactness, which confines most of their activities to a relatively small area within boundaries that should be discernible archaeologically. An examination of material evidence from the three extensively examined plantation sites is expected to reveal a pattern of settlement similar to that described in the earlier discussion of the occupance form.

Each of the three sites was examined through the use of data gathered in extensive archaeological sampling. The stratified, systematic, unaligned samples conducted at Middleton Place and Hampton and the systematic and random sampling carried out at Limerick were centered around architectural evidence that implied the presence of a plantation settlement. At Middleton Place (Fig. 5.1), one standing brick structure and the foundations of two others lie at the end of a branch road leading from a colonial period through road paralleling the Ashley River. The structures lie on a high bluff overlooking the river, and the intervening space has been modified with artificial terracing, impoundments, rice fields, and gardens. The foundations of the central structure at Middleton Place indicate that it was a symmetrical building with a hall and tower in the center of the front facade. Its Palladian plan suggests an early eighteenth-century high-status residence. This period of construction is substantiated by ceramic evidence from the site (Lewis and Hardesty 1979:24, 33). The archaeological excavations covered a large portion of the site, including the area of the main house, its dependencies, and a wide area to the south of these structures.

At Hampton (Fig. 5.1), the main house and one of its dependencies still stand. They are situated at the end of a branch road leading from the main road paralleling the South Santee River. The house, situated on a bluff above the river, is a large, two-story, frame structure originally constructed with the plan of a double house. It was subsequently expanded with the addition of symmetrical wings and a large pedimented portico extending across the entire front of the original building (Fig. 8.17). Interior details, such as the wallcoverings, carved woodwork, and other decorative features (Foley 1979:36–43), testify to the high-status of its occupants. The dependency is also of frame construction. Apparently built in several stages, the structure is dominated by a central brick chimney pile whose multiple hearths identify it as a kitchen (Foley 1979:63). Ceramic evidence from the site indicates that the European occupation of Hampton began around 1730, although the architecture of the main house suggests a construction data closer to the middle of the eighteenth century (Lewis 1979a:36; Lewis and Haskell 1980:62–63). Archaeological investigations at Hampton were conducted over a wide area to the west of the main house and in the vicinity of the main house area.

Structural remains at Limerick (Fig. 5.1) were encountered during an archaeological survey for a railway right-of-way on the west side of the East Branch of the Cooper River. Subsequent testing of the site defined the limits of the past settlement and guided the final phase of work, which involved intensive sampling and the excavation of structural features, including the main house foundations (Lees

FIGURE 8.17   The main house at Hampton plantation on the South Santee River. (SCDPRT photograph.)

1980:16–20). Because of the spatial limitations imposed by the construction project, the portion of the site examined was restricted to a linear path through the settlement area. Areas outside of this zone were investigated, however, and collections were made from several nearby locations. The principal area of investigation included the sites of several structures, one of which was a large double house. An avenue flanked by live oak trees led from this structure to the through road along the river, implying that the structure was a main house. Ceramic and architectural data reveal that Limerick was occupied by English settlers in the first quarter of the eighteenth century (Lees 1980:89).

SYMAPs of structural materials at Middleton Place, Hampton, and Limerick is apt to be mirrored in the distribution of structural artifacts on these three sites. Spatial patterning in these data may be observed in SYMAP displays of artifact intensities similar to those employed in the analysis of the Camden archaeological materials. When combined with the distribution of intact structural remains and visible ruins, structural artifact patterns should reveal the locations of buildings at these settlements. It is anticipated that their layout will be typical of plantations in general.

SYMAPs of structural materials at Middleton Place, Hampton, and Limerick have provided a key to the locations of structural remains at these three sites. At Middleton Place, the distribution of brick shows the location of the main house and its northern dependency, whose foundations are also visible. The standing southern dependency flanks these two structures. At least eight other concentrations of structural materials lie to the south and southwest of the main house complex (Fig. 8.18). Their distribution suggests the presence of several rows of buildings oriented at a right angle to the main house and its dependencies. This clustered, geometric arrangement follows the predicted pattern for plantation settlements.

The distribution of structural remains at Hampton reveals heavy concentrations of these artifacts in the vicinity of the main house and kitchen and in six other locations lying to the west of these structures (Fig. 8.19). Another concentration lies to the northeast of the main house in a position opposite the kitchen. Its symmetrical placement suggests that it represents the remains of the other dependency of the main house complex. The majority of the structures at Hampton are not situated immediately to the side of the main house as at Middleton Place because a topographic depression lies there. This feature, which has been modified to form an artificial impoundment, separates these structures from the main house complex by a short distance. The structures themselves appear to exhibit a typical plantation layout, since they are arranged in a geometric pattern aligned with the axis of the main house complex (Lewis 1979a:50; Lewis and Haskell 1980:46–47).

At Limerick, the distribution of structural materials identified the location of the main house and another eighteenth-century building a short distance to the side of it (Fig. 8.20). Additional exploratory excavations outside the project corridor

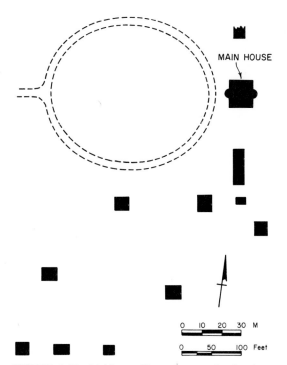

FIGURE 8.18 Middleton Place, showing the distribution of structures. (Source: Lewis and Hardesty 1979:37.)

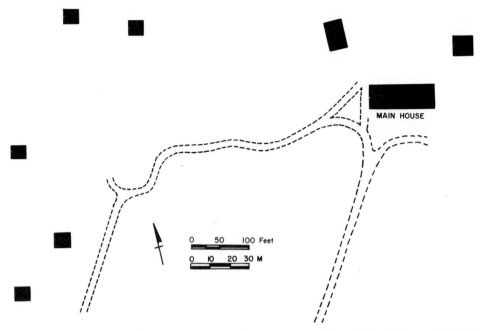

FIGURE 8.19   Hampton, showing the distribution of structures. (Source: Lewis 1979a:51; Lewis and Haskell 1980:32.)

uncovered the locations of two other early structures. One lay northwest of the house in a position suggestive of a dependency. The existence of its expected opposite number could not be determined, because the area northeast of the main house had been severely disturbed. Footings of a large structure were found to the west of the house (Lees 1980:99–120). Although only a portion of the Limerick site was explored, the distribution of structures there indicates the presence of a main house complex and a spatial layout of activities similar to that anticipated in plantation settlements.

ACTIVITY PATTERNING

The three basic components of a plantation settlement are the main house complex, which includes the owner's residence, its service activities, and the plantation's administrative offices; agricultural and other specialized activity areas, where production of various plantation commodities is carried out; and housing for the plantation's labor force. At Middleton Place and Hampton, the main house complexes have been identified by the architecture of their central structures. Architectural and archaeological evidence has defined the location of each main house and its symmetrically placed dependencies. The remaining components of the plantation settlements left behind almost no surface architectural evidence and must be identified largely on the basis of archaeological data. In order to establish the existence of

production areas and slave housing, it will be necessary to recognize activity patterning in the sample data collected at these two sites and in material data gathered in the
more intensive excavations at Drayton Hall, Spier's Landing, Spring Grove, and
Yaughn.

In the following discussion, we examine data from Middleton Place and
Hampton in terms of functionally significant artifact classes. Variation in artifact
class occurrence is likely to be related to the presence of different types of activities.
The association of patterns of activity class variation with particular areas should
permit the identification of activity loci at these plantation settlements. The spatial
form of these patterns should also allow us to observe the arrangement of activities
on each site. Functional artifact patterns derived from these data may then be
compared to patterns observed at the other sites where more complete architectural
remains and larger samples of the material contents are available. An examination of
data obtained from these intensive excavations should help not only in identifying
the past activities carried out at these sites but also in refining the original patterns.

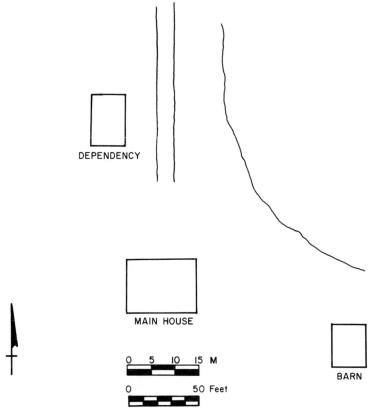

FIGURE 8.20   The structures at Limerick. (Source: Lees 1980.)

Domestic versus Specialized Activity The basic distinction between activities on a plantation involves those of a domestic and nondomestic, or specialized, nature. Domestic activities, evidenced by the occurrence of subsistence artifacts, should be confined to the main house and the workers' living areas, but specialized production activities, including animal husbandry, repair and processing, and storage, are likely to be located elsewhere on the site. Although specialized production areas may be expected to contain the discarded by-products of these activities, the quantities of artifacts comprising the Technological activity category would have been far less than those generated by domestic activities. As we have seen, the lower rate of discard and a high retention rate for tools and other artifacts associated with specialized activities in general resulted in their low rate of appearance in the archaeological record. This rate is apt to appear smaller because of sampling error in small samples such as those conducted at Middleton Place and Hampton. Consequently, the occurrence of specialized activities has been measured by the relative frequencies of artifacts falling within the Subsistence and Subsistence–Technological activity categories. The occurrence and distribution of these activities at the two plantation sites should be revealed by the extent to which each activity set is present throughout the site.

The Middleton Place and Hampton sites have been divided into units of analysis

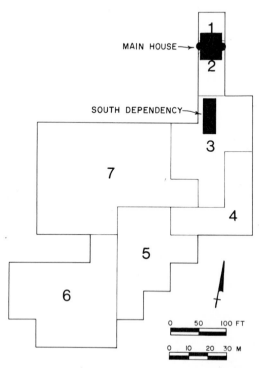

FIGURE 8.21 Structure-based activity areas at Middleton Place. (Source: Lewis and Hardesty 1979:45.)

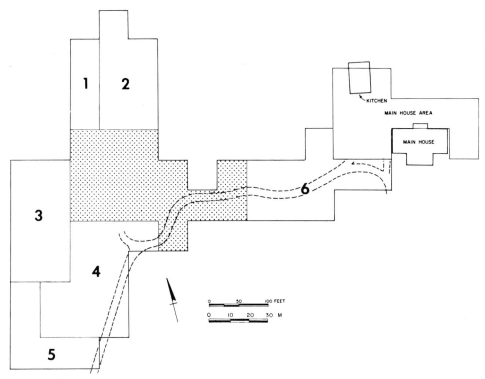

FIGURE 8.22 Structure-based activity areas at Hampton. (Sources: Lewis 1979a:53; Lewis and Haskell 1980:48.)

based on the distribution of structural artifacts (Figs. 8.21 and 8.22). Each unit includes those sample data assumed to have been associated with a structure or group of structures and which are likely to encompass activities carried out at these locations. A comparison of the frequencies of occurrence of artifacts belonging to activity categories in each area should indicate the general distribution of domestic and specialized activities at the sites. Table 8.11 illustrates the frequencies of artifacts in each category by area at Middleton Place and Hampton.

An examination of the percentage frequencies of artifacts in each activity category reveals wide variation among Subsistence and Subsistence–Technological activity artifacts at both sites, a nearly constant frequency of Technological activity artifacts at Hampton, and sharply varying frequencies of this category at Middleton Place. When compared graphically (Fig. 8.23), the percentages of the two larger categories fall into several clusters in a continuum, with two areas set apart from the others. In all but one area, Subsistence artifacts constitute over half of the archaeological materials recovered. The highest relative frequency of Subsistence artifacts occurs in Area 7 at Middleton Place. Four areas (4 and 6 at Middleton Place and 4 and 5 at Hampton) also exhibit high frequencies of artifacts falling into this activity category. Areas 1, 3, and 6 at Hampton cluster slightly below this group. A third

TABLE 8.11 Comparison of percentage frequencies of activity category artifacts by area at Middleton Place and Hampton[a]

Activity category	Area							Main[b] house
	1[b]	2	3	4	5	6	7	
				MIDDLETON PLACE				
Subsistence	—	—	—	71.2	44.7	71.4	74.1	58.2
Subsistence–Technological	—	—	—	28.5	29.6	28.4	25.5	41.2
Technological	—	—	—	0.3	25.7	0.2	0.4	0.6
				HAMPTON				
Subsistence	65.0	56.7	63.4	69.2	72.9	65.8	—	56.2
Subsistence–Technological	35.0	43.2	36.1	30.7	27.0	34.1	—	43.6
Technological	0	0.1	0.1	0.1	0.1	0.1	—	0.2

[a] Sources: Lewis (1979a), Lewis and Hardesty (1979), Lewis and Haskell (1980).

[b] Middletown Main House comprises areas 1, 2, and 3.

cluster contains the main house areas at both plantations and Area 2 at Hampton. Area 5 at Middleton Place is characterized by a large amount of refuse from a Technological activity, which distinguishes its contents from those of all other areas at both sites.

If we assume that the relationship between Subsistence and Subsistence–Technological activity artifacts reflects the degree to which domestic activities predominated in a particular area, then the first two clusters delineated in Figure 8.23 would appear to distinguish living areas from those devoted to specialized activities. A comparison of the frequency relationships of artifacts by activity category at Middleton Place and Hampton with those obtained from the structure-based activity areas at Camden and Ninety-Six shows that the contents of Clusters 1 and 2 are similar to those areas assumed to have been centers of domestic or mixed domestic–specialized activity at the other sites. The frequencies found in Cluster 3, on the other hand, compare favorably with those in areas believed to have contained specialized activities.

Area 5 at Middleton Place contains a great deal of slag produced as a by-product of a specialized activity, presumably smithing. As a consequence, both Subsistence and Subsistence–Technological activity artifact frequencies are lower here than in other areas. If we substract the Technological activity artifacts to simulate a specialized activity that produced no substantial by-product, then the relative frequencies of its other components are similar to those found in other presumed specialized activity areas at both plantation sites as well as Camden and Ninety-Six (Fig. 8.23).

The main house areas at Middleton Place and Hampton present a seemingly enigmatic situation in that they have been identified architecturally as living areas, yet exhibit the lowest percentage frequencies of Subsistence activity artifacts. This phenomenon is likely to be the result of several factors. First, although a domestic structure, it was a home to a relatively small number of persons. The extent of domestic activities producing subsistence refuse there was probably no greater than that associated with less substantial European colonial residence structures. Second, in addition to its use as a domicile, the main house area was also the site of administrative and other specialized activities, most of which would not have left a substantial by-product. Finally, because the main house was the central element of a plantation settlement and a focal point for displaying wealth and stylistic taste, discard activities that normally would have taken place near living areas would have been carried out elsewhere.

The disposal of secondary refuse constitutes the primary process by which the accumulation of subsistence discard occurs. If this process is directed away from the immediate area in which it is generated, as is likely to have been the case at a main house, then the archaeological component composed of such materials is expected to be greatly reduced. Subsistence–Technological activity artifacts, on the other hand, are not produced generally by secondary refuse deposition. Rather, they accumulate as a result of abandonment, loss, or other modes of unintentional disposal. Consequently, the size of the artifact component representing these activities should be relatively larger at the site of a main house than at the sites of other living areas with

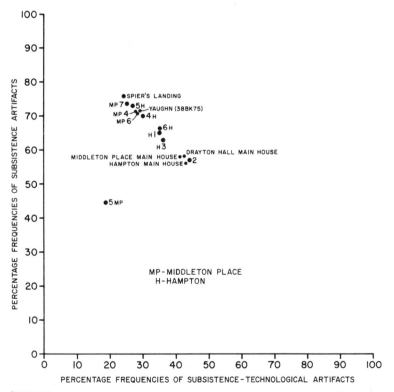

FIGURE 8.23   Activity areas at Middleton Place, Hampton, Drayton Hall, Spier's Landing, and Yaughn. (Sources: see text.)

their adjacent secondary refuse deposits. This disparity should be reflected in the relative percentage frequencies of Subsistence and Subsistence–Technological activity artifacts, as is the case at Middleton Place and Hampton.

A similarly high relative percentage frequency of Subsistence–Technological activity artifacts occurs also in Area 2 at Hampton. The area's location away from the main house complex, coupled with an absence of high-status architecture, implies that its contents are not a result of the processes outlined above. Instead, it is likely to have been a specialized activity area where a lesser amount of domestic activity took place.

The analysis of archaeological data from Middleton Place and Hampton has permitted a division of the structure-based activity areas there into clusters likely to represent domestic and specialized activity loci. In order to further differentiate past activities within these sites and identify particular aspects of plantation settlement, it is necessary to examine the distribution of other categories of material evidence. The two principal domestic activity areas on a plantation settlement are the owner's house and the slaves' dwellings. Although the presence of standing architectural remains at Middleton Place and Hampton has identified the owner's house, the status of the inhabitants of both areas may also be discernible through an analysis of the archaeological record they produced.

High versus Low Status   It is assumed that certain artifacts indicative of high status may be found in association with living and other activity areas used by high-status persons. The distribution of such items is complicated by the fact that they are usually in themselves highly valued objects that are subject to a high rate of retention. For this reason, the occurrence of high-status artifacts in the archaeological record is not as often the result of discard and abandonment as is the case with less valuable artifacts. Rather, their appearance is nearly always a consequence of loss.

Only two such items were recovered in the excavations at Middleton Place. They consist of a white-metal stringed instrument tuning knob and a fragment of marble veneer. Both were found in the main house area, and their presence there implies a high-status occupation in this area (Lewis and Hardesty 1979:47). A total of 51 high-status artifacts was found at Hampton, all of which came from the main house area or the area adjacent to it. These items include 37 fragments of lead-glass drinking glasses, three wine glass fragments, an abalone button, and 10 hand-painted, purple delft tile fragments (Lewis and Haskell 1980:52).[7]

Another artifact that is likely to be linked to status within the colonial plantation context is Oriental porcelain, an imported ware that gained increasingly in popularity during the eighteenth century. Its use was particularly associated with the tea ceremony, an English social custom in which people of both sexes gathered to

---

[7]The purple delft fireplace tiles are included as high-status artifacts because of their apparent association with the living areas of persons of high socioeconomic status in the colonial American South and their general absense in those of others. For example, of the nearly two dozen structures excavated at Brunswick Town, North Carolina, only the ruins of the governor's house and that of another prominent person yielded this artifact (South, personal communication, 1979).

exchange information, engage in conversation, and court while consuming the beverage (Roth 1961:70). The tea ceremony and its required use of porcelain had become commonplace in British colonial North America in the second half of the century. This makes the archaeological occurrence of this ceramic unreliable as a status marker in most colonial settlements.

In a plantation settlement, however, only a small portion of the population, its owners and managerial staff, were English, and the occurrence of the tea ceremony is likely to have been restricted to the areas they occupied. The remainder of the plantation population was not ethnically British and is not believed to have participated extensively in this ceremony in slave living areas. Consequently, the use of porcelain by these two groups may be expected to have been dramatically different. In addition, with the exception of Colono ware, most ceramics used on the plantation were obtained and distributed by the owner or manager. This centralized acquisition of ceramics is likely to have further systemized the kinds of ceramics used and served particularly to restrict the flow of porcelain to those individuals of higher status. Plantation slaves, particularly household servants whose work regularly placed them in close proximity to the behavior of such high-status persons, may be expected to have become acculturated to the use of porcelain and have begun to acquire it in small quantities by the close of the colonial period (Otto 1977:106).

Archaeologically, it is predicted that porcelain will occur in deposits associated with living areas of both manager and worker on the plantation. Differences in the use patterns of this ware make it very likely that a great deal of disparity will exist in

TABLE 8.12   Frequencies of occurrence of
porcelain by area at Middleton Place and Hampton[a]

Area	Total European ceramics (%)
Middleton Place	
Main House[b]	18
4[b]	20
5	10
6[b]	9
7[b]	7
Hampton	
Main House[b]	20
1	1
2	2
3	4
4[b]	7
5[b]	4
6	12

[a] Sources: Lewis and Hardesty (1979:48); Lewis and Haskell (1980:54).
[b] Denotes domestic activity area.

the occurrence of porcelain between these two areas. For this reason, the areas within and adjacent to the main house complex should exhibit a higher frequency of porcelain than other areas at Hampton and Middleton Place.

Table 8.12 shows the predicted variation in the presence of porcelain away from the structure-based activity areas at Middleton Place and Hampton. The main house areas at both sites and adjacent Area 4 at Middleton Place exhibit markedly higher percentage frequencies of porcelain than do all other domestic activity areas. The consistency of this frequency suggests a similarity in the use rate of this artifact. The occurrence of the next highest frequencies of porcelain in those areas closest to the main house areas reflects the concentrated use of this artifact in one portion of the settlements. The pattern of differential porcelain occurrence at Middleton Place and Hampton mirrors the deposition pattern of individual high-status artifacts and the appearance of high-status architecture on both sites.

On the basis of the distribution of Subsistence and status-related artifacts, it has been possible to identify the locations of three key elements of plantation settlements at Middleton Place and Hampton. These archaeological data have delineated areas of high- and low-status domestic occupation and specialized activity areas on both sites. Figure 8.24 illustrates the distribution of these areas relative to the layout of buildings whose locations have been based on structural data. Middleton Place is characterized by a complex of high-status domestic structures that constitute the main house group and by several clusters of low-status domestic structures that lay peripheral to it. Between and somewhat separated from the domestic structure groups stood a specialized activity structure. At Hampton, the main house complex is separated from the lower-status domestic structures and specialized activity structures by an intervening pond. The classification of activity areas at Middleton Place and Hampton as domestic does not imply that they served exclusively in this capacity. Indeed, most of their activity category artifact frequencies fall within the limits of those areas at Camden that are likely to have contained other activities as well. Such a combination of activities may indicate the dual usage of areas and structures resulting from housing laborers close to their places of work. The presence of combined specialized and domestic structures was not uncommon on colonial plantations elsewhere in the American South, where house servants and those associated with household industries and crafts were often quartered in or adjacent to structures devoted to these activities (Anthony 1976:13–14).

Functional Variation in the Main House Area Perhaps the best example of a combined activity area is the main house area itself. Within this complex, specialized activities should be associated primarily with the dependency structures. These activities may be identified archaeologically by observing variation in the occurrence of functionally significant artifact classes within the complex. On the basis of such a comparison, it should be possible to distinguish archaeological patterning related to the distribution of past activities.

The most common specialized activity likely to have produced a recognizable archaeological by-product occurred in the kitchen where food was processed, pre-

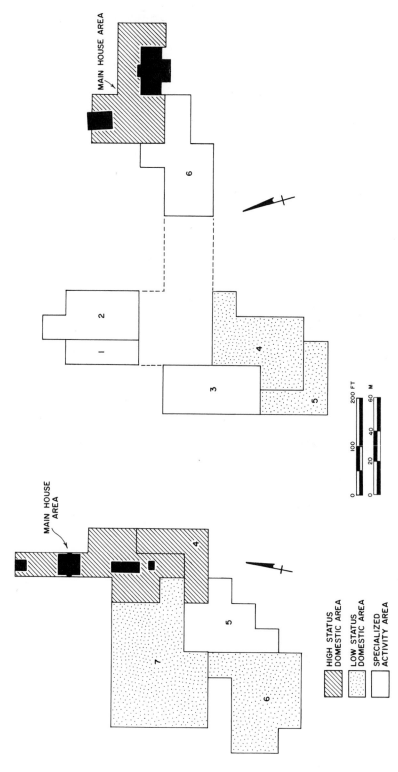

FIGURE 8.24 Status association with activity areas at Middleton Place and Hampton. (Sources: see text.)

TABLE 8.13 Percentage frequencies of faunal material to total nonceramic artifacts at Middleton Place and Hampton[a]

Site	Percentage frequency
Middleton Place	
North dependency	30
Main house	12
South dependency	13
Hampton	
West dependency	6
Main house	3
East dependency	14

[a] Sources: Lewis (1979a); Lewis and Hardesty (1979); Lewis and Haskell (1980).

pared, and, to some extent, stored. Relatively large quantities of kitchen refuse are expected to have been generated by such activity. Even if much of it was discarded away from the main house complex, evidence of kitchen activities is likely to have accumulated in or near its place of occurrence from intentional and unintentional disposal. Kitchen artifact debris should include faunal debris accrued as a result of food preparation, European ceramics associated with processing, preparation, and storage of food, and Colono pottery. The latter was apparently used for food preparation in both high- and low-status contexts (Ferguson 1980; Baker 1972:14), as a supplement to European wares. The occurrence of these materials in the archaeological record at Middleton Place and Hampton is shown in Tables 8.13 and 8.14.

Table 8.13 indicates that at both sites one or more of the dependencies has a markedly higher frequency of faunal remains.[8] This implies a greater intensity of food disposal, as might be expected in a kitchen area. The identification of the north dependency at Middleton Place and the east dependency at Hampton as kitchens is further supported by the relative frequencies of occurrence of Colono ware, which is highest in the same areas (Table 8.14). The higher relative occurrence of European serving ceramics at the main houses and the Middleton Place south dependency suggests that the serving and consumption of food was a more typical activity here and that living areas were probably situated in these structures.

The identification of domestic and specialized activity, high and low status, and specialized domestic activity at the extensively sampled sites of Middleton Place and

[8]At Hampton the nearly identical frequencies of faunal remains and serving wares in the east and west dependencies suggest that both would have served as kitchens. Because it is unlikely that both would have been in use simultaneously, their occupations may have been sequential. A comparison of mean ceramic dates obtained from a comparison of materials from the east and west areas indicates that the median dates of their occupations were 1742 and 1786, respectively. This 40-year discrepancy implies the earlier use and abandonment of the east dependency as a kitchen after which the west dependency assumed this role.

TABLE 8.14   Percentage frequencies of European processing and Colono ceramics versus European serving ceramics at Middleton Place and Hampton[a]

Site	European processing and Colono ceramics (%)	European serving ceramics (%)
Middleton Place		
North dependency	66	34
Main house	48	52
South dependency	36	64
Hampton		
West dependency	35	65
Main house	30	70
East dependency	36	64

[a] Sources: Lewis (1979a); Lewis and Hardesty (1979); Lewis and Haskell (1980).

Hampton has suggested the presence of functionally significant archaeological patterning capable of identifying plantation activities at a general level. In order to examine these patterns further, we may now look at data recovered from four other isolated colonial-period rural settlements on the Lower Coastal Plain. Because of their association with a geographical region characterized by a predominance of plantation agriculture during the eighteenth century, they are likely to represent components of plantation settlements. Likewise, they should exhibit evidence of plantation behavior similar to that encountered at Middleton Place and Hampton.

The first of these sites, Drayton Hall, contains the large, brick Palladian mansion described earlier. This structure lies at the terminus of an oak-lined road connecting it with the highway paralleling the west bank of the Ashley River. Its architecture and location identify the building as the main house of a plantation settlement, the other structures of which are no longer standing. Archaeological investigations at Drayton Hall were conducted to gather architectural information about the main house and adjacent structures and to obtain material data relating to the lifestyle of their inhabitants (L. Lewis 1978:10). Intensive excavations within and to one side of the house revealed the foundations of a dependency lying to the south of the mansion (Fig. 8.25). Ceramic evidence revealed that the site was occupied by the middle of the eighteenth century (L. Lewis 1978:57).

Because architectural information indicated that a main house complex is present, it is anticipated that archaeological data obtained here will exhibit patterning reflecting the role of this plantation component. A comparison of the percentage frequencies of Subsistence, Subsistence–Technological, and Technological activity-category artifacts at Middleton Place and Hampton have shown that the main house areas there produced a relatively lower frequency of Subsistence category artifacts than other domestic areas at those sites (Table 8.11). Although specific activities are

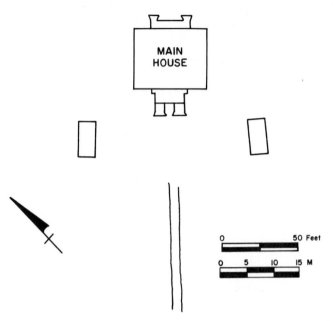

FIGURE 8.25   Structures in the main house complex at Drayton Hall. (Source: L. Lewis 1978:16–17.)

not identified by this pattern, it seems to indicate a reduced role for domestic activity and the discard of its by-products here. Frequencies of activity-category artifacts from Drayton Hall may be compared to those from these two sites to determine if the observed pattern occurs here as well. The similarity of the frequencies (Table 8.15) suggests a common pattern of material evidence denoting activity areas of like function within a plantation settlement.

As a main house complex, the Drayton Hall site is also expected to yield evidence of its inhabitants' high status within the larger plantation settlement. At Middleton Place and Hampton, high status was measured by the relative proportion of porcelain contained in the archaeological deposits associated with the structure-based activity at each site. It was noted that in each main house complex, porcelain constituted 18–20% of the total European ceramics recovered, a percentage fre-

TABLE 8.15   Comparison of percentage frequencies of activity category artifacts at the main house areas of Middleton Place, Hampton, and Drayton Hall[a]

Activity category	Middleton Place	Hampton	Drayton Hall
Subsistence	58.2	56.2	58.2
Subsistence–Technological	41.2	43.6	41.8
Technological	0.6	0.2	0.1

[a] Source: L. Lewis (1977).

quency well above that found in all other areas of both sites. At Drayton Hall, porcelain makes up 18% of the European ceramics in the main house area, a frequency comparable to that observed at the other plantations. The occurrence of this frequency of porcelain here supports our assumption regarding a high-status occupation at Drayton Hall.

Main house complexes at Middleton Place and Hampton also yielded evidence of internal activity patterning, particularly that relating to the preparation and consumption of food. Since one of the dependencies at Drayton Hall is also likely to have been a kitchen, artifact patterning reflecting this activity is likely to be in evidence if this structure was excavated. The extent to which food preparation or consumption activities were carried out at the main house and its dependency were measured using the same criteria as at Middleton Place and Hampton. At Drayton Hall, faunal material accounts for 15% of the nonceramic artifacts in the main house and 28% in the dependency. Similarly, the greatest percentage frequency of Colono and European processing ceramics (33%) also occurs in the dependency (L. Lewis 1977).

A comparison of the statistical relationships between certain functionally significant classes of artifacts obtained in the intensive excavations at Drayton Hall has revealed patterning similar to that encountered on the two extensively sampled plantation sites. These patterns reveal the status of the sites' inhabitants and intrasite variation in the occurrence of specialized domestic activities. The fact that material data have permitted the identification of Drayton Hall as a plantation main house complex implies that other components of this colonial settlement type may also be recognized on the basis of the patterning derived from the results of sampling. Consequently, an examination of archaeological remains at several other sites likely to represent domestic plantation components should reveal material patterning showing their past function. Four such sites are examined below.

Domestic Plantation Components The Spier's Landing site (Fig. 5.1) consists of the subsurface remains of a small structure that rested on posts with a wattle-and-daub chimney at one end and four pit features, one of which lay within the structure. Ceramic evidence indicates the site was occupied as early as 1790 (Drucker and Anthony 1979:90, 96, 150).

At the Yaughn site (Fig. 5.1), several structures set on posts were discovered. Ceramic evidence indicates that the Yaughn site was occupied after 1780 (Thomas R. Wheaton, personal communication, 1982). The structures were arranged in roughly linear fashion as though set out according to a plan (Fig. 8.26). Such a layout is characteristic of plantation settlements, and its appearance here is suggestive of this occupance form. Substantial artifact collections were obtained from the structures, which permits an analysis of activities associated with these architectural features. Because of the architectural similarity of the post structures, they are assumed to have had a similar function and are examined together by site.

The Spring Grove site (38BK359) is represented by an intensive surface collec-

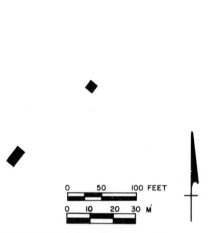

FIGURE 8.26   The Yaughn site, showing structure locations. (Source: Garrow *et al.* 1981.)

tion conducted at the site of an isolated rural settlement with associated structural ruins. Ceramic evidence indicates that it was occupied in the last quarter of the eighteenth century (Anthony and Drucker 1983).

In order to establish the function of the Spier's Landing and Yaughn sites as plantation domestic areas, it is necessary to make a comparison of Subsistence, Subsistence–Technological, and Technological activity artifacts from each site and those areas of Middleton Place and Hampton assumed to have contained lower-status domestic occupations. The percentage frequencies of activity category artifacts at each of these sites is shown in Table 8.16. When plotted on a graph (Fig. 8.23), the frequencies from all but one site cluster into two groups near the upper end of the Subsistence axis. The sites falling into the lower cluster exhibit frequencies closely approximating those found in the lower-status living areas at Middleton Place and Hampton and those associated with combined domestic–specialized ac-

TABLE 8.16   Comparison of percentage frequencies of activity category artifacts at the Spier's Landing, Yaughn, and Spring Grove sites with lower status domestic areas at Middleton Place and Hampton[a]

| Activity category | Spier's Landing | Yaughn | Middleton Place | | | Hampton | |
			Area 4	Area 6	Area 7	Area 4	Area 5
Subsistence	75.5	71.1	71.2	71.4	74.1	69.2	72.9
Subsistence–Technological	24.2	28.6	28.5	28.4	25.5	30.7	27.0
Technological	0.3	0.3	0.3	0.2	0.4	0	0.1

[a] Sources: Drucker and Anthony (1979); Lewis (1979a); Lewis and Hardesty (1979); Lewis and Haskell (1980); Thomas R. Wheaton, personal communication, 1982.

tivity structures at Camden. The other cluster of frequencies lies close to those frequencies exhibited by the areas at Camden assumed to have been used solely as domestic living areas. On the basis of this comparison, it is possible to assign a combined domestic–specialized activity function to the Spier's Landing and Yaughn sites. As such, they are both likely to have been components of larger plantation settlements. Their identification as slave living areas should be reflected in the relative occurrence of porcelain.

At Middleton Place and Hampton, a comparison of the percentage frequencies of porcelain to total European ceramics has revealed that the quantity of this artifact varied dramatically throughout the site. Its occurrence was highest in the main house area and markedly lower in all other domestic areas, indicating the differential use of porcelain between high- and low-status residents of plantation settlement. The association of relatively high frequencies of porcelain with occupants of the main house complex at these two sites is paralleled by the results of excavations at the main house area at Drayton Hall. It is anticipated that lower frequencies comparable to those found at lower-status domestic areas at Middleton Place and Hampton will distinguish the archaeological record from similar components of other plantation settlements. The layout and architecture of Spier's Landing and Yaughn suggests that they represent plantation components, and the high frequencies of Subsistence activity artifacts indicate that the structures housed domestic activities. The low status of the inhabitants of Spier's Landing, Yaughn, and Spring Grove is reflected in the percentage frequencies of porcelain to other European ceramics as shown in Table 8.17. These figures reveal that the frequency range of porcelain here is well below the 10% upper limit of porcelain occurrence in the lower-status domestic areas of Middleton Place and Hampton. On the basis of these data, we may conclude that these three sites include similar settlement components that were probably slave houses attached to plantations.

Archaeological investigations at the sites of seven dispersed, rural, colonial period settlements have produced architectural and archaeological evidence that all were plantations. Extensive sample excavations at the sites of Middleton Place and Hampton have not only permitted the definition of settlement form but also the

TABLE 8.17 Frequencies of occurrence of porcelain at the Spier's Landing, Yaughn, and Spring Grove sites[a]

Site	Total European artifacts (%)
Spier's Landing	1.0
Yaughn	1.9
Spring Grove	0.8

[a] Sources: Anthony and Drucker (1983); Drucker and Anthony (1979:49); Thomas R. Wheaton, personal communication, 1982.

delineation of archaeological patterning linked to the functions of various components of the plantation settlement. Data gathered in these investigations have identified both high- and low-status domestic areas and those associated with nondomestic activities. These results were compared with information obtained from intensive excavations at five other sites to determine if these also represent elements of plantation settlements. Archaeological data derived from these sites show patterning similar to that observed at the two extensively examined plantations. The occurrence of common patterning demonstrates the existence of the predicted settlement types and a correspondence between the results obtained from sample excavations and those of a more intensive nature.

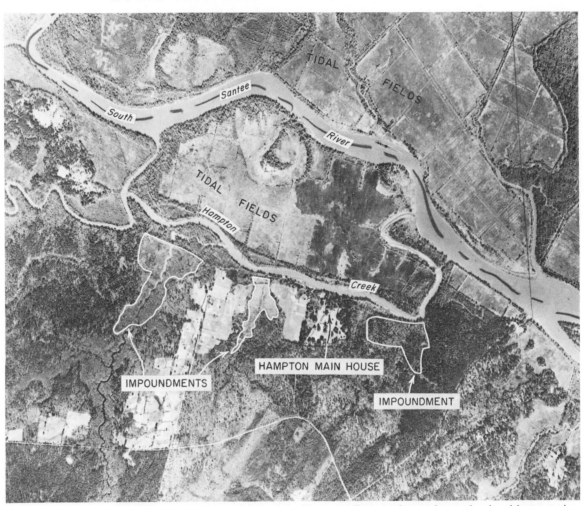

FIGURE 8.27 Vertical aerial photograph of Hampton, illustrating large-scale agricultural modification in the surrounding landscape. Both impounded fields and tidal irrigated fields are illustrated. (Source: USDAASCA 1950.)

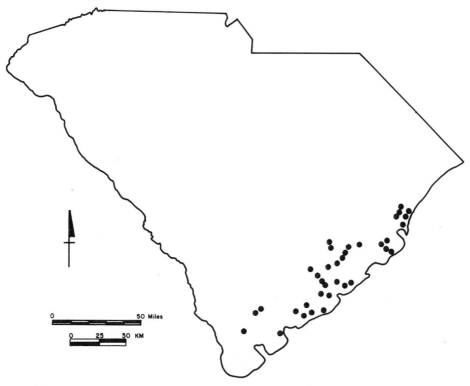

FIGURE 8.28   Distribution of plantation settlements in South Carolina in 1800 based on material evidence. (Sources: see text.)

THE DISTRIBUTION OF PLANTATIONS

The plantations identified on the basis of their archaeological remains above probably represent only a small portion of those that existed in South Carolina during the colonial period. A glimpse of the geographical extent of this settlement type may be seen in the distribution of other kinds of physical evidence associated with its occurrence. Such evidence consists of surviving architecture, primarily the large, rural Palladian houses and their symmetrically placed dependencies and other landscape elements related to large-scale agricultural production.

An examination of the landscapes of Middleton Place, Hampton, and Limerick reveals evidence for a type of agricultural activity associated with plantations. At each site, extensive modifications were carried out to create large, irrigated fields capable of accommodating agricultural production on a massive scale. A vertical aerial photograph of Hampton illustrates several such modifications (Fig. 8.27). The first consists of stream impoundments to create fields by flooding their shallow drainages. A more extensively employed irrigation technique involved the use of canals and dikes to to take advantage of the tidal flow of the coastal rivers for irrigating and draining large areas of adjacent low-lying land. Although these land-scape features cannot be dated precisely on the basis of material evidence alone, their proximity to eighteenth-century plantation sites strongly implies an association with these past settlements.

An areal comparison of the evidence for intensive agricultural irrigation, to-gether with that for surviving plantation architecture, indicates the extent to which these two forms of settlement data share a common distribution. Figure 8.28 shows a pattern with settlement concentrated primarily on the Lower Coastal Plain and particularly along the major coastal rivers. Eighteenth-century plantation farming does not appear to have extended into the Upper Coastal Plain or the Piedmont regions, and its distribution complements that of farms which were largely confined to the interior (Fig. 8.16). The concentration of plantation farming in the riverine region of the Coastal Plain implies that constraints imposed by the environmental and transport requirements of large-scale commercial production of available staple crops limited the geographical extent of this type of agriculture and its accompany-ing settlement form during the colonial period.

SETTLEMENT FUNCTION AND DISTRIBUTION: A SUMMARY

On the basis of archaeological evidence, it has been possible to discern that each of the principal settlement types usually associated with insular frontier colonization was present in eighteenth-century South Carolina. When plotted on a map, the locations of these settlements illustrate the overall patterning at the close of the colonial period and the spatial arrangement of the hierarchical structure of settle-ment. The entrepôt of Charleston, characterized by its size, accessibility to the metropolitan area, and the presence of a variety of centralizing institutions and elaborate status differentiation, lay in a central position on the South Carolina coast. Two smaller coastal settlements, Beaufort and Georgetown, and the inland settle-ment of Camden have been identified as frontier towns on the basis of their size and layout and by the presence of certain centralizing institutions and some internal status differentiation. Their locations reflect placement as secondary economic cen-ters to permit the consolidation of trade and administrative control over a large portion of the colony.

The absence of frontier towns in the western interior indicates the later settle-ment of this area. By the time it was occupied in the second half of the eighteenth century, the frontier town of Augusta had arisen as a regional center and controlled much of the developing trade in this part of South Carolina. Although outside our area of study because it lies in the neighboring colony of Georgia, Augusta's exis-tence is crucial to understanding the gap in the material record for settlements of this type west of Camden.

An analysis of the archaeological record has permitted the identification of the two larger types of frontier settlements in South Carolina. Likewise, several exam-ples of smaller types, nucleated and dispersed settlements, have also been discerned on the basis of this form of evidence. The sites of three eighteenth-century nucleated settlements have been examined. All lie in the Piedmont or the Piedmont–Upper Coastal Plain transition zone, suggesting a concentration of this settlement type in the interior. Archaeological evidence from Ninety-Six, Long Bluff, and Pinckneyville has permitted the recognition of a distinct layout characteristic of smaller commercial settlements. Their placement at central locations in the overland trade and communications network, combined with evidence for the existence of specialized activities, reveals the integrative role of nucleated settlements in this frontier region.

Dispersed settlements are by far the most common type in a frontier region. Archaeological investigations, however, have identified only a few such settlements in South Carolina. Architectural and archaeological data have allowed three farm settlements to be examined in detail. It is likely, however, that a large number of isolated, rural, domestic structures dating from this period also represent this type of settlement. In general, farm sites are confined to the Upper Coastal Plain and Piedmont regions, which implies that this form of agricultural production was most adaptive in the interior.

Archaeological investigations have also identified the sites of eight plantation settlements. These excavations have shown distinctive patterns of architecture as well as activity content and distribution that characterized the plantation as an occupance form. Architectural attributes associated with plantations have allowed a number of additional sites to be identified. Their distribution indicates that this type of dispersed settlement was found largely along the major river valleys of the Lower Coastal Plain. Associated with this zone of settlement is evidence for extensive agricultural land modification, marking the development of large areas for commercial agricultural production.

The complementary distribution of farm and plantation settlements appears to indicate the existence of at least two principal regions of agricultural production. Farming was carried out over a wide area of the interior in a variety of environments. The wide distribution of farm sites implies an overland system of transport is apt to have served this area. Evidence of such a road network and the placement of larger interior settlements at strategic locations within it support this assumption. The association of plantations with the courses of large, navigable coastal rivers, on the other hand, suggests that waterborne transport dominated this region, a statement corroborated by the occurrence of shipwrecks in many of these watercourses.

The development of the two agricultural regions in colonial South Carolina appears to have been a sequential process in which the area adjacent to the coastal entrepôt was occupied first. The successful exploitation of this coastal riverine zone through plantation farming appears to have resulted in an initial expansion along the Lower Coastal Plain, a trend observable in Figures 8.2–8.5. Only when this was complete did movement into the interior begin in earnest. With it came the development of a different mode of commercial agricultural production more suitable to a region where environmental factors affecting cultivation and transport were unlike those encountered on the coast.

Despite the development of two contrasting agricultural economies characterized by settlement patterns, the South Carolina frontier developed as a single area of colonization internally integrated by a trade and communications network focused on a single entrepôt. Settlements in this region correspond to types normally associated with insular frontier regions. South Carolina's entrepôt, frontier towns, nucleated settlements, and dispersed settlements have been shown to have played roles similar to their counterparts described in the insular frontier model. So far, we have observed this settlement as a synchronic phenomenon in which individual settlements have been identified as they existed at the apex of their development. Insular frontier change, however, is an evolutionary process that must be examined over time. In order to explore this process diachronically, it is necessary to examine settlements as changing, developing entities, the evolution of which should exhibit the dynamic changes inherent in the colonization gradient.

9

The Colonization Gradient and a Summary
of the Archaeological Analysis

The process of insular frontier colonization involves both the creation of new settlements as the frontier expands and the modification of earlier settlements within the colonial area. Settlements within an area of colonization may be ranked in order of their complexity according to a hierarchical arrangement known as the colonization gradient. Components of the gradient may be recognized by observing the region as a whole at any time during its development or by noting the changes in individual settlements as they change through time.

If a frontier region is viewed synchronically, the newer settlements, furthest from the entrepôt along the transport network, should be the least complex. Conversely, settlements of greater complexity will be located increasingly closer to the focal point of the colony. As the area of colonization expands through time, less-complex settlements formerly on the periphery are incorporated into the growing network of trade and communications and adapt to their new position by taking on additional roles. The development of this network may also remove advantages possessed by other settlements, causing their decline and abandonment. Processual changes inherent in the colonization gradient reflect the evolution of a frontier region and the settlements in it through the time and space. The results of these changes should be discernible in the material record of some of the settlements we have examined.

251

HYPOTHESIS 11: THE COLONIZATION GRADIENT

Viewing the Gradient as a Spatial Phenomenon

An examination of the distribution of settlement in colonial South Carolina should permit us to observe the colonization gradient as a spatial phenomenon as the frontier expanded. In general, the entrepôt should lie in a central location at the edge of the occupied area most closely accessible to the metropolitan area. The periphery of settlement expanding outward from it should always consist of dispersed settlements. When larger settlements develop, they should appear within an area already occupied and serve as focal points for activity there. If both frontier towns and nucleated settlements are present, the latter should be situated closest to the edge of settlement. The development of central settlements should occur throughout the period of frontier growth, with new settlements appearing as the zone of dispersed settlement expands.

The colonization gradient and its changing appearance as the colony expands may be illustrated by plotting the locations of central frontier settlements on a series of maps (Fig. 9.1). Although the incomplete nature of the present material data has left many gaps in our knowledge of settlement locations, particularly the smaller settlements, the overall pattern is similar to that predicted in the model. Charleston, which had developed as the entrepôt by 1700, was surrounded by dispersed settlements at this time (Fig. 9.1A). By the time Georgetown and Beaufort had emerged as the colony's first frontier towns in the 1730s, settlement had already spread inland from the coast (Fig. 9.1B). These two settlements lay at the centers of developing regions, each with an expanding hinterland. By 1760, dispersed settlement had moved far into the interior; however, only after another decade did Camden arise as a frontier town in this region. Ninety-Six, a nucleated settlement, appeared at about this time, as did Long Bluff on the Pee Dee River (Fig. 9.1C). Pinckneyville, farther to the north, did not develop as a nucleated settlement at this time. It appeared in the 1780s, well after this part of the colony had been occupied by dispersed settlement (Fig. 9.1D). The distribution of complex settlements exhibited an overall pattern similar to that anticipated. The frontier towns lay closest to the entrepôt and the nucleated settlements were closer to the periphery of settlement. Dispersed settlement surrounded all the other settlement types and formed the milieu in which they developed as the frontier expanded. In addition to forming the greater part of the settlement throughout the area of colonization, dispersed settlement always constituted the earliest occupation of new lands. The material remains of settlement in eighteenth century South Carolina clearly illustrate the spatial aspect of the colonization gradient in this insular frontier region.

The Colonization Gradient in Temporal Perspective

In order to observe the colonization gradient as a process of change, an individual settlement that had attained the complexity of a frontier town or entrepôt

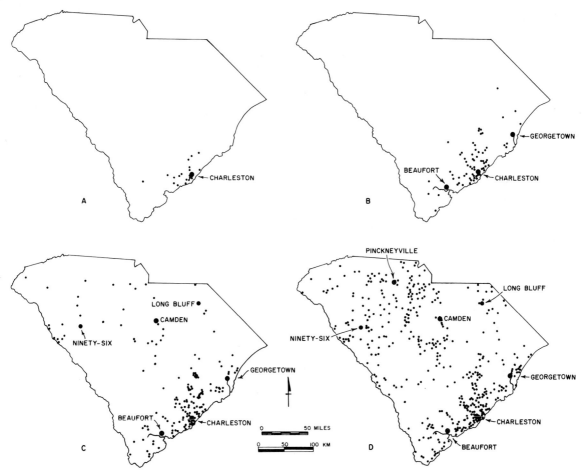

FIGURE 9.1   The association of central settlement appearance and the overall spread of settlement in South Carolina during the eighteenth century: A, 1700; B, 1740; C, 1770; D, 1800. (Sources: see text.)

may be examined. If complete, data from such a site should yield evidence of the settlement's growth from a smaller dispersed settlement with a primarily domestic agricultural function to a larger settlement containing the multiple functions of an economic and political center. Only one such settlement has been extensively examined in South Carolina, the frontier town of Camden.

Camden is likely to have originated as a small dispersed settlement that grew to its optimum size during the colonial period. Later its site was gradually abandoned as its population shifted northward to the location of the present city. The form of Camden's growth during the frontier period should be discernible in the distribution of datable archaeological materials recovered from the site of this settlement. An analysis of ceramic artifacts obtained in the sample excavations revealed that the site's most intensive occupation occurred about 1791 and that the range of that

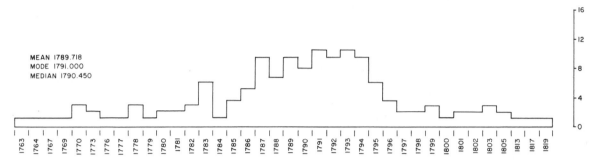

MEAN 1789.718
MODE 1791.000
MEDIAN 1790.450

FIGURE 9.2 Frequency distribution of mean ceramic dates of excavated sample units at Camden. (Source: Lewis 1976:82.)

occupation lasted from about 1750 to 1820 (Lewis 1976:82). A frequency distribution of sample unit mean ceramic dates by year forms a unimodal curve with a mode of 1791. This indicates a gradual growth before and a similar decline after this data (Fig. 9.2). If we assume that Camden reached its maximum size prior to 1791, its development as a frontier town is likely to have occurred during the previous 40 years.

It will be necessary to determine the sequence in which the site was occupied in order to trace Camden's growth. Our previous discussion of Camden indicated that the town consisted of a number of activity areas, each of which was centered on a structure or group of structures. If we assume that each of these represents a unit of occupation that arose separately from those around it, the beginning dates of each area's occupation should indicate the temporal order of their appearance. This

TABLE 9.1 Occupational ranges of activity areas at Camden[a]

Area	Estimated ranges[b]	Mean ceramic date
1	1770–1820	1793
2	1759–1820	1792
3	1762–1820	1785
4	1759–1820	1790
5	1763–1820	1789
6	1762–1820	1790
7	1765–1820	1787
8	1744–1820	1791
9	1750–1820	1794
10	1765–1820	1795

[a] Source: SIR.

[b] The ranges have been calculated using the mean ceramic dating formula and the bracketing tool described in the text.

sequence should, in turn, reveal the morphological development of the settlement through time and permit us to observe Camden's growth as a frontier town.

Ceramic evidence, because of its temporal sensitivity, may be used effectively to calculate the occupational range of each of the 10 structure-based activity areas at Camden. These ranges are shown in Table 9.1. The date ranges clearly indicate a sequential pattern of settlement at Camden. Based on ceramic evidence, Camden's earliest occupation occurred in the 1740s and encompassed only a small portion of the townsite, Area 8 (Fig. 9.3A). In the following decade several other areas were settled adjacent to Broad Street (Fig. 9.3B). These produced a linear settlement composed of perhaps as many as five structures (cf. Fig. 8.1). During the decade of the 1760s, the greater part of the townsite was occupied (Fig. 9.3C), with only its northwest corner left to be settled after 1770 (Fig. 9.3D).

Camden's growth followed the pattern anticipated for frontier towns in insular frontier regions. Beginning as an isolated rural settlement on a through road in the eighteenth century, Camden expanded along this thoroughfare, and within the next quarter century it had grown into a town of at least two dozen structures arranged in a grid pattern. The early townsite was abandoned in the early nineteenth century as settlement shifted northward. Although the postcolonial site has not been explored archaeologically, material evidence of the expansion of Camden is present in the

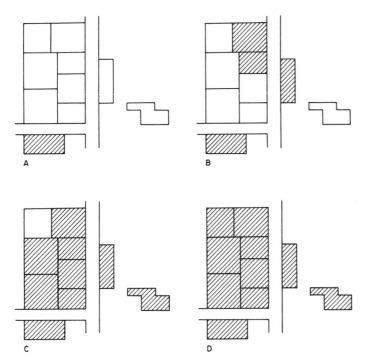

FIGURE 9.3   Camden's growth in the eighteenth century as evidenced by archaeological dates of occupation: A, before 1750; B, 1750–1759; C, 1760–1769; D, after 1770. (Source: Lewis 1976.)

form of numerous structures built in the early 1800s (Kirkland and Kennedy 1926; Schulz 1972; Sweet 1978; SWPC 1972). Using the distribution of structural evidence as a guide, it was possible to estimate the size of Camden in the early nineteenth century. Figure 9.4 illustrates the spatial extent of Camden by 1830. This map is

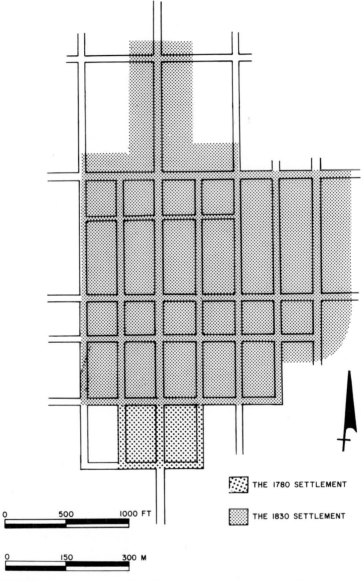

THE 1780 SETTLEMENT

THE 1830 SETTLEMENT

0   500   1000 FT

0   150   300 M

FIGURE 9.4 Camden in 1830. The occupied area of the antebellum town clearly reveals not only its substantial growth over the size of the earlier settlement, but also the abandonment of the eighteenth century townsite. (Source: Schulz 1972:79.)

superimposed on the present street grid which follows the orientation of the colonial settlement. The growth of the town in this relatively short time is obvious and shows the further evolution of Camden into a regional center in the postcolonial period.

The temporal aspect of the colonization gradient is clearly recognizable in the changing settlement pattern of Camden, a successful frontier settlement that passed through several stages of growth to become a frontier town. Camden's success was undoubtedly due to its maintaining a central position in the trade and communications network throughout the colonial period. This condition enabled it to emerge as a focus of political and social activities as well as an economic center. The inability of other frontier settlements to maintain such a central role appears to have led to their failure. Ninety-Six, Long Bluff, and Pinckneyville were all nucleated settlements that emerged in the interior during the last half of the eighteenth century, declined subsequently, and were abandoned. The sites of the last two were never reoccupied and their central functions shifted, presumably, to other settlements emerging as colonial centers. The time of their decline is reflected by the terminal dates of the temporal ranges of ceramic artifacts recovered at their sites. As we have seen, these ranges suggest that decline and abandonment occurred in the first quarter of the nineteenth century, which indicates the settlements' demise was just after the close of the frontier period.

The distribution of complex frontier settlements on the colonial landscape and their development over time witnessed the operation of the colonization gradient in South Carolina. Camden, with its direct link to the entrepôt, was the largest of the interior settlements and emerged as a frontier town. It lay in a position central to the three nucleated settlements identified archaeologically, Ninety-Six, Long Bluff, and Pinckneyville, and this geographical situation allowed it to serve efficiently as a focus of trade and communications throughout this area. Camden's development from a small, dispersed rural settlement provides an example of the colonization gradient as a temporal process. Its growth illustrates the evolution of frontier settlements as their roles change in response to the changing economy of the colonial region. Camden, like many settlements of the frontier period, remained a regional center, while others did not. Expanding population density, the introduction of new agricultural commodities, and shifting networks of transport in the area of colonization resulted in an increasingly more complex level of socioeconomic integration and a restructured settlement hierarchy. This development marked the culmination of the colonization gradient in South Carolina and established the settlement pattern that would characterize the state until the present century.

SUMMARY OF THE ARCHAEOLOGICAL ANALYSIS

In this and the previous four chapters we employed 11 archaeological hypotheses to examine material evidence from South Carolina to demonstrate that this region evolved as an insular frontier during the eighteenth century. These hypotheses were organized according to five subject headings, each of which dealt with a separate aspect of the insular frontier process. The archaeological analysis produced data that support the test implications for each hypothesis, thereby demonstrating the occurrence of the insular frontier process. In the remainder of this chapter, we shall summarize and synthesize the results of this analysis and address a few of their implications.

The Colony's Establishment

Hypotheses concerned with the colony's establishment have focused on demonstrating the transplantation of a foreign society to an overseas area of colonization and the subsequent creation of a permanent settlement there. A colonial society is characterized both by cultural continuity with the parent state and innovation resulting from adaptation to the physical and social environment of the frontier area. Cultural continuity and change was observed through an examination of two categories of artifacts commonly found throughout the region, ceramics and architecture. Ceramic use in early South Carolina mirrored that of the homeland, and the extensive use of British ware has clearly identified the colony's social and economic affiliation. The chronological sensitivity of these artifacts permitted the placement of settlement sites within the temporal framework of British colonization in North America. It also enabled us to observe the spatial distribution of settlement through time in the area of colonization. Ceramic artifacts also were useful in measuring technological innovation and adaptation on the frontier. To supplement imported English ceramics, the inhabitants of colonial South Carolina obtained and used wares representing three colonial ceramic traditions with roots in Germany, England, West Africa, and aboriginal America.

The surviving architecture of the colonial period offered another form of material evidence with which to measure cultural continuity and change on the frontier. Contemporary English Palladian architecture provided a dominant stylistic theme for this colonial area, particularly in the urban coastal settings, but was modified extensively to adapt it to the climate of the region and the function of various structures. Colonial architecture was also influenced by a tradition of log construction that developed in the northern colonies and diffused southward. Colonial building was marked also by the extensive use of wood in both traditional and log architecture. Wood largely replaced other building materials employed in contemporary Europe and appears to have been an adaptive use of an abundant resource.

The establishment of the colony is also reflected in the long-term nature of its settlement. An examination of a number of extensively investigated archaeological sites revealed the existence of overlapping occupations lasting from the last half of the seventeenth century to the close of the colonial period at the end of the eighteenth century. The data also permitted the delineation of likely sites for the colony's entrepôt. The identification of the entrepôt is critical to the investigation of a frontier region because, as the earliest permanent settlement site, it constitutes a point of origin from which subsequent expansion can be measured.

Spatial Patterning

The next two hypotheses were centered on the definition of spatial patterning within the area of colonization as a whole. The entrepôt is situated at the center of the expanding settlement network of a colonial region. The locations of three potential entrepôt settlements on the South Carolina coast could be narrowed to one, Charleston, because of its earlier time of settlement. In order to identify it as such on the basis of material evidence, it was necessary to demonstrate that Charleston was the largest settlement and that it possessed the centralizing institutions associated with the entrepôt's function as the colony's social, economic, and political center and principal link with the metropolitan area. Available material data from all three sites was largely architectural, yet a study of structural remains was sufficient to reveal both the size and content of the settlements. The distribution of structures demonstrated Charleston's markedly greater size. The presence of a variety of specialized activity structures identified it as having contained the greatest number of centralizing institutions in the region. Charleston clearly emerged as the entrepôt of South Carolina.

Because economic expansion within a colonial region centers on the entrepôt, the settlement pattern that develops generally assumes a dendritic form with a transportation network linking all parts of the area to the entrepôt. An examination of the distribution of standing structures, archaeological sites, and cemeteries in South Carolina dating from the latter part of the colonial period provided a graphic view of the pattern of frontier settlement in its most developed stage. The settlement pattern revealed was similar to that predicted. Settlement extended inland along and between the major river drainages as far as the borders of the present state. Traces of colonial roads associated with these sites were also mapped to determine probable overland transport routes, and early shipwrecks and landings in rivers were plotted to estimate the extent of water transport in colonial South Carolina. These data indicated a dual system of transport, composed of a dendritic pattern of overland routes linking Charleston with the interior and a coastal riverine system tying Charleston and the settlements of the Lower Coastal Plain together.

Expansion

In addition to providing information relevant to the form of the South Carolina frontier, material data from this region also were employed to investigate change in the area of colonization through time. The expansion of this area is a major element of the insular frontier process as is the development of distinct types of frontier settlements. In order to study this process in South Carolina, two hypotheses were examined. The first assumed expansion to have been a continuous process throughout the colonial period. Settlement expansion during this time was explored using maps of the distributions of standing structures, archaeological sites, and cemeteries at regular intervals throughout the eighteenth century. A comparison of these maps revealed an initial expansion along the coast from the area of earliest settlement, followed by gradual movement into the interior along the major river drainages. The northwest section of the province was the last area to be settled in the closing years of the colonial period. The three-stage settlement of South Carolina was seen as a response to economic factors that favored the exploitation of the riverine coastal region before expanding into the interior, which required an additional system of overland transport. The avoidance of the northwest resulted from substantial groups of potentially hostile aboriginal peoples who were not removed until the third quarter of the eighteenth century.

The settlement of insular frontier regions is characterized by a distributional trend toward even spacing. This reflects adjustments to increasing population density and competition for land. A comparison of nearest-neighbor values for settlement in South Carolina showed that a trend from clustered toward evenly spaced distribution continued throughout the colonial period and revealed the gradual filling in of open areas left vacant by initial expansion.

Settlement Pattern and the Distribution of Activities

Three hypotheses relating to individual settlement form and content were examined to determine if the various settlement types normally found in insular frontier regions were associated with South Carolina. The sites of various historic settlements provided material data upon which to identify frontier towns, nucleated settlements, and dispersed settlements. The function of these frontier settlements is closely related to their size, layout, and content. An examination of these factors was carried out using data derived from historical and archaeological analogs of contemporary settlements. An analysis of archaeological and architectural information showed the presence of three frontier towns: Georgetown and Beaufort on the coast and Camden in the interior. Three nucleated settlements were also identified: Ninety-Six in the west, Pinckneyville in the north, and Long Bluff to the east on the Pee Dee River. Dispersed settlements of two types were found associated with the colonial landscape of South Carolina. Farms were by far the most common, constituting the bulk of interior settlements, but plantations dominated the riverine coastal region of the colony. Because each settlement type represents agricultural adaptations differing in scale and organization, the differential occurrence of farms and plantations was assumed to denote distinctly different agricultural economies on the coast and in the interior. This economic disparity also corresponded with the differential expansion of settlement and the limits imposed by environmental factors on plantation farming in the eighteenth century. These obstacles are likely to have resulted in the initial resistence to expansion inland from the Lower Coastal Plain.

The Colonization Gradient

Finally, the dynamic aspect of frontier settlement was investigated by seeking evidence for the colonization gradient. This phenomenon was verified spatially by noting the differing complexity of colonial settlements during the colonial period in terms of their geographical positions relative to the focus of colonial activity, the entrepôt. As anticipated, the distribution of settlements showed the frontier town of Camden to have been closest to the entrepôt in terms of the overland transport network, with the three nucleated settlements located closer to the outer boundaries of settlement and the dispersed settlement extending to the edge of the frontier. As a temporal process, the colonization gradient was examined at the site of Camden because this frontier town was expected to have passed through all stages of less-complex settlement growth. Camden was found to have originated as a dispersed settlement, expanded into a nucleated settlement, and finally attained its maximum size and complexity as a frontier town, all within a relatively short period. By illustrating a sequence of increasingly more complex settlement forms corresponding to those observed over the region as a whole, the evolution of Camden demonstrated the occurrence of the colonization gradient as a developmental process reflecting the stages of growth observed synchronically in the overall settlement pattern of the region.

South Carolina as an Insular Frontier

The archaeological evidence presented tends to support the hypotheses for the occurrence of insular frontier change in South Carolina. An examination of available material data provided sufficient information regarding both static and dynamic aspects of this frontier process and produced results comparable to those derived from the documentary study of the same historical phenomenon presented in Chapter 3. Although omissions occur regarding particular details in the results of both studies, their conclusions are the same with respect to basic characteristics of change observed. For example, the lack of material evidence for specific documented settlements and the apparent absence of data relating directly to the precise nature of certain economic activities has denied neither the existence of those settlement types in the area of colonization nor the fact that several forms of agricultural production took place.

Although omissions of particular information do not impair our ability to distinguish the general characteristics of frontier change, they do reveal inadequacies in the data base employed. This can result from either the absence of data pertaining to particular aspects of a past society or a failure on the part of the investigator to collect such data. Thus, when we observe that material evidence has provided a more comprehensive and accurate picture of settlement than have historical accounts of this process, it may indicate that no such documentary information survived or merely that such evidence never was compiled. Similarly, the absence of material data relating to examples of the settlement types discussed points to obvious gaps in our knowledge reflecting the present incompleteness of archaeological research in South Carolina. The ability of each type of research to illuminate the other illustrates the complementary nature of documentary and archaeological research, and demonstrates the obvious advantages to be gained from employing both in the investigation of general as well as particular questions.

The accessibility of certain types of information made possible the delineation of the process of insular frontier colonization in South Carolina. These include chronological and settlement pattern data for the region as a whole and evidence relating to the layout and composition of individual settlements. These data provided temporal and spatial parameters for the study of processual change and information relating to the development of specific components within this milieu. The comprehensive nature of insular frontier change makes it amenible to analyses employing regional data as well as more specific evidence. Studies of this and other processes of colonization must consider both to be effective.

South Carolina is not unique in that insular frontier change took place here or that its occurrence is discernible in terms of material evidence. Our ability to observe this change archaeologically demonstrates that processes of frontier colonization can be detected on the basis of its material remains and that the process itself is a valid generalization useful in interpreting the evolutionary history of colonial regions. The insular frontier model may be used to explore the development of other such areas to determine if colonization followed this particular adaptive strategy and under what range of conditions this process may have occurred. We have seen, however, that insular frontiers are the result of one type of process of colonization. Thus, when investigating the development of a colonial region about which little is known, or whose development is at variance with the process described above, it is necessary to consider alternate models to that of insular frontier change. Such models characterize processes of cosmopolitan frontier colonization and their occurrence should be discernible in the form and structure of the material record. These frontier processes often preceded and coexisted with insular frontier development, and although more transient since they would have produced no permanent colonial society, represent equally significant types of frontier settlement. It is now appropriate to consider additional frontier processes.

10

Beyond the Insular Frontier

INTRODUCTION

In the previous chapters we have dealt with a singular process of colonization, one that is associated with the permanent settlement of new lands by immigrant agriculturalists. Insular frontier colonization is one of the dominant processes associated with the expansion of Europe and has potential usefulness in analyzing the development of most areas occupied by intrusive Old World populations. The insular frontier model is not intended to describe other types of colonization that accompanied European expansion. Cosmopolitan frontiers are regions of specialized economic activity which exhibit little of the fundamental change associated with insular frontiers. Instead they reflect the variability inherent in their specific functions. The need to describe and explain the range of variation encompassed by this phenomenon requires the creation of an additional frontier model or models, a point that this chapter addresses.

It is beyond the scope of this book to develop and test comprehensive models of cosmopolitan frontier change. It is, however, our intent to begin an inquiry into this important aspect of colonization. Before attempting to analyze cosmopolitan frontier change, we must examine first its general role as a part of an expanding world economy. It should then be possible to analyze processes of change accompanying it and to isolate significant socioeconomic variables linked to these processes. On the basis of this information, we may infer the manner in which the organizational structure of societies found in cosmopolitan frontier areas might adapt to their roles in the world economy. A knowledge of these adaptive strategies should permit us to make inferences regarding the structural organization of settlement in these regions and the manner in which it is likely to be revealed in the material record. From these results, the state of current knowledge about this type of colonization process may be assessed, and this will allow us to determine what information is necessary to construct usable models of cosmopolitan frontier development.

EXPANDING THE FRONTIER CONCEPT: COSMOPOLITAN FRONTIER CHANGE

Within an expanding world economy, colonization follows two general courses. Insular frontier development is associated with the permanent occupation of regions by agriculturalists and is marked by the process of fundamental change described in Chapter 2. Cosmopolitan frontier change follows a different course. Unlike their agricultural counterparts, cosmopolitan frontiers arise to accommodate specialized, extractive economic activities in peripheral areas of the world economy. Because of their limited interests, these frontiers are often short term and impermanent. Their close economic ties with the homeland result in an absence of the insularity found in frontiers characterized by permanent settlement. Therefore, cosmopolitan frontiers experience little indigenous change (Steffen 1980:*xvii*). This is not to imply that change does not occur in such areas, but rather that it is of a significantly different type (Hardesty 1982). Cosmopolitan frontier change is an adaptation to the economic system in which it plays a major role rather than an adaptation to the economic and social milieu of peripheral areas. As a consequence, cosmopolitan frontiers exhibit a greater degree of cultural uniformity despite their varied environments.

The uniformity of cosmopolitan frontier settlement is manifested both in the conscious effort of colonists to maintain behavioral patterns of the parent society and in the development of similar organizational structures to facilitate the various types of extractive activities. Frontier scholars (e.g., Hardesty 1982; Leyburn 1935; Steffen 1980) have stressed both the structural similarity and cultural continuity of cosmopolitan frontiers in their discussions of six basic types of colonization.

Trading Frontiers

The first type of cosmopolitan frontier is devoted to trading. As the name implies, these frontiers involve capitalist activities oriented toward the large-scale acquisition of native commodities for a home market through trade. An example of a trading frontier is that associated with the fur trade in colonial North America (Phillips 1961). Here, as on other trading frontiers, the production of a noncompetitive staple permitted this colonial activity to form an integral part of the mercantilist economy. In order to carry out these activities efficiently, each nation attempted to eliminate competition within its own trading community through regulation and the granting of monopolies. This aided the capitalist traders by assuring them a market for their product, while it assisted the state by exploring and occupying potential imperial acquisitions. Trading frontiers also produced similar economic organizations, in particular the joint-stock company and the factory system.

The joint-stock company, brought together capital from many sources to finance individual ventures. This permitted the amassing of capital to support costly and often risky ventures by distributing costs, profits, and losses; yet was flexible enough to expand and contract in response to the scale of business activity. The factory system, which granted monopoly rights to individual companies, eliminated competition, and allowed centralized control of the full range of activities related to the production, processing, and shipment of frontier commodities to be maintained by a single manager in a permanent place of operation. Such control fostered the coordination of trading activities within the colonial region and increased the efficiency of the entire system of production (Steffen 1980:36–38). Although its organization was rigidly controlled, the structure of the system had to be fluid in order to deal with the transitory nature of trading operations. The impermanent nature of the traders' interaction with the frontier environment, coupled with their close ties to the parent company and the specialized nature of their work, produced a static system and failed to provide the impetus for fundamental change associated with insular frontier regions (Steffen 1980:46–47).

Ranching Frontiers

Ranching constitutes a second type of cosmopolitan frontier. Like fur trading frontiers, these regions were characterized by a behavioral continuity that reflects their lack of insularity. Ranching, or livestock raising, is essentially a form of industrial agriculture like the plantation. It is, however, a separate form of adaptation utilizing a different kind of habitat and is characterized by its own distinct features. The latter derive from the three variables most closely tied to this activity: livestock, land, and markets (Strickon 1965:230). Livestock raising is a land-extensive activity that is not economically competitive with agriculture for the same amount of land. This is because forage for livestock requires a larger land base per calorie of food obtained than would be needed to produce an equal amount of plant food directly usable by man. Consequently, this activity is confined either to areas that are outside or on the fringe of agricultural settlement where transport costs make farming economically unprofitable by comparison or to pockets within permanently settled regions that are unsuitable for agriculture (Strickon 1965:255). Regions of the first category would constitute areas of cosmopolitan frontier settlement.

The cosmopolitan nature of ranching frontiers may be seen in the organization of commercial livestock raising in such areas. Ranching is a transient activity geared toward an external market. The requirements of marketing and the necessity for efficient management to gain a maximum return on investment encourage close ties with the national economy rather than indigenous development. Frontier livestock raising is a short-term high-return investment activity that is an extension of the capitalist entrepreneurial pattern developed in the metropolitan area. Historically, those individuals involved in its management have had only a tenuous association with its physical location, because the latter is merely a setting for production and not the region in which the changes that fostered this production mode took place. In North America, the close association of ranching and the larger national business environment is also reflected in the simultaneous economic change undergone by both in response to technological and marketing pattern changes in the latter part of the nineteenth century (Steffen 1980:64–47).

Although livestock raising persists as part of an integrated diversified economy in nonfrontier regions where ecological and economic conditions permit, ranching as a frontier activity is a specialized extension of the homeland economy. Because they remain tied to and managed by external capitalist interests and thereby maintain a continuity with the parent culture, these regions fall within the domain of cosmopolitan frontier settlement.

Exploitative Plantation Frontiers

Exploitative plantation frontiers (Leyburn 1935) are similar to those devoted to ranching in that they represent areas of industrial agricultural production that are managed by and closely linked with capitalist economic interests in the metropolitan area. Exploitative plantations differ from those associated with insular frontier regions for several reasons. First, residence by those who control production in the former is transient or, as in the case of West Indies sugar plantations (see Chapter 3), absentee. These plantations are transitory, short-term, profit-oriented enterprises intended to exploit a colonial area for the production of noncompetitive commodities. Externally financed, their economic success is not felt in the colony, but profits return to and are reinvested in the core state. The colony is merely a region of extractive production. The intrusive population is limited to management and some temporary specialized technological personnel and does not include their family units. They form a minority among the native or imported foreign laborers and generally establish enclaves which maintain close social ties with the homeland and inhibit the fundamental change characteristic of insular frontier colonization. Like ranching frontiers, exploitative plantation frontiers are tightly bound in the national economy, and fluctuations in the latter can bring about the success or failure of this type of cosmopolitan frontier.

Exploitative plantation frontiers form the model for tropical colonization, described earlier (Chapter 2), since they typify the type of European commercial settlement established in these regions. Such plantations arose in tropical areas because they provided an environment in which a number of noncompetitive commodities could be produced. Labor was obtained either by commandeering native populations or importing hostage groups from other peripheral areas. Because agriculture was a more efficient means of production than ranching and the tropical regions where it was carried out were undesirable for permanent settlement by Europeans, such areas often remained competitive economically. Although retaining the impermanence and external economic and social orientation of cosmopolitan frontiers, exploitative plantations became the most permanent example of this type.

Industrial Frontiers

Industrial frontiers, which include mining, lumbering, and other similar extractive activities, are the next form of cosmopolitan frontier. Like the types discussed above, industrial frontiers are a transient form of economic activity, often of very short duration, conducted by persons temporarily residing in the region, and linked closely to external markets in the core state. Similarly, these settlements experience little fundamental change through time. Uniformity here is maintained through participation in a common activity and a need for market efficiency. Consequently, technological change and innovation spread quickly on the industrial frontier but only so far as they effect higher product quality or greater rates of production (Hardesty 1982).

The cosmopolitan nature of industrial frontiers is reflected in the factors that connected activities in these regions with the core state economy more closely than that of the other types discussed above. Its specialization and consequent lack of self-sufficiency, its temporary nature and dependence on imports, and its often changing technology served to decrease the region's degree of insularity from the national culture and thwart indigenous development (Steffen 1980:89). Behavior on industrial frontiers may be seen clearly as an adaption almost solely to the region's role as a producer of raw commodities rather than to its isolation and the necessity of coping with a new social and physical environment.

Military Frontiers

Military frontiers are found in areas undergoing cosmopolitan frontier colonization. Unlike the other frontier types described above, they are not settled in order to extract or otherwise obtain resources but as an adjunct to these economic activities. Military frontiers are established to provide protection for other colonial activities by pacifying the regions in which the latter take place. Military camps and forts house soldiers to protect, and often to oversee, the conduct of frontier activities and to serve as places of refuge in the event of danger (Prucha 1958:xiii). They are also used to maintain a national presence in areas not yet colonized and serve as bases for exploration and future settlement.

Military frontiers are the type linked most closely with the parent state because they represent one of its agencies. The components of such a frontier represent direct control by the core state in areas where its expansion is threatened either by aboriginal groups or other colonial states. Consequently, military frontiers are not found in all peripheral areas. Because they are linked organizationally to a central source and not to the occurrence of an economic resource, military frontiers may encompass part of a number of cosmopolitan frontier regions. Similarly, their political rather than economic role links their establishment, expansion, and abandonment to factors other than those normally affecting the development of other cosmopolitan frontiers.

Transportation Frontiers

Transportation frontiers, like military frontiers, are associated with the establishment of cosmopolitan frontier regions, yet they are not a part of them. Instead, they represent the intrusive society's links between frontier regions or between such regions and the homeland. Unlike other cosmopolitan frontiers, the areas involved here include no resources to be exploited. They consist only of transportation routes and the settlements necessary to maintain them. Often the latter include garrisons to protect lines of communication and, in such cases, a transportation frontier may be subsumed with a military frontier. This is not always the case, however, and non-military transportation frontiers, such as those supporting the pony express and overland mail routes and the various railroads in the American West, are examples of this type of frontier. Because their existence was tied to the maintenance of the routes they served, transportation frontiers, like their military counterparts, rose and declined as a result of external factors.

PROCESSES OF COSMOPOLITAN FRONTIER CHANGE

The Characteristics of Cosmopolitan Frontiers

Cosmopolitan frontier settlements may be identified by their close association with the economy of the colonizing state and by an absence of fundamental change resulting from adaptation to a new environment. The lack of insularity is apparent in the six frontier types as are several other characteristics. To explore processes of cosmopolitan frontier change, it is necessary to enumerate functional similarities showing the areas' participation in a common experience. What are the central characteristics of cosmopolitan frontier change?

First is the maintenance of close ties with the core state economy. For of each of the six frontier types, success is dependent solely on the ability to produce a marketable commodity for export to a settled region. Because of this specialized role, its survival remains heavily dependent on outside support and attempts need not be made to establish a subsistence base in the colony. Management is by core-state capitalists who are often in absentia. There is also a rapid turnover of settlers, for whom colonization and residence on the frontier is usually only a temporary occupation. Settlers also maintain a social contact with the homeland that reinforces the economic bond between the two regions. The strength of this bond is also reflected in the organization of the colony as a production unit and in its development as an element of the larger core state economy. Cosmopolitan frontier form and change both reflect the region's economic role in a world system.

The nearly complete dependence upon and consequent close ties with the homeland affect the nature of continuity and change in cosmopolitan frontier regions. We have already noted the degree of uniformity, or standardization, in cosmopolitan frontiers resulting from an attempt to extend the culture of the core state into these areas. The continuous flow of material items and a constant transfer of information makes possible not only the maintenance of an imported environment resembling that of the homeland (Ostrogorsky 1982:81) but also the rapid and widespread dissemination of innovations within the area of cosmopolitan frontier colonization. All cosmopolitan frontier regions, even those containing the same type of activity, will not be identical because each involves an adaptation to circumstances encountered in a specific environment. The general similarity of their adaptations, however, seems to indicate the occurrence of common processes of cosmopolitan frontier colonization as well as those peculiar to individual cosmopolitan frontier types. Cosmopolitan frontier processes denote a region's role as an integral part of an expanding state economy, a role that is tied to a larger sequence of overall colonial development.

The role of cosmopolitan frontiers in the expansion of Europe is suggested by Meinig's (1976) model of sequential colonial growth discussed earlier (see Chapter 2). In this scheme, colonization is seen as a process of increasing economic and social complexity, which ranges from initial transient contact with a colonial region to its permanent settlement by a self-sufficient immigrant agricultural population. The final stages of settlement are always preceded by the establishment of commercial activities of the type associated with cosmopolitan frontiers. Consequently, the latter may be seen as a transitory form of colonial settlement in regions later developed as insular frontiers, though not a stage in the evolution of the latter. The rapid growth and decline of cosmopolitan frontiers in areas of subsequent agrarian settlement suggests that activities associated with the former are less competitive economically. The transplantation of one form of frontier activity for another indicates the relative productivity of each, given the same degree of security and accessibility to markets. If a colonial region is accessible to agriculture and possesses adequate transport links, the greater efficiency of this form of production per unit of land favors a switch to commercial plant cultivation and, if this activity is in the hands of immigrant colonists, the development of an insular frontier region.

We have observed the process of transition in the case of ranching, which as a land-extensive activity cannot compete with agriculture in terms of food produced per given amount of land. Most other cosmopolitan frontier activities are also land-extensive and require either large amounts of land to acquire the commodity produced, as in the case of furs or animal skins, or specific resource sites, such as mines, that are located sporadically over a region. Such activities are generally unable to compete economically with agriculture if the regions they occupy become available for and are capable of supporting the latter. For example, in colonial South Carolina, insular frontier settlement followed an initial occupation of the region as a cosmopolitan fur trading frontier (see Chapter 3). Similarly, livestock raising preceded agricultural settlement in many portions of this area (Crane 1929:108–110, 185, Gray 1933:151). While the transition from cosmopolitan to insular frontier was generally peaceful here, it was often accompanied by social disruption. The celebrated conflict between ranchers and homesteaders in the American West and its inevitable outcome is a classic example of the problems potentially accompanying the transition from cosmopolitan to insular frontier settlement.

Cosmopolitan frontier regions may continue to persist alongside those of insular frontier settlement if the former areas are not accessible to agriculture, have inadequate transport links, or produce a commodity of unusually high market value (such as certain mineral resources). Improved agricultural technology, increased demand, improved transport, and an exhaustion of resources could change this situation dramatically and make such areas available for settlement as secondary frontiers (Prescott 1965:38–39). An example of such resettlement is the agricultural colonization of the Great Plains west of the ninety-eighth meridian. Lack of water, efficient transport, and materials for fencing and building allowed this area to thrive as a ranching frontier for several decades. Technological innovations overcame these environmental obstacles by 1880 and permitted the region's rapid settlement as an insular frontier (Kraenzel 1955:125–126). Many cosmopolitan frontier regions lie beyond the environmental limits of efficient crop growing and remain devoted to nonagricultural activities as long as the acquisition of the commercially valuable resources remains economically feasible. These areas consist of agriculturally marginal zones accessible to fur trading, ranching, and the production of various raw industrial commodities. There are also agricultural regions that may remain cosmopolitan frontiers. These are exploitative plantation frontiers. Activities associated with this type of settlement differ from those of other cosmopolitan frontiers in several ways that permit their development as long-term colonial institutions. First, the role of the exploitative plantation as a large-scale producer of noncompetitive crops places them in environments suitable to their cultivation. In the case of European expansion, these areas were generally found in the tropics, an area generally avoided by small farm settlement because of its perceived unsuitability for the production of European crops.[1] Second, exploitative plantations exhibit an intensity of land use that rivals that of farming settlements associated with insular frontiers. Because of their size and potential for large-scale organizational efficiency, exploitative plantations possess an economy of scale that permits them to achieve greater productivity than many other forms of agriculture, particularly in the growing of

[1]The environmental suitability of insular frontier regions in colonial North America was an important factor in their selection. Their physical and climatic similarity to Europe and adaptability to European crops were features stressed in their promotion to perspective immigrants. See Merrens (1969) for a discussion and examples of promotional literature relating to South Carolina.

specialized staple crops. Although able to compete economically with insular frontier agriculture in the production of foodstuffs, exploitative plantations are geared toward specialized staples that cannot be grown in temperate environments. Because of their separate requirements the two forms of frontier agriculture have seldom competed for the same environmental resources. This form of cosmopolitan frontier settlement will remain an economically efficient frontier adaptation on the periphery of the world economy as long as demand for its products remains high and the political and social conditions of production are maintained.

In general, cosmopolitan frontiers retain close economic, social, and political ties with the parent state, exhibit a standardization that allows a rapid diffusion of adaptive innovation rather than fundamental change, and in regions amenable to agricultural settlement by immigrant farmers, constitute a transitory adaptation that is unable to compete economically with and is usually superceded by insular frontier colonization. These organizational similarities appear to transcend the differences in resource bases supporting each type of cosmopolitan frontier and suggest the operation of common developmental processes at a general level. Such processes are adaptations to the basic ecological conditions encountered in cosmopolitan frontier colonization, and they are likely to reflect evolutionary economic trends occurring in societies involved in this situation. The processes to be discussed here are not intended to be all inclusive, but they should help establish the dimensions of this type of frontier change. The content, spatial orientation, and temporal development of these processes can also provide a basis for approaching cosmopolitan frontiers through the study of their material remains. What kinds of processes, then, tend to be found in cosmopolitan frontier regions?

Defining Processes of Change

Processes of cosmopolitan frontier colonization are related to the adaptation of complex societies to the economic environment of frontier regions created solely for the exploitation of their resources. This adaptation appears in the form and sequence of events described in the characteristics of frontier colonization discussed above. Processes may be abstracted from these characteristics by considering the functional and ecological significance of behavior associated with them. In a recent examination of industrial frontiers, Hardesty (1982) identified several processes of change that appear to apply equally well to other types of cosmopolitan frontiers. These processes are linked to the role of such regions in the world economy and permit the nature of these frontiers to be defined as components of a larger system.

The first process relates to the nature of adaptation and change in cosmopolitan frontier environments. Because activities in these frontiers are oriented toward the efficient commercial exploitation of a particular area, functional behavior, or that having adaptive value (see Dunnell 1978), is likely to fall within a narrow range in response to the restricted variability of the cosmopolitan frontier environment. The process of *adaptation* appears to follow a sequence modeled by Kirch (1980). Here adaptation occurs as selection sorts out behavioral variants through differential reproduction to allow the increase of those best able to solve environmental problems. Adaptation is seen as a three stage sequence. In the first stage, the colonists arrive with a behavioral assemblage adapted to conditions in the homeland. Diversity of individual behavior within the immigrating group is low. Experimentation within the area of colonization results in a diversification of behavior that characterizes the second stage. Intensified selection pressure brought about by the colonial environment sorts out and eliminates all but the most fit innovations. The range of behavior is reduced again in the third stage of the adaptation process (Hardesty 1982). In the case of cosmopolitan frontier colonization, the narrow range of activities associated with its extremely specialized role is likely to restrict behavior to a much greater degree than in an economically diverse insular frontier. This results in the cultural standardization characteristic of these regions.

Cosmopolitan frontier change is sudden and widespread, and innovation diffuses rapidly throughout the area of colonization. The pattern of change is not continuous but steplike and nearly simultaneous throughout a region. This suggests a process of discontinuous evolution dominated by sudden replacements and extinctions. Discontinuous change found here is suggestive of the model of *punctuated equilibria* developed to explain similar change in the paleontological record (Gould and Eldredge 1977). The model describes a process of change in which populations evolve gradually but that, when viewed on long time scales, is characterized by rapid appearance and disappearance of species. Although it is an infrequent event resulting from a long process of evolution, the appearance of a new species is profound. It may be better adapted to a changed environment and may rapidly replace older species that are less so. These relatively rapid changes appear as jumps or "punctuations" in the long-term fossil record.

Hardesty (1982) has suggested that if the time scale is recalibrated to take into consideration the faster rates of change in cultural behavior over biological variables, this process may be used to explain the punctuated pattern of cosmopolitan frontier change. The rapidity of individual and corporate decision-making associated with cosmopolitan frontier development dramatically compresses the generational time scale of biological evolution. Thus change here may be observed as the short-term phenomenon characteristic of these regions.

To examine the form of adaptation in a frontier region within the framework of this biological analogy, Hardesty (1981) proposed substituting the term *cultural species* for its biological counterpart. This recognizes the paramount role of cultural behavior in solving environmental problems and focuses attention on the social group as the primary unit of adaptive change. In cosmopolitan frontier regions, a trading post, ranch, or industrial colony would constitute a member of such a cultural species. Adaptive change is brought about through successful technological or organizational modifications in these species. The rapidity by which such changes occur and are diffused mark the punctuations in the rate of an area's evolution as a frontier.

Although the cosmopolitan frontier is characterized by cultural standardization arising from its specialized economic role, it is not completely homogenous. Each type of cosmopolitan frontier adapts differently than the others because it is organized in a manner to permit the most efficient exploitation of a particular resource. Consequently, it develops and modifies its own cultural species as a means of accomplishing this task. Variation within one type of frontier results from the necessity of adapting a standard technology to the demands of local environments. The necessity of such adaptation depends on the degree to which environmental control is permitted by the available technology and the extent to which integration with the national economy exists. Therefore, the process of *differentiation* does not occur uniformly on all frontiers (Hardesty 1982). The operation of this process is apparent if one examines the histories of individual cosmopolitan frontier regions.

The differentiation of technology on industrial frontiers was studied by Hardesty and Edaburn (1982) who traced its development on the silver mining frontier of central Nevada. Between 1860 and 1880, immigrant miners adapted to the differing nature of ore concentrations by modifying available mining and milling processes into two separate, more efficient processes. Three decades later, advances in industrial technology permitted a greater degree of control over the environmental variables that had brought about the earlier technological divergence. A single more efficient mining technology then became dominant throughout the region.

The differentiation of organization may also be linked to the degree of environmental control in a frontier region. An example of this is found on the trading frontier of the northern plains of the United States and Canada. The differential adaptation there was not a result of contrasting physical environments but a different degree of integration between the trading companies and the national economies of their respective states. In Canada, for example, traders were licensed by the government, and centralized posts were maintained. Competition between companies and the intrusion of European trappers were avoided to guarantee as much stability as possible in the trading relationship. As a consequence, trade in a variety of commodities was maintained for over a century. In contrast, the trade on the northern plains of the United States was not regulated as closely as its Canadian counterpart. A lack of overall integration within the national economy resulted in a series of loosely organized and often competitive short-term operations that lacked the stability necessary to carry out successful trade for a long duration (Lewis 1942).

Colonization, especially of cosmopolitan frontiers, represents an adaptation to the exploitation of commercial resources in peripheral areas of the world economy. Because of this emphasis on economic utility, the existence of the colony is closely related to its ability as a cultural species to exploit a given environment. The manner in which such regions are occupied, abandoned, and reoccupied reflects the process of colonization.

Hardesty (1982) has suggested that Charnov's (1976) marginal value theorem from optimal foraging theory is applicable to explaining this process. The theorem states that an optimal predator will remain in the *patch,* or area it occupies, until its rate of intake (the marginal value) drops to a level equal to the average of intake for the habitat as a whole (Krebs and Davies 1978:43). Because the average intake is net, the cost of moving among patches and acquiring resources in a patch must be subtracted from the resources accumulated.

A cosmopolitan frontier region may be seen as an archipelago of patches consisting of industrial commodity sites, rangelands, or hunting and trapping territories. Colonists may be expected to occupy each patch only until its net yield drops below that likely to be obtained from the average in that frontier area. Several variables affect the rate of patch movement. These include variability and size of the patch, the technological efficiency of exploitation, transportation cost, and market price. The rate of patch movement may be lessened by minimizing transport cost which maximizes all the other variables. Because technology, transportation cost, and market price are subject to change, the duration of patch occupation may be extended and abandoned patches recolonized (Hardesty 1982).

The process of colonization also varies with the nature of the resource exploited. Basically, there are two types, renewable and nonrenewable. Renewable resources, such as timberlands, trapping territories, and rangelands, may be reoccupied at regular intervals. On the other hand, nonrenewable resources, such as ore deposits, are generally used until exhausted or until their exploitation is economically impractical. Such patches are reoccupied only if improved technology or higher market prices again make this possible. Because of the drastic manner in which such economic variables change, cycles of abandonment and recolonization are irregular in occurrence and are less predictable than use cycles in renewable resource patches (Hardesty 1982).

The four processes outlined above would appear to account for the characteristics of cosmopolitan frontier change discussed earlier. The process of adaptation links the development of a standardized culture in the area of colonization to the selection of behavioral variants best able to solve the environmental problems posed by adapting a narrow economic venture to conditions imposed by the environment of a particular frontier region. The sudden appearance and rapid diffusion of change reflects the process of punctuated equilibria, which accounts for replacement of existing technologies and methods of organization by newer more adaptive ones that arise infrequently and as a result of forces external to the colony. The term *cultural species* refers to such agents of change. It compares their evolutionary role to that of biological species that appear periodically and cause similar punctations in the fossil record. Despite the uniformity imposed by the cosmopolitan frontier's economic role, the process of differentiation acts to permit adaptive variation in response to particular conditions encountered in the frontier region. The nature and duration of such adaptations indicates the degree of technological control over the local environment and the region's integration with the national economy. Finally, colonization describes the process of occupying, abandoning, and reoccupying resource areas, or patches, and helps explain the transitory nature of cosmopolitan frontier settlement. The specialized nature of activities on these frontiers place a lower marginal value on a given patch than would be the case if the area were occupied by a more diversified insular frontier colony. This usually results in a great deal of movement between patches, a shorter tenure of occupation, and inevitably, the abandonment of these regions as their exploitable resources diminish, leaving them vacant and often open to settlement as insular frontiers.

The similarity of cosmopolitan frontiers lies in the occurrence of common characteristics of change and their underlying processual causes. These reflect the colonies' overall functional similarity resulting from their role as producers of specialized commodities on the periphery of a world economy. This economic role has been responsible for the development of a number of parallels in the organization of cosmopolitan frontier societies, while their specialization has kept them distinct as separate types, each possessing its own adaptive strategy. These adaptive characteristics are likely to be revealed in behavioral patterning associated with each type of frontier. This patterning should be discernible to the observer of an existing society as well as to the archaeologist studying its material remains.

COSMOPOLITAN FRONTIERS AND THE ARCHAEOLOGICAL RECORD

The investigation of cosmopolitan frontier colonization, like that associated with insular frontiers, may be conducted through the examination of various forms of data. We have divided these broadly into documentary and historical sources to explore each separately. This interpretation of data is useless without some type of overriding explanatory framework within which to analyze it. Because we are interested here in investigating cosmopolitan frontier change through the material record, it is imperative that we first develop such a framework. Ideally, this framework should take the form of a model; however, as we are not attempting to treat cosmopolitan frontier change in this depth here, a more limited approach may be employed. Before examining the archaeological aspect of change, it will be necessary to refine further the precise nature of the phenomenon we are about to explore.

An examination of cosmopolitan frontier colonization revealed that a variety of activities were carried out in these regions. Although all reflect the operation of a set of common processes, the behavioral manifestations of these processes often take separate courses in response to the diverse and specialized nature of the particular colony. Up to this point, we have concentrated on the general aspects of cosmopolitan frontier colonization. Based on this knowledge, it should be possible to construct a model similar to that developed for insular frontier colonization (see Chapter 2). Such a model would have to consider only those aspects held in common by all cosmopolitan frontiers. This ignores the variety of behavior associated with each frontier type. In order to investigate cosmopolitan frontier change to adequately consider this variation, it may be more useful to develop several models covering each of the cosmopolitan frontier types outlined earlier in this chapter. In short, the investigation of cosmopolitan frontier colonization may best be accomplished through the use of six separate models, each specifying the manner in which general cosmopolitan frontier processes are revealed in terms of the six types of specialized frontiers. The construction of these models is necessary if we are to examine cosmopolitan frontier situations in a systematic manner. They are particularly useful if we intend to extract behavioral information from the archaeological record.

Although the development of comprehensive cosmopolitan frontier models is beyond the scope of this chapter, we may still explore certain aspects of this type of frontier change through the medium of material evidence. One means of accomplishing this requires that we focus on certain general aspects of colonization that are likely to be evident in the nature and distribution of the archaeological record. Because cosmopolitan frontier societies are a product of the economic and social processes that govern their existence, their structure and organization are likely to reflect their basic role as producers of specialized commodities. Two basic elements of structure that are relatively easily discernible in the archaeological record are *settlement pattern* and *activity composition*. The nature and distribution of settlements are crucial aspects of cosmopolitan frontier development and should be characterized by recognizable material by-products. We must first determine the context in which they were produced to address the nature of these by-products. In other words, we must define the layout and composition of settlement for each of the six cosmopolitan frontier types before attempting to ascertain how these might be revealed archaeologically.

Each type of cosmopolitan frontier colonization is a result of the interaction of four processes (adaptation, punctuated equilibria, differentiation, and colonization) on an intrusive society playing a very specialized economic role in a peripheral region. Because of the different role played by each frontier type, these processes are likely to produce a somewhat dissimilar structure characterized in each case by its own layout and composition. The latter are indicated by the settlements of a region. These processes also account for change in certain cosmopolitan frontiers, a condition that is likely to alter structure and, consequently, settlement pattern and composition. To discover the nature of settlement distribution and content, it is necessary first to examine the structure of each of the six cosmopolitan frontier types. Once the structure of each frontier type has been defined, we then explore the manner in which settlement pattern and composition are likely to appear in the archaeological record.

The distribution and composition of settlements in cosmopolitan frontier regions reflects the specialized orientation of these areas. Settlements of each frontier type are established to extract and process commercial products obtained in the area of colonization and to supply and maintain these extractive activities. Consequently, settlement pattern and composition are linked to variables governing these activities: (1) the nature and location of the resources, (2) their accessibility, (3) the available extractive and transport technology, (4) distances to markets, (5) the presence of hostile groups (including competing colonial states), and (6) the processing requirements of the product. A basic similarity in the organization of production in each is likely to produce a common settlement pattern containing functionally similar components. Hence, we should expect different frontiers of the same type to exhibit little variation in settlement pattern and content. It should be possible to model the distribution and composition of settlement in the context of the organizational structure in which each type operates.

The structure of each of the six cosmopolitan frontier types shows the operation of the frontier processes on the tasks undertaken by each type of colonization. In our discussion of structure, we described briefly the organization of settlement for each type of frontier, linking the inclusion of particular settlements to the network of activities associated with the frontier's overall task. The presence of these settlements and their relationship to one another within a network of trade and communications is reflected in both the distribution and composition of settlements in cosmopolitan frontier regions. We may summarize these for the six types of cosmopolitan frontiers in the following discussion.

The Structure of Cosmopolitan Frontier Change

TRADING FRONTIERS

Perhaps the most far-reaching and transient cosmopolitan frontier is devoted to trading. The goal of trade is the acquisition of items through exchange with aboriginal groups. This form of frontier settlement requires only the presence of the trader and his stock of supplies and a transportation link between his post and the source of supply. Although a variety of goods is an integral part of the trade, their procurement is not, and consequently, adaptive behavior here does not involve the employment of a complex or extensive procurement technology.

In general, trading frontiers have been oriented toward obtaining a marketable product or products native to the area where the trade is carried out. Once established, the frontiers exist as stable entities as long as a market for these items remains. Only when the latter declined or the trade products ceased to be available did the activity cease and the role of the region in the larger economy change. The exhaustion of a trade commodity or an increased market demand may also bring about an expansion of the trading system and permit the creation of new trading posts and the enlargement of the frontier region.

The organization of trading frontiers requires a minimal presence by the intensive society and a fairly simple structure. This would include the trading posts where trade goods and native products were stockpiled prior to and after exchange. Trade routes on the frontier need only allow the movement of goods and are likely to be unimproved. The resulting settlement pattern is likely to consist of widely separated sites of specialized economic function situated in or at the edge of trading territories. These may or may not be situated on natural transport routes, such as rivers, but should be in accessible locations. Activities should reveal the rather narrow function of the settlements and be confined largely to the trade and the traders' subsistence. Because of the autonomy and similar function of trading settlements, the range of activities should vary little from site to site within a frontier region unless an additional function, such as defense, is present. This simplified and repetitive pattern is likely to characterize the archaeological record of trading frontier areas.

As the most geographically dispersed and most thinly populated form of colonization, trading frontiers are expected to exhibit a settlement pattern characterized by a small number of settlements thinly distributed along the periphery of the area of colonization. These settlements may be located along natural routes of transportation, such as navigable water courses where available, yet they are unlikely to be associated with an elaborate man-made system of roads. Settlements are likely to be small and consist of buildings necessary to store trading commodities, house the traders, and maintain the latter between times of resupply.[2] In some areas, trading centers may be attached to military forts for protection. Although they constitute part of somewhat larger settlements, this should not alter their content.

Because trade involves a reciprocal arrangement between the intrusive society and resident aboriginal groups, settlements belonging to the latter may also be included as part of the overall pattern in a trading frontier area. The actual nature and distribution of aboriginal settlements will vary with their level of sociocultural integration; however, groups participating in, and to some extent acculturated by, the trade should be present in the general vicinity of the trading settlements. Occasionally, villages even grew up adjacent to a trading post as was the case at Fort Prince George, where evidence of a large Cherokee settlement was found (SIR).

Trading frontiers are linked with the core state economy through an entrepôt which serves as the focal point for the trading system as a whole. The size of the area served by a single entrepôt may vary immensely. For example, in the early eighteenth century, Charleston, South Carolina served trading areas in many parts of the American Southeast (Crane 1929:108–109), but a half century later, St. Augustine was the center of a trading network confined to British East Florida (Mowat 1941:135–36). As a result, such settlements often lie well outside the trading areas they serve and may also represent a component of another area of colonization.

The relatively simple settlement pattern of trading frontiers should allow them to be recognized easily on the basis of material evidence, but because of the size and highly dispersed nature of its component settlements, the discovery of individual sites may require intensive regional survey. Because of their specialized nature, sites should be recognizable through an analysis of their archaeological contents.

The diagnostic activities associated with trading frontier settlements center around the storage and handling of specialized trade artifacts that are either not found nearby or are employed in much smaller quantities elsewhere. Consequently, the sites of settlements associated with trade, principally the trading posts, should exhibit a higher, patterned frequency of occurrence of this class of artifact. In an examination of six Canadian trading post sites, Forsman and Gallo (1979) found

---

[2]See, for example, Spalding's Lower Store in Florida (Lewis 1969) and Rocky Mountain House in British Columbia (Noble 1973).

that a comparison of arbitrarily defined artifact groups[3] produced an exceptionally high percentage frequency range of occurrence (41.26–93.07%) of items classified under the "Clothing" group. A closer examination of the contents of this group reveals that it is composed largely of beads, an item used primarily for trade (Forsman and Gallo 1979:247). It is likely that the pattern the sites exhibit, though not functionally derived on purpose, is in effect measuring these settlements' participation in the Indian trade. A comparison with other known trading post sites in North America[4] has shown that at sites from which trade beads were recovered, a similarly high percentage frequency of clothing group artifacts was present. Thus, the occurrence of specialized items would indicate that trading frontier settlements may be identified on the basis of their material record.

The specialized function of these settlements is also reflected in the relatively low frequency range of "Kitchen" artifacts. This group consists mostly of domestic artifacts similar to those in the Subsistence activity category discussed earlier (see Chapter 8). The small size of a domestic activity component at trading frontier sites and its lower occurrence at specialized activity sites in insular frontier regions suggests a parallel pattern of secondary domestic activity in both cases.

The patterning described here clearly reflects the function of the settlements whose sites were examined. It illustrates the occurrence of general patterns capable of identifying the composition of settlements on a frontier characterized by little variation in settlement function. It should be possible, moreover, to predict additional artifact patterning linked to other variables of the trade to identify its nature and development over time. These and other factors must be considered in developing a comprehensive model of trading frontiers.

RANCHING FRONTIERS

Ranching, like trading, is a geographically extensive activity requiring a relatively small number of colonists. Unlike trading, ranching is concerned with the actual production of a commodity (livestock) rather than exchange. Because of the relatively low return in food per unit of land utilized, ranching requires large amounts of rangeland. The amount of land needed to support each head varies with the environment of a region and, together with the market demand for livestock, affects the size of territory required for this activity (Clark 1956:745; Strickon 1965:234). Because economies of scale also permit labor costs per head to decrease as land size increases (Carpenter *et al.* 1941:45), efficient production favors the enlargement of holdings. The large land requirements for grazing result in dispersed

---

[3]The artifact groups used in Forsman and Gallo's study are based on those employed by South (1977) in developing his "Carolina" and "Frontier" patterns to differentiate colonial settlements in British North America. The categories are the kitchen, architecture, furniture, arms, clothing, personal, tobacco pipes, and activities artifact groups.

[4]These sites include Fort Colville, Washington (Chance and Chance 1979); Fort Christianna, Virginia (Beaudry 1979); and Spalding's Lower Store, Florida (Lewis 1969).

settlement pattern. Webb (1931:229) estimated that ranches in the American Great Plains, for example, were scattered at intervals of 20 to 50 miles (32–80km) or more.

The ranch is the primary settlement unit on this type of frontier because it is the center from which livestock production is carried out. These settlements are linked to the larger world economy through a series of market towns whose presence is also part of the overall settlement pattern of ranching frontiers. These settlements are termini of other forms of transport such as railroads and serve as livestock shipping points and supply centers for the ranching frontier region. Generally they are located as close to the region as possible. Although livestock are capable of being driven over unimproved terrain to market, the effect of driving on their physical condition limits the distance they can be moved economically. Consequently, the opening of new ranching frontiers is usually accompanied by the appearance of new market settlements along its fringe. The sequential rise of railroad "cow towns" in the American West following the Civil War is an example of this development (Kraenzel 1955: 106–109). Lying on the periphery of a ranching frontier, such settlements may serve only the specialized economic interests of the area. If the ranching frontier lies close to settled insular frontier regions, as in the colonial Atlantic Seaboard, established entrepôts may serve also as livestock marketing centers. In addition to marketing centers, small supply towns may arise in or adjacent to ranching frontiers. These are widely scattered and are generally situated along the major transportation routes out of the area of colonization (Roosevelt 1899:6).

Ranch settlements are generally devoted solely to this activity. Each represents the control component of a spatially dispersed activity and usually involves a relatively long-term occupation. A ranch may grow according to the needs of production, but it usually includes only structures related to its specialized function. The ranch operated by Theodore Roosevelt in Dakota Territory in the 1880s was typical of such settlements. It included a ranch house, stable, sheds for equipment, hayricks, pens, horse and cow corrals, and several other miscellaneous outbuildings (Roosevelt 1899:25–26).

The composition of ranching frontier settlement is likely to be reflected in the patterning of their artifacts as well as in the architectural content. Ranching's specialized function is likely to have resulted in the deposition of a smaller Subsistence artifact component than at domestic settlements generally. A specialized artifact component similar to that found in trading frontiers is not anticipated (Fontana 1967:61), however, because the activities of ranching, like farming (see Chapter 8), do not produce a substantial by-product.[5]

Specialized marketing centers for livestock may also be recognizable archaeologically by the presence of the limited range of economic activities centered there. These might include livestock holding and transport facilities, as well as financial

---

[5]See Chapter 8 for a discussion of farm sites. The anticipated low occurrence of specialized ranching artifacts is evident in at least one excavated ranch site, Johnny Ward's ranch in Arizona (Fontana and Greenleaf 1962).

institutions to oversee sales and credit, stores, repair facilities, hotels, and buildings devoted to entertainments. These settlements would lie along or at the end of trans-portation links and at the termini of established livestock routes, the presence of which may be discerned through an examination of physical evidence (such as roads, rivers, and railroad tracks or their beds) still present on the landscape.

Because of its dispersed layout and relatively uniform content, the settlement pattern of ranching frontiers should be readily apparent. The ranches and market centers are linked by a system of roads and trails which though unimproved are likely to become permanently marked by the heavy traffic passing over them. As a consequence, many livestock trails in open country even though abandoned are still traceable, especially when aided by the use of aerial photography. By combining such evidence with that obtained from settlement sites, it should be possible to gain a fairly complete picture of certain ranching frontier regions and their contents through an analysis of material evidence. A comparative study of such regions and their settlement components should yield archaeological and spatial patterns capable of defining these elements more closely and allowing the researcher to observe their development over time.

EXPLOITATIVE PLANTATION FRONTIERS

In contrast to other types of cosmopolitan frontiers, exploitative plantation regions are characterized by an intensive use of land and the employment of large numbers of laborers. Like the other frontiers, they are engaged in the production of specialized commodities for a larger national market. Because it is an agricultural activity, the exploitative plantation involves more complex processes of production than takes place on either the trading or ranching frontiers. Here crops are grown (often on a highly modified landscape), harvested, and processed (often with the aid of complex industrial equipment), workers are housed, specialized support activities carried out, and the administration of the entire operation planned and coordinated.

The location of exploitative plantations is usually more environmentally selec-tive than other types of agricultural frontiers because of the particular requirements of cultivation and transport. Due to their emphasis on noncompetitive staple pro-duction, these frontiers have commonly been situated within the tropical environ-mental zones in which such crops can be grown. Crops like sugar, rice, tobacco, coffee, tea, rubber, and other cultigens whose products became an integral part of European life could not be grown elsewhere, and their production often guided expansion into suitable regions.

Although the overall location of exploitative plantation colonies is strongly influenced by the environmental limits of the commodities produced, the actual form of the frontier is governed by several variables. Specialized staple crops may be grown only where there exist specific environmental conditions, including such particular factors as soil type, elevation, amount of rainfall, native groundcover, and susceptibility to erosion. Accessibility to market is another factor in locating these settlements. Because the cost of production and transport must be borne by market demand, expansion is controlled. This affects both the size and form of settlement. The transportation network of an exploitative plantation frontier region is centered in an entrepôt. It also serves as an enclave for European proprietors whose plantations are often managed by hired resident overseers.

The development of rubber growing in southern Vietnam by the French offers an example of exploitative plantation colonization. In the early years of the twentieth century, planting began in the "grey lands" of the Mekong Delta. Although the soils here varied extensively, their proximity to the entrepôt of Saigon encouraged their development. By the 1920s, rubber production has passed the experimental stage, and increased market demand encouraged adequate investment to allow expansion into the more productive but remote "red lands" to the north (Thompson 1937:17). The rubber-producing region expanded to its environmental limits in the 1930s (McIndoe 1969:4). Economies of scale fostered an early consolidation of rubber holdings, forced out native competition, and resulted in the domination of the market by several large European joint stock companies (Robequain 1944:207). This process of isolating staple crop production on large forign-owned enclave plantations is paralleled in other exploitative plantation frontiers where different crops were involved. For example, the development of coffee and sugar in the Dutch East Indies and Indonesia, rubber in Indonesia and in British Malaya, and sugar in the West Indies (Geertz 1963:59–61; Robequain 1944:207; Thompson 1937:17) were all accompanied by the development of an exploitative plantation economy that appears to be characteristic of these regions in general. Indeed, if South Carolina had been settled merely for the production of rice in the coastal region with imported labor (see Chapter 3), it too may have become such a cosmopolitan frontier area.

The settlement pattern of exploitative plantation frontiers is expected to reflect the structure of this type of region. It should consist primarily of the entrepôt and the plantations. Native settlements, some of precolonial origin, may also be present. Because the center of European activity in such areas is the entrepôt, the foci of social, political, and economic activities are there. The relatively permanent nature of these frontiers and the desire to recapitulate the culture of the homeland in the enclave often result in an extraordinary display of European lifestyle in the entrepôt. On the plantations themselves, this trend should be far less evident. Here life is focused on specialized production and involves a largely, and sometimes totally, non–European population. Plantation activities reveal the settlement's specific role in this type of cosmopolitan frontier.

The exploitative plantation colony is characterized by a geographically compact size with the segregation of production activities on the plantations and residence enclave activities in the entrepôt. Because of the sedentary nature of these colonies, their settlements can be more permanent than on other cosmopolitan frontiers. Settlement distribution and composition indicate the structure of a region devoted to long-term specialized production. The narrow limits imposed by production serve to inhibit the fundamental change usually accompanying prolonged settlement.

Archaeologically, an exploitative plantation frontier should be marked by the presence of a series of plantation settlements situated within a limited environmental zone. Because of the need to transport relatively bulky agricultural produce to the entrepôt, the plantations would have been located along a well-developed transport network such as a river, canal system, or a railroad. The individual plantations are likely to consist of the same basic components as plantations located in insular frontier regions (see Chapter 8); however, their size should tend toward the economic maximum. The absence of a resident colonial proprietor may eliminate the high-status European domestic component found on owner occupied plantations. Plantation layout and architecture may vary, but all are expected to exhibit a regular arrangement to facilitate production.

Artifact patterning should show the occurrence and arrangement of specialized and domestic activities within the settlement and the status and ethnicity of its occupants. On exploitative plantation settlements, patterning reveals the relatively limited European presence. For example, ceramic collections from a twentieth century rubber plantation in the grey lands near Saigon, Vietnam consisted almost entirely of inexpensive Chinese, Vietnamese, or other Indochinese wares in forms that reflect the Oriental origin and lower economic status of their users (Lewis 1980b). Similarly, a study of sugar plantation workers' cemeteries in Barbados revealed mortuary practices and artifacts identifying their African origin and subservient status (Handler and Lange 1979). In both cases, European wares were in a minority and contrasted with the pattern found on insular plantations in South Carolina, where European wares regularly formed more than half the ceramics recovered (see Chapter 8).

Architectural evidence at exploitative plantation sites should also reveal information about their composition. These remains permit an investigation to ascertain settlement size and layout and the various components of the plantation, particularly specialized processing equipment related to staple crop production. Architecture may also provide clues to status within the plantation community and identify the ethnic origins of inhabitants. For example, documentary architectural studies of exploitative plantations in the New World have revealed that elements of African architecture were often employed in the construction of slave dwellings. These elements involve the form and design of the buildings and should be recognizable through an examination of the archaeological record (Handler and Lange 1978).

The form and content of an exploitative plantation frontier region may be discussed by studying the distribution of the material remains of settlements. Such an examination should also yield evidence of the transportation network linking the plantations and show the location of the entrepôt. The latter is likely to contain processing and shipping facilities, a large portion of the region's colonial population, and a foreign section occupied by non–European groups. Material evidence of these is apt to be present at the sites of such settlements. Archaeology may provide data relating to both settlement pattern and composition in exploitative plantation regions by permitting the identification of material patterning related to key structural elements of this type of colonization. The utility of this data source should also allow us to address a variety of questions concerning additional aspects of exploitative plantation frontiers.

INDUSTRIAL FRONTIERS

Industrial frontiers are created to exploit the nonagricultural resources of a region. This is accomplished through the application of industrial technology and continues as long as the resources remain economically feasible to extract. Because the activities of an industrial frontier are focused on particular resources, production is situated in those locations where their resources naturally occur. Similarly, the colonial population is also concentrated there. The dispersal of production permits the immediate conversion of the raw resource, be it ore, oil, or lumber, into a form that can be economically transported. The distribution of activities together with the technological, scheduling, and labor requirements of production result in a structure that contrasts with those of other cosmopolitan frontier types.

The exploitation of finite natural resources or those that are renewable after a lengthy interval requires the continual expansion of and movement of settlement within the area of colonization. Within this context, levels of activity may rise and fall markedly with the discovery, extraction, exhaustion, and abandonment of resource patches. Consequently, the large, unfree labor forces employed by exploitative plantations are uneconomical here and the labor force is hired by the task. Such labor may involve native groups as in French Indochina (Thompson 1937:16) and imported foreign workers, such as the Chinese in the American West (Lee 1960). Members of the intrusive colonial society constitute the majority of workers (Temple 1972:64).

Because of the transient mode of resource exploitation, a resource-based pattern of settlement evolves. Settlements in an industrial frontier include camps, where resource collection and processing occur; at least one entrepôt, which serves as a processing, collection, and redistribution center linking the colony with the outside world; and sometimes, intermediate supply centers, which are often attached to the camps and move with them. The impermanence of the resource base requires the movement of camps and results in their periodic abandonment (Ostrogorsky 1982:81). The well-known ghost towns of the American West (see, for example, Florin 1961) are usually examples of abandoned industrial frontier settlements. Because of this movement, the course of transportation networks was also frequently altered, and transport in such regions was usually accomplished by a means that involved the lowest capital outlay. For example, much of the mining frontier in the American Southwest was served by unimproved overland routes (Winther 1964:43), and the railroads that carried logs from western lumbering frontiers were usually temporary arrangements characterized by poor roadbeds and inexpensive equipment not found elsewhere (Bruce 1952:358–359). Because several types of extractive activities may exist within a single region possessing multiple resources, settlements and transportation networks of more than one industrial frontier activity may occur there either simultaneously or sequentially.

How might industrial frontier regions be identified archaeologically? Unlike other cosmopolitan frontiers that are oriented toward the exploitation of a region, industrial frontiers involve the extraction of resources at specific sites. Consequently, the settlement pattern of these frontiers would be organized around the location of these resource sites, and the requirements of linking them to entrepôts where their products may be collected and shipped would be satisfied. Settlement composition would reflect the technological requirements of resource extraction and processing as well as the need to maintain and supply the labor force necessary to maintain production. Change, of course, plays an important role here. Resource depletion and technological innovation results in the abandonment of old extraction sites and the opening of new ones, causing the settlement pattern to shift and the function of individual settlements to change dramatically.

Because industrial frontiers include a variety of technological activities, no one distribution of settlement is typical. All these regions, however, should exhibit the three basic settlement types discussed above. Settlement composition is likely to mirror the functional similarity of settlement types on all industrial frontiers as well as differences related to the specific tasks performed to extract and process the particular resources of each region.

Resource extraction sites are probably the most numerous and most easily recognizable settlements in an industrial frontier region. Their material record should be characterized by both a technological component and one devoted to housing and maintaining the colonists. The former is generally recognizable on the basis of its architectural and artifactual contents. Such structures as mines (Teague 1980) and mills (Teague and Shenk 1977) have distinctive forms and contain artifacts related to the extractive and processing activities carried out there. The high cost of moving or retrieving many items, especially if they are heavy and bulky, can make their removal uneconomical, if not impractical, and result in the accumulation of a great deal of diagnostic artifacts on these sites. This rate of abandonment is accelerated by the rapid movement and technological change inherent in industrial frontier development. Resource extraction and processing areas should be marked by a specialized activity component and by little if any domestic refuse and should contrast markedly with workers' living areas where such artifacts dominate. Living areas constitute the other element of resource extraction sites and should exhibit diagnostic architecture and a recognizable artifact component. The ethnicity of the laborers residing there may also be detected in the archaeological record by analyzing variation in the occurrence of particular artifacts. For example, the presence of Chinese miners and loggers in the American West is revealed by the form and origin of the ceramics recovered from their living areas (Elston *et al.* 1980; Elston *et al.* 1982; Teague and Shenk 1977).

Because of the rapid expansion of industrial frontiers, the cycle of settlement founding and abandonment is shorter than on many other cosmopolitan frontiers. Consequently, the development of these regions may be discernible through a spatial study of settlement distribution over time. The material remains of the settlements involved here should provide data useful in analyzing aspects of cosmopolitan frontier change not discernible on the other, more stable frontier types. Such studies may reveal patterning relating to such diverse subjects as the rate and nature of technological change, processes of abandonment, the acculturation of ethnic groups, the growth and change of transport systems, and the relationship of frontier expansion and contraction to market demand. By examining broader concepts within the context of the industrial frontier, it should be possible not only to increase our knowledge of cosmopolitan frontiers in general but to utilize more fully archaeological methodology in studying this larger process of colonization.

MILITARY FRONTIERS

Unlike other forms of cosmopolitan frontier colonization, military and transportation frontiers do not arise in response to a desire to exploit the economic resources of a peripheral area. Rather, they come into being in order to protect, regulate, or maintain transport and communications links to, and political control over other frontier regions. In effect, they support cosmopolitan frontier expansion but do not actively participate in its primary production. Because of their supportive function, the structure of military and transportation frontiers is tied to factors different than those affecting other cosmopolitan frontiers.

Military frontiers are created to establish political control over a region of peripheral settlement. Consequently, its settlements are situated to control transportation routes and other strategic locations dominating access into and within such regions. The pattern of settlement may vary in response to environmental factors and the nature of perceived threats, but all settlements within such a frontier should exhibit a military function.

Military frontiers often overlap other types of cosmopolitan frontier regions, and nonmilitary settlements are found among and often adjacent to forts, camps, and other sites of frontier military activity. Many military posts have served as focal points for the Indian trade such as Fort Prince George on the Cherokee frontier in northwestern South Carolina (Ivers 1970:70). Others, like the forts along the Santa Fe Trail and other overland routes in western North America, acted to protect transportation and immigration into these regions and served as distribution points supporting their economic development as zones of frontier colonization (Winther 1964:4). Forts established in areas that later became insular frontiers were often the nuclei of civilian settlements that retained the names of their military predecessors. Fort Worth, Texas; Fort Smith, Arkansas; Fort Gibson, Oklahoma; Dearborne, Michigan; Des Moines, Iowa; Missoula, Montana; and Walla Walla, Washington are but a few examples of such settlements in the American West. Although military frontiers may later become areas of insular settlement, they are usually not coexistant with them because of the military's specialized role. Consequently, military frontier settlement is not subject to the fundamental change characteristic of insular frontier areas, and instead its structure is likely to reflect the principal task of maintaining an armed presence of the national government on the periphery of expansion.

The role of military frontiers is also shown in the pattern and composition of its settlements. Because of the regulatory and protective tasks of military settlements, they are usually placed at strategic locations along principal transportation routes of the region, often in the same locations occupied by transportation frontier settlements. Their positions are intended to permit the defense of the region against a particular perceived threat, and their settlement pattern should indicate the nature of that threat. In the English colony of Georgia, for example, military frontier settlements were grouped on the coastal islands to protect this southernmost frontier region from the Spanish in adjacent Florida (Manucy 1962b:4–7). These settlements were built as strong defensive positions to withstand well-organized attacks by the forces of a competing European state and serve as bases to support offensives against them (Duffy 1975:21–22). In contrast, the forts of the United States Government in the American West were generally isolated and without extensive defensive works. Potential threats here did not come from other states but from less-complex, nomadic aboriginal societies that could be engaged by mobile field forces in sporadic informal or guerilla warfare rather than in set battles to control the position occupied by the fort. Because they served as supply bases supporting police activity rather than as defensive positions, the role of these forts contrasted with that of those in colonial Georgia, and each region was characterized by a somewhat different settlement pattern.

Military frontiers, because of their specialized nature, consist of settlements for maintaining troops and supplies to be used to protect economic activities in adjacent cosmopolitan frontier areas. The function of military settlements should be apparent in their material record. Because of the standardization and unique forms of military artifacts, the presence of such items would be requisite to identifying military settlement sites.

A specialized function is also likely to be reflected in a relatively low frequency of domestic activity artifacts on extensively excavated settlement sites. The size of this component may be recognized roughly by observing the occurrence of two artifact groups—Kitchen and Architecture—used by South (1977) in his analysis of historic sites. A relatively higher percentage frequency of the former is characteristic of Carolina Pattern sites, which are, in fact, those of insular frontier settlements sites (South 1977:107), and indicates a higher domestic component of these settlements (see Chapter 8). In contrast, the relative sizes of Kitchen and Architecture groups is reversed on Frontier Pattern sites, all but one of which are military frontier settlements (South 1977:145). A comparison of the percentage frequency ranges of these artifact groups in the Frontier Pattern and the group frequencies at several other extensively excavated military frontier sites (Table 10.1) reveals that the latter fall within the range of the pattern. The similar patterning of artifact group occurrence at military frontier sites indicates that their smaller domestic component is clearly discernible and suggests that the specialized function of military frontier settlements is recognizable in their material record.

Finally, the structure of military frontier settlements should be observable in their architecture. The layout of military settlements mirrors the rigid, hierarchical organization of the groups that occupy them. As a result, structures and activity areas are arranged in a regular, geometric order around a central parade ground, which serves as a focus of activity within the settlement. Structures devoted to

TABLE 10.1 Comparison of artifact group frequencies at military frontier sites with the frontier pattern

Frontier pattern artifact group ranges (%)[a]	Artifact group frequencies from military frontier sites (%)			
	Fort Towson, Oklahoma[b]	Fort Washita, Oklahoma[c]	Fort Townsend, Washington[d]	Fort Atkinson, Nebraska[e]
Kitchen 10.2–45.0	33.7	27.8	31.1	20.3
Architecture 29.7–74.3	64.7	69.8	67.6	62.2

[a] South (1977:107,145).
[b] Lewis (1972).
[c] Penman (1975).
[d] Thomas and Larson (1977).
[e] Carlson (1979).

specific activities may be identified on the basis of their form and content, particularly those buildings having a specific military role such as magazines, barracks, or blockhouses. Perhaps the most characteristic type of military architecture is fortification. This can take on a number of forms, ranging from simple fortified structures to elaborate defensive works intended to withstand seiges (Duffy 1975). The presence of distinctive architecture together with the use of specialized artifacts clearly show the distinctive function of military frontier settlements. The regions they encompass should be plainly recognizable in a study of the archaeological record.

TRANSPORTATION FRONTIERS

Transportation frontiers, like military frontiers, are composed of specialized activity settlements whose function is not tied directly to the production of frontier commodities. They maintain flows of information and goods within and between frontier regions. Thus transportation frontier settlements are not expected to contain the specialized production activities found in other cosmopolitan frontier settlements. Instead, they should reflect their limited role as transportation and communications nodes and contain only those activities associated with the movement of commodities and information. Transportation frontiers contain way stations, stage coach and overland mail stations, railroad stops, boat landings, commodity transfer points (Winther 1964), and other settlements devoted to maintaining transportation on the frontier. The existence of a transportation frontier is dependent solely on the cosmopolitan frontier regions whose products pass through it. Consequently, changes in the latter can affect dramatically the role of transportation frontiers and result in their alteration, abandonment, or incorporation into other frontier regions.

The settlement pattern of transportation frontier settlement is likely to be linear in form. It follows the courses of the networks linking cosmopolitan frontier areas with one another and the outside world. Such settlements are likely to be placed on roads, rivers, railroads, or other routes. Because their role is to support transport, the locations of these settlements are placed to best accomplish this task. As a result, most are isolated, special activity settlements such as those represented by the stage stops of the Butterfield Overland Mail between Texas and California (Conkling and Conkling 1947), the stations of the Pony Express between Missouri and California (Majors 1893), and the refueling stops of the Great Northern Railway and other railroads traversing the mountains of western North America (Wood and Wood 1979). Because of their location and limited function, transportation frontier settlements should exhibit aspects of form and content that are recognizable in the archaeological record.

The architecture of transportation frontier settlements is likely to reflect their specialized roles (Ehrenhard 1973). Settlements intended to support transport activities are usually composed of buildings designed for specific purposes. For example, the stage station at Gila Bend, New Mexico consisted of several specialized structures that served to accommodate passengers, feed a relatively large number of people, and care for stock and equipment (Berge 1968:240), all activities associated with its role as a transport settlement. Similarly, railroad refueling stops would be characterized by specialized structures designed to store fuel, water, and sand, to accommodate passengers, and to maintain equipment.

An analysis of artifacts is likely also to reveal information relevant to the role of transportation frontier settlements. Because of the specialized nature of certain forms of transport, such as the railroad, the presence of particular items or groups of items should be adequate to identify the function of the settlement in which they are found. Artifact patterning may also yield clues to a settlement's past role. In a comparison of four transportation frontier settlements in Nevada,[6] Hardesty (1979:120–122) found that ogives formed by the percentage frequencies of various artifact categories show a similarity suggesting a common pattern on these sites. Comparative analysis of collections from additional transportation and other cosmopolitan frontier settlement sites should aid in refining these and other patterns in the archaeological record.

Archaeological Approaches to New Frontiers

Because of the diversity of cosmopolitan frontier change, modeling this form of colonization is a far more complex task than that associated with the study of agricultural expansion in insular frontier regions. We have seen that cosmopolitan frontiers represent generally short-term, economically specialized occupations whose roles are closely tied to the economic development of the parent state. This close linkage favors the retention of existing economic, political, and social institutions and discourages the fundamental change characteristic of insular frontier societies. Such a lack of insularity does not bring about a cultural sameness in all

[6]These sites are the two pony express stations at Cold Springs and Sand Springs, the Rock Springs stage station, and the Rock Springs telegraph station.

cosmopolitan frontier regions. Variation in the kind of economic activities associated with different regions indicates the existence of distinct cosmopolitan frontier types, six of which have been identified. Each type is affected differently by the processes of frontier change. Each is characterized by an organizational structure manifested in the distribution and composition of its settlements. These phenomena are discernible in the material record, and an attempt has been made to outline the form each is likely to assume in the six types of frontiers. Based on our discussion of cosmopolitan frontiers, several broad statements may be made regarding the nature of their settlement and possible directions for archaeological research.

It is apparent that cosmopolitan frontier colonization is associated with a variety of procurement strategies designed to obtain a diverse range of commodities. These strategies include means of production appropriate to the collecting and processing of particular commodities prior to their shipment out of the area of colonization. Because production is a site specific activity, its nature is reflected in the form of settlement within the region where production takes place.

Settlement pattern is affected directly by the requirements of production. Settlement associated with the procurement of a commodity obtainable over a wide area and which needs little modification prior to shipment tends to be distributed over the area of colonization or placed in central locations within it. Ranching and trading frontiers exhibit settlement patterns of this type. Conversely, the procurement of commodities that require extensive processing are found only in certain locations resulting in a clustered settlement pattern centered on those areas where the desired commodities may be most easily obtained. Industrial and exploitative plantation frontiers exhibit settlement distributions revealing these variables. Settlements associated with nonproduction aspects of cosmopolitan frontier colonization, such as those found in military and transportation frontiers, owe their distribution to other variables. These involve the need to protect or maintain order within an area of colonization and to effect the movement of commodities from these regions to the core state. Consequently, military frontier settlements are stratically placed for purposes of control, while transportation frontiers employ a settlement pattern designed to support the flow of commodities and supplies out of and into other areas of colonization.

The composition of cosmopolitan frontiers also reflects the nature of production. Settlements that serve as sites of complex production processes are expected to be larger and more diverse than those associated with relatively simple procurement modes. Of the frontier types we have examined, industrial and exploitative plantation frontiers are characterized by settlements larger and more elaborate than those found in other colonial areas. In both cases, these settlements include multistage procurement activities, often involving complicated industrial technology, where at least preliminary processing is completed prior to shipment out of the area of colonization. Settlements such as ranches and trading posts, where little or no processing is carried out, are smaller and less complex, as are those belonging to frontier types not involved directly in production.

Several aspects of cosmopolitan frontier colonization have been touched on briefly with reference to archaeology. These deal with the temporal component of colonization and the relationship between procurement strategy and change. Two questions of immediate interest center around the rate and nature of technological change and the duration of settlement. These vary from one cosmopolitan frontier type to another and appear to be related to factors such as the nature of the commodity extracted, the state of production technology, and the availability of adequate transportation. For example, some cosmopolitan frontiers, such as those concerned with ranching or trading, employ strategies that are less likely to be made more efficient through technological change than are those strategies involved with more complex industrial frontiers. As a result, the former may be expected to undergo technological change at a much slower rate than the latter. Similarly, procurement strategies linked to rapidly exhausted resources or to those that are renewable only after a substantial period of regeneration are likely to produce settlements of shorter duration than strategies involved with the exploitation of relatively permanent resources. Thus, a rubber plantation might be expected to be occupied over a substantially longer period than either a mining town or a lumber camp.

These temporal regularities seem to manifest behavioral patterning that is linked to the organizational structure of each frontier type. As in the synchronic, spatial phenomena observed earlier in this chapter, patterns of temporal change should also be identifiable in the material record. Archaeological studies of change differ in that they require the observation of data over time. This diachronic approach permits the investigation of the dynamic processes of colonization that must be included as an integral part of a cosmopolitan frontier model.

As we have seen, the specialization inherent in insular frontier colonization makes the use of a single model inappropriate. Instead, the development of six parallel models appears to offer the best approach to analyzing the growth of such regions. We have examined several aspects of colonization with regard to each of the cosmopolitan frontier types and identified regularities related to the nature of the diverse procurement strategies involved. These regularities appear in synchronic variables such as settlement pattern and composition and seem likely to be reflected in dyachronic phenomena like rate of change and duration of occupation. Material correlates of the former have been outlined, and those for the latter inferred. Both spatial and temporal aspects of cosmopolitan frontier change should be discernible in the archaeological record.

The development of cosmopolitan frontier models is still far from complete. Further research is needed to isolate all of the variables affecting each of the frontier types defined in our discussion. A more intensive investigation and comparative study of each type will provide a clearer picture of its organizational structure as well as the interrelationship between that structure and the role the colony plays in the larger world economy. Variation within a particular frontier type occurs also, and its causes must be clarified in terms of the interaction of such variables as procurement technology, environmental conditions, and ethnic diversity. Only when these factors are understood will it be possible to predict accurately the distribution, layout, and content of all cosmopolitan frontier settlements. The evolution of these frontiers through time is also poorly understood as are the variables that influence their change. Because of the emphasis on cultural continuity in these frontiers, this aspect of their existence has until recently been largely ignored, though often acknowledged. Hardesty's (1982) adaptation of the marginal-value theorem in predicting rates of abandonment and recolonization has introduced a needed methodological framework for approaching change within an economic–ecological context. Finally, the development of adequate models requires a knowledge of the interrelationship of different frontier types, particularly those that perform a role secondary to the production of commodities. The linkages between individual cosmopolitan frontiers and their ties with insular frontiers and semiperipheral regions can help define further their function within the world economic system and provide a basis for modeling frontier change as a general phenomenon.

11

Conclusions

The study of frontiers allows an examination of human behavior at several levels. On the one hand, it provides a macroevolutionary scheme for exploring the general development of an important component in the expanding world economy. It also allows particular events to be explained by placing them in the context of larger processes of change. This book has investigated frontiers through the use of a comparative model of colonization. Because of the complexity of this phenomenon, our model focused on only a portion of the total frontier experience. It has dealt with insular frontier colonization, a process associated with the expansion of agricultural societies and their permanent occupation of new lands. As a focus of this study, the British colony of South Carolina on the Eastern Seaboard of North America was chosen. This region underwent settlement as an agricultural colony in the eighteenth century and was a peripheral area of the European world economy.

The insular frontier model was examined using several separate forms of evidence. The employment of both documentary and material evidence pertaining to the South Carolina frontier permitted us to examine not only the accuracy of the model but also the capability of each form of data to elicit independently information relating to culture process. The results of this inquiry demonstrate the usefulness of employing comparative models in the study of regional histories and, in particular, the importance of developing adequate models to analyze such complex and widespread processes as insular frontier colonization. The potential for creating additional frontier models to examine other types of colonization was explored and appears to offer equally worthwhile possibilities for further research; however, the development and testing of such models lies outside the scope of the present volume.

The successful employment of the insular frontier model has wider implications of both methodological and substantive interest. These pertain to the use of archaeology, or material culture in general, in studies of large-scale change and process; the importance of a regional approach to the study of such change; and the role of frontier studies in exploring the expansion of Europe and the histories of its colonial areas. Such topics are significant to historical archaeology because they bear upon its role in investigating the evolution of complex, stratified societies and explaining the development of much of the modern world as an outcome of European expansion and colonization.

ARCHAEOLOGY AND COLONIZATION

Archaeological analysis played a substantial role in the study of insular frontier colonization in South Carolina. By examining this form of data independently of the documentary record, it has been possible to demonstrate its utility in recognizing the characteristics of insular frontier change in the absence of other types of evidence. Our ability to extract such information derives from a relatively tight control over analogies regarding key variables. These include artifact use and function, settlement layout and distribution, and chronological change in the form and composition of both of these as well as a knowledge of processes relating to artifact use and deposition. A knowledge of these variables allows the investigator to obtain material data capable of yielding information relating to both temporal and spatial aspects of colonization.

The model of insular frontier change requires the examination of hypotheses concerning the diverse aspects of colonial development. In order to approach a variety of questions, which range from regionwide spatial distributions to intrasite activity patterning, a wide range of material evidence collected from a broad geographical area is needed. This information could be obtained from archaeological sources alone; however, regions the size of an area of colonization have seldom been examined extensively by archaeologists. South Carolina is no exception. Architecture and cemetery inscriptions were the two supplemental forms of material data employed to overcome gaps in the archaeological record. Both are useful sources of behavioral information (see Deetz and Dethlefsen 1965; Glassie 1975) and should be recognized as integral parts of the material record in historic sites research. Because these data have often been collected separately from archaeological surveys, they can provide a more extensive geographic coverage of a region.

The analysis of archaeological evidence requires the recognition of patterning related to a number of spatial and temporal variables of frontier colonization. Such patterns are the result of the regular and systematic deposition of artifacts produced by particular activities. Because these activities are directly related to the function of a settlement and reflect variation in space as well as time, the recognition of functional patterning can provide clues to the evolution of a region and its components.

Two types of settlement patterns have been useful in our research. The first deals with the temporal affiliation of a site or its component parts. Archaeologically sensitive artifacts, in this case ceramics, were found to vary in a patterned way on British and British colonial sites of the eighteenth century. By comparing the relative frequencies of ceramic types present at a site with the use spans of these artifacts, a mean date can be ascertained quantitatively (see South 1972a). A comparison of time spans of types present can also permit the beginning and ending dates of an occupation to be determined. If these dates are calculated for individual sites and the latter displayed on a map of the area of colonization, the spatial distribution of dates allows us to observe regional patterns of settlement and their change over time.

The recognition of functionally significant spatial patterning also played a significant role in our research. In order to identify site function, several types of archaeological patterning were investigated. The first involves the recognition of artifact and architectural patterns characteristic of activities whose occurrence is linked to settlement function. Patterns of domestic and specialized activity occurrence were used to identify all of the settlement types normally associated with insular frontier regions. In addition to studies of site content, an examination of size and layout also was useful in determining settlement function. Functionally significant settlement patterns have been identified through material evidence based on comparative information from contemporary European and British colonial sources. The association of these patterns with particular settlements permitted the recognition of the latter. In at least one case, analysis of site form over time allowed us to observe the functional evolution of a key colonial settlement, the frontier town of Camden.

The availability of material data from South Carolina has affected the extent to which pattern-based studies could be carried out. In addition, a dearth of comparative archaeological data from colonial agricultural regions has limited the breadth of certain analogies used in constructing the archaeological test implications examined. Despite these and other shortcomings, enough material data exist to demonstrate that the archaeological study of frontier regions need not be inhibited by limited source materials. Archaeological evidence will never be "complete" in the sense that it contains all the material used by a past culture or all the components of a settlement system. The available data, however, are adequate to provide information about cultural processes such as frontier change if this evidence is employed in the testing of hypotheses for which specific types of data are required (see Binford 1968:18–20).

Our ability to derive information relating to the insular frontier process on the basis of material evidence demonstrates the utility of archaeological methodology in providing an independent information base. Archaeological hypotheses bearing on the characteristics of insular frontier change were constructed without reference to historical sources pertaining directly to South Carolina. Similarly, analogies used in deducing implications by which to examine these hypotheses were developed independently of such sources. Consequently, the conclusions regarding frontier change in this region could have been arrived at in the absence of an extensive documentary record. Demonstrating the capability of archaeological methodology to elucidate phenomena of culture process is not new or unique to this discussion (see Binford 1968:14–16; South 1977:300, 318; Thomas 1973), nor is it intended to be. Rather our goal is to show the applicability of archaeology to the study of processes of frontier change. The analysis of material data from South Carolina permitted us to accomplish this in a carefully controlled manner.

THE REGIONAL APPROACH TO FRONTIER STUDIES

It is impossible to speak of colonization and insular frontier change without reference to the spatial aspect of these processes. As an element of an expanding world economic system, a colony plays a role dictated by its position in the trading network relative to the system's core. Similarly, the functions of insular frontier settlements are determined by their geographical position within the economic network of the region. These functions change as an area expands, new settlements are created, and transportation routes shift. These changes permit variation in role to be observed as both a temporal and spatial phenomenon.

A regional approach is necessary to study colonization archaeologically. A consideration of the region is a key element in the investigation of past cultural systems. It has long been recognized that a regional approach is necessary for defining the content, structure, and range of these cultures (Binford 1965:426). Research problems focused on cultural processes must be formulated to include the areal distribution as well as the sequential occurrence of phenomena involved. Likewise, archaeological methodologies aimed at investigating such processes must be designed to incorporate material data distributed differentially over the area occupied by a past society. The archaeological study of colonization must deal with a temporal process also possessing an extensive spatial dimension. Consequently, it must employ a methodology capable of obtaining data reflecting the content, structure, and range of the frontier society and the economic system of which it is a part.

Colonization is not a homogeneous process, and its form and composition vary with the role it plays in the world economy. The insular frontier process described above is basically one of agricultural expansion into and the permanent settlement of new lands. Settlement occupies a wide area and includes a variety of functionally distinct units, indicating the economic and social diversity of these regions. In contrast, cosmopolitan frontiers represent processes involving the largely temporary exploitation of limited resources. Settlement here reveals the specialized economic role played by these regions and tends to be confined to similar units situated so as to best exploit the area's resources. The content, structure, and range of these two kinds of frontiers are strongly dissimilar, and research questions addressed to the investigation of either must show an awareness of these differences. In developing the insular frontier model and discussing the six types of cosmopolitan frontiers, it was necessary to employ research questions focused on such critical factors as settlement distribution in time and space, activity patterning and settlement function, and the spatial organization of the colony as a social and economic entity. These questions are aimed at distinguishing the salient characteristics of each frontier type, and they represent the use of a research methodology capable of exploring both temporal and spatial aspects of the frontier as a region.

Because a frontier region involves such a large area and so many settlements, a complete investigation of its archaeological contents would be too lengthy and expensive to be practical. Even the cost of completely excavating individual settlements can be prohibitive if their sites are large. If portions of the site are inaccessible or destroyed, this task is impossible. These problems of data accessibility may be overcome if a representative sample of evidence relating to the research questions can be obtained. The substitution of partial for complete coverage of data must be controlled whenever possible to permit the reliability of information to be measured in terms of probability. Statistical sampling was employed in the investigation of a number of insular frontier settlements. The sampling strategies used were designed to obtain specific types of evidence which bear on questions of settlement size, form, layout, composition, and time of occupation, factors which are important in ascertaining the content and structure of the frontier region. Although perhaps somewhat less reliable because of their nonstatistical basis, various types of settlement surveys provided adequate information from which to observe settlement pattern and the range of colonization through time. The accuracy of the spatial patterning revealed in these data is reflected by the degree to which it anticipates statistical trends in the settlement of insular frontier regions. The use of sampling played a major role in obtaining the material evidence necessary to observe the occurrence of the insular frontier process. Its success here underlines the potential role of sampling in providing representative data for the study of cosmopolitan frontier colonization as well as other regional processes of change.

FRONTIER STUDIES AND THE EXPANSION OF EUROPE

The settlement of the New World after the fifteenth century represents one facet of a larger phenomenon known as the expansion of Europe. At the center of the expansion lies the emergence of the capitalist world economy, which provided the impetus for the development of new resource areas. Insular frontier colonization is a crucial process in the growth of this economy. An examination of the role of colonization in the world economy should help contribute to our understanding of the latter as a whole and increase our ability to interpret regional histories in terms of larger processes related to the economy's growth.

Frontiers, as zones of resource extraction, form a part of the periphery in a world economic system, but all peripheral areas do not remain frontiers. A frontier represents a peripheral region during the time it evolves from a newly occupied area to one characterized by stable economic adaptation. All frontiers, of course, do not develop toward this end.

Cosmopolitan frontiers, because of their specialized and impermanent nature, are relatively unstable regions in the long run. Their general inability to compete economically with agriculture usually confines them to the more marginal areas of the periphery. Although they may serve to open new territories to permanent settlement, cosmopolitan frontiers tend not to evolve into insular frontier regions and do not represent a stage of that colonization process.

Insular frontier colonization, however, is the first stage of more complex peripheral area development. This process ushers in the permanent occupation of a region that may lead eventually to its achieving core status within the world economy. The completion of the colonization process, though, does not always mark the area's emergence from its peripheral status. For example, South Carolina was colonized during the eighteenth century and had become a stable agricultural region by the close of this period. It remained a peripheral area throughout the following century, producing agricultural commodities for an industrial core centered in Europe and later the northern United States.

Other insular frontier regions followed a different course. New England, for example, developed from a producer of raw materials into a semiperipheral area as early as the eighteenth century because of its entrance into the trans-Atlantic carrying trade to supplement weak markets for its goods (Wallerstein 1980b:237). In the following century, the industrialization of this region accompanied its rise to core status. Paynter (1982) recently attempted to examine its transition from semiperiphery to core by observing the evolving settlement pattern of a portion of this region, the Connecticut River Valley in Massachusetts during the period 1800–1850. Based on the assumption that elites in a stratified society tend to perpetuate their position by controlling access to strategic resources crucial to the production and circulation of surplus, he modeled the intensification of such a region in terms of their tendencies to maximize control over the settlement pattern and minimize transport costs by concentrating settlements and production. Settlement pattern and land use data from this region were compared using several quantitative models designed to measure relative settlement concentration and wealth accumulation. These analyses revealed a chronological trend from dispersion toward aggregation around a single industrial center dominating the region.

It will be recalled that another study of the Connecticut River Valley prior to this time showed that the settlement pattern of this region followed a trend from random toward even spacing, a trend similar to that observed in colonial South Carolina (Swedlund 1975). This pattern of dispersed economic and political foci appears to mark the stabilization of both areas as postfrontier peripheral regions. At this stage each region reached a similar threshold in its economic development. Both passed through a common sequence as insular frontier regions, but as components of a larger developing economic system, each would take on a different role in response to its position in this world economy.

The evolution of a colonial region from an insular frontier to a core area is a complex process of change. It involves the initial expansion of an agricultural society into a territory, which is followed by the establishment of a stable economy geared to the production of exports to core markets. The area's emergence from its peripheral status is marked by an accumulation of surplus and the development of mechanisms for accelerating its accumulation. This evolutionary process is reflected in the form and composition of the region's settlement. An examination of its structure is capable of revealing patterning linked to the area's position in the world economic system. Portions of this process were observed in two separate areas in British colonial North America on the basis of patterning derived from documentary and material evidence. It is likely that such patterning is a widespread phenomenon, at least within the British world system, and should permit the recognition of an area's economic role as an element of this larger entity.

The process of change from periphery to core incorporates within a single region all of the geographically separate structural elements of a world economic system, much as the colonization gradient reveals the various settlement elements of an insular frontier region in the progressive development of a single settlement. Because both of these processes possess a temporal as well as a spatial apsect, it is possible to observe each process in terms of either of its forms. In the insular frontier region of South Carolina, for example, it was possible to detect the colonization gradient in time and space. On a larger scale, the periphery–core process was observed as a temporal phenomenon in the Connecticut River Valley. Taken together, both regions may be seen to represent elements of this process in space.

The occurrence of the insular frontier process and the periphery–core process as both spatial and temporal phenomena reflects the fact that in an area of colonization and a world economy respectively, the roles of settlements or regions are based on their relative access to the central element of each system. In the case of a colony, this is the entrepôt, and the center of a world economy is its core. Differential access changes as expansion occurs in each system, resulting in the promotion of some and the stabilization of others. The nature of this change was examined in models designed to explore colonization and the expansion of Europe as phenomena of growth. Consequently, those aspects of continuity, such as the failure of frontier settlements to develop beyond their original form or the stabilization of a region as a peripheral area, were neglected. Because processes of stability play such a prominant role in postfrontier development, they constitute a topic that deserves more attention if we are to examine regional and national growth as outcomes of European expansion.

The processes of frontier colonization can help explain local developments associated with the establishment of peripheral areas. By employing a model of frontier change in the examination of a specific region such as South Carolina, the area's history may be seen in a wider social and economic context. Rather than consisting of a series of unique events that took place in relative isolation as a local adaptation, a colony's history may be viewed as a local response to conditions imposed by the region's peripheral status. For example, settlement in the South

Carolina interior can be seen as a movement intended to accommodate growth by settling pioneers in the nearest available territory. An examination of the structure and content of settlement reveals, however, that expansion was carried out in a manner that expedited the area's development as a zone of commercial agricultural production geared to an extensive outside market. This role is characteristic of developing peripheral areas in a world economy. An understanding of the workings of the world economy permits local events to be seen as elements of larger processes that are economic and ecological responses to the expansion of state systems. Knowledge of such processes is an asset in defining the scope of local and regional histories and in assessing their roles with regard to wider colonial developments. A processual approach facilitates a comparison of colonial histories, permitting the recognition of wider patterns of change that can aid in explaining both large- and small-scale aspects of colonization through a variety of data bases. The potential for archaeological research in the study of expansion and colonization has only begun to be realized. It should prove a major source of information about a process that played such an important role in the making of the modern world.

References

COLLECTIONS AND RECORD GROUPS

Cemetery Records (CR)
> Manuscript Division, South Caroliniana Library, University of South Carolina, Columbia.

Nathaniel Greene Papers, Papers of the Continental Congress (NGPPCC)
> South Carolina Archives, Columbia, microfilm.

National Register File (NRF)
> South Carolina Department of Archives and History, Columbia.

Site Inventory Record (SIR)
> Institute of Arcaheology, University of South Carolina, Columbia.

South Carolina Department of Archives and History (SCDAHSF)
> Survey Files. Columbia.

South Carolina Department of Parks, Recreation, and Tourism (SCDPRT)
> Hampton Plantation State Park File. Columbia.

South Carolina, Records of the Commons House of Assembly (SCRCHAJ)
> Journals, 1692–1776, 79 volumes. South Carolina Archives, Columbia, manuscript.

South Carolina, Records of the General Assembly (SCRGAABJR) Acts, Bills, and Joint Resolutions, 1691–1972. South Carolina Archives, Columbia, manuscript.

South Carolina, Records of the Secretary of State Land Grants (SCRSSLGCS) Colonial Series, copies, 1694–1776, 43 volumes. South Carolina Archives, Columbia, manuscript.

United States Department of the Interior, Office of Archaeology and Historic Preservation, Inventory (USDIOAHPI)
> Inventory of sites in the Richard B. Russell Project area. Institute of Archaeology and Anthropology, University of South Carolina, Columbia.

MAPS AND ATLASES

Cook, James
 1773   A map of the province of South Carolina with all the rivers, creeks, bays, inletts, islands, inland navigation, soundings, time of high water on the seacoast, roads, marches, ferrys, bridges, swamps, parishes, churches, towns, townships, county parish district, and provincial lines. . . . (Map 81 × 78 cm, scale ca. 1:600,000. London.)

Coram, T., and J. Akin
 1802   [Map of the State of South Carolina] engraved for Drayton's History of South Carolina. (Color map 50 × 48 cm, scale 1:1,013,760. Charleston and Philadelphia.)

DeBrahm, William
 1757   A map of South Carolina and a part of Georgia containing the whole sea-coast; all the islands, inlets, rivers, creeks, parishes, townships, boroughs, roads and bridges: As also several plantations with their names and the names of their proprietors. (Color map on 2 sheets each 69 × 122 cm, scale 1:316,800. T. Jefferys, London.)

Dickey, Henry, Davenport, Riggs, and Bergen
 1818   [Spartanburg, South Carolina, survey of land grants.] (Color map 110 × 135 cm, scale not given. Manuscript in Library of Congress, Geography and Map Division, Washington.)

Faden, William
 1780   A map of South Carolina and a part of Georgia, containing the whole sea-coast; all the islands, inlets, rivers, creeks, parishes, townships, boroughs, roads, and bridges; as also several plantations with their proper boundary lines, their names, and the names of their proprietors. Composed from surveys taken by the Hon. William Bull, Esq. Lieutenant Governor, Captain Gascoign, Hugh Bryan, Esq. and William DeBraham Esq. Surveyor General of the South District of North America, republished with considerable additions, from the surveys made and collected by John Stuart Esq. His Majesty's Superintendant of Indian Affairs. (Color map on 4 sheets 136 × 123 cm, scale *ca.* 1:320,000. London.)

Hunter, George
 1730   The Charecke nation by Col. Herberts map & my own observations with the path to Charles Town, its course & (distance measured by my watch) the names of ye branches, rivers and creeks, as given them by ye traders along that nation, May 21, 1730. (Map 42 × 66 cm, scales vary. Geography and Map Division, Library of Congress, Washington.)

Mills, Robert
 1825   *Atlas of the State of South Carolina.* Baltimore: John D. Toy. Reprint edition 1965, Columbia: Robert Pearce Wilkins and John D. Keels, Jr.

Moll, Herman
 1715   A map of the improved part of Carolina with the settlements, etc. *Inset on* A new and exact map of the dominions of king of Great Britain on ye continent of North America. . . . In *The world described; or, a new and correct set of maps: Showing the several empires, kingdoms, republics . . . in all the known parts of the earth.* London: J. Bowles. (Map 31 × 27 cm, scale 1:348,480.)

Mouzon, Henry
 1775   An accurate map of North and South Carolina, with their Indian frontiers, shewing in a distinct manner all the mountains, rivers, swamps, marshes, bays, creeks, harbours, sandbanks and soundings on the coasts, with the roads and Indian paths, as well as the boundary or provincial lines, the several townships and other divisions of the land in both the provinces, the whole from actual surveys by Henry Mouzon and others. (Color map on 2 sheets each 50 × 142 cm, scale *ca.* 1:530,000. London: Robert Sayer and J. Bennett.)

Myer, William E.
 1928   The trail system of the southeastern United States in the early colonial period. (Color map 33 × 39 cm, scale 1:1,267,200. *In* Indian trails of the Southeast. *Annual Report of the Bureau of American Ethnology* 42:727–857.)

Sautier, C. J.
  1769a   Plan of the town of Halifax in Halifax County, North Carolina. (Map 51 × 43 cm, scale 1:3,240. North Carolina Department of Archives and history, Raleigh, photostat.)
  1769b   Plan of the town and port of Brunswick in Brunswick County, North Carolina. (Map 56 × 44 cm, scale 1:3,120. North Carolina Department of Archives and History, Raleigh, photostat.)
  1769c   Plan of the town of Wilmington in New Hanover County, North Carolina. (Map 52 × 42 cm, scale 1:3,240. North Carolina Department of Archives and History, Raleigh, photostat.)
  1770a   Plan of the town of Cross Creek in Cumberland County, North Carolina. (Map 51 × 43 cm, scale 1:2,232. North Carolina Department of Archives and History, Raleigh, photostat.)
  1770b   Plan of the town of Salisbury in Rowan County, North Carolina. (Map 50 × 43 cm, scale 1:4,464. North Carolina Department of Archives and History, Raleigh, photostat.)
South Carolina Archives
  n.d.   Guide maps to development of South Carolina parishes, districts, and counties, from maps in South Carolina county inventories made by the W. P. A. Historical Records Survey. (Columbia, typescript.)
U.S. Department of Agriculture, Agricultural Stabilization and Conservation Service
  1950   Vertical aerial photograph, CDW-GD-52, Georgetown County, South Carolina. (Photo 29 × 29 cm, scale 1:15,840.)

LITERATURE CITED

Abbitt, Merry W.
  1973   The eighteenth century shoe buckle. In *Five artifact studies, Colonial Williamsburg Occasional Papers in Archaeology* 1:25–53.
Anthony, Carl
  1976   The big house and the slave quarters, part 1: Prelude to New World architecture. *Landscape* 21(1):8–19.
Anthony, Ronald W., and Lesley M. Drucker
  1980   An archaeological reconnaissance of the proposed J. E. Locklair Memorial Airport, Dorchester County, South Carolina. Report prepared by Carolina Archaeological Services for the Dorchester Country Aeronautics Commission, Columbia.
  1983   Cultural resources investigations at Spring Grove plantation, Berkeley County, South Carolina. *Carolina Archaeological Services, Resource Studies Series,* in preparation.
Architects' Emergency Committee
  1933   *Great Georgian houses of America,* volume 1. New York: Kalkhoff Press. Reprint edition 1970, New York: Dover Publications.
Arensberg, Conrad M.
  1961   The community as object and sample. *American Anthropologist* 63: 241–264.
Asreen, Robert
  1975   An archeological survey of proposed widening of U.S. 52 between Monck's Corner and Kingstree, South Carolina. *University of South Carolina, Institute of Archeology and Anthropology, Research Manuscript Series* 74.
Baker, Steven G.
  1972   Colono-Indian pottery from Cambridge, South Carolina, with comments on the historic Catawba pottery trade. *University of South Carolina, Institute of Archeology and Anthropology, Notebook* 4(1):3–30.
Barka, Norman F.
  1973   The kiln and ceramics of the "poor potter"of Yorktown: A preliminary report. In *Ce-*

ramics in America, edited by Ian M. G. Quimby. Charlottesville: The University Press of Virginia. Pp. 291–318.

Bartram, William
  1958   *The travels of William Bartram.* Naturalist's edition edited and annoted by Francis Harper. New Haven: Yale University Press.

Barzun, Jacques, and Henry F. Graff
  1962   *The modern researcher.* New York: Harcourt, Brace & World.

Beaudry, Mary C.
  1979   Fort Christanna: Frontier trading post of the Virginia Indian Company. Paper presented at The Twelfth Annual Converence on Historic Site Archaeology, St. Augustine, Florida, October 19, 1979.

Beresford, M. W., and J. K. S. St. Joseph
  1958   *Medieval England, an aerial survey.* Cambridge: The University Press.

Berge, Dale L.
  1968   The Gila Bend stage station. The Kiva 33(4):169–243.

Berkeley–Charleston–Dorchester Regional Planning Council
  1979   *Historic preservation inventory.* Charleston.

Bernheim, G. D.
  1872   *History of the German settlements and of the Lutheran Church in North and South Carolina.* Philadelphia: The Lutheran Bookstore. Reprint edition 1972, Spartanburg: The Reprint Company. 1972.

Berry, Brian J. L.
  1967   *Geography of market centers and retail distribution.* Englewood Cliffs: Prentice-Hall.

Binford, Lewis R.
  1964   A consideration of archaeological research design. *American Antiquity* 29(4):425–441.
  1968   Archaeological perspectives. In *New perspectives in archaeology,* edited by Sally R. and Lewis R. Binford. Chicago: Aldine. Pp. 5–32.
  1965   Archaeological systematics and the study of culture process. *American Antiquity* 3(2): 203–210.
  1978   Dimensional analysis of behavior and site structure: Learning from an Eskino hunting stand. *American Antiquity* 43(3):330–361.
  1980   *Nunamiut ethnoarchaeology.* New York: Academic Press.
  1981   Behavioral archaeology and the "Pompeii premise." *Journal of Anthropological Research* 37(3):195–208.

Bivins, John F., Jr.
  1972   *The Moravian potters in North Carolina.* Chapel Hill: The University of North Carolina Press.

Blanding, Abram
  1820   *Plans and progress of internal improvement in South Carolina.* Charleston: W. P. Young and Son.

Bloch, Marc
  1953   *The historian's craft.* New York: Knopf.

Blouet, Brian W.
  1972   Factors influencing the evolution of settlement patterns. In *Man, settlement and urbanism,* edited by Ruth Tringham and G. W. Dimbleby. London: Gerald Duckworth and Co. Pp. 3–15.

Bohannan, Paul, and Fred Plog (editors)
  1967   *Beyond the frontier: Social processes and cultural change.* Garden City, New Jersey: Natural History Press.

Brockington, Paul E., Jr.
  1980   Cooper River rediversion archeological survey. *University of South Carolina, Institute of Archeology and Anthropology, Research Manuscript Series 169.*

Brown, Marley R. III
1973 Ceramics from Plymouth, 1621–1800: The documentary record. In *Ceramics in America*, edited by Ian M. G. Quimby. Charlottesville: The University Press of Virginia. Pp. 41–74.

Brown, Richard Maxwell
1963 *The South Carolina Regulators*. Cambridge, Massachusetts: The Belknap Press of the Harvard University Press.

Bruce, Alfred W.
1952 *The steam locomotive in America, its development in the twentieth century*. New York: Bonanza Books.

Buckley, Walter
1967 *Sociology and modern systems theory*. Englewood Cliffs, New Jersey: Prentice-Hall.

Caldwell, Joseph R.
1974 Preliminary report, archeological investigation of Fort Charlotte, McCormick County, South Carolina. *University of South Carolina, Institute of Archeology and Anthropology, Notebook* VI (2):45–56.

Calmes, Alan
1968 The British Revolutionary fortifications of Camden, South Carolina. *Conference on Historic Site Archaeology, Papers* 2:50–60.

Carlson, Gayle F.
1979 Archaeological investigations at Fort Atkinson (25WN9), Washington County, Nebraska, 1956–1971. *Nebraska State Historical Society, Publications in Anthropology 8.*

Carpenter, G. A., M. Clawson, and C. E. Fleming
1941 *Ranch organization and operation in northeastern Nevada*. Carson City: Nevada State Printing Office.

Carrillo, Richard
1972 Archeological excavations at Pinckneyville, site of Pinckney District, 1791–1800. *University of South Carolina, Institute of Archeology and Anthropology, Research Manuscript Series 25.*
1980 Green Grove plantation: Archaeological and historical research at the Kinlock site (38Ch109), Charleston County. Report prepared for the South Carolina Department of Highways and Public Transportation, Columbia.

Carrillo, Richard, Joseph C. Wilkins, and Howell C. Hunter, Jr.
1975 Historical, architectural, and archeological research at Brattonsville (38YK21), York County, South Carolina. *University of South Carolina, Institute of Archeology and Anthropology, Research Manuscript Series 76.*

Casagrande, Joseph B., Stephen I. Thompson, and Philip D. Young
1964 Colonization as a research frontier. In *Process and pattern in culture, essays in honor of Julian H. Steward*, edited by Robert A. Manners. Chicago: Aldine. Pp. 281–325.

Catawba Regional Planning Council
1975 *Historic sites survey, York County*. Rock Hill, South Carolina.
1976a *Historic sites survey, Union County*. Rock Hill, South Carolina.
1976b *Historic sites survey, Lancaster County*. Rock Hill, South Carolina.
1976c *Historic sites survey, Chester County*. Rock Hill, South Carolina.

Caywood, Louis R.
1955 Green Spring plantation archeological report. Prepared for the Virginia 350th Anniversary Commission and the Jamestown–Williamsburg–Yorktown Celebration Commission.

Central Midlands Regional Planning Council
1974 *An inventory and plan for the preservation of historical properties in the Central Midlands region*. Columbia, South Carolina.

Central Piedmont Regional Planning Commission
1971 *Survey of historic sites, Chester County*. Rock Hill, South Carolina.

Chambers, J. D., and G. E. Mingay
  1966   *The agricultural revolution, 1750–1880.* London: B. T. Batsford.
Chance, David H., and Jennifer V. Chance
  1979   Kettle Falls: 1977, salvage archaeology in and beside Lake Roosevelt. *University of Idaho, Anthropological Research Manuscripts Series 53.*
Charnov, E. L.
  1976   Optimal foraging: The marginal value theorem. *Theoretical Population Biology* 9:129–136.
Childe, V. Gordon
  1942   *What happened in history.* Harmondsworth: Penguin Books.
Chorley, R. J., and P. Haggett
  1968   Trend surface mapping in geographical research. In *Spatial analysis, a reader in statistical geography,* edited by Brian J. L. Berry and Duane F. Marble. Englewood Cliffs: Prentice-Hall. Pp. 195–217.
Clark, Andrew H.
  1956   The impact of exotic invasion on the remaining New World mid-latitude grasslands. In *Man's role in changing the face of the earth,* edited by William L. Thomas, Jr. Chicago: University of Chicago Press. Pp. 737–762.
Clark, Grahame
  1952   *Prehistoric Europe; the economic basis.* London: Methuen.
  1953   The economic approach to prehistory. *Proceedings of the British Academy* 39:215–238.
  1957   *Archaeology and society, reconstructing the prehistoric past.* London: Methuen.
Clark, Philip J., and Francis C. Evans
  1954   Distance to nearest neighbor as a measure of spatial relationships in populations. *Ecology* 35(4):445–453.
Clow, A., and N. L. Clow
  1958   Ceramics from the fifteenth century to the rise of the Staffordshire potteries. In *A history of technology,* volume 4, *the industrial revolution, c. 1750 to c. 1850,* edited by Charles Singer *et al.* New York: Oxford University Press. Pp. 328–357.
Clowse, Converse D.
  1971   *Economic beginnings in colonial South Carolina.* Columbia: University of South Carolina Press.
Coleman, Kenneth
  1976   *Colonial Georgia, a history.* New York: Charles Scribner's Sons.
Colquhoun, Donald J.
  1969   Geomorphology of the Lower Coastal Plain of South Carolina. *South Carolina State Development Board, Division of Geology,* MS-15.
Combes, John D.
  1969   Archeological salvage operation in the Keowee-Toxaway project nears completion. *University of South Carolina, Institute of Archeology and Anthropology, Notebook* 1(1):7–8.
Conkling, Roscoe P., and Margaret B. Conkling
  1947   *The Butterfield Overland Mail, 1857–1869,* 3 volumes. Glendale, California: Arthur H. Clark.
Consulting Associates
  1976   South Carolina-future for her underwater past. Report prepared for the South Carolina Underwater Research Council, Columbia.
Cook, H. T.
  1923   *The Hard Labor section.* Greenville: By the author.
Cooke, C. Wythe
  1936   Geology of the Coastal Plain of South Carolina. *U. S. Department of the Interior, Geological Survey, Bulletin 867.*

Cotter, John L.
  1958   Archeological excavations at Jamestown Colonial National Historical Park and James-
          town National Historic Site, Virginia. *U. S. Department of the Interior, National Park
          Service, Archeological Research Series* 4.
Crane, Verner W.
  1929   *The southern frontier, 1670–1732.* Ann Arbor: University of Michigan Press. Reprint
          edition 1956, Ann Arbor Paperbacks.
Crockett, Nancy
  1965   The old Waxhaw graveyard. Manuscript on file, South Caroliniana Library, University of
          South Carolina, Columbia.
Crowder, Louise Kelly
  1970   *Tombstone records of Chester County, South Carolina and vicinity,* volume 1. Chester,
          South Carolina: By the author.
Dalcho, Frederick
  1820   *A historical account of the Protestant Episcopal Church in South Carolina.* Charleston: E.
          Thayer.
Darby, H. C.
  1973   The age of the improver: 1600–1800. In *A new historical geography of England,* edited by
          H. C. Darby. Cambridge: University Press. Pp. 302–388.
Daugherty, Lawton
  1961   Little River–Dominick Presbyterian Church, 1761–1961. Manuscript on file, South Car-
          oliniana Library, University of South Carolina, Columbia.
Daughters of the American Revolution, Old Cheraws Chapter
  1977   *A Guide to markers of old St. David's Cemetery, Cheraw, South Carolina.* Cheraw, South
          Carolina: By the author.
Dawson, C. A.
  1934   The settlement of the Peace River Country, a study of a pioneer area. In *Canadian frontiers
          of settlement,* volume 6, edited by W. A. Mackintosh and W. L. G. Joerg. Toronto:
          MacMillan Co.
Deagan, Kathleen
  1978   The material assemblage of 16th century Spanish Florida. *Historical Archaeology*
          12:25–50.
Deetz, James J. F.
  1971   Archeology as a social science. In Current directions in anthropology, edited by Ann
          Fischer. *American Anthropological Association, Bulletin* 3(3), part 2:115–125.
  1973   Ceramics from Plymouth, 1635–1835: The archaeological evidence. In *Ceramics in Amer-
          ica,* edited by Ian M. G. Quimby. Charlottesville: The University Press of Virginia. Pp.
          15–40.
Deetz, James J. F., and Edwin Dethlefsen
  1965   The Doppler Effect and archaeology: A consideration of the spatial aspects of seriation.
          Southwestern Journal of Anthropology **21**:196–206.
DeJarnette, David L., and Asael T. Hanson
  1960   The archeology of the Childersburg site, Alabama. *Florida State University, Notes in
          Anthropology* 4.
Derrick, Samuel M.
  1930   *Centennial history of the South Carolina Railroad.* Columbia: The State Company.
Dethlefsen, Edwin S.
  1981   The cemetery and culture change: Archaeological focus and ethnographic perspective. In
          Modern material culture: The archaeology of us, edited by Richard A. Gould and Michael
          B. Schiffer. New York: Academic Press. Pp. 137–159.

DeVorsey, Louis R.
    1966   *The Indian boundary in the southern colonies*. Chapel Hill: University of North Carolina Press.

Dickens, Roy S., Jr., and William R. Bowen
    1980   Problems and promises in urban historical archaeology: The MARTA Project. *Historical Archaeology* **14**:42–57.

Doar, David
    1936   Rice and rice planting in the South Carolina lowcountry, edited by E. Milby Burton. *Contributions from the Charleston Museum* 8:7–42.

Dodd, William E.
    1921   *The cotton kingdom, a chronicle of the old South*. New Haven: Yale University Press.

Dougenik, James A., and David E. Sheehan
    1976   *SYMAP user's reference manual*. Cambridge, Massachusetts: Harvard University, Laboratory for Computer Graphics and Spatial Analysis.

Downing, A. J.
    1850   *The architecture of country houses*. New York: D. Appleton & Co. Reprint edition 1969, New York: Dover Publications, Inc.

Doyon, Georges, and Robert Hubrecht
    1964   *L'architecture rurale & bourgeoise en France*. Paris: Vincent, Freal et Cie, Editeurs.

Drake, Elizabeth C., and Jacquelyn M. Rainwater
    1970   Cemetery Records of Marlboro County, South Carolina. Manuscript on file, South Caroliniana Library, University of South Carolina.

Drayton, John
    1802   *A view of South Carolina, as respects her natural and civil concerns*. Charleston: W. P. Young. Reprint edition 1972, Spartanburg: The Reprint Company.

Drucker, Lesley M.
    1980   Cultural resources inventory of selected areas of the Oaks and Laurel Hill plantations, Brookgreen Gardens, Georgetown County, South Carolina. Report prepared by Carolina Archaeological Services for Brookgreen Gardens, Columbia.

Drucker, Lesley M., and Ronald W. Anthony
    1979   The Spiers Landing Site: Archaeological investigations in Berkeley County, South Carolina. Report prepared by Carolina Archaeological Services for the U.S. Department of the Interior, Heritage Conservation and Recreation Service, Contract Number 5767(78). Columbia.
    1980   Cultural resources survey of the Pinckney Island National Wildlife Refuge, Beaufort County, South Carolina. Report prepared by Carolina Archaeological Services for the U.S. Department of the Interior, Heritage Conservation and Recreation Service, Contract Number A-55035(79). Columbia.

Drucker, Lesley M., and Rebecca G. Fulmer
    1981   Cultural resources investigations for Union Camp's proposed Eastover mill tract, Richland County, South Carolina. Report prepared by Carolina Archaeological Services for Environmental Research and Technology, Inc. and Union Camp Corp., Columbia.

Duffy, Christopher
    1975   *Fire and stone, the science of fortress warfare 1660–1860*. Newton Abbot, Devon: David and Charles.

Elston, R., D. L. Hardesty, and S. Clerico
    1980   Archaeological investigations on the Hopkins Land Exchange. Report prepared by Intermountain Research, Inc.

Elston, R., D. L. Hardesty, and C. Zeier
    1982   Archaeological investigations on the Hopkins Land Exchange, Part 2. Report prepared by Intermountain Research, Inc.

Garrow, Patrick H., Jack E. Bernhardt, and Jana Kellar
1979   Archaeological investigations at the Low Ridge (38BK372) and Deer Field (38BK373) sites, Cross generating station, Berkeley County, South Carolina. Report prepared by Soil Systems, Inc., Atlanta.

Dunnell, Robert C.
1978   Style and function: A fundamental dichotomy. *American Antiquity* 43(2):192–202.

Earle, Carville
1978   A staple interpretation of slavery and free labor. *Geographical Review* 68(1):51–65.

Earle, Carville, and Ronald Hoffman
1976   Staple crops and urban development in the eighteenth-century South. *Perspectives in American History* 10:7–80.

Ebenezer Memorial Association
1975   *Directory of Ebenezer Presbyterian Church Cemetery, Town of Ebenezer, York County, South Carolina.* By the author.

Eden, Sir Frederick Morton
1973   An estimate of the member of inhabitants in Great Britain and Ireland (1800). In *The population controversy,* edited by D. V. Glass. Farnborough, Hampshire: Gregg International Publishers Limited.

Edwards, Everett E.
1940   American agriculture-the first 300 years. In *Farmers in a changing world, the yearbook of agriculture* 1940. Washington: U.S. Department of Agriculture, Government Printing Office. Pp. 171–276.

Egnal, Marc, and Joseph A. Ernst
1972   An economic interpretation of the American Revolution. *William and Mary College Quarterly,* Series 3, 29(1):3–32.

Ehrenhard, John E.
1973   The Rustic Hotel, Fort Laramie National Historic Site, Wyoming. *Historical Archaeology* 7:11–29.

Eleazer, J. M.
1955   *Our land is our life, conservation of South Carolina's natural resources.* Columbia: State Department of Education.

Elzas, Barnett A.
1903   *The old Jewish cemeteries at Charleston, S. C.* Charleston: Daggett Printing Company.

Ernst, Joseph A., and H. Roy Merrens
1973a   The South Carolina economy of the middle eighteenth century: A view from Philadelphia. *West Georgia College, Studies in the Social Sciences* 12:16–29.
1973b   "Camden's turrets pierce the skies.": The urban process in the southern colonies. *William and Mary College Quarterly,* Series 3, 30(4):549–574.

Fairbanks, Charles H.
1973   The cultural significance of Spanish ceramics. In *Ceramics in America,* edited by Ian M. G. Quimby. Charlottesville: The University Press of Virginia. Pp. 141–174.

Favrelli, Rudy J., and Joy Putnam Favrelli
1978   Landscapes and gardens for historic buildings. Nashville: American Association for State and Local History.

Ferguson, Leland G.
1977   An archeological-historical analysis of Fort Watson: December 1780–April 1781. In *Research strategies in historical archeology,* edited by Stanley South. New York: Academic Press. Pp. 41–71.
1980   Looking for the "Afro" in Colono-Indian pottery. In *Archaeological perspectives on ethnicity in America,* edited by Robert L. Schuyler. Farmingdale, New York: Baywood Press. Pp. 14–28.

Flatres, P.
    1971   Hamlet and village. In *Man and his habitat, essays presented to Emyr Estyn Evans,* edited by R. H. Buchanan *et al.* New York: Barnes and Noble. Pp. 165–185.
Flinn, M. W.
    1965   *An economic and social history of Britain, 1066–1939.* New York: MacMillan.
Florin, Lambert
    1961   *Western ghost towns.* Seattle: Superior Publishing Company.
Fogel, Robert William
    1971   Railroads and American economic growth. In *The reinterpretation of American economic history,* edited by Robert William Fogel and Stanley L. Engerman. New York: Harper & Row. Pp. 187–203.
Fogel, Robert William, and Stanley L. Engerman
    1974   *Time on the cross, the economics of American Negro slavery.* Boston: Little, Brown and Company.
Foley, David Michael (editor)
    1979   *A master plan for Hampton Plantation State Park.* Division of State Parks, South Carolina Department of Parks, Recreation, and Tourism, Columbia.
Fontana, Bernard L.
    1967   The archaeology of post-18th century ranches in the United States. *Historical Archaeology* **1**:60–63.
Fontana, Bernard, and J. Cameron Greenleaf
    1962   Johnny Ward's ranch: A study in historic archaeology. *The Kiva* **28**(1–2).
Forman, Henry Chandlee
    1948   *The architecture of the old South, the medieval style, 1585–1850.* Cambridge: Harvard University Press.
Forsman, Michael R. A., and Joseph G. Gallo
    1979   The problem of archaeological diversity, synthesis, and comparison. *Conference on Historic Site Archaeology, Papers* **13**:238–252.
Fox, H. S. A.
    1973   Going to town in thirteenth century England. In *Man made the land, essays in English historical geography,* edited by Alan H. R. Baker and J. B. Harley. Newton Abbot, Devon: David & Charles. Pp. 69–78.
Friis, Herman R.
    1940   A series of population maps of the colonies and the United States, 1625–1790. *American Geographical Society, Mimeographed Publication* 3.
Frothingham, E. H., and R. M. Nelson
    1944   South Carolina forest resources and industries. *U. S. Department of Agriculture, Miscellaneous Publications* 552.
Garrow, Patrick H., Thomas R. Wheaton, Jr., and Amy Friedlander
    1981   Cooper River rediversion canal, historic sites archaeology, draft report. Prepared by Soil Systems, Inc. for Interagency Archeological Services-Atlanta, Contract Number C-59550(79).
Geertz, Clifford
    1963   *Agricultural involution: The process of ecological change in Indonesia.* Berkeley: University of California Press.
Georgia, State of
    1805   List of goods suitable for the State of Georgia and Indian and Spanish trade, St. Marys, Georgia. Manuscript in P. K. Yonge Library of Florida History, University of Florida, Gainesville.
Gipson, Lawrence Henry
    1936   *The British Empire before the American Revolution,* volume 1, *Great Britain and Ireland.* Caldwell, Idaho: Caxton Printers.

Glassie, Henry
    1968   *Pattern in the material folk culture of the eastern United States.* Philadelphia: University of Pennsylvania Press.
    1975   *Folk housing in middle Virginia.* Knoxville: University of Tennessee Press.

Glover, Beulah
    1939   Tombstone inscriptions, Colleton County. *South Carolina Historical Magazine* 40:36–39.
    1972   *In memory of: Inscriptions from early cemeteries.* Walterboro, South Carolina: The Press and Standard.

Glover, William L.
    1940   The Heyward family burying ground at Old House, near Grahmville, S. C. *South Carolina Historical Magazine* **41**:75–80.

Goodyear, Albert C.
    1975   An archeological survey of the proposed alternate three route, southern alternate, of the southwestern Columbia beltway between I-26 and South Carolina 48. *University of South Carolina, Institute of Archeology and Anthropology, Research Manuscript Series 77.*

Gould, J. D.
    1972   *Economic growth in history, survey and analysis.* London: Methuen and Co.

Gould, R. A.
    1971   The archaeologist as ethnographer: A case from the Western Desert of Australia. *World Archaeology* 3(2):143–177.

Gould, S., and N. Eldredge
    1977   Punctuated equilibria: The tempo and mode of evolution reconsidered. *Paleobiology* 3:115–151.

Gray, H. Peter
    1976   *A generalized theory of international trade.* New York: Holmes and Meier Publishers.

Gray, Lewis Cecil
    1933   *History of agriculture in the southern United States to 1860,* 2 volumes. Carnegie Institute of Washington. Reprint edition 1958, Glouchester, Massachusetts: Peter Smith.

Grayson, William John
    1960   Recollections of an island boyhood. In *Port Royal under six flags,* edited by Katherine M. Jones. New York: Bobbs-Merrill Company. Pp. 144–151.

Green, Fletcher M.
    1972   *The role of the Yankee in the old South.* Athens: University of Georgia Press.

Green, H. J. M.
    1961   An analysis of archaeological rubbish deposits. *Archaeological News Letter* 7(3):51–54.

Green, Stanton W.
    1980   Broadening least-cost models for expanding agricultural systems. In *Modeling change in prehistoric subsistence economies,* edited by T. Earle and J. Ericson. New York: Academic Press. Pp. 209–241.

Greene, Evarts B., and Virginia D. Harrington
    1932   *American population before the Federal census of 1790.* New York: Columbia University Press.

Greene, Jack P. (editor)
    1970   *Great Britain and the American colonies, 1606–1763.* Columbia: University of South Carolina Press.

Gregg, Alexander
    1867   *History of the old Cheraws.* New York: Richardson and Company. Reprint edition 1965, Spartanburg: The Reprint Co.

Griffin, John W.
    1962   Archaeological explorations at the Oldest House, 1954. In Evolution of the Oldest House, by Frederik C. Gjessing *et al. Florida State University, Notes in Anthropology 7.* Pp. 31–42.

Grimm, Jacob L.
   1970   Archaeological investigations of Fort Ligonier, 1960–1965. *Annals of the Carnegie Museum* 42.

Grove, David
   1972   The function and future of urban centres. In *Man, settlement, and urbanism,* edited by Ruth Tringham and G. W. Dimbleby. London: Gerald Duckworth and Co. Pp. 559–565.

Haggar, Reginald G.
   1968   *The concise encyclopedia of continental pottery and porcelain.* New York: Frederick A. Praeger.

Haggett, Peter
   1966   *Locational analysis in human geography.* New York: St. Martin's Press.

Haggett, P., A. D. Cliff, and A. Frey
   1977   *Locational analysis in human geography.* New York: Wiley

Hall, A. D., and R. E. Fagen
   1956   Definition of system. *General Systems* 1:18–28.

Hammond, Harry
   1883   *South Carolina, resources and population, institutions, and industries.* Charleston: Walker, Evans, & Cogswell.

Handler, Jerome, and Frederick Lange
   1978   *Plantation slavery in Barbados: An archaeological and historical investigation.* Cambridge: Harvard University Press.
   1979   Plantation slavery on Barbados, West Indies. *Archaeology* 32(4):45–52.

Hardesty, Donald L.
   1979   The Pony Express in central Nevada: Archaeological and documentary perspectives. *Bureau of Land Management, Nevada State Office, Cultural Resource Series* 1.
   1980   Historic sites archaeology on the western American frontier: Theoretical perspectives and research problems. *North American Archaeologist* 2(1):67–81.
   1981   Recovery of historical archaeological data in Bullfrog Claim and mining sites: Nye County, Nevada. Report prepared by University of Nevada, Reno.
   1982   Evolution on the industrial frontier. In *Frontiers and boundary processes,* edited by Stanton Green and Stephen Perlman. New York: Academic Press. In press.

Hardesty, Donald L., and S. L. Edaburn
   1982   Technological systems on the Nevada mining frontier. Paper presented at the 1982 meeting of the Society for Historical Archaeology, Philadelphia.

Harley, Lillian H., Pattie W. Heaton, and Lillian D. Kizer
   1978   *Cemetery inscriptions of Dorchester County, South Carolina,* Volume 1. St. George, South Carolina: The Dorchester Eagle-Record Publishing Company.
   1979   *Cemetery inscriptions of Dorchester County, South Carolina,* Volume 2. St. George, South Carolina: The Dorchester Eagle-Record Publishing Company.
   1980   *Cemetery inscriptions of Dorchester County, South Carolina,* volume 3. St. George, South Carolina: The Dorcester Eagle-Record Publishing Company.

Harrington, J. C.
   1952   Historic site archeology in the United States. In *Archeology of eastern United States,* edited by James B. Griffin. Chicago: University of Chicago Press. Pp. 335–344.

Harris, R. Cole
   1977   The simplification of Europe overseas. *Annals of the Association of American Geographers* 67(4):469–483.

Haskel, Daniel, and J. Calvin Smith
   1846   *A complete descriptive and statistical gazetteer of the United States of America.* New York: Sherman & Smith.

Herold, Elaine B.
   1981   Historical archaeological report on the Meeting Street office building site, Charleston, S. C. Report prepared by the Charleston Museum, Charleston.

Herold, Elaine B., and Stanley G. Knick, III
  1979   An archaeological reconnaissance of proposed power transmission lines for the Santee-Cooper Cross Generating Plant. Report prepared by the Charleston Museum, Charleston.
Herold, Elaine B., and Elizabeth Thomas
  1981   Historical archaeological survey of the First Citizen's Bank and Trust project on south Market Street, Charleston, S. C. Report prepared by the Charleston Museum, Charleston.
Herskovits, Melville J.
  1948   *Man and his works, the science of cultural anthropology.* New York: Alfred A. Knopf.
Heyward, Marie H.
  1929   Tombstone inscriptions from Holy Cross Church, Stateburg, S. C. *South Carolina Historical Magazine* 30:50–59.
Hill, James N.
  1972   The methodological debate in contemporary archaeology: A model. In *Models in archaeology,* edited by David L. Clarke. London: Methuen and Co. Pp. 61–107.
Hilliard, Sam Bowers
  1975   The tidewater rice plantation: An indigenous adaptation to nature. *Geoscience and Man* 12:57–66.
  1978   Antebellum tidewater rice culture in South Carolina and Georgia. In *European settlement and development in North America: Essays on geographical change in honor and memory of Andrew Hill Clark,* edited by James R. Gibson. Toronto: University of Toronto Press. Pp. 91–115.
Hirsch, Arthur Henry
  1928   *The Huguenots of colonial South Carolina.* Durham, North Carolina: Duke University Press.
Hofstadter, Richard
  1968   *The progressive historians: Turner, Beard, and Parrington.* New York: Alfred A. Knopf.
Hole, Frank, and Robert F. Heizer
  1977   *Prehistoric archeology, a brief introduction.* New York: Holt, Rinehart and Winston.
Holschlag, Stephanie, L., and Michael J. Rodeffer
  1976a   *Ninety Six: The stockade fort on the right.* Ninety Six, South Carolina: Ninety Six Historic Site.
  1976b   *Ninety Six: Siegeworks opposite star redoubt.* Ninety Six, South Carolina: Ninety Six Historic Site.
  1977   *Ninety Six: Exploratory excavations in the village.* Ninety Six, South Carolina: Star Fort Historical Commission.
Holschlag, Stephanie L., Michael J. Rodeffer, and Marvin L. Cann
  1978   *Ninety Six: The jail.* Ninety Six, South Carolina: Star Fort Historical Commission.
Honerkamp, Nicholas, R. Bruce Council, and M. Elizabeth Will
  1982   An archaeological assessment of the Charlestown Convention Center site, Charleston, South Carolina. Report prepared by the Jeffrey L. Brown Institute of Archaeology, University of Tennessee at Chattanooga for the National Park Service, Contract #C-54060(81).
Hoskins, W. G. (Editor)
  1970   *History from the farm.* London: Faber and Faber.
Hough, Perry B.
  1963   Bennett, Hammond, Hughes, and Conners family records. *South Carolina Historical Magazine* 64:220–226.
House, John H.
  1977   Survey data and regional models in historical archeology. In *Research strategies in historical archeology,* edited by Stanley South. New York: Academic Press. Pp. 241–260.
House, John H., and David L. Ballenger
  1976   An archeological survey of the Interstate 77 route in the South Carolina Piedmont. *University of South Carolina, Institute of Archeology and Anthropology, Research Manuscript Series* 104.

Howe, George
    1870   *History of the Presbyterian Church in South Carolina,* volume 1. Coumbia: Duffie &
            Chapman.
Hudson, John C.
    1969   A locational theory for rural settlement. *Annals of the Association of American Geogra-
            phers* 59:365–381.
Hughes, Quentin
    1974   *Military architecture.* London: Hugh Evelyn.
Hunneycutt, Dwight J.
    1949   The economics of the indigo industry of South Carolina. Unpublished M.A. thesis, Depart-
            ment of History, University of South Carolina.
Hurst, John G.
    1971   A review of archaeological research. In *Deserted Medieval villages,* edited by Maurice
            Beresford and John G. Hurst. London: Lutterworth Press. Pp. 76–144.
Ivers, Larry E.
    1970   *Colonial forts in South Carolina, 1670–1775.* Columbia: University of South Carolina
            Press.
Jervey, Clare
    1906   *Inscriptions on the tablets and gravestones in St. Michael's Church and graveyard,
            Charleston, S. C.* Columbia: The State Co.
Johnson, Louise R., and Julia Rosa
    1971   *Inscriptions from the churchyard, 1773–1932, Prince George Winyah, Georgetown,
            South Carolina.* Georgetown, South Carolina: by the author.
Jones, Emry
    1966   *Towns and cities.* London: Oxford University Press.
Jordan, Terry G.
    1980   Alpine, Alemannic, and American log architecture. *Annals of the Association of American
            Geographers* 70(2):154–180.
Katzman, Maicin T.
    1975   The Brazilian frontier in comparative perspective. *Comparative studies in society and
            history* 17(3):266–285.
Kennedy, Robert MacMillan
    1935   *De mortuis, concerning those that lie in the old burial grounds in and about Camden, S. C.*
            Columbia: The State Company.
Kimball, Fiske
    1922   *Domestic architecture of the American colonies and of the early republic.* New York:
            Charles Scribner's Sons. Reprint edition 1966, New York: Dover Publications.
Kirch, P.
    1980   The archaeological study of adaptation: Theoretical and methodological issues. In *Ad-
            vances in archaeological method and theory,* volume 3, edited by Michael Schiffer. New
            York: Academic Press. Pp. 101–156.
Kirkland, Thomas J., and Robert M. Kennedy
    1905   *Historic Camden,* volume 1, *Colonial and revolutionary.* Columbia: The State Printing
            Co.
    1926   *Historic Camden, volume 2, Nineteenth century.* Columbia: The State Co.
Klein, Rachel
    1981   Ordering the backcountry: The South Carolina Regulation. *William and Mary College
            Quarterly,* Series 3, 38(4):661–680.
Kniffen, Fred B.
    1936   Louisiana house types. *Annals of the Association of American Geographers* 26:179–193.
    1965   Folk housing: Key to diffusion. *Annals of the Association of American Geographers*
            55:549–577

Kniffen, Fred B., and Henry Glassie
    1966   Building in wood in the eastern United States. *Geographical Review* 56(1):40–66.
Kohn, David
    1938   *Internal improvement in South Carolina, 1817–1828.* Washington: By the author.
Kraenzel, Carl Frederick
    1955   *The Great Plains in transition.* Norman, Oklahoma: University of Oklahoma Press.
Krebs, J. R., and N. B. Davies
    1978   *Behavioral ecology.* London: Blackwell Scientific Publications.
Kristof, Ladis K. D.
    1959   The nature of frontiers and boundaries. *Annals of the Association of American Geographers* 49:269–282.
Lachicotte, Alberta Morel
    1955   *Georgetown rice plantations.* Columbia: The State Commercial Printing Co.
Lancaster County Historical Commission
    1974   *Inscriptions from old cemeteries in Lancaster, S. C.* Lancaster, South Carolina: Tri-County Publishing Company.
Lang, James
    1975   *Conquest and commerce, Spain and England in the Americas.* New York: Academic Press.
Laslett, Peter
    1972   Mean household size in England since the sixteenth century. In *Household and family in past time,* edited by Peter Laslett and Richard Wall. Cambridge: University Press. Pp. 125–158.
Lawson, Dennis T.
    1974   *A guide to historic Georgetown County, South Carolina.* Georgetown, South Carolina: The Rice Museum.
Lee, Henry
    1869   *Memoirs of the war in the Southern Department of the United States,* edited by Robert E. Lee. New York: University Publishing Company. Reprint edition 1969, New York: Arno Press.
Lee, R. H.
    1960   *The Chinese in the United States of America.* Hong Kong: Hong Kong University Press.
Lees, William B.
    1980   Old and in the way: Archeological investigations at Limerick plantation, Berkeley County, South Carolina. *University of South Carolina Institute of Archeology and Anthropology, Anthropological Studies* 5.
Lees, William B., and James L. Michie
    1978   Reconnaissance survey of the proposed Berkeley County wastewater system plant site, Robert E. Lee tract, Berkeley County, South Carolina. *University of South Carolina, Institute of Archeology and Anthropology, Research Manuscript Series* 132.
Lepionka, Larry
    1979   Fort Lyttelton: Excavations 1978. Manuscript on file, South Carolina Department of Archives and History, Columbia.
Lewis, Kenneth E.
    1969   The history of archeology of Spalding's Lower Store (PU-23), Putnam County, Florida, Unpublished M.A. thesis. Department of Anthropology, University of Florida.
    1972   1971 archeological investigations at Fort Towson, Oklahoma. *University of Oklahoma, Oklahoma Archeological Survey, Studies in Oklahoma's Past 2.*
    1975a   *The Jamestown frontier: An archaeological view of colonization.* Ph.D. dissertation, University of Oklahoma. University Microfilms, Ann Arbor.
    1975b   The north parade ground structure. In *Fort Washita from past to present, an archaeological report,* edited by Kenneth E. Lewis. *Oklahoma Historical Society, Series in Anthropology* 1:34–75.

1975c   Archeological investigations at the Kershaw house, Camden (38KE1), Kershaw County, South Carolina. *University of South Carolina, Institute of Archeology and Anthropology, Research Manuscript Series* 78.

1975d   Archeological investigations at the colonial settlement of Long Bluff (38DA5), Darlington County, South Carolina. *University of South Carolina, Institute of Archeology and Anthropology, Research Manuscript Series* 67.

1976   Camden, a frontier town in eighteenth century South Carolina. *University of South Carolina, Institute of Archeology and Anthropology, Anthropological Studies* 2.

1977a   Sampling the archeological frontier: Regional models and component analysis. In *Research strategies in historical archeology*, edited by Stanley South. New York: Academic Press. Pp. 151–201.

1977b   A functional study of the Kershaw house site in Camden, South Carolina. *University of South Carolina, Institute of Archeology and Anthropology, Research Manuscript Series* 110.

1978   An archeological survey of Long Bluff State Park, Darlington County, South Carolina. *University of South Carolina, Institute of Archeology and Anthropology, Research Manuscript Series* 129.

1979a   Hampton, initial archeological investigations at an eighteenth century rice plantation in the Santee delta, South Carolina. *University of South Carolina, Institute of Archeology and Anthropology, Research Manuscript Series* 151.

1979b   The Guillebeau house, an eighteenth century Huguenot structure in McCormick County, South Carolina. *Institute of Archeology and Anthropology, University of South Carolina, Research Manuscript Series* 145.

1980a   Pattern and layout on the South Carolina frontier: An archaeological investigation of settlement function. *North American Archaeologist* 1(2):177–200.

1980b   Ceramics from the Plantation site, a twentieth century settlement in southern Vietnam. *Asian Perspectives* XXIII(1):99–145.

1981   The Camden jail and market site: A report on preliminary investigations. *University of South Carolina, Institute of Archeology and Anthropology, Research Manuscript Series* 171.

Lewis, Kenneth E., and Donald L. Hardesty
1979   Middleton Place: Initial archeological investigations at an Ashley River rice plantation. *University of South Carolina, Institute of Archeology and Anthropology, Research Manuscript Series* 148.

Lewis, Kenneth E., and Helen Haskell
1980   Hampton II: Further archeological investigations at a Santee River rice plantation. *University of South Carolina, Institute of Archeology and Anthropology, Research Manuscript Series* 161.

Lewis, Lynne G.
1977   Drayton Hall artifact provenience data. Manuscript on file, National Trust for Historic Preservation, Washington.

1978   *Drayton Hall: Preliminary archaeological investigation at a low country plantation.* Charlottesville: University Press of Virginia.

Lewis, Oscar
1942   The effects of white contact upon Blackfoot culture; with special reference to the role of the fur trade. *American Ethnological Society, Monograph* 6.

Lewis, Pierce F.
1975   Common houses, cultural spoor. *Landscape* 19(2):1–22.

Leyburn, James G.
1935   *Frontier folkways.* New Haven: Yale University Press.

Linton, Ralph
    1936   *The study of man.* New York: Appleton-Century Crofts.
Lipscomb, Terry W.
    1973   South Carolina Revolutionary battles: Part I. *Names in South Carolina* 20:18–23.
    1975   South Carolina Revolutionary battles: Part III. *Names in South Carolina* 22:33–39.
    1977   South Carolina Revolutionary battles: Part V. *Names in South Carolina* 24:13–18.
    1978   South Carolina Revolutionary battles: Part VI. *Names in South Carolina* 25:26–33.
    1980   South Carolina Revolutionary battles: Part VIII. *Names in South Carolina* 27:16–20.
Lister, Florence C., and Robert H. Lister
    1974   Maiolica in colonial Spanish America. *Historical Archaeology* 8:17–52.
    1976   A descriptive dictionary for 500 years of Spanish-tradition ceramics (13th through 18th centuries). *Society for Historical Archaeology, Special Publication Series* 1.
Littlefield, Daniel C.
    1981   *Rice and slaves, ethnicity and the slave trade in colonial South Carolina.* Baton Rouge: Louisiana State University Press.
Lockwood, Thomas P.
    1832   *A geography of South Carolina.* Charleston: J. S. Burges.
Logan, John H.
    1859   *A history of the upper country of South Carolina,* 2 volumes. Charleston: S. G. Courtnay & Co. Reprint edition 1960, Spartanburg: The Reprint Co.
Logan, Trisha
    1980   A preliminary archeological survey of McConnell's Landing road, Forest Service Road 204-D. U. S. Forest Service, Columbia.
Longacre, William A.
    1971   Current thinking in American archaeology. In Current directions in anthropology, edited by Ann Fisher. *American Anthropological Association, Bulletin* 3(3), part 2:126–138.
Lossing, Benson J.
    1860   *The pictorial field-book of the Revolution,* 2 volumes. New York: Harper and Brothers. Reprint edition 1969, Spartanburg: The Reprint Co.
Lowcountry Council of Governments
    1979   *Historic resources of the Lowcountry, a regional survey.* Yamassee, South Carolina.
Lower Savannah Council of Governments
    1972   *A survey of the historic sites in the Lower Savannah region.* Aiken, South Carolina.
Lunn, John
    1973   Colonial Louisbourg and its developing ceramics collection. In *Ceramics in America,* edited by Iain M. G. Quimby. Charlottesville: The University Press of Virginia. Pp. 175–190.
Lurie, Nancy Oestreich
    1959   Indian cultural adjustment to European civilization. In *Seventeenth-century America,* edited by James Morton Smith. Chapel Hill: University of North Carolina Press. Pp. 33–60.
McClendon, Carlee T.
    1977   *Edgefield death notices and cemetery records.* Columbia: The Hive Press.
McIndoe, K. G.
    1969   A preliminary survey of rubber plantations in South Vietnam. *Development and Resources Corporation, Vietnam Working Paper* 3.
McIntosh, David Gregg
    n.d.   Reminiscences of early life in South Carolina. Manuscript on file, Special Collections, James A. Rogers Library, Francis Marion College, Florence, South Carolina.
MacLeod, William Christie
    1928   *The American Indian frontier.* New York: Alfred A. Knopf.
Majors, Alexander
    1893   *Seventy years on the frontier.* Minneapolis, Minnesota: Ross and Haines.

Manucy, Albert
    1962a   *The houses of St. Augustine, notes on the architecture from 1565 to 1821.* St. Augustine, Florida: The St. Augustine Historical Society.
    1962b   The fort at Frederica. *Florida State University, Department of Anthropology, Notes in Anthropology 5.*

Margolis, Maxine
    1977   Historical perspectives on frontier agriculture as an adaptive strategy. In Human ecology, edited by Victoria Reifler Bricker. Special issue of *American Ethnologist* **4**(1):42–64.

Meinig, D. W.
    1976   Spatial models of a sequence of Transatlantic interactions. *XXIII International Geographical Congress, International Geography, '76,* Section 9: *Historical Geography.* Moscow. Pp. 30–35.

Meriwether, Robert L.
    1940   *The expansion of South Carolina, 1729–1765.* Kingsport, Tennessee: Southern Publishers, Inc.

Merrens, H. Roy
    1964   *Colonial North Carolina in the eighteenth century, a study in historical geography.* Chapel Hill: University of North Carolina Press.
    1969   The physical environment of early America, images and image makers in colonial South Carolina. *Geographical Review* **59**(4):530–556.

Merrens, H. Roy (Editor)
    1977   *The colonial South Carolina scene, contemporary views, 1697–1774.* Columbia: University of South Carolina Press.

Middleton, Margaret Simms
    1941   Inscriptions from the graveyard of Lewisfield plantation on Cooper River. *South Carolina Historical Magazine* **42**:81–82.

Miller, David Harry, and William W. Savage, Jr. (editors)
    1977   Introduction to *The character and influence of the Indian trade in Wisconsin, a study of the trading post as an institution,* by Frederick Jackson Turner. Norman: University of Oklahoma Press.

Miller, J. Jefferson, and Lyle M. Stone
    1970   Eighteenth century ceramics from Fort Michilimacinac, a study in historical archeology. *Smithsonian Studies in History and Technology 4.*

Mills, Robert
    1826   *Statistics of South Carolina.* Charleston: Hurlbut and Lloyd. Reprint Edition 1972, Spartanburg: The Reprint Co.

Mintz, Sidney W.
    1959   The plantation as a socio-cultural type. In Plantation systems of the New World. *Pan American Union, Social Science Monographs* **7**:42–49.

Mitchell, Joseph B.
    1962   *Decisive battles of the American Revolution.* Greenwich: Fawcett Publications, Inc.

Mood, Fulmer
    1945   The concept of the frontier, 1871–1898, comments on a select list of source documents. *Agricultural History* **19**(1):24–30.

Moragne, W. C.
    1857   *An address delivered at New Bordeaux, Abbeville District, South Carolina, November 15, 1854 on the 90th anniversary of the arrival of the French Protestants at that place.* Charleston: James Phynney. Reprint edition 1972, McCormick: McCormick County Historical Society.

Mowat, Charles L.
    1941   St. Augustine under the British flag. *Florida Historical Quarterly* **20**(2):131–150.

Muller, John
    1746   *A treatise containing the elementary part of fortification, regular and irregular*. London: J. Nourse. Reprint edition 1968, Ottawa: Museum Restoration Service.

Murdock, George Peter
    1949   *Social structure*. New York: MacMillan.

Muse, Jenalee
    1980   An archeological survey of the Walnut Grove plantation located in Compartment 191, Wambaw District, Francis Marion National Forest, U.S. Forest Service, Columbia.

Neely, Juanita Henderson
    1959   *Neely family history*. By the author.

Neill, Wilfred
    1968   The Galphin trading post at Silver Bluff, South Carolina. *Florida Anthropologist* 21(2–3):42–54.

Nelson, William H.
    1961   *The American Tory*. Boston: Beacon Press.

Newton, Milton B., Jr.
    1971   Louisiana house types, a field guide. *Museum of Geoscience, Louisiana State University, Melanges* 2:1–18.
    1972   *Atlas of Louisiana, a guide for students*. Baton Rouge: Louisiana State University Press.

Nigel, Harvey
    1970   *A history of farm buildings in England and Wales*. Newton Abbot, Devon: David & Charles.

Noble, William C.
    1973   The excavation and historical identification of Rocky Mountain house. *Canadian Historic Sites: Occasional Papers in Archaeology and History* 6.

Noël Hume, Ivor
    1962   An Indian ware of the colonial period. *Quarterly Bulletin of the Archaeological Society of Virginia* 17(1):2–14.
    1969   *Historical Archaeology*. New York: Alfred A. Knopf.
    1970   *A guide to artifacts of colonial America*. New York: Alfred A. Knopf.

Norton, William, and E. C. Conklin
    1974   Land use theory and the pioneering economy. *Geografiska Annaler* 56B(1):44–56.

Olmsted, Frederick Law
    1957   A tobacco plantation in Virginia. In *The plantation South*, edited by Kathrine M. Jones. Indianapolis: The Bobbs-Merrill Co., Inc. Pp. 49–55.

Orser, Charles E.
    1979   Ethnohistory, analogy, and historical archaeology. *Conference on Historic Site Archaeology, Papers* 13:1–24.

Ostrogorsky, Michael
    1982   An Idaho model of frontier settlement. *North America Archaeologist* 3(1):79–83.

Otto, John Solomon
    1977   Artifacts and status differences—A comparison of ceramic differences from planter, overseer, and slave sites on an antebellum plantation. In *Research strategies in historical archeology*, edited by Stanley South. New York: Academic Press. Pp. 91–118.

Page, William
    1927   Notes on the types of English villages and their distribution. *Antiquity* 1(4):447–468.

Palmer, Arlene M.
    1976   *A Winterhur guide to Chinese export procelain*. New York: Crown Publishers.

Pan American Union
    1959   Appendix: Summaries of workshops. In Plantation systems of the New World. *Social Science Monographs* 7:188–196.

Patten, John
   1973   Urban life before the Industrial Revolution. In *Man made the land, essays in English historical geography,* edited by Alan R. H. Baker and J. P. Harley. Newton Abbot, Devon: David & Charles. Pp. 127–139.
Paynter, Robert
   1982   *Models of spatial inequality, settlement patterns in historical archeology.* New York: Academic Press.
Pee Dee Regional Planning and Development Council
   1972   *Historic preservation survey and plan.* Florence, South Carolina.
Peet, Richard
   1970–
   1971   Von Thünen theory and the dynamics of agricultural expansion. *Exporations in Economic History* 8:181–201.
Penman, John T.
   1975   Hospital complex. In Fort Washita from past to present, an archaeological report, edited by Kenneth E. Lewis. *Oklahoma Historical Society, Series in Anthropology* 1:145–198.
Peters, Kristen Lynn Stevens
   1982   Remote sensing for historical archaeological applications. Unpublished M.A. thesis, Department of Anthropology, University of South Carolina.
Petty, Julian J.
   1943   The growth and distribution of population in South Carolina. *South Carolina State Planning Board,* Bulletin 11. Reprint edition 1975, Spartanburg: The Reprint Co.
Phillips, Paul Christler
   1961   *The fur trade,* 2 volumes. Norman: University of Oklahoma Press.
Phillips, Ulrich Bonnell
   1908   *A history of transportation in the eastern cotton belt to 1860.* New York: Columbia University Press.
   1929   *Life and labor in the old South.* Boston: Little, Brown, and Co.
Pinckney, Eliza Lucas
   1977   A letter from Eliza Lucas Pinckney, 1785. In *The colonial South Carolina scene, contemporary views, 1697–1774,* edited by H. Roy Merrens. Columbia: University of South Carolina Press. Pp. 145–146.
Pomfret, John E.
   1970   *Founding the American colonies, 1583–1660.* New York: Harper & Row.
Prescott, J. R. V.
   1965   *The geography of frontiers and boundaries.* Chicago: Aldine.
Price, Barbara J.
   1982   Cultural materialism: A theoretical review. *American Antiquity* 47(4):709–741.
Price, Cynthia R., and James E. Price
   1978   Pioneer settlement and subsistence on the Ozark border: Preliminary report on the Widow Harris Cabin Site Project. *Conference on Historic Site Archaeology, Papers* 12:145–169.
Price, Edward T.
   1968   The central courthouse square in the American county seat. *Geographical Review* 58(1):29–60.
Prucha, Francis Paul
   1958   *Army life on the western frontier.* Norman: University of Oklahoma Press.
Prunty, Merle, Jr.
   1955   The renaissance of the southern plantation. *The Geographical Review* 45(4):459–491.
Quimby, George I.
   1966   *Indian culture and European trade goods.* Madison: University of Wisconsin Press.
Ralph, Elizabeth K., and Henry Borstling
   1965   Instrument survey of Camden, South Carolina, August 2–7, 1965. Manuscript on file, Camden Historical Commission, Camden, South Carolina.

Ramsay, David
    1809   *The history of South Carolina,* 2 volumes. Charleston: David Longworth. Reprint edition 1960, Spartanburg: The Reprint Company.

Rathje, William L., and Michael McCarthy
    1977   Regularity and variability in contemporary garbage. In *Research strategies in historical archeology,* edited by Stanley South. New York: Academic Press. Pp. 261–286.

Ravenel, Theodore D.
    1936   The last days of rice planting. *Contributions from the Charleston Museum* 8, edited by E. Milby Burton. Charleston, South Carolina. Pp. 43–50.

Rawick, George P.
    1972   *The American slave: A composite autobiography,* volume 1, *from sundown to sunup, the making of the black community.* Westport, Connecticut: Greenwood Publishing Co.

Readling, James M.
    1970   *History of Hopewell Presbyterian Church, Claussen, South Carolina, 1770–1970.* Columbia: R. L. Bryan Co.

Redfield, Robert, Ralph Linton, and Melville J. Herskovitts
    1936   Memorandum for the study of acculturation. *American Anthropologist* 38:149–152.

Redman, Charles L., and Patty Jo Watson
    1970   Systematic intensive surface collection. *American Antiquity* 35(3):279–291.

Rees, Peter W.
    1975   Origins of colonial transportation in Mexico. *Geographical Review* 65:323–334.

Reid, Mary Ritter
    1977   Survey of Williamsburg Presbyterian Cemetery, Kingstree, South Carolina. Manuscript on file, Special Collections, James A. Rogers Library, Francis Marion College, Florence, South Carolina.

Renfrew, Colin
    1972   *The emergence of civilization: The Cyclades and the Aegean in the third millenium* B.C. London: Methuen & Co., Ltd.

Reps, John W.
    1965   *The making of urban America, a history of city planning in the United States.* Princeton: Princeton University Press.
    1972   *Tidewater towns, city planning in colonial Virginia and Maryland.* Williamsburg, Virginia: The Colonial Williamsburg Foundation.

Robequain, Charles
    1944   *The economic development of French Indo-China.* London: Oxford University Press.

Rogers, George C., Jr.
    1969   *Charleston in the age of the Pinckneys.* Norman: University of Okalhoma Press.

Roosevelt, Theodore
    1899   *Ranch life and the hunting-trail.* New York: The Century Co. Reprint edition 1966, Ann Arbor: University Microfilms.

Roth, Rodris
    1961   Tea drinking in eighteenth century America: Its etiquette and equipage. *United States National Museum, Bulletin* 225.

Rowse, A. L.
    1957   Tudor expansion: The transition from medieval to modern history. *William and Mary College Quarterly, Series* 3, **14**(3):309–316.

Runnette, Mabel
    1936   Inscriptions from the gravestones at Stoney Creek Cemetery near Yamassee, Beaufort County, S. C. *South Carolina Historical Magazine* 37:100–110.
    1937   Inscriptions from graveyards in Beaufort County. *South Carolina* Historical Magazine 38:16–20.
    1950   Epitaphs from Beaufort County. *South Carolina Historical Magazine* 51:171–174.

Russell, S. Gayle, Lesley M. Drucker, and Rebecca G. Fulmer
    1981   Archaeological testing and architectural interpretation of the Homestead house kitchen, well, and servants' dwelling, and the Revolutionary house spring at Historic Brattonsville, York County, South Carolina. Report prepared by Carolina Archaeological Services for the York County Historical Commission, Columbia.
Sahlins, Marshall D., and Elman R. Service
    1960   *Evolution and culture.* Ann Arbor: University of Michigan Press.
Salley, A. S., Jr.
    1925   Tombstone inscriptions at Belle Isle plantation. *South Carolina Historical Magazine* **26**:158–161.
    1936   The true story of how the Madagascar gold seed rice was introduced into South Carolina. *Contributions from the Charleston Museum,* edited by E. Milby Burton 8:51–53.
Salmon, Merrilee H.
    1976   "Deductive" and "inductive" archaeology. *American Antiquity* **41**(3):376–381.
Santee–Wateree Planning Council
    1972   *Historic preservation plan and inventory, Santee-Wateree Planning Council.* Sumter, South Carolina.
Schenck, David
    1889   *North Carolina, 1780–81, being a history of the invasion of the Carolinas.* Raleigh: Edwards & Broughton. Reprint edition 1967, Spartanburg: The Reprint Co.
Schiffer, Michael B.
    1972   Archeological context and systemic context. *American Antiquity* **37**(2):156–165.
    1976   *Behavioral archeology.* New York: Academic Press.
Schiffer, Michael B., Theodore E. Downing, and Michael McCarthy
    1981   Waste not, want not: An ethnoarchaeological study of reuse in Tucson, Arizona. In *Modern material culture: The archaeology of us,* edited by Richard A. Gould and Michael B. Schiffer. New York: Academic Press. Pp. 67–86.
Schulz, Judith J.
    1976   The hinterland of Revolutionary Camden, South Carolina. *Southeastern Geographer* **16**(2):91–97.
Scurry, James D., and Mark J. Brooks
    1980   An intensive archeological survey of the South Carolina State Port Authority's Belleview plantation, Charleston, South Carolina. *University of South Carolina, Institute of Archeology and Anthropology, Research Manuscript Series* 158.
Scurry, James D., J. Walter Joseph, and Fritz Hamer
    1980   Initial archeological investigations at Silver Bluff plantation, Aiken County, South Carolina. *University of South Carolina, Institute of Archeology, Research Manuscript Series* 168.
Sellers, Leila
    1934   *Charleston business on the eve of the American Revolution.* Chapel Hill: University of North Carolina Press.
Shepard, Anna O.
    1956   Ceramics for the archaeologist. *Carnegie Institution of Washington, Publication* 609.
Shepherd, James F., and Gary M. Walton
    1972   Trade, distribution, and economic growth in colonial America. *Journal of Economic History* **32**(1):128–145.
Simms, William Gilmore
    1843   *The geography of South Carolina.* Charleston: Babcock and Co.
Simons, Albert, and Samuel Lapham, Jr. (editors)
    1927   *Charleston, South Carolina.* New York: Press of the American Institute of Architects, Inc.
Sirmans, M. Eugene
    1966   *Colonial South Carolina: a political history, 1663–1763.* Chapel Hill: University of North Carolina Press.

Sloane, Eric
    1967   *An age of barns.* New York: Ballantine Books.

Smith, Alice R. Huger, and D. E. Huger Smith
    1917   *The dwelling houses of Charleston, South Carolina.* Philadephia: J. B. Lippincott Company.

Smith, Daniel
    1793   *A short description of the Tennessee Government, or the territory of the United States south of the River Ohio, to accompany a map of that country.* Philadelphia: Mathew Carey, Bookseller. Reprint edition 1974, Spartanburg: The Reprint Co.

Smith, Danny H.
    1981   A survey of the cemeteries between the Black and Santee Rivers in Williamsburg County. *Three Rivers Historical Society, Williamsburg County Series* 3.

Smith, George
    1779   *An universal military dictionary.* London: John Millan.

Smith, Hale G.
    1956   The European and the Indian, European-Indian contacts in Georgia and Florida. *Florida Anthropological Society Publications* 4.

Smith, Henry A. M.
    1909   Historical notes, the grave of William Washington. *South Carolina Historical Magazine* 10:181–183.

Smith, Henry Nash
    1950   *Virgin land, the American West as symbol and myth.* Cambridge: Harvard University Press.

Smith, Julia Floyd
    1973   *Slavery and plantation growth in antebellum Florida, 1821–1860.* Gainesville: University of Florida Press.

Snowden, Yates (Editor)
    1920   *History of South Carolina,* 5 volumes. Chicago: The Lewis Publishing Company.

Soltow, J. H.
    1959   Scottish traders in Virginia, 1750–1775. *Economic History Review* 11:83–98.

South, Stanley
    1962   An archaeological examination of Indian Hill on the campus of the Citadel, Charleston, South Carolina. Manuscript on file, North Carolina Department of Archives and History, Raleigh.
    1963   Exploratory excavation of a brick kiln at Town Creek, Brunswick County, North Carolina. Manuscript on file, N.C. Department of Archives and History, Raleigh.
    1964   Analysis of the buttons from Brunswick Town and Fort Fisher. *Forida Anthropologist* 17(2):113–133.
    1965   Anthropomorphic pipes from the kiln waster dump of Gottfried Aust-1755–1771. *Florida Anthropologist* 18(3), Part 2:49–60.
    1967   The ceramic forms of the potter Gottfried Aust at Bethabara, North Carolina, 1755 to 1771. *The Conference on Historic Site Archaeology, Papers* 1:33–52.
    1970a   Exploratory archeology of Ninety-Six. *University of South Carolina, Institute of Archeology and Anthropology, Research Manuscript Series* 6.
    1970b   Exploratory excavations at the Price house (38SP1). *University of South Carolina, Institute of Archeology and Anthropology, Research Manuscript Series* 5.
    1971a   A comment on alkaline glazed stoneware. *Conference on Historic Site Archaeology, Papers* 5:171–185.
    1971b   Exploratory archeology at Holmes' fort, the blockhouse, and jail redoubt at Ninety Six. *Conference on Historic Site Archaeology, Papers* 5:35–50.
    1972a   Evolution and horizon as revealed in ceramic analysis in historical archaeology. *Conference on Historic Site Archaeology, Papers* 6:71–116.

1972b   Archeological excavation at the site of Williamson's fort of 1775, Holmes' fort of 1780, and the town of Cambridge of 1783–1850. *University of South Carolina, Institute of Archeology and Anthropology, Research Manuscript Series* 18.

1974   Palmetto parapets, exploratory archeology at Fort Moultrie, South Carolina, 38CH50. *University of South Carolina, Institute of Archeology and Anthropology, Anthropological Studies* 1.

1975   Fickle forts on Windmill Point: Exploratory archeology at Fort Johnson, South Carolina. *University of South Carolina, Institute of Archeology and Anthropology, Research Manuscript Series* 81.

1977   *Method and theory in historical archeology.* New York: Academic Press.

1978   Pattern recognition in historical archaeology. *American Antiquity* 43(2):223–230.

1979a   Historic site content, structure, and function. *American Antiquity* 44(2):213–237.

1979b   The search for Santa Elena on Parris Island, South Carolina. *University of South Carolina, Institute of Archeology and Anthropology. Research Manuscript Series* 150.

1979c   Architectural data "rescue" at the Guillebeau house. In the Guillebeau house: An eighteenth century Huguenot structure in McCormick County, South Carolina, by Kenneth E. Lewis. *University of South Carolina, Institute of Archeology and Anthropology, Research Manuscript Series* 145. Pp. 77–95.

1980   The discovery of Santa Elena, *University of South Carolina, Institute of Archeology and Anthropology, Research Manuscript Series* 165.

1982   Exploring Santa Elena, 1981. *University of South Carolina, Institute of Archeology and Anthropology, Research Manuscript Series* 184.

South, Stanley, and Michael Hartley
1980   Deep water and high ground: Seventeenth century low country settlement. *University of South Carolina, Institute of Archeology and Anthropology, Research Manuscript Series* 166.

South Carolina Appalachian Council of Governments
1972   *A survey of historic places in the South Carolina Appalachian region.* Greenville, South Carolina.

South Carolina Historical Magazine
1913   Historical Notes 14:112–114, 171–174.

1917a   Inscriptions from the churchyard of old Prince Frederick Winyah, at Browns Ferry, Black River 18:91–95.

1917b   The inscriptions on the gravestones at Sheldon Church 18:180–183.

1925   Inscriptions on tombstones, private burying grounds, on the Santee River in old St. Stephens Parish, S. C. 26:113–121.

1926   Historical notes. 27:181–188.

1937   Inscriptions from family burying ground at Yeamans Hall 38:99–103.

Spicer, Edward H. (editor)
1962   *Perspectives in American Indian culture change.* Chicago: University of Chicago Press.

Steel, Sophie B., and Cecil W. Trout
1904   Historic dress in America, 1607–1870, 2 volumes, New York: Benjamin Blom.

Steffen, Jerome O.
1980   *Comparative frontiers: A proposal for studying the American West.* Norman: University of Oklahoma Press.

Stephenson, Robert L.
1975   An archeological preservation plan for South Carolina. *University of South Carolina, Institute of Archeology and Anthropology, Research Manuscript Series* 84.

Stevenson, Marc
1981   Pattern in pattern recognition? *Conference on Historic Site Archaeology, Papers* 14. 35–47.

Steward, Julian H.
1955   *Theory of culture change, the methodology of multilinear evolution.* Urbana: University of Illinois Press.

Stoddard, Mrs. David
   1963   Union County, S. C., cemetery records. *South Carolina Genealogical Register* 1(1):3–26.
   1965a   *Greeville County, S. C., cemetery records*, volume 1. Pass Christian, Mississippi: Willo
               Institute of Genealogy.
   1965b   *Spartanburg County, S. C., cemetery records*, volume 1. Pass Christian, Mississippi: Willo
               Institute of Genealogy.
   1966a   *Laurens County, S. C., cemetery records*, volume 1. Pass Christian, Mississippi: Willo
               Institute of Genealogy.
   1966b   Laurens County cemetery records. *South Carolina Genealogical Register* 4(3):157–168.
Stone, Gary Wheeler
   1970   Ceramics in Suffolk County, Massachusetts inventories 1680–1775—a preliminary study
               with divers comments thereon, and sundry suggestions. *Conference on Historic Site Ar-
               chaeology, Papers* 3:73–90.
Stoney, Samuel Gaillard
   1937   *Charleston, azaleas and old bricks*. Boston: Houghton Mifflin Company.
   1938   *Plantations of the Carolina Low Country*. Charleston: The Charleston Art Association.
   1944   *This is Charleston, a survey of the architectural heritage of a unique American city*.
               Charleston: Charleston Art Association.
Strickland, Robert N.
   1971   Camden Revolutionary War fortifications (38KE1): The 1969–70 excavations. *Institute
               of Archeology and Anthropology. University of South Carolina, Notebook* 3(3):55–71.
   1976   Archeological excavations at Camden, 1971–1973. Manuscript on file, Camden Histor-
               ical Commission, Camden, South Carolina.
Strickon, Arnold
   1965   The Euro-American raching complex. In Man, culture, and animals, the role of animals in
               human ecological adjustments, edited by Anthony Leeds and Andrew P. Vayda. *American
               Association for the Advancement of Science, Publication* 78. Pp. 119–258.
Sutherland, Stella H.
   1936   *Population distribution in colonial America*. New York: Columbia University Press.
Swedlund, Alan C.
   1975   Population growth and settlement pattern in Franklin and Hampshire Counties, Mas-
               sachusetts, 1650–1850. In Population studies in archaeology and biological anthropology:
               A symposium, edited by Alan C. Swedlund. *American Antiquity, Memoir* 30. Pp. 22–33.
Sweet, Ethel Wylly
   1978   *Camden, homes and heritage*, with an architectural appendix by Henry D. Boykin II.
               Camden, South Carolina: Kershaw County Historical Society.
Taaffe, E. J., R. L. Morrill, and P. R. Gould
   1963   Transport expansion in underdeveloped countries: A comparative analysis. *Geographical
               Review* 53:503–529.
Tarleton, Banastre
   1787   *A history of the campaigns of 1780 and 1781, in the southern provinces of North America*.
               London: T. Cadell. Reprint edition 1967, Spartanburg: The Reprint Co.
Taylor, Richard L., and Marion F. Smith (assemblers)
   1978   The report of the intensive survey of the Richard B. Russell dam and lake, Savannah River,
               Georgia and South Carolina. *University of South Carolina, Institute of Archeology and
               Anthropology, Research Manuscript Series* 142.
Teague, George A.
   1980   The Reward Mine and associated sites. *Western Archeological Center, Publications in
               Anthropology* 11.
Teague, George A., and Lynette O. Shenk
   1977   Excavations at Harmony Borax Works, historical archeology at Death Valley National
               Monument. *Western Archeological Center, Publications in Anthropology* 6.
Temple, John
   1972   *Mining, an international history*. New York: Praeger Publishers.

Thirsk, Joan
    1973   Roots of industrial England. In *Man made the land, essays in English historical geography*, edited by Alan R. H. Baker and J. B. Harley. Newton Abbot, Devon: David and Charles. Pp. 93–108.

Thomas, David Hurst
    1973   An empirical test of Steward's model of Great Basin settlement patterns. *American Antiquity* **38**(2):115–176.

Thomas, Robert S., and Lynn Larson
    1977   Archaeological testing at Old Ford Townsend State Park (45JE26). *University of Washington, Institute for Environmental Studies, Office of Public Archaeology, Reconnaissance Report* 12.

Thompson, Edgar T.
    1959   The plantation as a social system. In Plantation systems of the New World. *Pan American Union, Social Science Monographs* 7:26–37.

Thompson, Stephen I.
    1970   *San Juan Yapacani: A Japanese pioneer colony in eastern Bolivia.* Ph.D. dissertation, University of Illinois. University Microfilms, Ann Arbor.
    1973a   Pioneer colonization, a cross-cultural view. *Addison–Wesley Modules in Anthropology* 33.
    1973b   Introduction: The anthropological study of the frontier. *Papers in Anthropology* **14**:1–5.

Thompson, Virginia
    1937   Indo-China—France's great stake in the Far East. *Far Eastern Survey* **6**(2):15–22.

Todd, John R.
    1931   Inscriptions from Brewton plantation near Yamassee. *South Carolina Historical Magazine* 32:238–240.

Townsend, Leah
    1935   *South Carolina Baptists, 1670–1805.* Florence, South Carolina: Privately printed. Reprint edition 1974, Spartanburg: The Reprint Co.

Trigger, Bruce G.
    1968   The determinants of settlement patterns. In *Settlement archaeology*, edited by K. C. Chang. Palo Alto, California: National Press Books. Pp. 53–78.
    1974   The archaeology of government. *World Archaeology* **6**(1):95–106.

Trinkley, Michael, and Lee Tippett
    1980   Archaeological survey of the proposed Mark Clark Expressway, final report, Charleston and Berkeley Counties, South Carolina Report prepared by the South Carolina Department of Highways and Public Transportation, Columbia.

Tumin, Melvin M.
    1967   *Social stratification, the forms and functions of inequality.* Englewood Cliffs: Prentice-Hall.

Turner, Frederick Jackson
    1891   The character and influence of the Indian trade in Wisconsin, a study of the trading post as an institution, *Johns Hopkins University Studies in Historical and Political Science,* Ninth Series 11–12. Reprint edition 1977, edited by David Harry Miller and William W. Savage, Jr., Norman: University of Oklahoma Press.
    1893   The significance of the frontier in American history, *Annual Report of the American Historical Association for the year 1893.* Pp. 199–227.
    1926   Geographic sectionalism in American history. *Annals of the Association of American Geographers* **16**(2):85–93.

Tuttle, William M., Jr.
    1967   Forerunners of Frederick Jackson Turner: Nineteenth-century British conservatives and the frontier thesis. *Agricultural History* **41**(3):219–227.

Upper Savannah Regional Planning and Development Council
    1972   *Upper Savannah historical program.* Greenwood, South Carolina.

Vauban, Sebastien LePrestre de
1740 *Mémoire pour servir d'instruction dans la conduite des sieges et dans la défense des places* [A manual of siegecraft and fortification]. Leiden; reprint edition 1968, translation and introduction by George A. Rothrock. Ann Arbor: University of Michigan Press.

von Thünen, Johann Heinrich
1966 *Isolated state; an English translation of Der isolierte Staat.* Translated by Carla M. Wartenberg. Editing and introduction by Peter Hall. Oxford: Pergamon Press.

Waccamaw Regional Planning and Development Commission
1971 Waccamaw, survey of historic places. Georgetown, South Carolina.

Wagley, Charles, and Marvin Harris
1955 A typology of Latin American subcultures. *American Anthropologist* 57(3):428–451.

Walker, Legare
1941 *Dorchester County.* Charleston: By the author.

Walker, Nannie McAliley
1939 *Roster of names of persons buried in old Purity Presbyterian Cemetery, Chester, South Carolina.* Columbia: The Letter Shop.

Wallace, David Duncan
1899 *Constitutional history of South Carolina from 1725 to 1775.* Abbeville, South Carolina: H. Wilson.
1951 *South Carolina, a short history, 1520–1948.* Columbia: University of South Carolina Press.

Wallerstein, Immanuel
1974 *The modern world system, capitalist agriculture and the origins of the European world economy in the sixteenth century.* New York: Academic Press.
1980a Theories, research designs, and empirical measures. In History and underdevelopment, essays on underdevelopment and European expansion in Asia and Africa, edited by L. Blussé *et al. Itinerario* 4(1):21–28.
1980b *The modern world system II, mercantilism and the consolidation of the European world economy, 1600–1750.* New York: Academic Press.

Waring, Joseph Ioor
1926 Tombstone inscriptions. *South Carolina Historical Magazine* 27:36–41.

Waterman, Thomas Tileston
1945 *The mansion of Virginia, 1706–1776.* Chapel Hill: University of North Carolina Press.

Waterman, Thomas Tileston, and John A. Barrows
1969 *Domestic colonial architecture of tidewater Virginia.* New York: Dover Publications, Inc.

Watkins, C. Malcolm
1973 Ceramics used in America: Comparisons. In *Ceramics in America,* edited by Ian M. G. Quimby. Charlottesville: The University Press of Virginia. Pp. 191–198.

Watkins, C. Malcolm, and Ivor Noël Hume
1967 The "poor potter" of Yorktown. *United States National Museum, Bulletin* 249, *Contributions from the Museum of History and Technology, Paper* 54:73–112.

Watson, Margaret J.
1970 *Greenwood County sketches.* Greenwood, S. C.: The Attic Press.

Watson, Margaret J., and Louise M. Watson
1972 *Tombstone inscriptions from family graveyards in Greenwood County, S.C.* Greenwood, South Carolina: Drinkard Printing Co.

Weaver, David C.
1977 The transport expansion process in Georgia and the Carolinas 1670–1900: A graphical analysis. *Proceedings of the Southern Studies Session, 32nd Annual Meeting of the Southeastern Division of the Association of American Geographers,* Knoxville, Tennessee. Pp. 29–47.

Webb, Walter Prescott
1931 *The Great Plains.* Boston: Ginn and Company.

Webber, Mabel L.
    1928   Inscriptions from the Independent or Congregational (Circular) Church yard, Charleston, S. C. *South Carolina Historical Magazine* **29**:55–66, 133–150, 238–257, 306–328.

Weigert, Hans W., Henry Brodie, Edward W. Doherty, John R. Fernstrom, Eric Fischer, and Dudley Kirk
    1957   *Principles of political geography.* New York: Appleton-Century-Crofts, Inc.

Weigley, Russel F.
    1970   *The Partisan war: The South Carolina campaign of 1780–1782.* Columbia: University of South Carolina Press.

Wells, Robin
    1973   Frontier systems as a sociocultural type. *Papers in Anthropology* **14**(1):6–15.

Whaley, E. D.
    1976   *Union County cememteries, epitaphs of 18th and 19th century settlers in Union County, South Carolina and their descendents.* Greenville, South Carolina: A. Press.

White, George
    1849   *Statistics of Georgia.* Savannah: W. Thorne Williams.

White, Leslie
    1959   *The evolution of culture.* New York: McGraw-Hill Book Company.

Widmer, Randolph J.
    1976   An archaeological survey of the proposed Esat Cooper and Berkeley Railroad, Berkeley County, South Carolina. *University of South Carolina, Institute of Archeology and Anthropology, Research Manuscript Series* 100.

Winius, George
    1980   Third World development, historians of the Expansion and "relevance." In History and underdevelopment, essays on underdevelopment and European expansion in Asia and Africa, edited by L. Blussé *et al. Itinerario* 4(1):77–84.

Winther, Oscar Osburn
    1964   *The transportation frontier, Trans-Mississippi West, 1865–1890.* New York: Holt, Rinehart and Winston.

Wood, Charles, and Dorothy Wood
    1979   *The Great Northern Railway.* Edmonds, Washington: Pacific Fast Mail.

Wood, Karen G.
    1977   An archaeological survey of South Carolina Electric and Gas Company's Williams–Mt. Pleasant 230 KV transmission line project, Charleston County and Berkeley County, South Carolina. Report prepared by the Laboratory of Archaeology, University of Georgia.

Wood, Peter H.
    1974   *Black majority.* New York: Alfred A. Knopf.

Woodall, J. Ned
    1972   *An introduction to modern archaeology.* Cambridge, Massachusetts: Schenkman Publishing Company.

Woodmason, Charles
    1953   *The Carolina backcountry on the eve of the Revolution, the journal and other writings of Charles Woodmason, Anglican itinerant.* Editing and introduction by Richard J. Hooker. Chapel Hill: University of North Carolina Press.

Zierden, Martha
    1981   An archeological survey of portions of Compartment 199, Wambaw District, Francis Marion National Forest. U.S. Forest Service, Columbia.
    1982   Preliminary management report: Archeological survey of Compartment 159, Francis Marion National Forest. U.S. Forest Service, Columbia.

Zelinsky, Wilbur
    1953   The log house in Georgia. *Geographical Review* **43**(2):173–193.

Zucker, Paul
    1959   *Town and Square, from the Agora to the village green.* Cambridge, Massachusetts: The MIT Press.

Index

329